D1087723

Union Power and American Democracy

The UAW and the Democratic Party, 1972–83

Dudley W. Buffa

Ann Arbor   The University of Michigan Press

For Karen

RHIS
HD
6515
.A8
B835
1984

Library of Congress Cataloging in Publication Data

Buffa, Dudley W., 1940–
  Union power and American democracy.

  Bibliography: p.
  Includes index.
  1. International Union, United Automobile, Aero-
space, and Agricultural Implement Workers of America—
Political activity—History.   2. Trade-unions—United
States—Political activity—History.   3. Democratic
Party (Mich.)—History.   4. Michigan—Politics and
government—1951–   . I. Title.
HD6515.A8B835 1984   322'.2'0973   84-11887
ISBN 0-472-10053-X

Quod praecipuum munus annalium reor ne
virtutes sileantur utque pravis dictis factisque ex
posteritate et infamia metus sit.

Tacitus Annals 3.65

Introduction

In 1948 the United Auto Workers (UAW), then still a part of the Congress of Industrial Organizations, followed the lead of state CIO president Gus Scholle and joined Democratic liberals in an effort to take control of the Michigan Democratic party. What had seemed a distant became an imminent prospect with the astonishing victory of G. Mennen Williams in the November gubernatorial election. Hicks Griffiths, who had served as Williams's campaign manager, was elected state party chairman, and within two years the new coalition had removed nearly all organized opposition in the district and county Democratic committees. Griffiths, whether because he wanted to or was forced to, accepted appointment to the bench and was replaced by Neil Staebler. Throughout the 1950s G. Mennen Williams served as governor, Staebler chaired the state party, and Gus Scholle spoke for the political interests of organized labor.

The unity of the liberal-labor coalition was disrupted in 1960, when G. Mennen Williams decided not to seek a seventh consecutive term and Michigan Democrats, for the first time since 1948, witnessed a contested primary for the gubernatorial nomination. Convinced that secretary of state James Hare would without difficulty defeat the relatively unknown lieutenant governor, John Swainson, the leadership of both the party and the merged American Federation of Labor and Congress of Industrial Organizations (AFL-CIO) were content to remain at least formally neutral. A number of UAW local union presidents, including, for example, Sam Fishman, ignored the professed neutrality of the international and, along with a great many new party activists, campaigned with energy and effect for Swainson. Swainson won the nomination and the election, and brought into positions of power in both the government and the party people who were more loyal to him than to the followers of Williams, Staebler, and Scholle.

Swainson's first term as governor was his last. In 1962 George Romney, the former head of American Motors who had begun and led a successful attempt to rewrite the Michigan Constitution, became the first Republican elected governor since 1946. With Swainson's defeat the importance of the state Democratic chairman, who would now become the leading spokesman for the Democratic party, increased. Gus Scholle and Neil Staebler both wanted to retain John J. "Joe" Collins, while Swainson and those who followed him supported Zolton Ferency. At the state convention Scholle could not deliver all of the AFL-CIO, and Staebler could no longer command the allegiance of party liberals. With the UAW, including both Leonard Woodcock and Douglas Fraser, in full support, Ferency defeated Collins and found himself in charge of a deeply divided party. When he left the chairmanship nearly five years later the party would be on the verge of destruction.

Ferency had been elected following the Democratic defeat of 1962. The processes of party disintegration were intensified and accelerated following the Democratic victory of 1964. Though George Romney was elected to a second term, the state legislature, for the first time in nearly thirty years, had Democratic majorities in both the house and the senate. The state Democratic chairman insisted that the Democratic legislature keep the party's long-standing promise and adopt a state income tax. The state AFL-CIO did not agree. Gus Scholle argued that the state did not yet need an income tax and that before one was adopted the state constitution should be amended to permit one that was graduated instead of flat-rate. Until that happened Scholle was perfectly willing to raise revenues by raising taxes on business. While Scholle spoke publicly for the AFL-CIO, the UAW privately expressed reservations. Unlike Scholle, the UAW had become increasingly willing to regard taxation more as a means by which to raise revenue in the most progressive way available than as a weapon in a continuing war between business and labor. Scholle, however, was permitted to have his way, and the UAW reluctantly supported the refusal of the Democratic majority to pass an income tax before the voters had a chance to repeal the prohibition on a graduated tax. Democratic legislators did not vote for a tax, but the voters did not have a chance to remove the prohibition, because the legislature, on a straight partisan division, failed by a single vote to obtain the two-thirds necessary to place it on the ballot. The voters did have a chance to elect members of the state house and senate, however, and they used it to return both chambers to Republican control.

The Democratic party lost more than their legislative majorities in 1966. G. Mennen Williams was defeated by Robert Griffin in a race for the Senate seat that had been held since 1954 by Patrick V. McNamara, and Zolton Ferency failed even to come close in his effort to capture the governorship from George Romney. Though Ferency, over the opposition of Scholle and Staebler, was elected to another term as chairman, the party officers opposed him at every turn. When he decided in 1967 to oppose publicly the renomination of Lyndon Johnson, even the UAW decided the party required a replacement. Ferency was compelled to resign, and State Senator Sander M. Levin, chairman of the senate Labor Committee and an experienced practitioner of the arts of compromise and conciliation, was chosen to fill out the unexpired portion of Ferency's two-year term.

Far more important to the long-term prospects of the Michigan Democratic party than the resignation of a state chairman was the almost simultaneous withdrawal of the UAW from the AFL-CIO. Though both labor organizations cooperated during the 1968 campaign, the dominant labor voice in the councils of the state party now belonged not to Gus Scholle but to Sam Fishman, director of the UAW's Michigan Community Action Program (CAP). Though without the UAW the state AFL-CIO was but a shadow of its former self, its ambitions did not diminish with its strength. When the UAW endorsed James McNeely, who had served as Levin's deputy, for state chairman in 1969, the AFL-CIO, now led by William Marshall, supported deputy secretary of state William Hettiger. McNeely won on the first ballot, and even the AFL-CIO was forced to recognize that the UAW was the single most powerful force in the Michigan Democratic party.

With the election of McNeely, the UAW demonstrated its ability to exercise influence in the party organization. In 1970 the union displayed its ability to affect the outcome of a Democratic gubernatorial primary when it opposed the nomination of Zolton Ferency. Convinced that the former state party chairman would not do appreciably better against William Milliken than he had against George Romney in 1966, and not entirely persuaded that it would be all to the good if he did, the UAW endorsed Sander Levin. Levin won the nomination and Milliken won the November election. Thus it was demonstrated that the UAW could determine the selection of the party chairman and provide perhaps a decisive advantage to a candidate in a Democratic primary, but it could not by itself, or even in combination with the AFL-CIO, elect a governor.

Through its own statewide political apparatus the UAW encouraged the active involvement of union members in the county and district Democratic committees that make up the semiautonomous units of the state Democratic party. Through the election of union members as precinct delegates the UAW regularly fielded the largest single bloc of delegates in many of the county and district conventions that selected delegates to both the state and national Democratic conventions. Through a well-developed ability to get its own members elected at every level of the party organization the UAW had become the most powerful part of the Democratic coalition. Elections, however, do not always or even very often result in an apportionment of power that reflects the numerical strength of every group in the electorate. In 1972 the national Democratic party, under the direction of George McGovern, proceeded to adopt rules that required precisely such an apportionment. The Michigan Democratic party, which had already had a reform commission of its own and already required that all official bodies in the party be divided equally between the sexes, made little formal protest against the extension of guaranteed representation to other groups that could lay claim to the need for what some called affirmative action and others called mandatory quotas.

Few seemed to notice, and fewer still were heard to object, that one consequence of the new arrangement, if it were really applied in all its mathematical exactness, would be the reduction of black participation from roughly 20 percent, the proportion of the black contribution to the Democratic electorate, to approximately 11 percent, its percentage of the Michigan population as a whole. This obvious political problem was ignored by the adherents of the new politics in the interest of a theory that proposed to produce perfect political equality. The enthusiasm aroused by the promise of guaranteed representation helped George McGovern win the Democratic presidential nomination; the attempt to implement the theory of proportional power nearly destroyed the Democratic party.

Having accepted the principle that power in the party should be apportioned on the basis of numerical strength in the population, the elected leadership of the state Democratic party found it impossible to resist the claim that a similar apportionment should be made among the slate of candidates the party was to nominate at its August state convention. The slate, however, was not large enough to accommodate the claimed entitlement of each group, and the party leadership was unable or unwilling to compel concessions. Immobilized by its new principles, the state party had become considerably less than the sum of its parts. The UAW decided to act on its own, while the party leadership refused to act at all. In consultation with the AFL-CIO, the union fashioned a separate slate of candidates and supported them in the convention. Every candidate on the union slate became the nominee of the Michigan Democratic party, and the UAW, in this instance at least, left no doubt that it had the power to dominate the Democratic party.

The history of the UAW and the Democratic party from its origins through the Democratic state convention in the summer of 1972 has been published in an earlier volume. This work continues that history from 1972 to 1983. Nineteen seventy-two marked the end of one era and the beginning of another in the union's involvement in party politics. Before 1972 the UAW acted as a participant, albeit the strongest one, in the Democratic coalition; after 1972 the UAW simply took over the leadership of the Democratic party.

At the state convention, when the party leadership was unable to produce agreement among the groups claiming representation on the basis of their percentage of the general population, the UAW abandoned persuasion and used power. But although the union could dominate the party it could not so easily influence the outcome of a statewide election. Democrats might be divided on the question whether to have a quota system within the party;

among the white residents of Oakland, Macomb, and Wayne counties there was little debate, and even less disagreement, about whether to permit the imposition of racial quotas in the public schools. Democratic members of Congress who normally commanded 70 or even 80 percent of the vote now found themselves, often for the first time in their lives, fighting for political survival. Black Democrats watched with growing cynicism and distrust as some of the most ardent opponents of segregation in the South tried to establish themselves as the most determined opponents of what seemed, at least to the courts, the best means of eliminating de facto segregation in the North. The New Deal coalition in which labor and blacks had joined together to support a program that promised economic benefits was in danger of being destroyed by a social issue that split along racial lines.

The 1972 election was decisive in convincing the political leadership of the UAW that the Democratic party could win elections only if it could win back the allegiance of the white blue-collar workers spread through the metropolitan suburbs of Detroit. Nothing was more important, then, than that the Democratic party be chaired by someone who had precisely the same point of view. The union did not have far to look. Though he had been chairman of the Oakland County Democratic party for less than a single term, Morley Winograd had already acquired a reputation as an intelligent and effective opponent of the new politics and the new rules of the Democratic party. With the endorsement of the UAW, Winograd was elected state chairman in February, 1973, and with the advice and assistance of Sam Fishman began almost immediately to move the party away from the left and toward the political center.

The candidate of the union had become the chairman of the party, but that was, if the most important, only the first step toward establishing complete control of the party. The chairman was placed under the obligation to consult with the party officers, most of whom were either members or employees of the UAW or the AFL-CIO, before he made any public statement on any public issue. The state central committee, which determined party policy between party conventions, was brought under union control through the ingenious device of a caucus in which labor, its allies, and those who wanted to remain in its good graces adopted a position on each matter scheduled to come before the central committee. Without any organized source of opposition, what was called the unity caucus decided before the central committee meeting what the central committee would do. With matters already decided, debate diminished and open dissent became almost as rare as it was useless. The Democratic party had become a subsidiary of the UAW.

The UAW had taken control of the party to return it to its historically successful emphasis on economic issues. The old Democratic coalition had acquired and kept political power on both the national and state levels because of its ability to appeal to electoral majorities concerned mainly with improving the material conditions of existence. Under its new leadership the Democratic party was not about to permit the Republicans to distract attention from economic questions. There was no hesitation, then, when it became possible to make a ballot proposal to eliminate the sales tax on food and drugs the principal issue in the 1974 gubernatorial campaign. William Milliken, the Republican governor, opposed repeal, while Sander Levin, the Democratic challenger, favored it and promised not to increase any other tax to compensate for the revenue that would be lost. The electorate repealed the tax and reelected the Republican. The UAW and the Democratic party, through a combination of chance and calculation, had for the first time in years been able to wage a campaign in which an economic question was put before voters undisturbed by busing, abortion, amnesty, or any of the other social issues that had sent so many Democratic candidacies down to inglorious defeat. But even though they had waged the battle on their own terms, they had lost. Controlling the party organization was one thing; controlling the Michigan electorate was quite another.

The defeat of Sander Levin in 1974 could of course be blamed on the candidate's own deficiencies. Levin had fallen behind the rest of the Democratic ticket in Oakland, Macomb, and western Wayne counties in 1970; he had fallen behind even further in those areas in 1974. If the party needed to field a stronger candidate, the UAW, through its control of the party and through its own political organization, was in a powerful position to put one forward. In 1976, however, neither the party nor the UAW did anything to influence the outcome of the Democratic primary to choose a candidate to run for the U.S. Senate seat that had been held for eighteen years by Philip A. Hart. The party continued its traditional policy of neutrality, while the UAW, which just a few months earlier had played a decisive part in the primary victory of Jimmy Carter, found itself unable to make any decision at all. Congressman James G. O'Hara had become one of the most effective legislators in the House, and as an Irish Catholic from Macomb county appeared to have the best chance of carrying the blue-collar suburban vote. Congressman Donald Riegle had the intense support of the union leadership in his own district and a reputation as a candidate who would do anything to win. Neither O'Hara nor Riegle, however, was thought to have much chance against Richard Austin, who, as secretary of state, had a statewide following and a well-known name. Austin, it was generally believed, would win the primary because he was the secretary of state and lose the general election because he was black. The UAW was unwilling to be drawn into a contest in which an endorsement would almost inevitably divide the union, and, if the endorsement was of either O'Hara or Riegle, divide it along racial lines. With both the party and the union neutral, Richard Austin, who was supposed to win the primary, lost; and Donald Riegle, who as a liberal was supposed to have little chance in the primary and none at all in the general election, won the nomination, and in November, a seat in the U.S. Senate.

Though the UAW and the Democratic party had been unable to win the gubernatorial election in 1974 and unwilling to become involved in the Senate primary in 1976, 1978 seemed to offer reasonable prospects of success. Without needing or wanting the endorsement of the UAW, William Fitzgerald, an Irish Catholic opposed to abortion, won the party's gubernatorial nomination and appeared to have an excellent chance to reclaim the lost Democratic allegiance of suburban working-class Catholics. Although Fitzgerald enjoyed the apparent advantage of belonging to the very constituency to which he appealed, the rejection of his candidacy by suburban voters approached abandonment. He lost the suburbs and nearly everything else as well. William Milliken became the first Republican in more than thirty years to carry Wayne County, as he swept every industrial county in the state. Fitzgerald, the candidate who was supposed to win back the blue-collar suburbs, was annihilated. Carl Levin, who because he was a liberal, a Jew, and the president of the Detroit Common Council, was given no chance of winning in the suburbs and therefore no chance of winning election to the U.S. Senate, defeated the incumbent Republican senator, Robert Griffin. In the three elections held since it took control of the Democratic party, the UAW had witnessed Democratic victories only when the Democratic candidates were supposedly too liberal to win.

The Democratic party had not yet succeeded in winning back the loyal electoral support of the white working class, and its effort to do so had caused serious difficulties with the black leadership in both the party and the UAW. In 1973 the UAW endorsed Mel Ravitz instead of Coleman Young in the Detroit mayoral primary on the theory that a black candidate could not defeat the conservative John Nichols in the general election. The black leadership of the union refused to honor the endorsement and instead supported the black candidate. Coleman Young became the first black mayor of Detroit, and the black community had a prominent and powerful public spokesman. In 1976 Young and Leonard Woodcock became two of the first public figures to endorse Jimmy Carter, and both received the rewards of foresight. Woodcock became the first American ambassador to the People's Republic of China, and Young became vice-chairman of the Democratic National Committee. Young was a friend and ally of the president, and Detroit began to receive more federal financial assistance. Detroit, however, also depended on the state, and no one needed to tell the mayor the importance of maintaining good relations with the state's Republican governor. In 1978, Coleman Young did little for William Fitzgerald, and, Morley Winograd charged, a great deal for William Milliken. Relations between the mayor and the state chairman were strained; they would become much worse.

Coleman Young was vice-chairman of the national Democratic party and the person with whom the Carter White House consulted before making any appointments or political decisions that involved or affected Michigan. Morley Winograd, however, had some power of his own. He was still state chairman, and he continued to enjoy the confidence and the support of the UAW. He had, moreover, a national position of his own as head of a commission appointed by the national party chairman to review and propose revisions in the rules under which the party selected delegates to the national convention. When the Winograd Commission finished its work, Coleman Young, who favored quotas, attacked Winograd for abandoning affirmative action. The chairman angrily denied the allegation.

Winograd left the chairmanship in 1979 to take a position in private business, but the split between the white leadership of the party and the black leadership of Detroit widened and deepened as Winograd and the UAW supported Edward Kennedy, and Coleman Young stayed with Jimmy Carter in the 1980 presidential primary. After the general election relations became even worse when the two black districts, the First and Thirteenth, walked out of a state central committee meeting in protest against Winograd's charge that Coleman Young and the black leadership wanted more than their fair share of representation among the Michigan members of the Democratic National Committee. Relations were broken off completely when the First and Thirteenth boycotted the state Democratic convention and then for the next two years held their own event instead of attending the annual Jefferson-Jackson Day dinner.

The black boycott of the Democratic party had begun because of a question of political representation; it ended because of a question of economic survival. The inflation of the last years of the Carter administration and the unemployment of the first years of the Reagan administration combined to produce economic calamity in Michigan. With the announcement that William Milliken would not seek reelection, Coleman Young faced the unpleasant prospect of a Republican administration in Washington and perhaps a conservative administration in Lansing. For its part, the UAW had witnessed in agonizing disbelief the decimation of its membership and was prepared to do whatever was required to elect a Democratic governor. The UAW, the AFL-CIO, the Michigan Education Association (MEA), Coleman Young, and most of the leadership of the state party agreed that the election of a Democratic governor depended on finding a candidate with the broadest possible appeal, and all of them ultimately endorsed the candidacy of Congressman James J. Blanchard. Though few knew it at the time, that result had been anticipated, and in some measure orchestrated, by Sam Fishman and Morley Winograd.

Contents

PART 1   The Labor Party

Chapter 1   The Trauma of 1972   3

2   Battle for Control   34

3   Democratic Centralism and the Movement to the
Center   58

**PART 2   The Union, the Party, and the
Electorate**

4   1974 and the Politics of Integrity   87

5   1974 and the Politics of Deception   116

6   The Year of the Long Shot, 1976   142

7   The Creation of a Gubernatorial Candidate, 1978   175

8   Winners and Losers, 1978   194

PART 3   Division and Victory

9   Black and White, Jew and Gentile   219

10   The Common Danger and the Politics of Necessity   252

Selected Bibliography   277

Index   281

PART 1
The Labor Party

CHAPTER 1

The Trauma of 1972

On March 24, 1970, in what Theodore White, with unusual hyperbole, called "an unprecedented public philosophical statement on the nature of America's communities,"[1] Richard Nixon defined the principles of his administration's policy on race, and in so doing disclosed the political direction of the Republican party. "The goal of this administration," he said, "is a free and open society. In saying this, I use the words 'free' and 'open' quite precisely." Freedom, for the president, meant both the "right to choose, and the ability to choose. The right to move out of a mid-city slum, for example, means little without the means of doing so." There was nothing about the president's definition of freedom that was likely to disturb anyone, except possibly those who claimed to find a sinister meaning in everything, no matter how mundane, Richard Nixon ever said. The president's understanding of the meaning of an "open society," however, was another matter. As if by design, it appeared to define "open" by the right to close:

> Similarly an "open" society is one of open choice—and one in which the individual has the mobility to take advantage of those choices. . . . We cannot be free, and at the same time be required to fit our lives into prescribed places on a racial grid—whether segregated or integrated, and whether by some mathematical formula or by automatic assignment.[2]

Freedom, which had been defined as the right and the ability to choose, was threatened by the imposition of racial restrictions, whether those restrictions took the form of segregation, i.e., the exclusion of someone on the basis of race, or of integration, i.e., the inclusion of someone on the basis of race. Freedom, according to Nixon, demanded the elimination of segregation, but—and this was the heart of the political message—it did not permit the introduction of compulsory integration.

If there was any doubt about the real meaning of the president's message the next paragraph supplied all the clarity required.

> An open society does not have to be homogeneous, or even fully integrated.

There is room within it for communities. Especially in a nation like America, it is natural and right that we have Italian or Irish or Negro or Norwegian neighborhoods; it is natural and right that members of those communities feel a sense of group identity and group pride.[3]

Nixon's endorsement of a society separated into its ethnic and racial parts provided the context for what otherwise would have appeared to be an attack on any form of racial distinction.

As we strive to make our schools places of equal educational opportunity, we should keep our eye fixed on this goal: to achieve a set of conditions in which neither the laws nor the institutions supported by law any longer draw an invidious distinction based on race. . . .[4]

This objective could be achieved by ethnic communities, or more simply and more broadly, white communities, in which every white student from an all-white neighborhood was admitted to the neighborhood school without regard to the color of his skin.

The day after Nixon announced his policy of opposition to both segregation and integration, a policy that was grounded in his belief that Americans supported desegregation but not racial integration, Philip A. Hart, the senior senator from Michigan, walked down the block from his home in northwest Washington and entered the Shoreham Hotel. It seemed to Hart, after he had entered the Shoreham and begun his speech to a meeting of the Civil Liberties Clearinghouse, that the president's statement of March 24 threatened not just a curtailment of the rights of a minority but the very existence of free institutions. The Nixon administration, by relaxing the government's commitment to racial equality, was removing the strongest bulwark of racial peace. Hart, who rarely raised his voice, attacked the president of the United States and did it with weapons he seldom employed, ridicule and irony. He began, however, with typical deference.

I am always hesitant to imagine myself in the position of a Negro. No white can do that successfully.

But as far as I am able . . . I would guess that I would feel today very much like a defendant listening to a prejudiced judge charge the jury.

The judge says to the jury all the right things about constitutional rights and liberties. It's those knowing winks he delivers that really bother you. The kind of knowing wink that says . . . "You-all know I have to say these things but you shouldn't feel you have to pay them any mind."

The Nixon administration was using the same well-understood deception on black citizens that southern judges and all-white juries had used on black defendants.

> The administration comes out four-square for school desegregation but . . . wink . . . Leon Panetta is forced out of office.
>
> The administration is heartily in favor of extending the voting franchise to every American citizen but . . . wink . . . it supports a watered-down Votings Rights Bill.
>
> The administration applauds all the historic civil rights decisions of the Supreme Court but . . . wink . . . Judge Carswell is the nominee to the bench.

The senator's most withering criticism was directed at that part of Nixon's statement of the preceding day in which the president had announced the administration's interpretation of equal educational opportunity. In words that he added to his written text while he waited to speak, Hart noted:

> And we, of course, have new federal guidelines for school desegregation, I guess. Depending on whom is interpreting the President's mystical message on school desegregation, the solution, we discover is to build up the black schools to parity with the white schools.
>
> Now that still gives us a net gain since 1954. Then it was "separate but equal." Now the watchword is "separate but *really* equal."

Despite a reputation for being somehow above politics, Hart had not only an appreciation for the art and its practice but—and this set him apart from those for whom politics was an end in itself—a clear understanding of the relation between political ambition and sound public policy. Without citing either *Federalist* No. 10 or *Federalist* No. 51, he summarized the thought of the two most famous and most influential portions of what is still the best commentary on the Constitution of the United States: "Our founding fathers . . . devised a system built on the premise that politicans will indeed act in their own interest. But most of the time, what is good for the politician is good for the nation." Unfortunately, the pursuit of political self-interest was not always sufficient to guarantee the public welfare. The Nixon strategy constituted "one of those times in American history when sound political consideration does not result in sound public policy." According to Hart:

> A southern strategy for a Republican President may be very sound politics. And that's what makes me uneasy. Because I have always comforted myself with the notion that sound politics usually could be depended upon to result in sound public policy. . . . And it is a little unnerving to see a major case . . . a really important issue . . . where it is not.

This, if true, was a dismal prospect. If civil rights came to carry a political cost to elected officials, elected officials would soon find ways and means to avoid any connection with the rights of unpopular or politically expendable minorities. Still, this was a "southern strategy for a Republican President" and his administration.

> The Republican administration, to all appearances is winning support . . . or a measure of support . . . from all those who have felt irritated, threatened, or angered by the black man's attempt to gain full citizenship.

> The Negro has been written off.

The Republican administration of Richard Nixon had "written off" black citizens, and Phil Hart had written off the Nixon administration. "I am not . . . going to plead with the administration to do an about face. . . . I have a feeling that they are pretty well set in their ways." Others would have to "continue to make it clear that the nation's long-term conscience can tolerate only one course . . . a continuing battle for equality." Hart looked to the Democratic Congress and to the coalition of groups that made up the civil rights movement.

> This movement must stay alive if our society is to survive. I know that sounds overblown and exaggerated. Everyone is certain that society will die if his particular project is not immediately undertaken. But in this case even a less partial source than myself might link racial justice to survival. And survival is too important to dismiss with a wink.[5]

A year and a half after Hart spoke in the Shoreham Hotel what he had feared had come to pass. If anything, he had not adequately foreseen the dimension of the difficulty. The willingness to support the demands of white constituencies instead of the constitutional guarantees of black minorities, which had begun as the southern strategy of the Republican president, quickly became the political tactic of a growing number of northern Democratic congressmen. What had seemed a clear issue of principle when civil rights meant a struggle for black freedom in the South became morally nebulous when the question was de facto school segregation in the North. Many who had refused to distinguish between a Stennis and a Fulbright on the ground that both had deplorable records on civil rights legislation became modern schoolmen constructing elaborate proofs to demonstrate that it was morally better to give up the defense of unpopular minority rights than to lose the power to help those same minorities in other ways.

In Michigan the Democratic party that in many respects had become the most integrated party organization in America, that had vigorously opposed and even voted against John F. Kennedy's selection of Lyndon Johnson in 1960 on civil rights grounds, and that had elected the first black in history to the Democratic National Committee in 1968 became irrevocably divided on the day in late September, 1971, when Federal District Judge Stephen J. Roth "ordered that a metropolitan-areawide desegregation plan be developed for Detroit, where he found the schools deliberately segregated."[6]

At first the state Democratic party appeared to ignore the obvious political dangers. The state party chairman, James McNeely, considered himself a liberal and believed the Democratic party had an unbreakable commitment to racial integration. McNeely also believed that the Michigan Democratic party could not be for civil rights only when there was no political price to be paid for the observance of principle. Not everyone agreed with this point of view, then or later, and not everyone was convinced that the chairman of a political party should so blithely ignore the demands of political necessity. McNeely, however, was determined, as he put it, "to find out who the real liberals really were."[7] Five days after Judge Roth issued his ruling, the Democratic state central committee held a long-scheduled meeting in Battle Creek. To his own immediate satisfaction, McNeely discovered that the "real liberals" included nearly everyone in attendance. The central committee adopted a resolution that stated: "We accept busing as an instrument for the immediate implementation of the court's ruling."[8] This resolution was signed by, among others, the attorney general of the state of Michigan. That signature alone may have sealed his political fate and deprived him of a seat in the Senate of the United States.

The Battle Creek resolution was adopted on Saturday, October 2. Two weeks later, on Saturday, October 16, the Macomb County Democratic party held its fifth annual Phil Hart Day Dinner in Mount Clemens. In all three of his campaigns for the Senate, Hart had done extremely well in Macomb County; in 1970, he had carried the county by a margin of more than three-to-one.[9] The congressman from Macomb County, James G. O'Hara, had been elected to his first term in 1958, the same year Hart was first elected to the Senate, and they had become good friends. Hart viewed O'Hara not only as a friend, but as one of the finest legislative craftsmen in the Congress. In 1965, while Hart served as floor leader on the Voting Rights Act in the Senate, O'Hara was one of the leading proponents of the bill in the House. For the first twelve years of their respective careers, they seldom disagreed on an issue and never differed on a principle. Both were called, and called themselves, liberal Democrats. But although they never exchanged a harsh or even unpleasant word on the subject, busing brought to an end this close collaboration between two unusually able public servants who had shared a common understanding of the public welfare. On that issue, O'Hara and Hart were separated by a distance that could never be bridged. What for Hart was a

matter of moral principle was for O'Hara, necessarily, a matter of sheer
political survival. Unlike Hart, O'Hara had to seek reelection in 1972, and he
had to seek it in a county that was perhaps more in fear of busing and more
angered by it than any other in the nation.[10] Hart knew the intensity of feeling
in Macomb County, and he knew that O'Hara was doing everything he could
to convince his constituents that he had opposed busing for years. He also
knew what he had known a year and a half earlier: that there are some issues
on which political self-interest does not lead to the public policy the country
ought to have.

Several hundred residents of Macomb County, most of them active
members of the Democratic party, were in attendance when Phil Hart rose to
speak at the dinner being given in his honor. He went immediately to the
central issue. "Why," he asked, "should good public schooling be an accident of geography? Is it right for rich kids to go to good schools while poor
kids go to inferior schools?" Hart clearly thought it was not: "Is it not more
moral to hold that all children in a state deserve an equal chance at good
public education, regardless of where they live or how much money their
parents make?" Most, if not all, of his mainly working-class Democratic
audience might have agreed with the abstract proposition that wealth and
location should not provide some with a good education while preventing
others from a chance at even an adequate one. But they did not have abstract
propositions in mind, and Hart knew it.

> Right now, the lightning rod for all school concerns and tensions is that yellow
> peril, the school bus. It is ironic—though perfectly understandable—that the tool
> that promises to be of least use in solving all our problems is the one that
> generates the greatest emotion.

Though busing was likely to be the least effective means of ending school
segregation, Hart was not prepared to reject it out of hand. In words that may
have been intended not only to make his own position clear, but to make
things easier for Jim O'Hara, he stated the principal reason for retaining
busing as a possible instrument of policy.

> I have heard a great many indisputably sound arguments against racial busing—
> many of them from Congressman Jim O'Hara. It is one of the rare issues on
> which we differ. He says it is never the right thing to do; I say it is right on those
> occasions when a Constitutional guarantee can't be delivered any other way.

Busing was to be used as a last resort, when it was the only means by which to
protect constitutional rights. The "sound arguments against racial busing"
that were being advanced by, among others, Jim O'Hara, were really more

political than constitutional. Hart mentioned several of them. Nothing was "sounder . . . than the concept of neighborhood schools," and it was "comforting to have your children close by. . . ." Moreover, no one should be "accused of bigotry" for being "reluctant to have your child bused . . . to a school where the education is the same or worse than the one within walking distance or if you think the new environment might be hostile."[11]

The arguments against busing were essentially concerned with the fears and the hopes of parents for their children. There were, however, arguments on the other side, and one of them "is overriding and it says that deliberate racial segregation in the public schools is wrong. That's been the law since 1954 and the morality, I think, is well established." There were others as well. One of them—that neither money nor race should entitle some to a better, and condemn others to a worse, education—had been mentioned at the beginning of his speech. Another went to the heart of the most important thing threatened by the whole busing controversy, the basic relationship between the races. If white parents vigorously opposed busing, and if most white public officials and the government they controlled followed the fears of their constituents and prohibited it, would it not be clear to black citizens that they might be tolerated but would never be fully accepted? Would it not appear that for all the talk about equality of opportunity and the brotherhood of man, no white, no matter what abstract principle he was willing to defend when the problem affected someone else, was the least bit color-blind when an improvement in the condition of blacks endangered his own way of life? For years a central tenet of the democratic dogma had been the belief in the limitless possibilities for constant improvement through the provision of massive doses of public education. Perhaps the most commonly believed equation of individual and social progress was the simple formulation that education was beneficial in proportion to its quality, and that money was the major, if not the sole, cause of educational excellence. It followed that educational opportunity was the greatest in those schools supported by the most money, and black parents, in Hart's judgment, knew where that was. "Blacks are convinced that money follows whites—that black kids don't get the same deal that white kids do unless they are going to school with white kids. And let's face it, they have about 100 years of experience to back up that belief." White opposition to busing as a legitimate and permissible means by which the judiciary could remedy racial segregation raised the basic question of good faith—or, rather, it raised the question whether white claims of good faith could ever have credibility. "So what happens," Hart asked, "when a responsible court finds that blacks are being segregated as deliberate policy and the only possible remedy—though a temporary one—is the bus?" Hart thought he knew the answer, and he gave it in the form of a question that he hoped would appeal to the conscience: "If we outlaw that tool, do we not signal that we are content with enforced segregation, a splitting of society between black and white?"[12]

When Phil Hart was the floor manager in the Senate for the 1965 Voting Rights Act he had faced the formidable difficulty of persuading the chairman of the Senate Judiciary Committee, James Eastland of Mississippi, who had once been described as "philosophically more inclined toward slavery than voting rights," to let the bill out of committee for the consideration of the full Senate. Eastland "could have bottled up the bill forever. But he didn't."[13] Clarence Mitchell of the NAACP thought he knew why:

> Phil Hart was our bridge to Eastland. He was indispensable. Somehow he was able to talk to Eastland and get him to lift the roadblocks. I don't know how he did it, but it was probably the same way Phil usually got things done. He was such an honest, such a fair man, that Eastland probably felt an obligation to act responsibly with him.[14]

The senator's honesty was unquestioned, and his fairness was almost legendary, but his ability to persuade Eastland, and the respect he received from those who disagreed most vigorously with him on matters of public policy, depended perhaps more on his natural dignity and reserve. He was the very antithesis of the gregarious American politician who remembers every name and forgets every friendship. It was the sort of personal reserve of which Walter Bagehot wrote: "In a popular assembly this sort of reserve rightly manipulated is a power."[15]

The dignity that had apparently appealed to the conscience of such an ardent segregationist as James Eastland, and the quiet reserve that the *Washington Post* believed had helped him to become by the end of his second term "the spokesman for the Senate's liberal Democratic bloc" at a time when that bloc carried substantial authority, were effective and useful in the Senate. But in Macomb County, among his own constituents, neither his personal character nor his obvious sincerity carried any weight in the face of the public's passionate fear of the new "yellow peril." Hart's speech was not greeted with an ovation or even normal applause. While some applauded without enthusiasm, most refused to give any sign that might be mistaken for approval. The major portion of this Democratic audience greeted the speech of Michigan's only Democratic senator with silent, sullen contempt. The fifth annual Phil Hart Day Dinner came to its awkward conclusion. It was the last such dinner the Macomb County Democratic party ever held.

While Phil Hart was willing to ask a white Democratic audience for courage and compassion as they faced the possibility of racial busing, the other white members of the Michigan congressional delegation, all of whom faced reelection from white constituencies, were less interested in public virtue than in political preservation. In 1972, only seven of the nineteen House members from Michigan were Democrats, and of the seven, two, John Conyers and Charles Diggs, were black congressmen from heavily black districts. The five white Democrats, Martha Griffiths, James G. O'Hara, Lucien Nedzi, William Ford, and John Dingell, all had districts that were mainly suburban and largely, if not exclusively, white. Griffiths, who in 1962 had warned President Kennedy that an executive order against housing discrimination could have devastating political consequences because suburban Democratic congressmen would lose white votes,[16] was not about to counsel political courage in 1972. Along with Ford, Dingell, Nedzi, and O'Hara, Griffiths voted in February "for a barrage of anti-busing legislation, even including one measure to deprive Federal funds for busing from those districts complying with court orders."[17] Donald W. Riegle, Jr., then a congressman and still a Republican, objected to the news coverage of this series of votes and claimed to be the only member of the Michigan delegation except Conyers to have voted against depriving districts of federal funds for complying with a judicial order.[18] Riegle's displeasure, however, was, until the publication of his book, *O Congress*, discreetly confined to his diary. Even then it was not at all clear what his position really was. On November 4, 1971, Riegle, along with every other member of the Michigan delegation except John Conyers, voted for the Broomfield amendment, which would delay the effect of any federal court order requiring busing until all appeals had been exhausted.[19] This would postpone, sometimes for years, the date at which any child could be bused to achieve racial integration. Seven months later, on June 8, 1972, the Flint congressman voted for adoption of the conference report on a higher education appropriation bill[20] that postponed implementation of court desegregation orders requiring busing of school children.[21] Moreover, the very day after he recorded his apparent willingness to be counted among the very few white liberals who had not "jumped on the anti-busing bandwagon," the congressman spoke to "eight young black mothers" in his district office. He inquired about their views on racial busing by posing a question that not everyone would find completely connected with reality: "If given the choice of equal resources for neighborhood schools in all black areas—or integrated schools with busing—they indicated by a vote of 7 to 1 they would prefer the upgraded neighborhood school."[22] What the answer might have been had the choice been between the schools as they were in black neighborhoods and integrated schools with busing was apparently something the congressman had no interest in ascertaining.[23]

The full force of the passion unleashed by the busing issue fell not on

Donald Riegle or Martha Griffiths but on the four white congressmen from the districts that were mainly suburban and immediately adjacent to Detroit. In areas where many of the most recent arrivals had lived in Detroit, where nearly all of the residents were white, and where the most difficult thing to find was someone willing to advocate school busing to achieve racial balance in the schools, organizations were created, sometimes as if by spontaneous generation, for the single purpose of preventing forced busing with whatever means were available. An Oakland County housewife, Irene McCabe, who had no previous history of political involvement and no prior record of civic accomplishment, became a household word as the principal spokesperson for the National Action Group (NAG). McCabe, whose major contribution to the public debate was to stand before an audience and unbutton her blouse to reveal a T-shirt inscribed with the acronym NAG, led an organization made up of thousands of suburban women, all of them white, who exchanged the obscurity of private life for the noise and notoriety of the public arena solely in order to preserve the sanctity of the neighborhood school. They had no interest in fashioning coalitions among diverse constituencies; they had no concern for other political issues; and they appeared oblivious to the distinctions between the major political parties. The ladies of NAG viewed busing as a direct threat to their way of life and an immediate danger to the physical and moral well-being of their children; they were in politics as an almost instinctive act of self-preservation. There were of course those who were perfectly willing to exploit the opportunity to achieve a larger fame and a wider following. L. Brooks Patterson, the attorney for NAG, was not content to restrict his advocacy to the courts. With the intense hatred that often characterizes those who find in nearly every political issue a source of moral outrage and a cause for righteous indignation, Patterson used busing first to become well known and then to become a candidate for Oakland County prosecutor, an office from which, he seemed to suggest, he could prosecute anyone who even dared suggest busing Oakland County children to Detroit public schools.

Patterson may have been the most demagogic of the busing opponents, and NAG the most famous of the antibusing organizations, but every suburban community had some kind of an organization, and every organization had someone making public statements and political demands. Nedzi, Dingell, Ford, and O'Hara were not slow to appreciate the significance of the demands or the unforgiving nature of those who made them. John Dingell, who had once refused to return a call from Walter Reuther because the president of the UAW was calling to ask his support on open-housing legislation, summed up the issue at a meeting in the sixteenth district in words somewhat reminiscent of Hobbes's famous description of the state of nature: "Busing is the meanest, hottest, nastiest, ugliest issue I've ever faced. It produces raw, boiling emotion."[24] Dingell's own contribution to moderation and reason was limited to his redundant insistence that he was "completely and entirely opposed to cross-district busing to achieve racial balance, and for first-class education for every child in this nation." The audience, described by the *Detroit News* as "conservative," was moved to applause when Dingell evidenced his credentials by asserting that he was "the only Michigan congressman to oppose the nomination of Judge Roth ten years ago."[25] That no one had ever even heard of busing to achieve racial integration in Michigan a decade earlier did nothing to diminish the effect this statement had on that audience. Roth was for busing and Dingell had voted against Roth. Dingell was on their side. Q.E.D.

What John Dingell understood, the others quickly learned: busing was something it was necessary to oppose totally and something that had to have been opposed from the very beginning. Total opposition required a willingness to do anything necessary to make sure that busing became impossible. The only way to do that was to amend the Constitution of the United States to prohibit the judiciary from employing racial busing for any purpose whatsoever. Suburban parents had little difficulty choosing between the tangible existence of the school down the street and the abstract propositions contained in the fundamental law of the country. Suburban congressmen, all of whom were lawyers, had little difficulty choosing between the passionate public demands of outraged constituents and private reservations about the propriety of altering the permanent legal framework for so transient a purpose. Lucien Nedzi, who had represented the Fourteenth District for ten years and who was the only member of Congress whom Phil Hart, who chose his words with unusual care, had ever publicly described as "great," yielded to necessity and "signed a discharge petition to pry a proposed constitutional amendment against busing out of the Judiciary Committee. . . ."[26] He also "voted for the Broomfield amendment to halt further court-ordered busing pending appeal."[27]

Nedzi, indeed, went further than any other Michigan Democrat except Martha Griffiths to build a record of opposition to busing. President Nixon's legislative solution to the busing problem was contained in two bills tied to each other in a curious fashion. The first bill, entitled the Student Transportation Moratorium Act, would bar implementation of all new busing orders until July 1, 1973, or until Congress passed the other bill, entitled the Equal Educational Opportunities Act. The latter bill would allow busing only as a limited last-resort remedy for segregation, and then only to the closest or next closest school to the student's home, and would appropriate $2.5 billion in federal funds for compensatory education programs in poor schools. George Meany called all of this "a cynical attempt to reward those who said 'never,' and to undermine the moral leadership of those citizens who endeavored to comply with the Constitution and the Supreme Court's 1954 decision."[28] The House, however, was listening to other voices. When the Equal Educational

Opportunities bill came up for a vote on August 18, 1972, Representative Louis Stokes, a black congressman from Cleveland, offered an amendment. It was the same amendment that had been used repeatedly and successfully in the past to nullify antibusing provisions. The amendment simply stated that nothing in the bill was intended to violate the Constitution. Now that busing was no longer the means of ending racial discrimination only in the South, 37 northern Democrats joined with 60 southern Democrats and 98 Republicans to defeat the Stokes amendment 178 to 195.[29] In the Michigan delegation even three Republicans—Riegle, Marvin Esch, and Philip Ruppe—voted for the amendment. Among the Democrats only Martha Griffiths and Lucien Nedzi were unwilling to declare that Congress had no desire intentionally to violate the Constitution of the United States.[30] After defeat of the Stokes amendment, the House passed the bill, 283 to 102. This vote, according to the *Congressional Quarterly,* represented "the largest showing of anti-busing strength in the House to date, but a liberal filibuster delayed Senate action and killed the bill."[31] Michigan Senator Philip A. Hart voted against the motion by Senator Proxmire to cut off debate.[32]

Nedzi had regularly rolled up majorities of 70 percent in his heavily Polish working-class district. This year, however, the Democratic congressman was opposed by a new organization that called itself Northwest Mothers Alert. It was no secret what they were on the alert for. Nedzi did everything he could to convince anyone who would listen that he was adamantly and unalterably opposed to busing, but a great many of those who had voted for him in the past refused to believe him. Fearful of association with any organization that was not clearly identified with opposition to busing, Nedzi accepted the assistance of the UAW but carefully contrived to hide the union's endorsement from public view. Though the name of the UAW was not to be found on any of the literature Nedzi used in the campaign, and though he himself had at least a recent record of legislative opposition to busing that could rival that of the most vociferous Republican opponent, the congressman was almost denied the nomination of his own party. In the most closely contested congressional primary in the state, and certainly one of the most closely contested in the nation, Nedzi won the Democratic primary by only 1,866 votes.[33] Had there not been several other candidates in the race who also opposed busing, Nedzi might not have won at all. In the general election, though he won by a larger margin, he came closer to losing to his Republican opponent than he ever had before.[34]

While Riegle complained about the failure of the media to report his record on busing accurately and then suppressed any inclination he might ever have had to state clearly what his position really was; while Dingell lamented the near violent irrationality let loose by the issue and then hurried not only to join but to incite the crowd; while Lucien Nedzi, who regularly faced down admirals and generals in hearings before the House Armed Services Committee, abandoned any concern for the integrity of the American Constitution rather than argue the necessity for moderation with his own constituents—while everyone else looked to his own immediate political advantage, Jim O'Hara tried at least to put the issue in the broader perspective of an essential principle of civil rights. In August, in testimony before the House Committee on Education and Labor, of which he was himself one of the most influential and effective members, O'Hara made the by now obligatory statement expressing his own long-held and irrevocable opposition to busing: "I am against busing—for whatever purpose—if the color of the student's skin becomes his bus ticket."[35] He then went on to reaffirm his opposition to separate schools for black and white: "I believe the unitary school system must be one . . . wholly and unreservedly blind to the color of the student's skin." For O'Hara it followed that nothing should be done that was in any way based on race. He expressly opposed

> any scheme by which any agency of government or, indeed, any private agency, can take people, look at the color of their skins and decide automatically what they are entitled to receive, where they can go to school, where or whether they will vote, or run for office, and how their government will treat them. That kind of a system is racism, and it is what I have always fought against. . . ."[36]

It was to O'Hara's credit that even in the midst of what politicians of both parties regarded as the most inflammatory issue they had ever seen, he sought to remind people that racial discrimination was intolerable and inexcusable. It is a mark of political intelligence to attempt to elevate as far as possible a passion that cannot be resisted. O'Hara did that, but he also understood that there was a limit to resistance. He ended his testimony by insisting that he was still fighting against racism: "And it is what I am fighting against today in seeking to ban—not to limit, not to mitigate, not to hold for a last resort, but to ban busing of school children on the basis of their race."[37]

The residents of O'Hara's Twelfth District, nearly all of whom lived in the blue-collar suburbs of Macomb County, were interested less in professions of opposition than in facts that would prove busing could be stopped and that would demonstrate that their congressman was doing everything possible to stop it. Once busing emerged as an issue it was almost too late for an incumbent congressman, especially a white Democratic suburban congressman, to do anything to prove he actually opposed it. Parents who were enraged at the prospect of having their children forcibly removed from their homes and neighborhoods and taken to a school in a dangerous part of Detroit were not inclined to believe any promise made by a politician who had permitted the possibility to occur in the first place. It was not "What are you going to do about it?'' but ''Why did you let it happen?'' For white suburban parents busing was like war; no one has great enthusiasm for permitting the people to pursue it who failed to prevent it.

O'Hara could not possibly satisfy those who demanded such explanations and insisted on such an accounting. He could only attempt to defuse the issue and disarm the opposition by the regular repetition of promises to support any and all efforts to legislate busing out of existence. At first he resisted the pressure to support a constitutional amendment, but finally it became irresistible, and one of the foremost parliamentary authorities in the Congress did what he had to do. Even then he tried to avoid acting on his decision by resorting to a subterfuge. He announced he would vote for a constitutional amendment when it came before the House. When it was discovered that he had not signed the petition to discharge the bill from committee, which meant that there might never be a vote in the House, several hundred angry citizens gathered in front of his district office in Mount Clemens and demanded his signature as the price of his reelection. With some regret, but no longer with any reluctance, O'Hara added his name to the growing list of those who were willing to petition for the opportunity to place a constitutional prohibition on busing. Like Lucien Nedzi, James O'Hara did everything he had to do to survive and very nearly failed. By less than half a percentage point, O'Hara managed to obtain another term in Congress.[38] Whether it was a permanent reprieve or simply a stay of execution remained to be seen.

Of all the suburban congressmen, Bill Ford had perhaps the easiest time of it in the general election. Looking back on it all two years later, Ford remarked that the fact that he had had a primary opponent seemed to have ''taken all the poison out. O'Hara had to go through it during the general but here, after the primary, the hatred seemed to go out of it.'' The Fifteenth District congressman, who was in many respects the most politically astute member of the Michigan delegation, managed to avoid at least some of the anger directed at his suburban colleagues, but he did not escape the wrath of one of his black colleagues from Detroit. John Conyers did not ordinarily go out of his way to observe congressional customs and traditions that concern the way members are to behave toward each other. As often as not, Conyers would use part of the time he devoted to what sometimes seemed a never-ending series of press conferences to castigate some member of Congress for an abysmal failure to uphold the constitutional rights of blacks and other minorities. These public attacks were almost always directed against southern reactionaries and northern Republicans. Though he had numerous and serious differences with members of the Michigan delegation, he usually refrained from making them a matter of public record. Just before the election, however, Conyers assailed those in the Michigan delegation who opposed busing because of what he called "pressure from the know-nothings and bigots in their districts." He was particularly displeased with Bill Ford, who, according to Conyers, "had the arrogance to assert to me that he was only doing what most black people want in opposing busing." Conyers thought he had a better idea of what black people wanted than a white congressman from the white suburbs did: "most black people don't wish him to help subvert the Constitution with an amendment that is unconstitutional on its face."[39] What Phil Hart had feared and had urged Democrats in Macomb County a year earlier to consider had come to pass. An issue that divided the suburbs from the central city and drove liberal legislators practically to offer to stand in front of a bus the same way and for the same political reason that George Wallace had once stood in front of a school house door in Alabama had diminished and nearly destroyed the willingness of black citizens and black congressmen to believe in a white commitment to civil rights and equal opportunity.

By promising whatever was necessary to stop the dreaded peril of inter-district busing, the incumbent Democratic members of Congress managed to secure reelection. Dingell, Ford, O'Hara, and Nedzi could go back to the Congress, where each of them exercised more than the ordinary amount of influence and received more than the normal degree of respect, and concentrate their considerable abilities on the business of legislation. Seven Michigan Democrats had stood for reelection to the House, and all seven had been returned for another term. But busing had cost the Democrats a seat—one they had not held, but one they had had every reasonable expectation of winning. In 1966, a one-term Democratic congressman with the unforgettable name of Billy Sunday Farnum had, like so many other freshman legislators first elected in the Johnson landslide of 1964, been defeated by a Republican challenger. Since then, Oakland County's two congressional districts, the Eighteenth and the Nineteenth, had both been held by Republicans. Jack MacDonald had a hold on the Nineteenth District that was only slightly less formidable than that which William Broomfield exercised in the Eighteenth. In 1970, MacDonald had defeated the Democratic candidate, Fred Harris, 91,763 to 63,175,[40] while Broomfield had annihilated former state AFL-CIO president Gus Scholle 113,309 to 62,081.[41] MacDonald and Broomfield were to Oakland County what Bill Ford and John Dingell were to western Wayne County. The major difference seemed to lie mainly in the fact that while busing could only hurt liberal Democrats in western Wayne, it could only help conservative Republicans in Oakland. Not content with the natural course of things, and apparently not satisfied with an unbroken record of opposition to busing and the entire liberal agenda, the Eighteenth District congressman made certain that one of the major pieces of antibusing legislation introduced in the House was named the Broomfield amendment. It seemed that nothing

save their own mortality was likely ever to deprive Broomfield and Mac-
Donald of seats in the House, so long as they wished to have them.

Thus, Oakland County had contained two congressional districts that
were difficult for Democrats to win. But through the judicious use of reapportionment, a Democratic legislature in Lansing created in the county one
district, the Nineteenth, that would be impossible for a Democrat to win, and
another, the Eighteenth, in which there would be a slight Democratic majority. The new Nineteenth District, moreover, contained the homes of both Jack
MacDonald and William Broomfield. While Broomfield and MacDonald engaged in a primary battle to determine which of them would continue in
office, Daniel Cooper, a state senator from Oak Park, was unopposed in the
Democratic primary in the new and now Democratic Eighteenth District.
Cooper did not have to face a Republican incumbent in the general election,
and his opponent was what Democratic candidates normally pray for, a Republican reactionary. Robert Huber had presented himself as a leading
spokesman for the conservative cause when Michigan conservatives could
have held a caucus in a closet. He had never given up. Elected to the state
senate, he had opposed nearly every moderate program suggested or supported by first George Romney and then William Milliken. In 1970 he had
contested the Republican nomination for the U.S. Senate with Romney's
wife, Lenore, and had come far closer than anyone had expected. Huber was a
conservative true believer. He cared nothing for the art of compromise and
knew nothing of the tactics required to build political coalitions. In 1972,
however, he needed to know nothing at all. The moral and political abso-
lutism of the arch-conservative became the most effective form of expediency
when the only issue that anyone cared anything about in Oakland County was
busing. Cooper had no chance. A liberal Democrat could not possibly convince anyone, much less an impassioned and infuriated majority, that he was
more likely to oppose busing from conviction than was a man who seemed to
question the propriety of the Bill of Rights. Huber went off to Congress,
where it quickly became clear that, as Republican minority leader John
Rhodes once said to Phil Hart, he had "not been elected because of his
intellect."

The loss of a congressional seat that had been made marginally Democratic through careful calculation and the prudent employment of political
power upset the expectations of those who had been most closely involved in
the process of reapportionment. Still, the district had been held previously by
a Republican, and the loss neither decreased the number of Democratic incumbents nor destroyed the career of a Democratic member of the House.
Moreover, though the Republicans continued to hold the Eighteenth District
seat, Robert Huber was not William Broomfield. Not only would Huber be
entering only his first term, and therefore be far less able than Broomfield had

been to claim the advantages of tenure and seniority, but his election had by his own admission been the result of the busing issue.[42] The disappearance of that issue might eliminate altogether his ability to escape the normal voting habits of a Democratic constituency. Once the furor and the fear subsided, an appeal could once again be made to the economic interests that had bound together the diverse elements of the Democratic coalition. The new Eighteenth District was still suburban, but unlike the old one, there were more blue-collar than white-collar suburbs within it. In two years another candidate would contest the district with Robert Huber and, if busing was no longer the central issue, could have solid grounds for confidence. Within weeks of Huber's victory, a young assistant attorney general was already laying plans for Huber's defeat. James Blanchard had no doubt he could win.

From the prespective of the Michigan Democratic party, the results of the 1972 congressional races were not nearly as bad as they might have been. All the incumbents had been reelected, and the inability to capture the new Eighteenth District could be seen as not so much a defeat as a temporary delay in the planned outcome of a successful scheme of reapportionment. There were no means of mitigating, however, the failure to deny a second term to United States Senator Robert Griffin. No Republican, even including George Romney, had managed to equal Griffin's capacity to antagonize the leadership of both the Democratic party and organized labor. As a congressman he had coauthored the famous Landrum-Griffin Act, which was designed to remove racketeering but which labor viewed as an attack on its independence and an attempt to reduce its political influence. Griffin's stunning victory in the Senate election of 1966 over G. Mennen Williams, who was already a living legend in the Democratic party, served only to increase the intensity with which the junior Senator from Michigan was hated by party regulars and union officers. That Griffin and Phil Hart enjoyed each other's company was as little known as it was irrelevant to the issue; Griffin was considered anti-labor, and labor was vehemently anti-Griffin. Democrats of every persuasion seemed united in their determination to defeat him in 1972. The prospects did not seem discouraging. Sander Levin had come within 44,000 votes of beating William Milliken for the governorship in 1970, and Milliken, it was widely believed, was infinitely more popular and therefore more difficult to defeat than Griffin. Unlike 1970 and 1966, 1972 was a presidential year, and the larger turnout would include more Democratic than Republican voters. If that was not enough, the Democratic candidate was going to be considerably more formidable than Sandy Levin. While Levin had served two terms in the state senate, the Democratic candidate for the U.S. Senate had been Michigan's attorney general for more than a decade. While Levin was losing by 44,000 votes to Milliken, the Democratic attorney general was winning elec-

tion to his fourth term by three quarters of a million votes, 1,644,348 to
893,438.[43] Frank Kelley seemed to have as good a chance to get to the Senate
as any candidate facing an incumbent could ever hope for.

Griffin expected a difficult reelection campaign and began preparing for
it within weeks after the 1970 general election. By December, a five-member
committee, including two Griffin assistants, Philip Van Dam and James De-
Francis, had begun what were to become regular weekly strategy meetings.
At first, and for the better part of a year, everyone on the committee assumed
that the campaign would try to direct public attention to Griffin's leadership
position in the Senate. Though Griffin was a Republican and Republicans
were a minority in the Senate, Griffin had led the fight to deny Abe Fortas
confirmation as chief justice of the Supreme Court. When he began, no one
seemed to believe he had any chance of success; when he had finished, Fortas
had been forced to resign from the court. At a time when many had purported
to see the emergence of an imperial presidency, Griffin could legitimately add
to the usual litany of advantages claimed by incumbents the fact that he had
taken a substantial step toward restoring the Senate's authority to advise and
consent. The reelection of Robert Griffin to the Senate was going to depend
on convincing a majority of Michigan voters that he was, as one of the least
elegant of his political slogans put it, "Michigan's muscle in the Senate."

If the strategy was simple and straightforward and showed little that was
innovative or even unusual, the tactics used to carry it out were so painstak-
ingly thorough as to border on the brilliant. George Romney had broken a
twelve-year Democratic hold on the governorship in 1962 by appealing not
only to independent voters and the Republican faithful, but to people who
considered themselves Democrats. In his two reelection campaigns, the Republican governor increased his majorities and enhanced his national reputation as a political power and a formidable presidential prospect by attracting
large numbers of at least nominally Democratic voters. Since the state, like
the nation as a whole, contained far more people who called themselves
Democrats than who called themselves Republicans, Romney's ability to
obtain support from the other party's normal electoral base opened new possibilities for Republican success. Romney's main political strategist, Walter
DeVries, had written a doctoral dissertation at Michigan State University on
lobbying activity in state government,[44] but as a political operative he turned
his attention to the problem of identifying those voters in the electorate who
considered themselves Democrats but who were likely to cast ballots for at
least an occasional Republican. DeVries was particularly concerned with
discovering the location of the largest groups of Democrats who would retain
their party identification by voting for Democratic candidates for local office
and the state legislature but would exercise their independence by voting for
"the man, not the party," at the top of the ticket. DeVries ultimately pub-

lished a small book detailing his findings and observations concerning the phenomenon that had come to be called "ticket-splitting."[45] Before publication, however, DeVries compiled his data and used it to assist the political fortunes of Republican candidates. After the election of William Milliken in 1970, DeVries once again analyzed the voting behavior of the Michigan electorate and isolated the ticket-splitters. He gave all of the data to the Griffin campaign.

Armed with the data supplied by DeVries, Philip Van Dam devoted four months to what in Democratic campaigns was never done systematically and was never even attempted before the campaign actually got under way. He developed a precise schedule that detailed to the hour where Griffin would spend his time during the 1972 campaign. Having studied thoroughly the voting statistics of every county and city in the state, he allocated a percentage of time to each portion of each county. He then translated the percentage into units of time by assuming that Griffin would spend two to three days a week campaigning when the Senate was in session and six days each week when it was not. Campaigns generally, and Democratic campaigns almost always, attempt to take advantage of events scheduled by others, but Van Dam's schedule relied almost entirely on self-generated events. The Griffin campaign was intended to be remarkably self-reliant. Instead of depending on some other Republican candidate to produce a crowd or some association to invite him to its event, Griffin would leave nothing to chance. Having determined the amount of time Griffin needed to spend in each locality, Van Dam had to know when it would be possible to spend that time. The management of every convention hall and motor lodge in Michigan was contacted and asked when their facilities would be available. Once he knew how much time Griffin would have to spend, where it had to be spent, and when it could be spent there, Van Dam calculated the area of media coverage each campaign appearance would attract. He made certain Griffin would never be in fewer than two separate media markets each day. In September Van Dam was finished, and nearly a year in advance of the general election campaign the scheduling memo was completed. Griffin now knew, for example, that in June and July of 1972 he would be spending a total of 10.5 days in the suburbs of western Wayne County. And what Van Dam scheduled in 1971 was almost exactly what Griffin actually did in 1972.[46]

The same month Van Dam submitted the scheduling memorandum, Judge Roth ordered development of a metropolitan desegregation plan for the Detroit schools. When Frank Kelley supported the state Democratic party's resolution approving busing as a means of carrying out school desegregation, Van Dam and several others involved in planning the Griffin campaign "thought Kelley made a mistake."[47] It was a mistake that could be exploited. There were those who apparently believed Griffin should exploit it in the most

dramatic fashion possible—suggesting, for example, that the senator go to
Pontiac and get on a school bus to demonstrate his opposition to busing.
Griffin, however, would have none of it. Neither he nor the members of his
Senate staff had any desire to get into a "racial thing." For a while Kelley's
support of the Battle Creek resolution, or, as it came to be called by those who
most vigorously opposed busing, and who perhaps sought to suggest something fundamentally radical, not to say subversive, the "Battle Creek manifesto," seemed to be the only thing the Republicans needed to emphasize.
When, a short time after he had given it his endorsement, Kelley disassociated
himself from his former position and began to oppose busing, the Griffin
strategists believed he had made his second major mistake. Now they could
direct public attention to the inconsistency and therewith raise the issue,
frequently lethal to a candidacy, of credibility. While Van Dam and James
DeFrancis were considering the most effective methods by which to contrast
Griffin's leadership in the Senate with Kelley's indecisiveness in Michigan,
Griffin, without discussing it with either of them in advance, issued a statement in Washington asserting his unalterable opposition to busing to achieve
racial balance in the public schools.

    Griffin opposed busing and, like so many of his Democratic colleagues
in the Michigan congressional delegation, eventually promised to vote for a
constitutional amendment prohibiting its use. Whether he was yielding to
political necessity, or was instead motivated by the belief that busing distracted from the issue of educational quality and threatened the deterioration
of the Detroit public schools through the exodus of white residents, Griffin's
opposition to busing was not based on racial prejudice nor designed to play on
racial fears among the electorate. Near the end of the campaign, for example,
Griffin appeared before a group of local leaders of antibusing organizations
and became embroiled in a heated exchange. The argument stemmed from his
statement that he believed in racial equality and would continue to support
civil rights legislation. He was "not going to do anything to go back on civil
rights," and, moreover, he was opposed to anyone who rejected busing from
a racial point of view. There were some in that audience who dissented from
this opinion and disagreed vehemently with Griffin's willingness to endorse
either racial equality or civil rights legislation.[48] Griffin's distaste for the
demagoguery, some of it with unmistakably racist overtones, employed by
Brooks Patterson, Irene McCabe, and other extremists connected with NAG
led to some deliberate deception on the part of the Republican campaign. The
frequent invitations to attend a NAG meeting or rally somewhere in southeastern Michigan were nearly always accepted. Almost as often there would
be some last-minute change in the senator's schedule that prevented his attendance. One antibusing rally that Griffin did attend had been organized by
Brooks Patterson to promote his own candidacy for Oakland County prosecutor. Nearly seven thousand people had turned out, and it seemed clear that

opposition to busing was on its way to becoming a mass movement no white politician could possibly resist. Very few, least of all Brooks Patterson, exhibited any serious interest in even trying to do so. Griffin spoke first and was content to deliver what had by then become his standard campaign speech. He spoke about his leadership in the Senate; he emphasized his ability to work in tandem with a Republican administration to improve economic conditions in Michigan; he stated his own opposition to busing and pointed out Frank Kelley's inconsistency on the issue. When he finished he left before hearing what Brooks Patterson might have to say. He disapproved of Patterson and despised the inflammatory tactics of NAG. That was personal. There was also a political reason. In what appeared to the very end to be a close race, a few black votes might make all the difference.

Frank Kelley had become attorney general by appointment and had retained the office through the approval of an electorate captivated by his denunciations of organized crime and his vociferous opposition to those who either harmed the public or abused the consumer. To be against crime is perhaps a dubious basis on which to claim distinction as an attorney general, but as Kelley and most others who have occupied similar positions well understood, it was an almost certain guarantee of reelection. Besides an unyielding refusal ever to do or say anything the slightest bit controversial, Kelley was among the most personable and outgoing practitioners of a profession in which those qualities are seldom in short supply. It was as difficult to dislike Kelley as it was to discover precisely what he believed in beyond the general conviction that Democratic candidates should always and everywhere be elected. In many respects he seemed more representative of an unreconstructed Tammany Hall than of the programmatic Michigan Democratic party. Kelley might not have any discernible intellectual commitments, but he did have political instincts, and although these usually led him to avoid discussing anything potentially disruptive, they were also basically decent. When the Democratic state central committee met in Battle Creek in September, 1971, and passed a resolution endorsing busing as an appropriate means for a court to use to end school segregation, Kelley saw no reason to oppose or separate himself from it. As Leon Cohan, Kelley's deputy and principal advisor, later put it, "that was simply one of the things the Democratic party did. No one even considered the possibility that there might be adverse political consequences."[49]

Once it became clear that there *were* political consequences, and that all of them were adverse, Kelley quickly became outspoken in his opposition to court-ordered busing. Early in the summer of 1972, he was even able to demonstrate his willingness to do something to prevent it. Judge Roth, who had determined in September that Detroit's schools were deliberately segregated, issued an order in June requiring preparation of a desegregation plan for Detroit and fifty-three suburban school districts. Then, on July 10, "Roth directed the state of Michigan to purchase 295 buses."[50] All of a sudden busing was no longer a future possibility. It was an immediate reality and, in the judgment of those who most vehemently opposed it, required immediate reaction. The attorney general of Michigan understood the consequences of delay as well as the benefits of swift and at least seemingly decisive action. On behalf of the state, Kelley appealed both of Judge Roth's orders to the Sixth Circuit Court of Appeals and obtained a ruling staying the implementation of the Roth plan until the Sixth Circuit had heard the state's case and reached a decision. The Roth decision was effectively postponed for months, and as no one doubted the issue would be appealed to the U.S. Supreme Court if the Circuit Court failed to rule against cross-district busing, probably for years.[51]

Having obtained the stay, Kelley tried to use it to argue that of the two candidates for the Senate only he had done anything to stop busing: "Senator Griffin thought he could be a successful one-issue candidate, but he hasn't gotten one single piece of legislation or resolution through the U.S. Senate on busing. We have secured the stay of Judge Roth's order. The public knows that."[52] Griffin, however, suggested that Kelley had displayed "incompetence" in the way he had handled the appeals of Judge Roth's rulings, and in what had become his principal line of attack, insisted it was "very difficult to say just exactly why Mr. Kelley does things from one day to the next, because he says different things than he has in the past."[53] Despite his claim that he and not Griffin had stopped or at least delayed the implementation of interdistrict busing, Kelley was clearly concerned. When to the surprise of nearly everyone Griffin accepted Kelley's challenge to debate, something incumbents seldom do and something Kelley himself had described two years earlier when he refused the challenge of the Republican candidate for attorney general as "the usual old-politics non-incumbent's ploy seeking publicity," Kelley insisted, "I'm prepared to debate him on busing, but in addition I want to talk about other issues."[54] Kelley had no interest in contesting the election with Griffin on the single issue of busing. Not only did he want the debate to include other issues, he also tried to obtain an agreement to a "moratorium" on any discussion of busing. Griffin rejected the proposal as "an affront to the intelligence of the voters of Michigan."[55] The proposal was a much more serious affront to Griffin's understanding of his own self-interest.

Kelley's success in obtaining a stay of Judge Roth's desegregation plan could offset in part, but could never entirely efface, either his approval of the Democratic party's resolution supporting busing or the charge that he had been inconsistent and insincere in replacing support with opposition. He was never able adequately to explain away the Battle Creek manifesto. His attempt to argue that he did not know what it meant seemed a confession of incompe-

tence, while his insistence that it was a party resolution, and not a document
he had actually signed, appeared to be the sort of technical quibble that
laymen believe lawyers use to evade the plain truth without penalty. A single
resolution, adopted by the Democratic state central committee on a matter no
one present considered politically significant or likely to escape the permanent
oblivion to which party resolutions were almost invariably consigned, followed Kelley like an albatross assigned by an inscrutable providence to fore-
shadow his fate. On an issue where so many people felt threatened personally,
there were intense demands for assurances of security for the future. At one
meeting in Macomb County every candidate present was asked to place his
hand on the Bible and swear he would never do anything to permit busing to
occur.[56] But the best and most certain guarantee of fidelity in the future was
faithful service in the antibusing cause in the past. Most politicians in most
elections constantly make the cynical but frequently correct observation that,
as the old line has it, the voters are not interested in what you have done for
them in the past but ask instead "What have you done for me lately?" This
time it was different, and both Kelley and Griffin knew it.

While Griffin avoided all but a few public meetings of antibusing groups,
Kelley spoke before them with some frequency. He had very little choice in
the matter. The busing issue affected mainly the southeastern metropolitan
area that traditionally was the heart of Democratic strength in the state. In the
part of the Sixteenth Congressional District closest to Detroit, an area known
as "downriver," Republicans were almost as difficult to find as a supporter of
busing. When local branches of NAG held meetings a thousand people would
turn out. The crowd, in the judgment of one field operative in the Kelley
campaign, constituted a "right wing hillbilly kind of movement. People
would get up and say things like, 'I'm from Alabama and I don't have
anything against blacks, but I lived with them and they're really dumb.' It was
incredible."[57] Kelley would accept an invitation to appear at these meetings,
and as the quintessential political animal would ask the staff person who had
responsibility for the area what kind of crowd it was and what they wanted to
hear. "It was like handing him a script." The script was easy to write. Kelley
would hammer away at how he had stopped the buses by his effective appeal
of Judge Roth's busing order and how Griffin had not been able to do anything
to stop the buses during his six years in the Senate. No matter how emphatically he asserted his opposition to busing, however, someone in the audience
always managed to ask the attorney general why, if he really opposed busing
on principle and not just because he wanted to get elected to the Senate, he
had signed the Battle Creek manifesto. The question was almost always
planted in advance by the Griffin campaign, which always knew when Kelley
was going to appear before a NAG meeting,[58] and it always produced whatever denials and explanations Kelley could invent at the time. After doing

everything he could to associate himself with the impassioned demands of an audience not all of whose members were perfectly free of a nearly rabid racism, the attorney general would leave and remark privately, "Those people are really scary—really crazy."[59]

Kelley was not content to confine his antibusing message to public meetings of the most vociferous opponents of Judge Roth's order. While he was insisting that the public debate be broadened to include issues other than busing, his campaign in western Wayne County seemed concerned with nothing else. In the Sixteenth District, campaign workers distributed door-to-door a tabloid that was designed to look like a local newspaper and carried the banner headline "Kelley Stops Buses."[60] Another headline linked Kelley with the district's popular antibusing congressman, John Dingell: "Kelley and Dingell Oppose Forced Busing." Others repeated once again that Frank Kelley had stopped the buses and asserted, with all the assurance of objective journalism, "Griffin Has Done Nothing." In Dearborn, where for a generation the city's all-white population had kept electing Orville Hubbard mayor because it understood exactly what he meant when he promised to keep the city clean, the Kelley campaign was only slightly more subtle. Busing was not mentioned at all in a flier prepared for distribution there. Instead, the attorney general was presented as the state's "Chief Crime Fighter," a label that appeared directly under a picture of Frank Kelley and Dearborn's police chief, Jack O'Reilly. What the authors of this apparently innocent communication intended, however, was something quite different. Dearborn, immediately adjacent to Detroit, feared nothing so much as the prospect of a black migration. With all the intensity of a completely sincere bigotry, its white citizens identified Detroit blacks with Detroit crime. Busing would bring blacks, and, it therefore followed, busing would bring crime. The "Chief Crime Fighter" would immediately be translated, or so at least was the hope and expectation of those who prepared the flier, into "Chief Opponent of Racial Busing." It was not a terribly ennobling effort, and it should be noted that there is no evidence that Frank Kelley had any personal knowledge that it was being done.

For those who worked in the Kelley campaign the busing issue produced not only inventive applications of human psychology but incredible frustrations. Perhaps no one became so frustrated as the campaign field director. Though James Blanchard, who worked on the attorney general's staff and had been in charge of the eighty counties outside the metropolitan area in the Levin campaign two years earlier,[61] was originally expected to be field director, the job had gone instead to Douglas Ross.[62] Ross's credentials supposedly included management of the successful Maryland Senate campaign of Joseph Tydings and authorship of a book on Robert Kennedy. He was by every indication a liberal Democrat and an effective political operative. He was undeniably energetic and unquestionably ambitious. He was also driven to the point of utter exasperation by the Griffin campaign's ability to exploit the busing controversy. At his wit's end, he remarked to one of his co-workers:

> Goddamn Griffin is just killing us on this busing issue. You know, they're really killing us on this stuff and they seem to be one step ahead of us all the way. You know what we should do—we should go over to the Griffin headquarters some night after they have closed—dig around in their trash and find out what's really going on inside that campaign.

One week later burglars broke into the offices of the Democratic National Committee in the Watergate office and apartment building in Washington, D.C.. Douglas Ross never mentioned his suggestion again.

Some of his staff seemed willing to do almost anything, and Kelley himself was willing to support any legislation or argue any point of law, to enhance his reputation for vigorous and effective opposition to busing. But there was one thing he would not do. While every white suburban congressman in Michigan agreed that busing was an evil so terrible that amendment of the Constitution of the United States was an appropriate and rational response to its threat, Kelley would not go along. Faced with unrelenting pressure to demonstrate that the Battle Creek manifesto was a temporary aberration from a sincere and deeply held conviction that busing was a moral wrong; confronted at every turn with Griffin's assaults on the competence of his efforts to halt busing in the courts; compelled to contest the election with an opponent who added to the advantages of Republican incumbency in the year Nixon ran against McGovern a willingness to change the Constitution if that was the price to be paid for electoral success; Frank Kelley refused to agree that the Constitution should be altered to assuage the fears of white suburban parents. Leon Cohan considered the very suggestion unthinkable: "We never would have done that."[63] It was perhaps not quite so simple.

The busing issue placed the Kelley campaign in a great dilemma. Congressmen such as Nedzi or O'Hara faced constituencies that were almost entirely white, and white suburban voters were so frightened by busing that nothing, including a constitutional amendment, seemed too radical or too dangerous if it appeared to provide protection against it. Kelley, however, was not running for Congress from a suburban district; he was running for the Senate in a state in which 11 percent of the population was black, and because of its normal habit of voting Democratic by margins of nine-to-one, a state in which considerably more than 11 percent of the Democratic vote in a state-wide election came from black precincts. Kelley could go a long way in his opposition to busing and do his best to out-Griffin Griffin on the issue, but he would retain black support only as long as he did not say something like "Governor Wallace was right" or come out in favor of a constitutional amendment against busing. If he did, he would run the danger, in the judgment of someone closely involved in the Senate campaign, of "blowing the coalition apart. Blacks saw the antibusing amendment as signaling total retrenchment from the Fourteenth Amendment."[64] The constitutional amendment was the cutting edge of the Senate campaign. If Kelley supported it, unknown numbers of black voters, along with those whites who might resent such an exercise in political expediency, might either stay away from the polls, or as a gesture of complete disgust, vote for Griffin. If Kelley did not support a constitutional amendment, Griffin, as well as the *Detroit News*, would rip into him for his failure to evidence unqualified and absolute opposition to busing, and undetermined numbers of white Democratic suburban voters might ignore party loyalty and support the Republican candidate.

It was a choice that was as unpleasant as it was unavoidable. The decision, nevertheless, was almost inevitable. No one who functioned in Democratic party politics at the state level counseled in favor of endorsing the constitutional amendment. The alternatives were understood, but they were not analyzed as equally applicable solutions. The Michigan Democratic party had put itself on record in support of busing, and while this had caused enormous difficulties, the leadership of the party was not the least bit inclined to abandon what it believed in order to promote a scheme almost certain to drive every prominent black Democrat out of the party. The state AFL-CIO, while not nearly as outspoken on the matter as George Meany was, was hardly going to endorse a proposal considerably more extreme than that on which Meany had lavished his considerable gift for invective. The UAW, which prided itself on its reputation as not only the most liberal but the most racially progressive union in America, had no interest in electing a Democrat to do the kind of harm to race relations that in its considered judgment was threatened by the amendment Senator Griffin endorsed. The whole institutional weight of the Democratic party, and the labor unions that were the principal sources of its strength, argued against what in any event did not promise much political advantage. There were those who would later look back and claim to discover in the reluctance to jeopardize the attachment of black voters the cause of Kelley's defeat and the source of blue-collar defections from the Democratic party. At the time, however, those were not the voices that were heard.

Despite the predominance of the busing issue[65] and Kelley's refusal to endorse the constitutional amendment the most strident opponents of busing demanded, the contest for the Senate entered the final few weeks in a virtual dead heat. The same polls that showed Kelley with a real chance of winning demonstrated certain defeat for the presidential candidacy of George McGovern. Kelley could not be expected to spend much time lamenting the impending victory of Richard Nixon when McGovern and the national party apparatus he had come to control had through their endorsement of busing only added to his difficulties. "Publicly," the *Detroit News* reported, "Kelley predicts victory for McGovern. Privately, he thinks McGovern will lose nationally and come close to Mr. Nixon in Michigan."[66] The *News* apparently found nothing ironic in Kelley's willingness to provide for publication his private views on the matter. Without any comment the paper quoted the Democratic senatorial candidate's claim that he would defeat Griffin because "a lot of people are going to feel mighty guilty about voting Republican for the presidency."[67] Kelley did everything he possibly could to separate himself from the self-destructing campaign of George McGovern. It had not been entirely a matter of chance that the keynote speaker at the Democratic state convention at the end of August had been the same Thomas Eagleton whom McGovern had supported "1,000 percent" before cutting him loose from the national ticket. Nor was it simply coincidence that McGovern literature was rarely carried by those distributing Kelley materials in the metropolitan area. McGovern was not invited into Michigan by the Kelley campaign or by organized labor. The state AFL-CIO, following the lead of George Meany and Al Barkan, did not even bother to endorse him. The UAW, though it had endorsed McGovern, and though Leonard Woodcock had even been willing to become McGovern's running mate,[68] devoted its considerable political skills to the task of depriving the McGovern organization in Michigan of any visible participation in any other Democratic campaign. To generate public attention and obtain support for Kelley's senatorial candidacy, the union used its influence and secured a visit not from George McGovern but from Edward Kennedy. When Kelley joined Kennedy at the Oakland Mall in front of a crowd estimated at between fifteen and twenty thousand, McGovern was not mentioned, busing was not discussed, and Kelley looked like he just might pull it off after all.

At the end of October, Griffin and Kelley debated before the prestigious Detroit Economic Club. Griffin knew what the major issue was and instinctively understood where Kelley was most vulnerable. He blasted him for never having really renounced the Democratic central committee's busing resolution of the previous year. Griffin charged that "my opponent joined in the Battle Creek manifesto which specifically referred to the Detroit metropolitan case and said, 'We accept busing as an instrument for immediate implementation of the court's rulings.'"[69] Griffin's attack was followed by an editorial in the *Detroit News* that matched the partisanship and the tactics of the Republican incumbent. Calling busing "the central issue of this Senate campaign," the *News* editorial writers repeated all of Griffin's charges and then concluded that "the best evidence suggests that if Frank Kelley went to the U.S. Senate, he would in the end turn up on the side of those who support busing."[70] Having in effect called the attorney general of the state of Michigan a liar, the *News* repeated its endorsement of Robert Griffin for a second term in the Senate. This astonished absolutely no one.

Kelley's prediction that there would be enough voters who were guilt-ridden over their vote for a Republican president to elect him to the Senate as an act of expiation fell short, though more than enough people met the eligibility requirements. Nixon, for example, "swamped Senator George McGovern by more than a 2-1 margin in the traditional Democratic stronghold of Macomb County."[71] The margin, however, was attributed not to McGovern's position on the war in Vietnam or to any of his famous proposals for the redistribution of the wealth of the country. In the judgment of the *Detroit News* and of nearly every experienced political operative in the area, the Macomb County voters who left their party to vote for Richard Nixon had something else in mind. Nixon carried two-thirds of the county vote by "riding the crest of the antibusing issue. . . ."[72] Robert Griffin rode the same issue to a second term. He defeated Frank Kelley 520,240 to 402,633. In the tri-county area Griffin obtained 42.5 percent of the vote.[73] The immediate question, and the ultimate problem, for the Democratic party was how to reclaim the allegiance of the white blue-collar voters who belonged to trade unions, lived in the suburbs, and until now had formed a reliable and indispensable element of the Democratic coalition. There were a few people who had been pondering this difficulty long before the voters had cast their ballots in the 1972 election.

Notes

1. Theodore H. White, *The Making of the President 1972* (New York: Atheneum, 1973), p. 226.

2. Quoted in ibid.

3. Quoted in ibid.

4. Quoted in ibid., p. 227.

5. Remarks of Philip A. Hart at Civil Liberties Clearinghouse, Washington, D.C., Shoreham Hotel, March 25, 1970.

6. *Congress and the Nation,* vol. 3 (Washington, D.C.: Congressional Quarterly Services, 1973), p. 514. Busing had only recently been approved by the Supreme Court as a constitutionally permissible means of desegregating schools. In *Swann v. Charlotte-Mecklenburg Board of Education,* 402 U.S. 1, a unanimous court declared: "desegregation plans cannot be limited to the walk-in school." *Swann,* however, had dealt with de jure school segregation—i.e., a dual system of schools, one for whites and another for blacks, in which students from the same area were divided on the basis of race. The case did not touch on the question whether a system of segregated schools that resulted from residential segregation was also unconstitutional. Thus, at the time Judge Roth issued his ruling, the Supreme Court had said nothing about whether

busing for the purpose of providing a remedy for de facto residential segregation was or was not constitutionally permissible. This question would remain unanswered for several years.

7. James M. McNeely, interview with author, May 14, 1973.

8. *Detroit News,* November 1, 1972.

9. State of Michigan, *Official Canvass of Votes 1970,* p. 53.

10. In the fall of 1971, Macomb County citizens voted fourteen-to-one in opposition to busing in a county referendum.

11. Remarks of Philip A. Hart at Fifth Annual Macomb County Phil Hart Day Dinner, Mount Clemens, October 16, 1971.

12. Ibid.

13. Joe Klein, "The Saint in the Senate," *Rolling Stone,* December 30, 1976.

14. Quoted in ibid.

15. Norman St. John-Stevas, ed., *The Collected Works of Walter Bagehot,* Vol. 3 (Cambridge, Mass.: Harvard University Press, 1968), p. 153.

16. Carl M. Brauer, *John F. Kennedy and the Second Reconstruction* (New York: Columbia University Press, 1977), pp. 106–7. In a letter to Lawrence O'Brien, White House congressional liaison chief, Griffiths argued there was "not enough time before the elections for 'the white areas to understand the full implications of this order,' for them to 'throw the rocks and settle down.'" "She knew of no Democratic Congressman from suburbia who believed he was in danger of 'losing colored votes; but he does feel such an order could cost white votes.' She sardonically concluded: 'In case the counsel of those seated less close to the fire than I am prevails, however, and I lose this election, would you mind asking the President if I can have the next Supreme Court vacancy, where I can legislate far from the prejudices of the precinct.'"

17. *Detroit Free Press,* February 24, 1972.

18. Donald W. Riegle, Jr., *O Congress* (New York: Doubleday and Co., 1972), p. 281.

19. *Congress and the Nation,* vol. 3, p. 34a.

20. *House of Representatives Report 92-1085.*

21. *Congress and the Nation,* vol. 3, p. 44a.

22. Riegle, *O Congress,* pp. 281–82.

23. To be against busing and for quality education was not even particularly inventive. On March 14, 1972, Florida voters, in a nonbinding referendum, overwhelmingly endorsed a constitutional amendment barring busing, and then, with a majority of 78 percent, affirmed the desirability of "providing an equal opportunity for quality education for all children, regardless of race, creed, color and place of residence, and oppose a return to a dual system of education." *Congress and the Nation,* vol. 3, p. 516.

24. *Detroit News,* November 3, 1972.

25. Ibid.

26. *Detroit News,* October 30, 1972.

27. Ibid.

28. *Congress and the Nation,* vol. 3, p. 517.

29. Ibid., p. 43a.

30. Ibid.

31. Ibid., p. 40a.

32. Ibid., p. 43a.

33. State of Michigan, *Official Canvass of Votes 1972*, p. 20.

34. Ibid., p. 70.

35. O'Hara, it must be recorded, had been "for years one of the leaders of the floor fights to cut anti-busing language out of appropriation bills." *Congress and the Nation*, vol. 3, p. 514.

36. *Lansing State Journal*, August 2, 1972.

37. Ibid.

38. State of Michigan, *Official Canvass of Votes 1972*, p. 70.

39. *Detroit News*, November 1, 1972.

40. State of Michigan, *Official Canvass of Votes 1970*, p. 69.

41. Ibid.

42. *Detroit News*, November 8, 1972.

43. State of Michigan, *Official Canvass of Votes 1970*, p. 51.

44. Walter DeVries, "The Michigan Lobbyist" (Ph.D. diss., Michigan State University, 1960).

45. Walter DeVries and Lance Tarrance, Jr., *The Ticket-Splitter: A New Force in American Politics* (Grand Rapids: William B. Eerdmans, 1972).

46. Philip Van Dam, interview with author, September 28, 1982.

47. Ibid.

48. Ibid.

49. Leon Cohan, interview with author, September 30, 1982.

50. *Congress and the Nation*, vol. 3, p. 513.

51. The busing issue was appealed to the Supreme Court, and a decision was rendered on July 25, 1974. *Milliken v. Bradley*, 418 U.S. 717 (1974).

52. *Lansing State Journal*, August 2, 1972.

53. Ibid.

54. Ibid.

55. Ibid.

56. Leon Cohan, interview with author, September 30, 1982.

57. Bernard M. Ryan, interview with author, September 7, 1982.

58. Philip Van Dam, interview with author, September 28, 1982.

59. Bernard M. Ryan, interview with author, September 7, 1982.

60. The tabloid was actually entitled "Suburban Viewpoint."

61. Hillel Levin, "The Next Deal: Jim Blanchard," *Monthly Detroit*, September, 1982, p. 58.

62. Blanchard played an advisory role in the campaign and was assigned the task of preparing demographic data on western Wayne County.

63. Leon Cohan, interview with author, September 30, 1982.

64. Bernard M. Ryan, interview with author, September 7, 1982.

65. Philip Van Dam, interview with author, September 28, 1982.

66. *Detroit News*, October 30, 1972.

67. Quoted in ibid. Kelley's point had a precedent. In 1964, while California voters were providing Lyndon Johnson with a two-to-one majority, they also chose to send

the Republican candidate, George Murphy, instead of the Democratic candidate, Pierre Salinger, to the U.S. Senate. That same year Michigan voters voted in overwhelming numbers against Barry Goldwater and then elected George Romney governor. What 1964 was to Republicans, 1972 was expected to be to Democrats. Kelley's argument seemed to follow logically. There was a difference between the two elections, however. In 1972 there was an intensely emotional issue at the state level, which had not been true in 1964.

68. The best description of the 1972 Democratic convention is that contained in White's *The Making of the President 1972*.

69. *Detroit News,* November 1, 1972.

70. Ibid.

71. *Detroit News,* November 8, 1972.

72. Ibid.

73. State of Michigan, *Official Canvass of Votes 1972,* p. 8.

CHAPTER 2
Battle for Control

A month after the 1968 election, in which Hubert Humphrey had faced nearly as much opposition from within his own, as he had from the Republican party, Sander Levin, acting chairman of the Michigan Democratic party, traveled to Battle Creek to attempt a reconciliation between liberal Democrats and the local union leadership. The liberals had done little in the general election that was helpful to Humphrey, and Larry Harbolt, who led the UAW in Calhoun County, had sworn vengeance. Obsessed by the desire to harm his political adversaries, Harbolt had decided to run for the chairmanship of the Calhoun County Democratic committee. There was little doubt that he intended to use the power of that office to deny participation in the party organization to those who had either actively opposed Humphrey's nomination or failed to support Humphrey's candidacy after the Democratic convention. If Harbolt won, the liberals would be driven out of the county party; if he lost, the liberals, who preached but seldom practiced the virtues of generosity and forgiveness, would doubtless do to labor what labor, or at least Larry Harbolt, wanted to do to them.

Levin had established decent relations with the liberals and he understood how to deal with labor. He treated Harbolt with courtesy and then turned him over to Russ Leach, a UAW political operative who had come from Detroit for the sole purpose of reminding the local union leader of his responsibilities. Leach drove alone with Harbolt from the Holiday Inn, where they had had dinner with Levin, to the Battle Creek Democratic headquarters, where the executive committee of the county party was scheduled to meet. Leach remarked that Harbolt's car, a late model Cadillac, indicated how well he had done with the union. The union had a policy, Leach proceeded to announce, that was designed to enhance the strength of the Democratic party. It was part of that policy to discourage union officials from becoming party officers; party office provided an incentive for people outside the union movement to become involved in the Democratic party. Leach, who even at dinner had constantly mentioned "Walter" as if Reuther were his closest friend, added that the president of the UAW personally endorsed this rule. There was nothing Harbolt could possibly say. When the two of them walked into the Democratic headquarters Harbolt quietly announced that in the interest of party unity he would not become a candidate for county chairman.

Leach had not told the entire truth. There were in fact numerous UAW officials who held formal positions in the Democratic party, and a few of them were even county chairmen. But he had been correct concerning the general policy and the principle that was the basis for it. The UAW did not want to find itself in control of a party organization that represented only itself. Walter Reuther had understood that in the American context a labor party was an impossibility and that to obtain the strength necessary for electoral success the Democratic party had to reach far beyond the confines of the UAW or even organized labor altogether. The union did not need formal positions of power to have influence in the party organization, and unless union possession of party offices was strictly controlled, it would find itself accountable for the actions and the attitudes of any UAW official who became a party officer. It might be true that a Larry Harbolt spoke only for himself when he announced to any Democrat who would listen his desire to drive the former supporters of Eugene McCarthy and Robert Kennedy out of the party, but the union would have a difficult time explaining why the statement of one of its own should not be taken as reflecting its position. The prospect of issuing denials every time a union official said something as a party officer that was in conflict with union policy was made even more unattractive by the knowledge that part of its political power depended on its ability to speak with a single voice and act with a single will.

Through the long gubernatorial tenure of G. Mennen Williams, the UAW had been content to leave the control of party affairs to state chairman Neil Staebler's practiced management. When, after John Swainson's single term in the executive office, Zolton Ferency took over the leading position in the party organization, the UAW remained a silent ally in the Democratic coalition. Not only did the union not seek to place any of its own officers in positions of formal authority in the state party structure, it almost invariably permitted its interests to be represented in the party by Gus Scholle, president of the state AFL-CIO. In 1968, however, two events occurred that would produce a permanent break with this policy of abstention from direct and regular involvement in party affairs. The decision by Walter Reuther to take the UAW out of what he had come to perceive as an increasingly conservative AFL-CIO reduced Scholle's position to that of a spokesman for an organization with less than half the membership of the UAW. The press and the general public might continue to attribute political significance to the statements of the Michigan AFL-CIO, but those who played leading parts in the Democratic party knew that power had shifted, and shifted in a dramatic fashion, from Scholle's office in Lansing to the citizenship department in

Solidarity House in Detroit. The UAW's withdrawal from the AFL-CIO might simply have diminished Scholle's political influence without altering the political tactics of the union, however, had it not been for the second event, the importance of which was not fully appreciated within the party or even within the union for some time.

In the late 1960s, the number of UAW regions in Michigan was increased from five to six. One obvious consequence of the creation of a new region was the sudden availability of a new regional directorship. Although the regional directors were elected by representatives of local unions in the region, Walter Reuther had no hesitation about taking a direct and usually decisive part in the selection process. There were several contenders for the new position, and one of them, the president of Local 136 in Wixom, had considerable political experience. Sam Fishman had been one of the most prominent union officers who had supported John Swainson in what had seemed at first a hopeless attempt to take the Democratic gubernatorial nomination away from the immensely popular secretary of state, James Hare, in 1960. Six years later he had accepted the unenviable assignment of managing the gubernatorial candidacy of Zolton Ferency against George Romney. Another contender to become regional director of what was designated Region 1-A was a leading official of Local 600, which proudly and accurately proclaimed itself the largest union local in the world. Marcellius Ivory had worked his way through the labyrinth of a local so large that its internal structure resembled a government bureaucracy. Along the way he had managed to improve his own education through a rigorous regime of study. He was one of the very few local union leaders who could quote from Shakespeare and the classics and do it without the appearance of pretense. Ivory's achievements were unusual, but his further advance in the union hierarchy depended not only on his abilities but on his race. Ivory was black, and all the regional directors were white. Reuther took a back seat to no one in his insistence on racial equality and found it embarrassing that the number of blacks in leadership positions was miniscule in proportion to the number who were union members. Fishman, who believed in racial equality with as much sincerity and dedication as Reuther, now found himself paying the price for the discrimination he had always opposed and which, as a Jew, he had sometimes suffered. There was not even a contest for the position. Reuther made the decision completely on his own. He informed the contenders that Ivory would be the new regional director, and Sam Fishman would become the new director of Michigan CAP, the political arm of the UAW in Michigan.

The new director of CAP represented the union in the leadership of the state party and witnessed the growing inability of that leadership to either provide direction or—and the two were obviously related—win elections. In

1968 Fishman watched as the Democratic party dissolved into warring factions, as liberals claimed moral superiority for their refusal to help Hubert Humphrey and then denied political responsibility for the election of Richard Nixon. Two years later, in 1970, he looked on while Republicans adroitly used the abortion issue and the question of public assistance to parochial schools to loosen the partisan attachments of working-class Catholic voters and deny the governorship to the Democratic candidate, Sander Levin. In 1968 and 1970 the party leadership had been unable to prevent defeat and division; in 1972 the leadership seemed unwilling even to try. The party chairman, James McNeely, had been elected in February, 1969, after serving as deputy chairman during the previous year-and-a-half while Sander Levin held the position of acting chairman, which had been given him by the party officers in 1967 following the forced resignation of Zolton Ferency. As second in command to Levin, a position he had held before in the Oakland County Democratic party, McNeely was efficient and effective, but his ability to carry out the decisions of others did not prepare him to make them on his own. Nineteen seventy-two would have challenged the ingenuity and exhausted the patience of the most experienced and resourceful party leader; it overwhelmed McNeely. Whenever it appeared that the chairman had the power to prevent a further deterioration of the party's ability to control or even influence events, he failed. In the fall of 1971 he not only permitted but eagerly advocated adoption of the Battle Creek manifesto. In the winter of 1972 he did nothing to retain the support of his own officers in opposing a presidential primary, one which George Wallace carried with more than 50 percent of the vote. Then, in August, 1972, he was unable to persuade the major groups in the party to agree on a common slate of candidates, and the UAW, with the support of the AFL-CIO, fashioned its own slate and then carried a majority of the convention delegates in support of those it endorsed. It would be an understatement to say that the chairman had lost the confidence of the labor movement. Fishman had reluctantly come to the conclusion that McNeely could be counted on to do the right thing only when the two of them were together. When he was alone, the party chairman seemed to have an uncanny ability to say or do something that would cause enormous damage and difficulty. There was absolutely no chance whatever that Jim McNeely would be allowed another term as chairman of the Michigan Democratic party. The UAW had proven in the August convention that it could carry a majority of delegates when it chose to do so, and after three elections in which Democrats had been defeated and two terms of a chairman who could not control, much less lead, the party, the UAW, or at least Sam Fishman, was ready for a more active role in party affairs.

For years the Democratic National Committee, like its Republican counterpart, had been composed of two members from each state. That the two delegates were required by the rules of the national committee to be divided between the sexes caused neither controversy nor even comment; the protests against quotas would come only when the principle of proportional representation was extended beyond gender to encompass differences of race. The Michigan Democratic party, like every other state party, had been represented on the committee by one man and one woman. Unlike any other state, however, Michigan was represented by a black man. At the 1968 Democratic convention, Neil Staebler, who considered the integration of the state party a major contribution of his long association with it, refused to run for another term as national committeeman so that Michigan might become the first state in American history to send a black to the national committee. Coleman Young, minority leader of the state senate, became the first black ever elected to the Democratic National Committee. Michigan Democrats, who were overwhelmingly white, were obviously willing to elect minority members to important positions of responsibility. Michigan, however, was both the first and the only state to elect a black to the DNC. For those who wanted to broaden the opportunities for political participation, the example of Neil Staebler scarcely seemed a secure foundation on which to build. Instead of goodwill, blacks and other minorities needed a guarantee of involvement at every level of the party organization. In 1971, the McGovern Commission proposed new party rules that appeared to do precisely that by requiring representation for a minority in proportion to its presence in the general population. This quota system, and despite the protestations of Commission members it was obvious even to them that it was a quota system, was for many a political impossibility. That was subject to debate. It was beyond dispute, however, that it would be mathematically impossible to meet the new requirements unless there were enough positions for the necessary allocations. The committee would continue to be almost exclusively white as long as membership was restricted to only two people from each state. The remedy, at least in the view of those who controlled things in 1972, was self-evident. The national committee was expanded, and although the only quota explicitly required continued to be equal representation of the sexes, reformers anticipated an easy and early inclusion of racial minorities. No one seemed much disturbed, if anyone even noticed, when one result of what was designed to secure minority representation was to diminish the black percentage of the Michigan delegation to the committee. There was another result. Although Douglas Fraser, who was then the UAW vice-president in charge of Michigan CAP, feared it would mean too close an involvement with the formal organization of the party, he eventually, if reluctantly, allowed Sam Fishman to become a candidate for one of the new positions on the committee. At the state Democratic convention in August, 1972, Fishman was elected to the

Democratic National Committee, and the UAW effectively abandoned its previous policy of abstention from formal party government. From now on the union would not only assist but would help to run the Michigan Democratic party.

The newly constituted committee was scheduled to meet in Washington on Saturday, December 9, to elect a new national chairman. On Friday evening Sam Fishman had dinner at the home of Congressman James O'Hara, and the conversation had little directly to do with the question of whether the next chairman would be Charles Manatt of California, who had the promised support of Leonard Woodcock, or a Texan who reminded some people of a polished version of Lyndon Johnson, Robert Strauss. Instead, O'Hara talked incessantly about the ordeal of the last election. Busing had come close to destroying his political career; it also seemed to have caused deep personal injury. It was as if O'Hara was suffering delayed reaction to a traumatic experience. He seemed uncertain whether he had handled the situation as well as he could have, and though he never said it, seemed worried that he might have yielded too much to political necessity. O'Hara was unusual; most members of the Congress would not have given a second thought to what they had done to win, so long as they had won. O'Hara's anguish was that of a New Deal liberal who had believed in the complete compatibility of the civil rights movement and the requirements of the American working class. He had always supported laws to guarantee the rights of minorities, and he had personally written some of the more impressive legislation designed to improve the condition of the wage-earner. Busing, along with other so-called social issues, threatened to disrupt and perhaps even to destroy permanently the coalition of liberals, minorities, and blue-collar workers that had made possible both the existing legal guarantees for racial equality and the improvement of the economic position of labor. Neither the congressman nor the director of Michigan CAP needed to be convinced that the Democratic party could not possibly survive a repetition of 1972.

Late that same evening, Robert Mitchell, who had served as deputy chairman of the state party under Jim McNeely, was talking to a friend in the hospitality suite of Charles Manatt at the Washington Hilton. Mitchell had resigned as deputy chairman a year earlier in order, as the phrase in vogue at the time put it, "to find himself." Those who represented the political interests of organized labor seldom had any doubts about who they were, and they found this explanation for Mitchell's departure unintelligible. They thought it stranger still when, after a brief sojourn in Charlevoix, he became involved in what was even by the standards of 1972 a bizarre attempt by Senator Mike Gravel of Alaska to run for the vice-presidential nomination of the Democratic party. Now that it was clear that McNeely would not be a candidate for another term as state party chairman, Mitchell was thinking about running himself. He had nothing to lose and, as he put it, not really too much else to do. Moreover, he might have a chance. He was well known throughout the state organization and, in his own estimation, could attract support in the outstate area, where he was likely to be the only candidate who was known at all. Liberals, especially those who had enthusiastically supported George McGovern, were likely to look with favor on a candidate who had worked for Gravel, the senator who had released to the public the contents of the famous Pentagon Papers by reading them into the *Congressional Record*. Mitchell wanted to discuss his prospective candidacy with Sam Fishman, but Fishman was much too busy that weekend making certain that Jean Westwood, McGovern's hand-picked national chairman, was replaced by someone who would move the party in a more moderate and more electorally viable direction. Woodcock had wanted Manatt, but Fishman was not disappointed with the election of Strauss. Neither Woodcock nor Fishman nor any other prominent official in the UAW wanted Mitchell.

Both the UAW and the AFL-CIO had agreed on the necessity of making certain McNeely did not have another two years to preside over the further deterioration of the Michigan Democratic party. Neither the UAW nor the AFL-CIO had any interest in having McNeely's deputy, who seemed even more closely connected with the liberal forces that were driving away union voters, preside in his place. But if it was certain Mitchell could not get labor support, it was not immediately clear who would. Paul Donahue, assistant to Congressman Lucien Nedzi, had a long history of party activity and had close ties to G. Mennen Williams. He had played a major role at the state level in the Humphrey presidential campaign in 1968 and displayed little sympathy for the ideological commitments of the new left. Donahue was the most experienced congressional district representative in the metropolitan area, and he had a shrewd instinct for the interests and emotions that motivated the different constituencies that composed the Democratic coalition. He had mastered the ethnic politics of the Fourteenth Congressional District and wanted to try his hand at reconciling the differences within the state organization.[1] Donahue did not have much difficulty convincing Bill Marshall, who had succeeded Gus Scholle as head of the state AFL-CIO, that he ought to be given the chance. Marshall despised McNeely, disliked Mitchell, and because he did not yet really know him, distrusted the third candidate in the race as another Oakland County liberal in the mold of Levin and McNeely. That Morley Winograd had run the Oakland County portion of Phil Hart's 1970 campaign and had then been elected county chairman did nothing to diminish Marshall's suspicion.[2]

Winograd had been running for the chairmanship much longer than either Mitchell or Donahue. He had begun campaigning for the job immediately after the November election; he had begun working toward it much earlier. Endowed with a mind that was both clear and quick, Winograd was one of the first to realize that McNeely had as little future with the state Democratic party as the party had with him. Winograd, however, had a major problem. He was still in his first term as Oakland County chairman, and outside his own county he was largely unknown. Without either Mitchell's broad acquaintance with party interests throughout the state's eighty-three counties or Donahue's decade of experience in state politics, he needed some device through which his considerable energies and remarkable organizational abilities could attract greater attention and a larger following. McNeely's difficulties provided Winograd with his opportunity. The state chairman's apparent abdication of political leadership meant that power in the party could be exercised by others. If the county and district chairmen, or at least those among them who were in control of the strongest organizations, acted in concert, they could determine party policy. Perhaps because he was the nearest thing to a full-time county chairman in the state, or perhaps because party politics had become the central preoccupation of his life, Winograd alone understood this and knew how to take advantage of it.

Winograd's first step was to organize what he called the tri-county chairmen's group, made up of the chairmen of the three metropolitan counties of Wayne, Oakland, and Macomb. The three counties together contained a majority of the members of the Democratic state central committee and, of greater significance for the future, a majority of the delegates to any Democratic state convention.[3] John Bruff, the Macomb County chairman, was Jim O'Hara's closest friend and his district representative. Bruff did not need Winograd to tell him that the state and national party were both in shambles and would have to be reorganized immediately after the election. Bruce Miller, chairman of the Wayne County committee, was a labor lawyer and one of Sam Fishman's closest personal friends. Miller's politics, described by his friends as farsighted and courageous and by his enemies as narrow and reactionary, were by any objective appraisal light-years away from the Democratic left. Though Winograd, Bruff, and Miller were county chairmen, none of them could be said to wield complete control in their organizations. Of the three, Miller had the least influence. Unlike both the Oakland and Macomb County organizations, the Wayne County committee was more in the nature of a loose alliance of the county's Democratic congressional district committees. The chairmanship provided Miller with both a title and a platform, but real power was retained by the chairmen of district committees. Although the three chairmen did not control and could not deliver all or even a majority of the state central members in the metropolitan region, together they constituted a power base that was quickly expanded. For example, by assuming a common position on the dispute over the party rules in 1972, the three chairmen attracted the allegiance of those Wayne County district chairmen who shared their position and were willing to join in a united front. As a result, the metropolitan area secured greater influence within the leaderless state party in 1972, and Morley Winograd acquired a wider reputation for 1973.

The establishment of an informal coalition of county and district chairmen had given Winograd the opportunity to become better known. It would not be the chairmen, however, who determined the identity of the next state chairman. Labor would undoubtedly play a major and perhaps decisive role, but it was not of a single mind. The AFL-CIO was leaning toward Paul Donahue, while the UAW gave no indication that it would make a decision before the state Democratic convention met the first weekend in February, if indeed it made one at all. Winograd might not be able to win without the UAW, but he certainly would have no chance to win if he waited to see what the UAW would finally decide to do. He barely waited for the November election before declaring his candidacy, and when he did, he already had in hand a detailed analysis of where he needed to conduct his search for delegate support. According to this analysis, the Detroit metropolitan area contained nearly 60 percent of the state Democratic vote. ''Any candidate for state party office, therefore, must enjoy substantial support in this area.'' The rest of the Democratic vote was ''unfortunately . . . spread over the remaining 95-odd percent of the state's area.'' It was not spread evenly, however. Almost three-quarters of the Democratic vote outside the metropolitan area was contained within twenty-two of the state's eighty-three counties. Put another way, twenty-five of the eighty-three counties accounted for 89 percent of the total Democratic vote. The campaign for the chairmanship could be conducted effectively by personal visits to these twenty-five. Telephone calls and letters to the party officers in the other fifty-eight counties would satisfy the requirements of political courtesy.[4]

Declaring that ''the Michigan Democratic Party should be in the mainstream of American politics,'' and that the major task of the party was to be ready for the next election ''with a well-developed organization,'' Morley Winograd spent the better part of the next two-and-a-half months visiting political leaders in the metropolitan area and party officials in the major counties outstate.[5] He left little doubt that he intended to break with the immediate past and even less doubt that the break was needed.

> I'm not impressed with the political sophistication of the state party, and didn't want to be frustrated another two years. . . . Some decisions which have been made by the state leadership have not been of much value to the Democratic Party. There was very little preparation for the campaign by the state party in basics like registration. There was also a failure to keep the different parts of the party together.[6]

The party needed a chairman who was devoted to what for most people, even people addicted to party politics, was the tedious, time-consuming, some would even say soul-destroying work of party organization. Winograd, who swore he actually loved it and had already acquired a reputation for being good at it, hammered away at his claim that "a lot of people feel that after the last four years, we need a chairman with organizational abilities." Because a "nuts and bolts" approach to party politics was in demand, it was, in Winograd's judgment at least, "not the time to quarrel over the ideology of the chairman." His own ideology was "irrelevant." If "I didn't solve the technical problems, any ideology in the world wouldn't matter."[7]

No matter how much he sought to portray himself as a political technician interested only in the organizational improvement of the Democratic party, Winograd, far better than most, had a clear understanding of the essential relationship between party organization and what some called party ideology. At least since 1972, when in the name of an ideology of egalitarianism the "new politics" wing of the party had altered the party structure and alienated millions of traditionally Democratic voters, those who spoke of the need for organization were talking about something considerably more fundamental than a more energetic voter registration program. If there were going to be enough Democratic voters to make registration a partisan advantage, the party had to be moved precisely where Winograd had already announced he wanted to move it, into the "mainstream of American politics." Nor was this the only reference to ideological considerations made by the candidate during his campaign. On December 18, Winograd, in remarks to the Marquette County Democratic women's caucus, stated in response to a question that he did not favor a quota system of the sort adopted by the McGovern Commission because, "unless you are willing to create innumerable categories of different socio-economic types in the party, quotas inevitably exclude some group." He added that "it was an artificial method for measuring how open to participation the party was and would end up in its implementation by becoming an end in itself that did not increase participation nor encourage an opening of the party."[8] In addition, he "spoke of party unity and said that, if we are to win elections in Michigan, we must not permit divisive issues such as busing and amnesty to tear us apart."[9] In other words, there were certain issues and certain ideologies that were incompatible with the creation of a political party organization capable of contesting elections with a decent prospect of success.

Throughout his campaign for the chairmanship, a campaign in which he claimed to have personally met 1,000 party activists,[10] Winograd continued to repeat his opposition to a quota system. In response to an inquiry from the party's educators caucus he wrote:

I believe the goal of reform should be to ensure that our party is open to

> participation by all and that people will be represented in the leadership in
> relation to their participation. I believe that quotas do not . . . accomplish this
> goal because without a quota for every imaginable group, someone will be
> excluded by rigid percentages.[11]

It is not difficult to understand why Winograd accompanied his insistence on
the overriding importance of party organization with adamant opposition to
the quota system that the party had adopted as part of the reforms proposed by
the McGovern-Fraser Commission. That system had been systematically used
to exclude much of organized labor and nearly all of the elected public
officials who had traditionally exercised power in the party. Liberal reformers
might find satisfaction in an arrangement that deprived Richard Daley of so
much as a seat on the floor of the 1972 Democratic National Convention;
those who were interested in the proven ability of Mayor Daley's Cook
County organization to deliver Chicago and, in one way or another, the state
of Illinois, could not. Quotas had been used to guarantee political power to
those who had not been able to assemble—that is to say, organize—constituencies large enough to provide equivalent power in open political competition. Not only had the reform rules and the quota system they were designed
to impose distributed power within the party in utter disregard of ability to
attract support among the electorate, many of the newly empowered groups
advocated some of the most divisive political positions ever devised. While
most of the traditional elements of the Democratic party, for example, might
agree that the civil rights of homosexuals ought to be protected, they would
also have argued that the best way to guarantee them was not to talk too much
about it. Advocates of gay rights, however, demanded proportional representation in the party and a platform declaring the unstinting support of Democrats everywhere for the full recognition and equal validity of "alternative
lifestyles." This did little to appeal to the opinion or the prejudices of a
majority of the American electorate.

Quotas were an organizational arrangement based on an ideological consideration that led to enormous negative electoral consequences. Winograd,
therefore, could base his opposition to quotas on the damage they had caused
the party organization. That however, at least on first impression, seemed to
imply that the party chairman should take the lead in determining which issues
should be used and which avoided as likely to help or hinder the party's quest
for majority support. Winograd appeared to be moving in this direction when
he suggested publicly that the party "not permit divisive issues such as busing
and amnesty to tear us apart."[12] Moreover, if effective organization required
an ideology acceptable to an electoral majority—and it was hard to see that
"moving the party into the mainstream of American politics" could mean
anything else—then neither Winograd nor anyone else could really function

as an ideological neutral. The imperatives of party organization seemed to demand a chairman who actively promoted a particular point of view on questions of public policy. Winograd, nevertheless, insisted that

> the Party Chairman should be someone who is neutral in factional and ideological disputes within the party; that means a willingness to put aside personal views and act only as spokesman for the Party when the Party has reached a common position and the differences have been resolved.[13]

Winograd's insistence on ideological neutrality was even more emphatic in a letter sent to party members shortly before the convention. He claimed to have heard repeatedly in his travels throughout the state five requirements for the next chairman, each of which he agreed with. The third requirement dealt with the neutrality issue.

> The party chairman should act as a spokesman for the party as a whole. That means he gives up his right to speak publicly on any important issue until he has consulted with all parts of the party; that is the price the chairman should be willing to pay. And he should be absolutely neutral in party fights so that the party remains a place where people come together to discuss their differences and where they stay united to battle Republicans.[14]

The next chairman, in other words, was to be a neutral spokesman of whatever policy emerged from whatever fights the various factions, with all their contending ideologies, might engage in. This remarkable restraint, moreover, was to be exercised at the same time the chairman was energetically pursuing the second requirement.

> We need party unity. And that means we have to bring back into the party those voters who chose to defect in 1972 without relinquishing any part of the coalition we now have.[15]

The chairman would restore the electoral strength of a refurbished Democratic organization by remaining absolutely neutral in struggles between those who advocated and those who opposed continuation of the policies that had driven out the voters it was now essential to win back. This, of course, made no sense at all, and Winograd knew it.

Morley Winograd never had the slightest intention of presiding over a Democratic party at war with itself; nor did he have any serious interest in becoming the public spokesman of a point of view that continued to repel sizeable segments of the blue-collar constituency essential to a viable Democratic coalition. Under the guise of broadening participation in the formulation of the state party's formal platform, Winograd argued for an organizational reform that would provide new opportunities for control. The women's caucus of the state party sent questionnaires to each candidate for the chairmanship and, among other things, asked how it might be possible to reconcile "conflicting ideologies among members." Winograd's answer was intriguing. He suggested that "the next Chairman should enact a program of more comprehensive discussion of the issues so that ideological differences are not allowed to build to a crisis at each Convention."[16] It was not plain on the face of it how "more comprehensive discussion" could serve to prevent "ideological differences" from creating the sort of political "crisis" that had occurred with such unfortunate effects at, for example, the 1970 state convention, when the party and its candidates had been put on record in favor of abortion and amnesty. On the contrary, there were quite a few Democrats, many of them holding leading positions in the labor movement, who believed there had been altogether too much discussion and debate of issues the mere mention of which could only improve the electoral prospects of Republicans. What Winograd understood by "a program of more comprehensive discussion," however, was rather different than what a follower of George McGovern or a friend of the New Democratic Coalition might have meant.

Winograd noted at the end of his answer to the question that his "own ideas on such a program are outlined in my answer to question #4." The fourth question read: "In previous years, the Party has passed resolutions on various controversial issues (e.g., birth control education, abortion law reform, amnesty, etc.), but it has failed to act on them. What steps would you take to implement the Party's platform?" With visions of enraged blue-collar Catholic voters doubtless dancing in his head, Winograd did not even bother to discuss how he would set about to implement a platform the specified planks of which had contributed mightily to the most massive defeat ever sustained by a Democratic candidate for the presidency. Instead, as he had noted in answering the other question, he presented his program for wider participation and broader discussion in the drafting of the party platform. He began by casting some doubt on the legitimacy of past platforms, including implicitly the one from which the women's caucus had selected its examples: "I do not believe what passes for a platform at Convention time is in reality a platform so much as a disjointed body of resolutions put together in the crisis atmosphere of a Convention." Winograd proposed instead "an attempt to work out a real platform in advance of Conventions to be thoughtfully discussed and debated when the convention occurs." A "real platform," in other words, was one arranged in advance of the convention; the platforms adopted in the past by delegates to the convention were not real ones at all. A "real platform," though it "should involve a large number of people," should be both more and less inclusive than past ones had been. On one hand,

"Public hearings should take place to help involve more of the community at large." On the other,

> a smaller drafting committee which includes those who would have responsibility in implementing the recommendations, particularly, our elected officials, should then provide a proposal to be discussed thoroughly by local County and District organizations before being recommended to the Convention by State Central.[17]

Both proposals appeared to broaden participation in the important business of drafting the party platform; not only convention delegates but the public and elected public officials would be included. Both proposals actually were designed to limit the likelihood of a party platform that failed to appeal to the broad middle ground and the large middle class of American politics. The influence of the liberal left wing of the party would be diluted in the first instance by public hearings in which, presumably, more moderate views would prevail. The ability of the liberal left wing to promote its own views in a state convention would be seriously curtailed when, instead of initiating proposals of its own, it could only respond to a draft prepared by those who had the greatest stake in the public acceptability of the party platform. More people would be involved, and the process would be more thorough. Power, however, would pass from those who could momentarily persuade convention delegates to those who controlled the relatively small membership of a drafting committee. Winograd spoke of participation; he understood power.

While the Oakland County chairman was promising ideological neutrality and promoting an organizational scheme designed to ensure ideological moderation, he was also actively seeking the support of the party's best-known and most influential members. Every Democrat who was a prominent public official or an important party leader was approached. With few exceptions, most notably the secretary of state, Richard Austin, who seemed intent on avoiding even a conversation,[18] Democrats who held elective office were more than willing to discuss the future of the party with Winograd. He visited with Detroit Mayor Roman Gribbs and former mayor Jerome P. Cavanagh, with whom certain "misunderstandings" were apparently resolved.[19] He spent time with members of the congressional delegation, and he held discussions with the Democratic leadership of the state legislature. He spoke with Phil Hart, who, as always, was neutral on internal party questions, and with the attorney general, Frank Kelley who, as usual, was not. Kelley, along with Speaker of the House William Ryan, majority floor leader Bobby Crim, and several other state legislators, endorsed him. With public officials Winograd was invariably courteous and affable; with a few party leaders he became belligerent and threatening. When Tom Baldini, perhaps the single most influential member of the Eleventh District congressional committee, joined Winograd for a drink in Marquette in the middle of December, he could not possibly have expected to hear what the candidate for the state chairmanship proceeded to tell him.

Failure to support a candidate who eventually wins is seldom the basis for a close and continuing political friendship. This is a proposition so obvious on the face of it that it rarely requires explicit expression. Whether out of irritation or frustration, Winograd, with the approval of his brother, Bernard, who was scarcely a source of restraint, decided to leave Baldini with no grounds for uncertainty about the inevitable consequences of a failure to provide assistance: "Either deliver the Eleventh or forget your career if we win anyway."[20] When he wanted to, Winograd could get to the heart of a matter with remarkable speed. On the off chance that Baldini might either forget the threat or dismiss it as a momentary aberration, Winograd, when he returned from his visit to the Upper Peninsula, wrote him a short letter, the central sentence of which read: "I trust you've had time to think further about our conversation and I look forward to hearing from you on where the Eleventh District might be headed."[21] Baldini did not reply, and Winograd had to wait for the first ballot at the state convention to discover Baldini's decision and to determine the direction the Eleventh district was taking.

Baldini might have been noncommittal, but many of the most influential county and district chairmen were not. John Bruff, chairman of the Twelfth Congressional District committee and the major force in the Macomb County Democratic organization, shared Winograd's vision of a party firmly committed to the political center, and had high expectations for his ability to organize the state party. Bruff solicited the support of other county and district chairmen, many of whom had come to know Winograd through the alliances formed during the party battles of the previous year. He did his work well. Two weeks before the convention convened, Bruff issued a press release declaring that "Leaders of the Michigan Democratic Party, including county and district chairmen, have announced their support for Morley A. Winograd as the new State Party Chairman." The release listed, in addition to Bruff, the chairmen of the Wayne, Kent, and Macomb county parties, as well as the chairmen of the Eleventh, Sixteenth, Eighteenth, and Second (Wayne) districts.[22] Far more important than the number of chairmen who had endorsed Winograd was the fact that counting Oakland County, where Winograd was still chairman, four of the five largest counties in the state, counties that together accounted for three-fifths of the Democratic vote, and therefore, three-fifths of the delegates at the Democratic state convention, seemed to be committed. Careful observers, or the adherents of Paul Donahue or Robert

Mitchell, might have noticed that the chairmen of the First, Thirteenth, Fourteenth, Fifteenth, and Seventeenth districts, all of which were in Wayne County and each of which contained more delegates than any of the districts listed in Bruff's release except the Sixteenth, were absent; county and district officers from the smaller counties and the more Republican districts of outstate Michigan would probably not be so discriminating. Winograd had what at least appeared to be powerful support among some of the most powerful leaders of the Democratic party.

With a meticulously planned campaign that had been conducted with unusual energy, Morley Winograd had secured the support of some of the state's most prominent Democratic public officials and obtained the endorsement of some of the most influential county and district committee chairmen. This was a necessary, but far from sufficient condition for election to the chairmanship. Neither public officials nor party leaders had the power to decide whether Winograd would or would not lead the party for the next two years. Labor had the power to make that decision, and within the house of labor the voice of the UAW would probably be decisive. When Winograd began to pursue the chairmanship openly immediately after the November election, he discussed his prospects with Ken Morris, director of UAW Region 1-B. Morris presided over the region that included Oakland County, and he knew more about the county chairman than did any of the other Michigan regional directors. Morris had made it possible for Winograd to become county chairman two years earlier, and he was willing to do what he could to help him become state chairman. Morris cautioned Winograd, however, that he could not promise UAW support. Sam Fishman was also encouraging when Winograd talked with him, but he too was careful to point out that no promises could be made about what the UAW might finally decide to do. At least part of the caution expressed by both Morris and Fishman was occasioned by the possibility that a fourth candidate might enter the race.

Michael Berry was an extremely successful attorney with a long and interesting history with the Democratic party. For years Berry chaired the Sixteenth District congressional committee, and through his leadership of what was one of the most heavily Democratic districts in the state, established friendships with some of Michigan's most prominent politicians and most influential labor leaders. When he added to his chairmanship of the Sixteenth District the chairmanship of the Wayne County Road Commission, he presided over one of the most formidable, and one of the least known, combinations of political and economic power ever placed under the control of a single individual in southeastern Michigan. Berry had yet another source of power: he was Lebanese and one of the most influential members of the Arab community. If he became a candidate for the state chairmanship, he would be difficult, though by no means impossible, to defeat. But no one could ever be quite certain what Michael Berry really wanted. His urbane and engaging exterior seemed calculated to mask a nature that took pride in its ability to dissemble. The enigmatic Mr. Berry seemed to enjoy the prestige of private influence much more than the sort of political career that might expose him constantly to public scrutiny. So long as he held out the possibility of a candidacy, however, he retained the backing of two UAW regional directors. Both Bard Young and Marcellius Ivory, who led the two regions, 1-E and 1-A, that encompassed all of western Wayne County, including the Sixteenth Congressional District and much of Detroit, would stay with Berry until and unless he decided not to enter the race. Whether he finally decided he had nothing to gain and perhaps something to lose by running for the chairmanship, or whether, as Winograd suspected, Ken Morris engaged in some internal maneuvering within the union to deny him labor support, Berry decided between Christmas and New Year's Day not to become a candidate.

With Berry out of it, Winograd had no serious competition for the support of the UAW. He entered the state convention with the endorsement of the union[23] and, with John Bruff's assistance, the support of a majority of those who held leadership positions in the party. He did not, however, come to the convention with enough support to defeat Paul Donahue and Robert Mitchell on the first ballot. Winograd fell 120 votes short of the 1,231 needed to win; Mitchell was only 239 votes behind him.[24] Mitchell had exceeded everyone's expectations by assembling a strange coalition of the disaffected. Appealing to the faithful followers of George McGovern not to desert their commitment to what some were already calling the politics of disaster and defeat, Mitchell had held the attachment of the Democratic left. Applauding the diligent effort of outstate and rural party workers and deploring the prospect of a third successive state chairman from the metropolitan suburbs of Oakland County, Mitchell had retained the allegiance of Democrats from the distant reaches of western and northern Michigan. Winograd could do nothing about his residence in Oakland County and was not about to become an advocate of busing, abortion, amnesty, gun control, or any of the other positions adamantly urged by liberals and overwhelmingly rejected by voters. His slogan, "Win With Winograd," might have only alliteration as a literary quality, but it sent a political message to the left that made him as unlikely to secure their support as he was unwilling to ask for it.

Mitchell's support seemed impervious to attack; Donahue's was another matter. While Mitchell had entered the convention trying to convince a majority of the delegates that "it's still a wide open race,"[25] Donahue had known that Winograd would win unless something was done to discredit him. Someone in the Donahue campaign somehow obtained the logo of the Winograd campaign from the printer and added a new message. Underneath the words

"Winograd: Let's Work Together To Win," the Donahue operative added "The 1972 Oakland County Election Record" that listed the county offices lost by Democratic incumbents. Suggesting that this was somehow entirely the fault of the county chairman, the message added: "With this fine record Winograd contends he is the man to organize the party for victory. What do you think?" When the flier was circulated among delegates late Saturday evening, reaction was predictable. Delegates who were supporting either Mitchell or Donahue considered it a shrewd tactical maneuver, while those backing Winograd professed outrage at a devious personal attack. The flier intensified emotions; it changed no minds. Donahue neither hurt Winograd nor helped himself. He still had very little support, and on the first ballot ran a poor third with only 312 votes. Most of the support Donahue did have, moreover, was controlled by the AFL-CIO.

Four years earlier, the AFL-CIO had also opposed the UAW's candidate with one of its own, but this time it was not motivated solely or even mainly by a desire to demonstrate its political independence and power. When Bill Marshall and the state AFL-CIO refused to endorse George McGovern, they were following the example and instruction of George Meany, but they had done it willingly, and in the case of a few of the members of the federation's executive board, almost gleefully. So far as the AFL-CIO was concerned, the liberal followers of first Eugene McCarthy and then George McGovern had managed in just four short years to elect Richard Nixon twice, and as if that were not bad enough, nearly destroy the Democratic party as a political organization. The state AFL-CIO wanted and demanded a movement away from the left and toward the center. Marshall, who had never done anything to cause anyone to confuse him with a member of the diplomatic corps, had expressed this otherwise respectable sentiment in words scarcely chosen to create a climate of conciliation and cooperation when, shortly after the election, he asserted it was "time the black caucus and the UAW stopped running the Democratic party." Marshall's remark was greeted by charges of racism from black legislators and stunned silence from the UAW.

Marshall thought Paul Donahue would move the party back toward the center. But while it was clear after the first ballot that Winograd did not have a majority, it was equally apparent that he had considerably more support than Donahue, who was running behind not only Winograd but Mitchell as well. Marshall may have then believed that Winograd was "probably another Oakland County flake,"[26] but he knew Mitchell much better, and knew him *actually* to be what he thought the Oakland County chairman *might* be. It was only a matter of time before the AFL-CIO would have to choose between Winograd and Mitchell, and there seemed little doubt what that choice would be. The UAW did not want to wait. At the end of the first ballot, Sam Fishman and Bill Marshall held a meeting. Fishman, who agreed completely with Marshall that the party had to be brought back to the center, had no trouble coming to an agreement with the president of the state AFL-CIO. Marshall, who had publicly insisted that "the time is past when the AFL-CIO can be looked to only when it is time to bail the party leadership out of trouble,"[27] wanted assurances that the AFL-CIO would be included in the internal decision making of the party. In exchange for Marshall's support of Winograd, the UAW promised that Dee Lyons of the AFL-CIO would be made the party's recording secretary.

Mitchell had succeeded in stopping Winograd on the first ballot, but he had needed the help of Paul Donahue and his bloc of AFL-CIO delegates to do it. Nevertheless, Mitchell could actually have won the chairmanship at that point had he carried all or even a substantial majority of the delegates from the two black congressional districts. The two districts together contained 356 votes—205 from the First District and 151 from the Thirteenth—but Mitchell, who had expected to carry both, trailed Winograd in each: by 90.5 to 79.5 in the First and by an incredible 108.4 to 15.5 in the Thirteenth. The reasons are intriguing. If the unions seemed to move in mysterious ways in this convention, the black delegations from the First and Thirteenth districts were a marvel of complication. Leadership in the black community was anything but united. John Conyers, who could almost always be counted on to oppose anything and anyone endorsed by the UAW, was backing Mitchell, as was Buddy Battle, president of UAW Local 600. Battle's boyhood friend, the minority leader of the state senate, Coleman Young, was neutral but privately betting on Winograd. Mitchell's support in the First and Thirteenth was not enough to deliver a majority of either district, however, once Ken Morris, a white UAW regional director, became involved. Morris knew that Marcellius Ivory and Buddy Battle were "mortal enemies." Battle was for Mitchell, so Morris had little difficulty persuading Ivory to go for Winograd. Proving that the power of a regional director exceeds that of any local union president, even the president of the largest local union in the world, Ivory delivered a majority of both delegations to Winograd.

Before the second ballot began, Donahue withdrew from the competition. In doing so, however, he failed or refused to throw his support to either Winograd or Mitchell. Those delegates who either belonged to or were influenced by the AFL-CIO had no guidance from Donahue about what they should do, and no clear message from the leadership of the union. Charlie Younglove, head of the Steelworkers, apparently had not been informed that Marshall was now supporting Winograd. On his own, he had already decided to abandon Donahue, and he proceeded to pull as many AFL-CIO delegates as he could off the floor in order to instruct them to switch to Winograd. Confusion was the order of the day. When the second ballot began and the roll call had already passed the Eleventh District, where Tom Baldini, whether because he had forgotten or because he remembered Winograd's threat, continued to hold a majority for Mitchell, someone discovered that nearly a dozen of Younglove's own Steelworkers had not voted for Winograd because no one had bothered to tell them what to do. The district asked to be repolled, and once this was done and it became apparent that Winograd now had a majority of a district that was supposed to be one of Mitchell's strongest, the slide began in earnest.

After Winograd's total passed the majority mark, and districts began to switch while there was still time to establish at least a feeble claim of loyalty to the winner, Mitchell conceded the inevitable: "This has been one hell of a fight, and I lost. Morley Winograd has a majority and he has my backing."[28] Winograd accepted the chairmanship from the convention, graciously acknowledged the formidable efforts of his two opponents, and made the obligatory promise to unify the party. Those who had greeted Mitchell's withdrawal with cries of "No, No, No, No, No, No"[29] were not about to respond with enthusiasm to calls for party unity. Labor had won, and although Bill Marshall might believe that the vote for Mitchell demonstrated that "Labor is weaker than in the past" within the party,[30] the liberal left was convinced that something more than a chairmanship had been lost.

The followers of McCarthy and McGovern had proclaimed the principle of open politics and had used it to acquire dominant power in the Democratic party. Labor elected Winograd to restore unity and then sought to diminish division by curtailing participation. Two-and-a-half hours of debate that had been allotted for discussion of rules and resolutions expired while the convention struggled through the unexpected second ballot for the chairmanship. When convention chairman Stuart Hertzberg announced that the interrupted discussion on resolutions would resume after the election of officers, liberals cheered. Once Winograd was elected, however, the worst fears of those who viewed labor as the major threat to the liberalization of the Democratic party seemed confirmed, as the convention was quickly adjourned and all resolutions referred to the consideration of the state central committee. Liberals suspected that Winograd and organized labor would make certain that what had not been discussed in convention would never be debated in the state central committee. They would soon learn that it is not always pleasant to be correct.

Since the formation of the liberal-labor coalition in 1948, six men had occupied the chairmanship of the Michigan Democratic party before the election of Morley Winograd. Three of them, Neil Staebler, Zolton Ferency, and Sander Levin, had become Democratic candidates for governor, and all had lost to Republican incumbents. Of the remaining three, Hicks Griffiths had been appointed to the bench, and John J. "Joe" Collins had used the extensive acquaintances and influence of a state chairman to build a lucrative insurance business. Only the unfortunate James McNeely had failed to obtain some political or personal advantage from the office. Unlike any of his predecessors, Winograd assumed office without any personal interest in either elective or appointive office. He was much more ambitious. He wanted nothing less than the radical reorganization of the Democratic party. Hicks Griffiths and Neil Staebler had helped give the state party the liberal principles of the New Deal. Zolton Ferency had sought to move the party even further to the left. Ferency had failed, but the leftward movement had continued with the growing influence of the followers of first McCarthy and then McGovern. What some saw as the inevitable and salutary liberalization of the Democratic party others viewed as an aberration that if not quickly corrected would be wholly destructive. Winograd began his first term with the clear intention of turning the party to the right, that it might once again come to occupy the political center.

He wasted no time. On the Saturday following his election he met with a small group of his closest allies and advisors. This was an inner circle that was open only to those who had demonstrated loyalty to each other and fidelity to common political principles. Sam Fishman headed the list of those invited, followed by Bruce Miller, John Bruff, Sheldon Klimist, Tom Gray, Bernard Winograd, and Stuart Hertzberg. Winograd had wanted to invite a friend from Oakland County politics, but Sam Fishman vetoed it on the ground that it was not yet certain that James Blanchard was politically reliable. John Bruff could not attend but sent Winograd a letter that set forth the objectives the new chairman should follow. None of the group that met that Saturday and continued to meet as the years passed and its membership increased, disagreed with what Bruff wrote. The state chairman, he advised, "should have an especially competent press person to help build an image for the Democratic Party as the party interested in issues of concern to white blue collar workers instead of *just* the young, poor, and black." That stated as concisely as possible the direction labor and its allies wanted the party to take. Bruff's other recommendations addressed the subject of party organization. "In respect to DSCC [Democratic State Central Committee], I would suggest the immediate appointment of a platform and resolutions committee and require all resolutions to be referred to said committee before action by DSCC." In the course of his campaign for the chairmanship Winograd had already proposed this method of providing for a more "thorough" discussion of issues. Bruff only added the obvious when he wrote: "Obviously, this committee must have reliable members." The next recommendation showed the way to greater control over the state central committee: "I would recommend that you build a state wide caucus of friends and loyal Democrats to support you and form a basis of a caucus at DSCC meetings and state conventions. Since you are State Chairman you will probably not be a member of this caucus but trusted friends should organize it." With adequate control over the organizational power of the state party, Winograd and his "trusted friends" could then at least give the appearance of sharing authority: "you should try dis-arming your opponents and enemies, i.e., Austin, Conyers, Irving [Helen Irving, chairman of the Fourteenth District], Marshall, etc. by consultation and involvement, so long as within safe areas of activities."[31] Bruff's remarkable letter said nothing that was not already understood by the group that met with Winograd that Saturday afternoon. Nor did it take long for Winograd and his allies to put into place everything Bruff had recommended.

Notes

1. In the résumé that accompanied the letter he sent to party activists to announce his candidacy, Donahue listed no fewer than thirty-seven different political positions he had occupied as a volunteer. These ranged in importance from Michigan campaign manager for Hubert Humphrey in the 1972 presidential primary to associate chairman of the Wayne County Democratic party's annual dinner-dance. It was impossible to think of a political organization or candidate that Donahue had neither worked for nor maintained "a solid and cordial working relationship with." Paul M. Donahue, résumé, 1973.

2. The extent of Marshall's dislike for those he considered responsible for the results of the 1972 election can hardly be overstated. Marshall released a statement analyzing the November election that made his position and his anger abundantly clear.

> Those struck by the "new politics" fervor were convinced of the greatness of their crusade because it worked after the 1968 Convention in taking control of the decision-making apparatus of the party. It worked in securing the May Primary in Michigan which the AFL-CIO cautioned and fought against, as it allowed the predictable massive Republican cross-over voting. When the Democratic presidential nominee was announced, it was final confirmation of the formula. And no one connected with pre-1968 political activity could caution against error or voice advice without being considered blasphemous.

> During the campaign, elected leaders of ethnic and labor groups were ignored in favor of chosen individual members of the respective groups, as though elected leadership were inherently tainted in some way, and individual members were 'pure,' though they spoke for no one. When elected leadership was not ignored, it was insulted.

William C. Marshall, press release, January 17, 1973.

3. Tom Gray prepared a memo for Morley Winograd to assist in the planning of the latter's campaign for the chairmanship in 1973. According to Gray's analysis, the three metropolitan counties together accounted for 57.1 percent of the state's base Democratic vote. Tom Gray, memo to Morley Winograd, n.d.

4. Tom Gray, "Targetting Memo for 1973 Chairman Campaign," n.d.

5. Morley Winograd, letter to Democratic party members, n.d.

6. *Royal Oak Daily Tribune,* January 1, 1973.

7. Ibid.

8. Morley Winograd, letter to Ginny Selin, January 17, 1973. This letter corrected a summary Selin had made of the Marquette meeting.

9. Marquette County Democratic women's caucus, December 18, 1972, Marquette. Summary of remarks of Morley Winograd at Marquette County Democratic women's caucus, Marquette, December 18, 1972.

10. *Royal Oak Daily Tribune,* February 1, 1973.

11. Morley Winograd, letter to Lillian Stoner, chairman, screening committee, educators caucus, Michigan Democratic party, January 28, 1973.

12. See note 9 above.

13. Morley Winograd, letter to Vicki Neiberg for the women's caucus of the Michigan Democratic party, January 11, 1973. This was in response to a questionnaire sent to candidates for the chairmanship by the women's caucus.

14. Morley Winograd, letter to "Fellow Democrats," n.d.

15. Ibid.

16. Morley Winograd, letter to Vicki Neiberg for the women's caucus of the Michigan Democratic party, January 11, 1973.

17. Ibid.

18. On three different occasions in December Winograd attempted to arrange a meeting with Austin and could not even get the secretary of state on the telephone. In a letter to Austin, Winograd, with some irritation, detailed the efforts he had made, efforts that included telephoning the secretary of state's office on Monday, December 11, when, "I called . . . every half hour starting at 9 a.m. and was told first that you hadn't arrived; later that you were in a conference; and finally, Walter Elliott, who had indicated earlier he would try and set something up for that morning, was left to tell me you had gone." Winograd continued his efforts to see Austin but remained unsuccessful. He was especially interested in meeting with Austin because "a number of your advisors have been criticizing me, who don't know me and haven't had the common courtesy to talk to me first. I'm sure this is not your position or your method of dealing with people." Morley Winograd, letter to Richard Austin, December 28, 1972.

19. Morley Winograd, letter to Jerome P. Cavanagh, January 24, 1973.

20. Morley Winograd, letter to author, October 12, 1982.

21. Morley Winograd, letter to Tom Baldini, January 5, 1973.

22. John Bruff, press release, January 24, 1973.

23. The Mitchell campaign correctly pointed out at the beginning of the convention that "the *UAW Executive Committee* has *recommended* Morley Winograd to their membership. A *UAW endorsement* of any candidate will *not* be made until Saturday night." ("Mitchell Newsgram," n.d. This was distributed to convention delegates as they arrived on the evening of Friday, February 2.) As the lawyers say, this was a distinction without a difference. A recommendation of the UAW executive board regarding a political endorsement to the politically active UAW members who made

up the membership that would vote on the recommendation had as much chance of being discarded as George McGovern had of winning the presidency on a recount. Mitchell knew this as well as anyone, but he also knew the advantages to be gained from planting the seeds of uncertainty wherever and however he could. In the same leaflet, Mitchell tacitly admitted that Winograd had the endorsement and attempted to use it against him: "While endorsements are important, it's the votes that count—this is the lesson we've learned from Sen. Ed. Muskie." Mitchell was obviously not appealing to the labor-led coalition of the center.

24. *Detroit Free Press,* February 6, 1973.
25. "Mitchell Newsgram," n.d.
26. Morley Winograd, interview with author, August 22, 1982.
27. William Marshall, press release, January 17, 1973.
28. *Oakland Press,* February 5, 1973.
29. *Detroit News,* February 5, 1973.
30. *Detroit Free Press,* February 12, 1973.
31. John Bruff, letter to Morley Winograd, February 8, 1973.

CHAPTER 3

Democratic Centralism and the Movement to the Center

Before the Michigan Democratic party could regain the political center, the New Democratic Coalition of "the young, the poor, and the black" had to be replaced with what Morley Winograd deliberately chose to call the "old coalition." In Michigan the "old coalition" meant "labor, blacks, industrial areas in both the metropolitan and outstate areas and suburban working-class Catholics."[1] Replacing one coalition with another was not simply a matter of rearranging the components of a verbal formula. The New Democratic Coalition had not acquired majority strength within the Michigan Democratic party, but neither was it a negligible force that would somehow disappear if simply ignored. It had yielded only to the organized strength of the UAW and the AFL-CIO at the August state convention and, as Winograd would never fail to remember, had fought persistently for Robert Mitchell in February. There were two ways to deal with this substantial liberal minority. One was to encourage its continued participation in a broad coalition, confident in the knowledge that it could not seriously affect the decisions or the direction of the party. This, of course, was the method normally and routinely prescribed by those who believe there are no limits to the range of political opinions that can be contained within a single political party. Winograd found this line of argument eminently unconvincing. If the party were to permit the participation of those who expounded views that antagonized and alienated a crucial segment of its normal constituency it would be committing collective suicide. Democratic liberals had driven substantial numbers of the white working class into the hands of Republican politicians eager to exploit their conservative instincts on social issues that seemed to threaten both the American family and the American work ethic. There was only one way to deal with the New Democratic Coalition, and that was to deprive them of any opportunity to influence any part of the party organization.

The decision to attempt the destruction of the influence of the new left was connected with the determination to increase the influence of organized labor. Winograd had been elected by the leadership, and he believed that the cornerstone of any electorally viable Democratic coalition had to be the membership, of organized labor. Whether the party would be able to defeat Republicans on the state level would be decided by the white blue-collar voters of the metropolitan suburban area. Their support would obviously be contingent on their belief that the Democratic, and not the Republican, party best represented their interests. Winograd and the leadership of organized labor were in complete agreement on the need to reclaim the political attachment of the blue-collar worker; they also agreed that this could be done only if labor played a larger role in party affairs. They agreed on something else as well. They wanted nothing even remotely resembling a repetition of the divisive issues of the last several elections. Sam Fishman and Bill Marshall had both been driven to distraction by Jim McNeely's propensity to make public statements that damaged the party's ability to retain the loyalty of blue-collar voters. Morley Winograd wanted to say nothing that could possibly harm the party or threaten the support of labor. No one had any hesitation about entering into an arrangement that was known to socialists as democratic centralism and became known to the press and the public as Morley Winograd's vow of silence. Within ten days of his election, Winograd and Fishman, without ever discussing it with the party officers, agreed that the chairman would make no public statements on public issues. The chairman would speak solely as the representative of the party. He would, in other words, speak only after the party as a whole had already spoken. Winograd, who loved to tell the story of how Ray Bliss had rebuilt the Republican party after the Goldwater debacle of 1964 by ignoring issues and working on organization, eagerly embraced an arrangement that would let him get on with his job.

When Winograd became chairman he inherited a staff that included, in addition to several clerical workers who had been with the party for years, a former reporter for the *Royal Oak Tribune*. Tom Gray had recently become the party's public relations director, and Winograd kept him on. Gray, who believed fervently in the desirability of moving the party away from the liberal left and toward the position of labor, decided that the new notion of collective leadership was too important to go unnoticed. At his urging Winograd called his first press conference; it was almost his last. When the new chairman walked into the Capitol in Lansing he and Tom Gray were filled with confidence. Winograd had just been elected state chairman after only two years as Oakland County chairman. He was bent on the thorough reorganization of the Democratic party, and no one, not the liberals and certainly not the press, was going to push him around. The capitol press corps had never seen anything quite like it. They had come to hear what the new, young chairman was going to say about himself and the Democratic party, and instead the new, young chairman announced that the purpose of the press conference was to announce that the new, young chairman of the Michigan Democratic party would not have any press conferences. Winograd explained that as the representative of the Democratic party he could state what the party position was on a matter when the party had taken a position, but where the party had not spoken he would not express a personal opinion. The press immediately decided to put this unprecedented policy to the test. Ignoring everything Winograd had just said, Robert Pisor of the *Detroit News* asked the chairman what his position was on the matter of busing to achieve racial balance in the public schools. Winograd, who was not going to be pushed around by anyone, responded, "No comment." Then the dam broke. Winograd was hit with a barrage of questions, more than two dozen in all, to each of which he replied, "No comment." Finally, he charged out of the room. Tom Greene, a Detroit television reporter, chased after him, asking more questions as the television camera captured it all on film. In answer to each question, Winograd, with increasing anger, screamed "No comment." Greene's final question, asked as Winograd turned a corner, was "Is it true that you are really a Republican?" In the background, out of sight of the camera, the fading voice of Morley Winograd was heard to utter, as if they were the last words he would ever speak in his lifetime, "No comment."

The whole episode had taken barely fifteen minutes, but it had consequences that lasted far into the future. That evening television viewers in the Detroit metropolitan area were treated to the curious spectacle of the new chairman of the Michigan Democratic party apparently running away from the press and its questions. Tom Greene, whose journalistic standards were evidenced by his stated determination, expressed shortly after the press conference, to "go after that guy," provided a commentary that was as close to satire as he knew how to come. The next morning readers all over the state, whether they opened the *Detroit Free Press* or the *Detroit News,* found stories depicting the remarkable, and so far as anyone could recall, unique refusal of a public figure to answer even a single question at his own press conference. Far worse for the chairman than either the television coverage or the newspaper stories was the reaction of Douglas Fraser, second in command of the UAW and chairman of UAW-CAP. Winograd had wanted to avoid any contact with the media, and though his first exposure had shaken his self-confidence, the public would soon forget what the chairman had done, if it even remembered who he was. Fraser, however, represented both the organization that had elected Winograd and a major portion of the electoral constituency that was absolutely crucial to the coalition he wanted to restore. Winograd's refusal to respond to questions from the press seemed to Fraser not a shrewd device by which to eliminate divisiveness within the party, but an embarrassing display of incompetence. As if to demonstrate his own ability to deal directly and publicly with any political situation, Fraser told the press that it might prove necessary for the union to find another Democratic party chairman. He left no room for doubt that he meant it might become necessary far in advance of the expiration of Winograd's two-year term. Winograd, who wanted nothing so much as to rebuild the state party on a foundation supplied by the labor movement, found himself, less than a month after his election, under fire from the highest levels of the UAW. It was not an auspicious beginning.

The press conference and its aftermath had been a chastening experience. One day everything seemed possible; a day later nothing appeared easy. Tom Gray had spent weeks developing and elaborating a theory demonstrating that a Democratic party transformed into what for all practical purposes would be a labor party could recapture the white working class by a policy deliberately designed to antagonize liberals and blacks. Gray believed that the "battle for the ring"—i.e., the suburban areas surrounding Detroit—could be won only by appealing directly to the interests, and if necessary, the prejudices of the white blue-collar Catholics who held the balance of power in statewide elections. Liberals might not feel comfortable with a party that, for example, vigorously opposed busing; but liberals, in the view of a political realist, were after all merely "flakes who had no idea what was going on in the world and therefore had no right in the party" in the first place.[2] Besides, liberals had no place else to go. They might not continue to participate actively in the reconstructed Democratic party, but they certainly were not likely to become part of a new Republican coalition. They would probably remain with the Democratic party and view their reduced influence as a temporary phenomenon; liberals always believed that the future belonged to them.

Liberals were not the only group that was likely to react adversely to the effort to adapt to the fears and adopt the attitudes of the suburban blue-collar voter. Blacks could not be expected to view with equanimity a policy that tied the civil rights platform of the Democratic party to the electoral demands of a white constituency that was largely identified by its fear of having black children commingle with their own. Gray was perfectly willing to face what so many Democratic politicians sought to avoid. White congressmen might fall all over each other to raise the flag against busing while assuring themselves and each other that this in no way represented a retreat from a dedicated commitment to civil rights. It did not require any very sophisticated analysis to understand that although white congressmen might believe this, the white constituencies they followed so slavishly on the busing issue could in fact lead them wherever they wanted to go. White constituencies that were eager, and white congressmen who were willing, to amend the Constitution of the United States to prohibit busing, did not appear to offer a reliable guarantee against alteration of the statutory law that constituted the civil rights progress of the

1960s. Gray understood the likely reaction of blacks; it was a price he, at least, was willing to pay.

Even more than liberals, blacks really had no other place to go. Liberals might occasionally drift off to support Republicans like John Lindsay who had reputations for progressive policies and liberal ideas. They might even discuss the possibility of a third-party movement based on the growing white-collar professional class. Blacks had neither the leisure nor the material resources to make these sorts of flirtations real possibilities. At worst they might be so disturbed by a new Democratic direction that they would decide not to vote at all. The black vote or at least substantial proportions of it might be lost, but— and this was decisive for Gray's theory—it would not be lost to the Republicans. The mathematics were simple, even if the politics were problematic at best. Any policy that convinced one suburban white to vote Democratic instead of Republican was a net gain, even if as a result of that policy one inner-city black stayed away from the polls. The Republicans would experience a net loss of one while the Democrats experienced no change at all. When, instead of single individuals, the calculation included tens of thousands, the electoral benefits became unmistakable. Levin had lost the 1970 gubernatorial election by 44,000 votes. If, by taking a position that caused 45,000 blacks to stay home, the party had been able to retain 45,000 voters who normally voted for Democrats but had voted for William Milliken instead, Levin's total would have been higher by only a thousand, but Milliken's would have been lower by a full 45,000. Levin would have been elected governor.

Gray seemed only to have worked out the implications of what many politicians, both white and black, had understood intuitively. Political success nearly always depends on an appeal to some popular prejudice. Political prudence, however, just as often requires silence about the calculations underlying the appeal. But silence was not compatible with Gray's intention. The most certain way to win back Democratic voters in the suburban ring around Detroit was deliberately to adopt policies designed to antagonize black voters. Any pretense that a policy would not injure blacks might succeed in convincing not black but white voters. Republicans had attracted Democratic voters because without a black constituency they were not inhibited in their advocacy of political positions that appealed to all-white constituencies. Democrats had a black constituency, and that had now become an apparent obstacle to winning back blue-collar defectors. It would not be enough to ignore the black voter; a successful appeal to white workers would have to be based on policies clearly antagonistic to black interests. Gray's strategy seemed to be based on a brutal realism; it was instead utterly unrealistic. It failed to acknowledge in any way those dimensions of human behavior that are not easily reducible to mathematics. It ignored entirely the possible public consequences of a policy so obviously based on a cynical view of the electorate. It had all the appearances of a Machiavellian strategy without any of the subtlety of Machiavelli. It was not, however, the integrity or the reputation of the Democratic party that put an end to the vision of a party based on the united and enthusiastic support of organized labor moving deliberately to antagonize black, in order to increase the number of white, voters. What Gray regarded as a mathematical certainty became a political impossibility after Douglas Fraser questioned the competence and threatened the career of Morley Winograd. Nothing really radical could even be considered while Winograd lacked the complete confidence of the UAW. Moderation once again became a virtue.

The first press conference had exposed the new state chairman to the animus of a press corps that was as unable to analyze a political situation as it was incapable of freeing itself from its own pretentions. The great majority of members of the press who covered the state capital saw politics almost exclusively in terms of personal ambition and private pressure. Politicians presented a curious spectacle that deserved to be watched with condescension, if not open contempt, so that the public could be protected from the depradations of a class that could never command respect. It was not uncommon to hear the reporters who participated each week on the local PBS program "Off the Record" laugh with comfortable self-assurance when the host, Tim Skubick, remarked that "No honest man was safe while the legislature was in session." Winograd had offended them by treating them with the same disdain with which they viewed most political practitioners. There was no danger that he could seriously discomfort them, however. He was dismissed as an errand boy of the labor movement who, given Fraser's response to his performance, would probably not have too many more errands to run. It became much more personal. There was no one the press enjoyed more than Zolton Ferency, because there was no one who more closely shared their opinion about the relative inconsequence of other politicians. They were always eager to hear the latest personal insult Ferency would present as insightful political analysis. When Ferency confirmed their belief that Winograd was the creature of the unions, they were pleased; when Ferency proceeded to observe that Morley Winograd even looked like Sam Fishman, they could barely contain themselves. Ferency and the press had both failed to understand that the most fundamental alteration of the state party since 1948 was in process of accomplishment. The press conference called to announce a policy of not having press conferences was only an unfortunate and momentary phenomenon of a movement toward labor control of the Michigan Democratic party. The methods employed to achieve this end, however, were not nearly as colorful as Ferency's superficial descriptions nor as easy to cover as what the press was normally content to report.

When Sam Fishman and Morley Winograd agreed to implement the principles of democratic centralism, they both understood that the party organization the chairman was to represent would be securely under the control of the UAW. The union had demonstrated its ability to exercise majority power in the two most recent Democratic state conventions. The political strength of the union was ultimately based on the approximately 600,000 members who were distributed throughout the six UAW regions into which Michigan had been divided. Four of the six were in the Detroit metropolitan area, which was both the industrial and the population center of the state. Blue-collar workers were the heart of Democratic voting strength, and the most Democratic districts contained the largest number of union members. Delegates to the Democratic state conventions and representation on the state central committee were both apportioned among the congressional districts on the basis of the Democratic vote in the preceding election. The most powerful congressional districts in the state party therefore contained the largest number of union members and the largest number of union political activists. Outside the metropolitan area, union membership constituted a smaller proportion of the population, but so did the normal Democratic vote. Moreover, some outstate areas, like Flint and Lansing, were heavily industrialized and heavily unionized. Even in the most rural and most Republican areas of the state, the UAW had representation. Precisely because the prospects for electing Democratic candidates in the Fourth, the Ninth, or the Tenth Congressional District seemed as imminent as the Second Coming, it was difficult to interest people in becoming active party members there. But every congressional district, including these, had not only union members but union staff people who had the continuing responsibility to increase the strength of the Democratic party.

The sheer size of the UAW would by itself have given it substantial influence within the party; the distribution of its membership provided it with the basis for influence in each of the nineteen congressional districts that sent delegations to state conventions and selected delegates to the state central committee. The UAW possessed the largest and most widely distributed private political organization in the state. For nearly a quarter of a century this organization had been placed at the disposal and employed at the direction of a political party led by people who had neither a formal affiliation nor a close personal identification with the union. The arrangement had worked with mutually beneficial results as long as a Democrat sat in the governor's office and the party confined itself to the business of reelecting the governor and reaffirming its commitment to the economic and civil rights policies of Democratic presidents. But now that the leadership of both the national and state Democratic party had begun to ignore the imperatives of electoral politics and to forget that the New Deal coalition was built on an understanding of the common economic interests of its constituent parts, the UAW had decided to use its strength to lead and no longer to follow the Democratic party. The election of Sam Fishman to the Democratic National Committee had signaled its new policy. The election of Morley Winograd had evidenced its power. The formation of the unity caucus demonstrated the mechanism by which the UAW could control and direct the Michigan Democratic party.

During Winograd's term as Oakland County chairman he had had little direct contact with Jim McNeely. Like most of his predecessors, McNeely acted in strict accordance with the apparent structural hierarchy of the state party. Under the textbook theory of party organization, the chairman and other officers of the state party were elected by vote of a state convention, delegates to which had been selected in party conventions in each of the nineteen congressional districts. The officers were in charge of the day-to-day workings of the party, but like the officers of a corporation, could only carry out the policy established by the membership. The membership, however, like the shareholders of a corporation, met infrequently; the party met in convention only twice every two years: once to adopt a party platform and nominate candidates for several state offices, and once to elect party officers. Between party conventions the power to make party policy was delegated to the Democratic state central committee, which, like the board of directors of a corporation, was elected by the members in district conventions and was accountable to them alone. From the beginning to the end of a two-year term, the chairman presided over meetings of the party officers and reported five times a year to the state central committee. McNeely, like his predecessors, viewed the state central committee as the source of the chairman's authority and its members as the keys to his power.

Winograd believed that the theory was wrong and actions based on it naive. He knew, even if McNeely and the others had not, that a member of the state central committee almost always owed his selection to an individual or an organization more powerful than himself. Winograd also knew that a seat on the state central committee conferred no discernible political influence on the person who held it. State central committee members really were delegates, and power really resided not in them but in those by whom they were delegated in the first place. No matter what a flow chart might appear to demonstrate, political power in the party was not in the state central committee membership but in the district and county organizations. Within those organizations, in turn, power was in the hands of the leadership. A state central member, if that position was the sole source of his strength, would never be able to bring pressure on a county or district chairman effectively. The county or district chairman, however, could almost always influence and could sometimes even control a member of that district's delegation to state central. As a county chairman, Winograd had used the other county and district chairmen to broaden his influence. As state chairman, he would use them to increase his control.

From the very beginning, Winograd replaced the state central members

with the county and district chairmen as the foundation of the state organization. Because the chairmen could usually influence their own delegates to
state central, there were fewer people with whom the state chairman had to
deal directly in order to control state central. Instead of speaking with each of
the state central members from, for example, the Sixteenth Congressional
District, Winograd would simply call the district chairman, Betty Burch, and
ask her to make certain that her people on state central understood what
needed to be done at the next meeting. For the first time county and district
chairmen were made to feel that they played a direct and significant role in the
state party organization. As more of them were drawn into the new arrangement, the influence of the state chairman increased. The prestige and the
political power of the county or district chairman came to be tied closely to his
or her relationship with the leadership of the state party. With a subtle grasp of
political psychology, Winograd understood that a county or district chairman
who began to help the state chairman exert influence over that district's
delegation to state central had become more the agent of the state party than
the representative of the local organization. What appeared to provide a
county or district chairman with greater power on the larger field of state
politics was paid for with diminished independence. If the county and district
chairmen served as the subordinate officers of the state chairman, the county
and district committees would become the subsidiary units of the state organization. By making what seemed a slight shift of emphasis from the state
central member to the county and district chairman, Winograd had begun a
major transformation of the entire party structure. Instead of a loose federation of county and district organizations, the state party was on the way to
becoming a centralized and hierarchical organization with the power to eliminate a cause of division or the possibility of challenge quickly and effectively.

The first step toward this change in the relationship between the state
party and the county and district organizations was taken two months after
Winograd's election. In April, the state central committee met for the first
time since the February state convention. The state convention had elected the
party officers; the state central committee was to elect officers-at-large. Unlike the party officers, the officers-at-large had no designated functions in the
state party. Instead, they were elected to represent either areas of the state that
would otherwise have no direct voice in party affairs or interests that were
important elements of the Democratic coalition. The election was over before
it began. Only one group had bothered to put together a slate of candidates,
and that group was formidable in the extreme. Not only the UAW and the
AFL-CIO but the chairmen of some of the largest Democratic county and
district committees had agreed to support it. John Bruff of Macomb County,
Betty Howe of Oakland, Robert Kleiner of Kent, Anthony Bielawski of Bay,
Betty Burch of the Sixteenth District, Vince Petitpren of the Fifteenth—all

the chairmen who were close allies of the labor movement and who had supported Morley Winograd for the chairmanship endorsed what was called the unity slate.

The state central committee meeting was scheduled for a Saturday afternoon in Midland. That morning those who supported the unity slate held a caucus. Each of the county and district chairmen who had joined with labor to create the slate of candidates attended, along with the state central members from their districts. The labor leadership was there, along with their political operatives. They had done their work with uncommon efficiency. Each UAW region had a political coordinator who worked both for the regional director and the director of the Michigan CAP. Each of them was a member of the state central committee, and all of them had contacted other members and made certain that those who had been convinced to support the slate attended the caucus. The unity caucus went through the exercise of formally endorsing the slate that its leading elements had already approved and then adjourned for lunch. It had the field to itself; there were no other organized groups within the state central committee. When the 120-odd members of the committee assembled in the afternoon, the entire slate was elected without opposition.

The unity caucus had been formed for the specific purpose of securing the election of officers-at-large who shared the political outlook of the chairman and the labor movement. The caucus had been eminently successful, and there seemed no reason not to employ it on a regular basis. At the next state central committee meeting the caucus met again. This time, however, it was thrown open to the entire membership of the state central committee. Instead of a private meeting of those who shared a common point of view, it became a public gathering open to any state central member regardless of his or her position on any particular question before the party. It was not, however, a public forum for open discussion but instead a remarkably successful attempt to eliminate the public expression of dissent and division.

While all members of state central had been informed that the unity caucus would meet before the state central meeting, the UAW-CAP coordinators, along with the county and district chairmen who were considered politically reliable, had been instructed to make certain that all the delegates who supported the leadership attended. The caucus would have a majority that followed the wishes of the party chairman and the labor leadership; it would also be chaired by three people selected by Sam Fishman and Morley Winograd. Ten years later Bruce Miller could still not understand why no one ever stood up and asked under what source of authority Betty Howe, John Bruff, and the Wayne County chairman served as convenors of the unity caucus.[3] While the three chairmen presided over the caucus and Sam Fishman and the rest of the labor leadership played prominent parts in its proceedings, the state chairman was nowhere to be seen. Morley Winograd never attended a meeting of the unity caucus. His absence was intended to create the impression that he was not connected with it, and that it was therefore an independent body organized to achieve a degree of consensus before the party officially acted.

For a long time no one but those who collaborated with Winograd in its organization quite understood what was going on. The unity caucus would meet, and when the state central committee convened in the afternoon, fliers would be circulated announcing the position of the caucus on the issues that the state central committee was about to consider. Attendance at the caucus increased as its influence became apparent; like moths to a flame, members were attracted to what appeared to be the source of real power in the party. Though the caucus never adopted any formal provision for a unit rule, those who attended increasingly followed the decisions of the group. Participation in the caucus seemed to require acquiescence in the will of the majority. Those who were actively involved in using the caucus to increase the influence of the leadership would suggest that it was only proper to support a group of which one was a member. As the power of the caucus increased with the addition of those who believed themselves bound by its decisions, it became even more difficult to dissent from its policies. As the caucus clearly dominated the state central committee, dissent became not only improper but imprudent. Though most members caught on to what the unity caucus really was within a year, it was by then a juggernaut that nearly everyone hastened to follow lest they be deprived of even association with the holders of political power.

The caucus served three main purposes, each of which was thought necessary to restore the strength of the Democratic party. The first and the easiest to achieve was to repair the division between the outstate and metropolitan areas of the state. It was a simple fact of political life that the majority of Democratic votes came from the industrial area of southeastern Michigan. As a consequence, the metropolitan area was also the source of majority power in the party. That it was a fact, however, did nothing to alleviate the distress of Democratic activists in western and northern Michigan. They could point to a fact of their own. Population was increasing in the outstate area, and more significantly, the Democratic vote was improving. In the belief that they deserved more recognition in the state party organization, they had formed the largest body of opposition to Winograd's election as state chairman. Through the unity caucus Winograd began to attach their loyalties, first by giving outstate areas more representation among the officers-at-large, and then—and this was far more important—by making certain that there was never a vote in which the state central committee divided on the basis of geography.[4]

The second purpose served by the unity caucus was eminently political and entirely consistent with what Winograd and the UAW were trying to achieve. At the February state convention Winograd's election had been accompanied by a successful labor-led effort to prevent debate on any controversial resolutions. Labor, at least, could not see much point in electing a chairman to restore unity if the party continued to divide itself by debating matters the mere mention of which was thought tantamount to Republican victory. Even while they were divided between Winograd and Mitchell, the UAW and the AFL-CIO had united and used every means of influence at their disposal to obtain adoption of a "resolution on resolutions" designed "to keep controversial proposals from coming to the convention floor for debate."[5] Seven hours had been spent in the rules committee on this single issue, and labor had lost. Even some normally reliable allies of the UAW thought this attempt to impose what its opponents called a gag rule was going too far. What labor lost in the rules committee, however, it won on the convention floor—or, more accurately, at the podium, when the convention adjourned before any resolutions could be brought up for discussion and debate. All the resolutions that had been before the convention were then referred to the state central committee. The unity caucus now served precisely the same function as the gag rule had been intended to serve at the state convention. Before any resolution came before the state central committee, it would be discussed by the caucus. If there was anything controversial about it, the caucus would simply decide that state central should not discuss it. Through the caucus, the party leadership could make certain that potentially divisive issues were handled "out of view of the press."[6]

The same power that permitted the unity caucus to prevent public discussion of divisive matters was also used to put in place the political line on which the old coalition could be restored. Those who advocated measures which, in the judgment of the group that controlled the caucus, might antagonize the white workers of the suburban ring and might therefore jeopardize the effort to recapture the political center, would not be permitted a public discussion in the state central committee. Those who opposed measures which, in the judgment of the party and labor leadership, would improve the prospects of building a Democratic majority in the electorate, would lose in the caucus and be able to offer only token resistance in the state central meeting, if they even bothered to stay and make what after the caucus decision could be no more than an empty gesture. For all practical purposes, the workings of the caucus paralleled what Tacitus described as the "classical pattern": "the view of the majority was suddenly found to be the view of everybody."[7] The party needed unity, and it required a new direction. The unity caucus gave it both. If the cost was a severe reduction of serious political debate and a growing unwillingness to give public expression to private opinion, it was a cost those who now held power did not find exorbitant.

A third purpose served by the unity caucus was connected with the second. Before the creation of the caucus labor had always held a caucus of its own before state central meetings. The labor caucus would take a position on at least the major issues coming before state central and, because of labor's power and because it aroused such intense feelings of fear and hatred in so many of its political adversaries, any vote of significance was seen as a measure of labor's strength or weakness. If the position advocated by labor carried a majority of state central delegates, it proved that labor owned the Democratic party; if labor lost, it demonstrated that the party had turned its back on the interests and the opinions of the working class. Labor, quite literally, could not win for losing. If it won a vote in state central, it was threatened with a loss of liberal and middle-class support in the party and in the electorate. If it lost a vote in state central, as for example when it was unable to prevent endorsement of a presidential primary in 1972, it could be forgiven its failure to view defeat as victory. The unity caucus provided a marvelous mask for the imposition of labor's control over the state central committee. None of the convenors was directly associated with labor, and each of them was a thoroughly reliable ally. The unity caucus was led by county and district party chairmen who would first engage in consultation with the political leadership of the UAW and then preside over a caucus containing a substantial majority of union members. Labor followed in the direction it wanted to go.

Labor controlled the unity caucus, and the unity caucus dominated the state central committee. The domination was total. From his election in February, 1973, until his resignation in October, 1980, Morley Winograd, in close and constant collaboration with Sam Fishman of the UAW, carefully determined in advance what the state central committee would decide. Nothing was left to chance. Every member and every alternate of the state central committee was methodically categorized on the basis of organizational affiliation and political attitude. A bare majority of the committee membership were associated with the UAW or the AFL-CIO. Those who were not connected with a union but were considered reliable allies were identified simply as "solid," while those who followed the precepts of the most recent version of a new politics were indelibly labeled "flakes."[8] All the meticulous preparation and all the exhaustive attention to the details of execution that the chairman devoted to the task of controlling the central committee accomplished the intended result. During the seven years of his chairmanship the central committee failed to follow the dictates of the unity caucus only twice, and both instances demonstrated not the weakness but the power of the chairman and his allies in the labor movement.

The first time the central committee ignored a decision of the unity caucus, the issue was one that clearly divided the new Democratic coalition of

McCarthy and McGovern from the old Democratic coalition. Shortly before the 1974 state convention the central committee met to approve the resolutions that would be brought before the convention. Under the organizational reforms initiated by the new chairman, nothing would be offered for the convention's consideration that had not received the prior approval of the state central committee, and though it was nowhere to be found in the party rules, the state central committee no longer approved anything without the prior permission of the unity caucus. The meeting of the central committee was held in Mount Clemens, and, because of the Macomb County location, John Bruff presided at the meeting of the caucus. One of the proposed resolutions endorsed severe penalties for the use of marijuana. It seemed to Bruff and to a majority of those in attendance that this would serve to signal a public repudiation by the party of at least one element of the famous trilogy of the 1972 campaign—acid, abortion, and amnesty—that had done so much to make life so difficult for so many Democratic candidates in, among other places, Macomb County. The caucus endorsed the resolution without hesitation. After the caucus adjourned, but before the state central committee convened, Tom Murray, chairman of the Washtenaw County committee, and Joe Finkbeiner, chairman of the Ingham County committee, approached Morley Winograd and complained about what the caucus had done. Winograd, of course, had not attended and could only ask what they were complaining about.

Murray and Finkbeiner were disturbed because a position against marijuana that might help the party in some areas would, in their judgment, hurt Democratic candidates for local office in Washtenaw and Ingham, the counties that contained the University of Michigan and Michigan State University, respectively. What might appeal to the working class might make the student vote more susceptible to the advances of left-wing third-party candidates. Winograd, who did not even smoke tobacco and who probably thought Colombian gold was a rare metal, would hardly have hesitated to sacrifice the strange desires of a small group of Ann Arbor pill heads and East Lansing freaks. He was not impressed by or even interested in an argument about the relative merits of marijuana use. He was impressed, however, and very much interested in the political reason Murray and Finkbeiner gave for their opposition to the action of the unity caucus. Winograd wanted to drive the new left out of the Democratic party, but he wanted to do it with their help, if he could. The unity caucus presented itself not as what it really was, a means by which to move the party away from where the new left had taken it, but as a device by which to make certain the party did nothing that could not be supported by everyone. This provided an effective veto over those proposals and policies that appealed only to a narrow segment of the population, but it did so in what on the surface at least could be defended as a politically neutral fashion. Murray and Finkbeiner now argued that the antimarijuana resolution violated that understanding by commiting the party to a position that would hurt Democratic candidates in their two counties. This was almost too good to be true. The chairmen of the two most liberal counties in the state were arguing for a policy of unanimity, a policy that would effectively prevent the left from ever bringing to public debate a resolution they supported and labor opposed. They were not arguing in favor of a resolution supporting decriminalization of marijuana; they only wanted the party to say nothing about the issue at all. Winograd could barely contain himself. Liberals were willing, even eager, to join in a concerted effort to keep liberals quiet. When state central convened and the antimarijuana resolution was brought up, more than a few of the members were surprised to hear Morley Winograd speak in opposition to the decision of the unity caucus. But once it became clear that the UAW was prepared to follow the new lead of the chairman, the prospect of massive emotional distress among central committee members faced with the necessity to make a decision for themselves vanished.

There was one other occasion when state central decided not to follow a decision of the unity caucus, and once again it was at the behest of the chairman. In 1975, a vacancy occurred on the Michigan delegation to the Democratic National Committee. It was regarded at the time as a position that had to be filled by a black. The central committee met at Three Rivers, on the western side of the state, and Betty Burch, chairman of the Sixteenth District and one of the most reliable friends of the UAW, presided at the morning meeting of the unity caucus. Whether out of a desire to please the union or a determination to prove she could handle difficult political problems, Burch proposed that the central committee fill the vacancy that day rather than postpone the selection of a new member of the national committee for two months, until the next meeting. Alex Ott, a UAW staff member from Flint, was the candidate of the union, but he was not the only candidate for the position. John Burton[9] of Washtenaw County also wanted to run, but he did not want to run so soon. He objected to having the election that day on the ground that adequate notice had not been given. Many of the delegates from the First and Thirteenth districts agreed with Burton and threatened to walk out if the election was not postponed. Winograd thought they had a legitimate argument. This was a position to be filled by a black Democrat, the meeting was being held 150 miles from Detroit, and there had been no prior announcement that the election would take place. He believed the election should be postponed. At the state central committee meeting in the afternoon, he called for a straw vote on whether the election should be held then or laid over to the next meeting. The voice vote was very close and the result uncertain. Winograd adroitly announced that because of that, the election should not be held until the next meeting. To a chorus of boos and jeers accompanied by loud cries suggesting that he was perhaps deficient in the fortitude necessary for the performance of his job, Winograd moved to the next item on the agenda. Two months later, when no one could object to the procedure and no one could legitimately threaten to disrupt party unity, the state central committee took the position of the UAW as its own and selected Alex Ott over John Burton by a margin of more than two-to-one.

Within months of his election as state Democratic chairman, Morley Winograd had converted a political organization that a year earlier had seemed on the verge of permanent fragmentation into a tightly controlled and efficient political structure. He had created a political body that without any formal authority provided the means by which labor could move the party to the political center without having to engage in formal and public battles with the liberal left. By the spring of 1973, with a majority of the membership of the state central committee, a unity caucus that made open dissent from the will of that majority almost a procedural impossibility, and a chairman who viewed the UAW as both the source of his own political power and the only certain source of the power necessary to revitalize the Democratic party, labor, which had been nearly driven out of the party in the summer of 1972, was firmly in command of the Michigan Democratic party. With a more efficient party organization and a more intelligent political direction, the labor-led party would doubtless recapture enough blue-collar voters to elect a governor in 1974. The next election, however, was not in 1974 but in 1973, and although it was not a race for statewide office, it would have enormous consequences for every statewide contest that followed. In the fall of 1973 the citizens of Detroit elected a mayor.

A week after Morley Winograd's election, the political reporter for the *Detroit Free Press*, Remer Tyson, wrote a lengthy analysis of labor's involvement with the Michigan Democratic party. He suggested that the impending city election would "spotlight labor's predicament in dealing with the ideals and practicality of Democratic politics." The predicament was really a conflict between a political judgment and a political fact. While "UAW leaders lean toward supporting Common Council president Mel Ravitz, a white liberal," the population of Detroit "is now almost half black." Support for Ravitz instead of a black candidate was predicated, according to Tyson, on the belief that "Secretary of State Richard H. Austin, a popular black politician who lost the mayoral race by only 6,000 votes four years ago, is the only prospective black candidate who can win." The UAW, which had vigorously campaigned for Austin in 1969, preferred Ravitz to Austin in 1973 because Austin would have to give up "his office of secretary of state, allowing Gov. Milliken to replace Austin with a Republican in advance of the 1974 governor's race." The UAW, in Tyson's explanation, believed Austin was the only black who could win and that an Austin victory was the only way the Republicans could capture the secretary of state's office, which, as Tyson pointed out, "provides more patronage to political parties than any other state office."[10] The prediction that the 1973 Detroit mayoral election would present the UAW with a predicament proved correct, but for reasons neither Tyson nor the UAW had ever imagined.

When Richard Austin decided not to try again for the honor of becoming the first black mayor of Detroit, the party and labor leaders who were mainly concerned with the retention of the patronage supplied by the secretary of state's office were not the only ones relieved. Austin had not been the first choice of every black leader in 1969, and four years later there were still considerable reservations about whether the first black mayor should be some-one whose political success owed so much to acceptance by the white estab-lishment. The moderation that led at least some labor leaders to believe Austin was the only black who had any real prospect of winning the city election in 1973 led at least some black leaders to wonder whether it would be a victory worth winning. There was something else. For all his political moderation and personal decency, and for all the support he had received from prominent whites and powerful organizations, Austin had only been able to attract 18 percent of the white vote in 1969. To say the least, it seemed doubtful that the white population of Detroit was now, four years later, awaiting with enthusi-asm the opportunity to demonstrate its racial toleration by embracing the candidacy of a black moderate.

Despite the good intentions and the energetic efforts of the white liberal and labor leadership, the white electorate had rejected Richard Austin by a margin of more than four-to-one. Nevertheless, Austin had nearly won, and in the judgment of a number of observers, had lost only because rain in the late afternoon reduced turnout in predominantly black precincts. An increase in the black turnout would have made Richard Austin and not Roman Gribbs mayor of Detroit. What had been true in 1969 would have even greater significance in 1973. The black proportion of the city population had in-creased during the intervening four years. No one, however, could really be certain precisely what the proportion now was. According to the 1970 census, blacks constituted 43.7 percent of the population. But everyone believed that whites were still leaving the city, and that as a consequence blacks were becoming a progressively larger percentage of a steadily diminishing popula-tion. There were really two questions. What was the black percentage of the population, and what would be the likely black percentage of the vote? The second question was hardly ever asked so long as the answer to the first continued to be that blacks were a minority in the city. Labor, the Democratic party leadership, and, as evidenced by Remer Tyson's observations, the press, believed the 1973 election would be decided by an electorate that contained a majority, if a diminishing one, of white voters. Robert Millender disagreed.

Though leadership of the black community was fragmented among different politicians, a variety of religious leaders, and a number of union officials, Robert Millender seemed to command the respect of everyone. He was one of those unusual people who devote themselves to a cause without any apparent personal ambition. He worked assiduously to improve the condition of blacks and he believed firmly in the principle of political self-reliance: the economic improvement of black people depended on the exercise of black political power. Almost alone, Millender believed not only that a black candidate could be elected mayor of Detroit in 1973, but that that result could be achieved with black votes alone. It is not too much to say that he believed it could only be done with black votes. Millender's theory was very simple. Unlike nearly everyone else, Millender believed Detroit had already become what nearly everyone else expected it to be in the future, a black city. If there was already a black majority in Detroit, the election of a black mayor depended entirely on making certain that a black majority in the population was also a black majority at the polls. The election of a black mayor depended on black turnout, and that, in the shrewd estimation of Robert Millender, would in turn depend on both the creation of an effective political organization and the presence of a black candidate who could mobilize the black community. Millender created much of the political organization himself; Detroit seemed to have created Coleman Young.

Like many of Detroit's black citizens, Coleman Young was born in the deep South. In 1923, when he was five years old, his family left Tuscaloosa, Alabama for Detroit, where his grandfather had come two years earlier in pursuit of the five-dollar day promised by Henry Ford. Coleman Young was raised in the Detroit ghetto where he witnessed both the prosperity that came even to Black Bottom during the 1920s and the Great Depression of the 1930s that devastated the city and destroyed any possibility of black economic improvement. Most of all he was a witness to discrimination, discrimination that was open, notorious, violent, and practiced without the slightest sense of remorse or the least bit of hesitation. The police, who were supposedly pledged to enforce the law, enforced instead their own version of white supremacy: any black could be beaten with impunity. In 1937, Young went to work at the Ford Rouge plant, where he was fired more than a dozen times for union organizing. Attracted by their teaching of racial equality, he joined the left-wing faction of the UAW that was dominated by the communists and vigorously opposed by the socialist faction led by Walter Reuther. When Reuther took control of the union the communists were driven out, and Coleman Young, who with the help of the president of the Detroit local,

Douglas Fraser, had become the first black on the Wayne County CIO council executive board, was removed from office. In a country in which segregation was still legal and discrimination a way of life, many whites considered blacks only marginally more acceptable than communists. As a black who was widely considered a communist, Coleman Young spent the better part of the next decade reduced to a daily struggle for survival. With the passage of time, however, memories faded, hatreds subsided, and Young had another chance. He took it. Elected as a delegate to the state constitutional convention in 1962, he established a reputation and a political base. Two years later he was elected to the state senate, and after reelection in 1966 became the senate Democratic leader.[11]

Coleman Young could have stayed in the state senate the rest of his life; the state constitution seemed to give him no other choice. It expressly prohibited anyone who held public office from accepting any other public position in the state during the term for which he was elected. Young or any other member of the state senate could run for Congress, but none of them could run for mayor of Detroit. Along with almost every other Democratic delegate, Young had fought against nearly every major provision eventually adopted by the Republican majority at the 1962 constitutional convention, and he was not about to lose twice. Although the prohibition seemed reasonably clear, clarity was very much a relative matter when it came to interpreting a document that seemed almost designed as a model of imprecision. The Michigan Supreme Court, in a decision that squarely contradicted its own recent ruling on the same question, cited former United States Supreme Court Justice Robert Jackson on the virtues and even the courage of inconsistency, and opened the path for Coleman Young to run for mayor.[12] Not everyone thought it was a path worth following.

When the supreme court rendered its decision and Coleman Young became a candidate for mayor, there were already two white candidates in the race, and the political attitudes of one of them had an enormous effect on the political calculations of the UAW. In 1969, the white candidate for mayor, Roman Gribbs, had been able to exploit the law-and-order issue without having even to mention it, by virtue of his position as the Wayne County sheriff. In 1973, John Nichols talked about almost nothing else, though his position as the city's police commissioner might have made his attachment to vigorous law enforcement sufficiently apparent. Nichols may not have been a racist, but the police department under his direction had established a pattern of harassment and intimidation that caused Young to remark, ''If there's one goddam thing I'm going to do when I get elected mayor, it's straighten out the police department.''[13] The police commissioner was viewed by blacks as racist and by labor as reactionary. If John Nichols became mayor, race relations would be dealt a potentially crippling blow, and labor would have little chance to exercise any discernible influence over city policy. Nichols's candidacy was opposed by blacks, liberals, and labor. This common opposition, however, instead of energizing the old Democratic coalition, led to a division between white and black within the UAW that was never fully repaired.

From the union's perspective, Nichols was a very serious threat. Richard Austin, with a name already well known to voters as a moderate mayoral candidate in 1969 and as the recently elected Michigan secretary of state, might have been able to defeat Nichols. Coleman Young, with his radical past and flamboyant manner, could not. Few whites had been willing to vote for the urbane, unassuming Richard Austin; far fewer would be willing to entrust the city to a man who could have played Rhett Butler in an all-black production of *Gone with the Wind*. Coleman Young could not get white votes, and in an election decided entirely on racial lines, John Nichols, a white reactionary, would unquestionably win. The fact that the proportion of black citizens was larger than four years earlier was given little significance. Blacks were still not a majority and every precinct captain with an eighth-grade education knew that the one law of politics that did not have an exception was that the percentage of eligible voters who both registered and voted was always and everywhere much lower among blacks than among whites. Coleman Young could not be elected by black votes alone, and he could not get enough white votes to make up the difference.

If the police commissioner met a white liberal instead of Young in the general election, his defeat was certain. Nichols would still face the almost total opposition of the black community, but he would be unable to exploit the racial fears of white voters. Mel Ravitz seemed to have everything that was required. He had impeccable liberal credentials and had attracted more votes than any of the other eight successful Common Council candidates in the last election. Ravitz would carry the black vote; he might even give Nichols a run for the white vote. For the leadership of the UAW, a white liberal was infinitely preferable to a white reactionary. There were those within the UAW who opposed the candidacy of Coleman Young not only because they believed he could not win the general election against Nichols, but because of his former involvement with the communist faction in the union. The socialists who had followed Reuther never found it possible to forgive or forget anyone who had ever been, as their political lexicon had it, a "Stalinist" or a "CPer." Even for them, however, Nichols, not Young, was the danger to be dealt with. To prevent the election of a mayor who would divide the city on racial grounds, the UAW endorsed Mel Ravitz and found itself dangerously divided between black and white.

Convinced that Coleman Young could not win and certain that Mel Ravitz could, the UAW made an endorsement that was immediately opposed by every major black leader in the union. Horace Sheffield, Nelson "Jack"

Edwards, Marcellius Ivory, Marc Stepp, and Buddy Battle, the five highest-ranking blacks in the UAW, ignored the endorsement and campaigned actively for Young. The union had put every black leader in an unbearable position. White officials of the UAW had only one loyalty. The union was the source of their influence and the basis of their prestige; the notion of a competing allegiance was unthinkable; the idea that race could be the object of such an allegiance unimaginable. For the black leadership of the UAW, however, race was a fact, and allegiance to it a moral imperative. Whites, who constituted an overwhelming majority, had no need to consider the effect of their action on the future of other whites or on the perception other whites as whites might have of them. Blacks had no choice. To a minority that had experienced every conceivable form of oppression and degradation, a black man's failure to help a black man who challenged a white bore all the marks of betrayal. The black leadership of the UAW might not believe Coleman Young would win, but it could scarcely retain the respect of the black community if it followed the direction of the white leaders of the union and worked for the election of Mel Ravitz or any other white candidate. If they turned their back on Young, and he failed by a small margin, no one would ever believe that it was not all their fault.

Though no black union leader protested when Walter Reuther, who did not live in Detroit, decided, without even bothering with a formal vote of the executive board, that the UAW would endorse Richard Austin in 1969, there was much objection when the executive board, a majority of whose members lived outside the city, endorsed Mel Ravitz in the 1973 mayoral primary. Buddy Battle claimed people outside Detroit had no business deciding what the union should do inside the city.[14] Though Battle never used this argument as the ground on which to exclude himself from decisions about political endorsements in other cities in his own region, he vigorously argued that the endorsement of Ravitz was procedurally flawed, and for that reason, not one that those, like himself, who lived in Detroit needed to follow. Though no one in the union took this line of argument for anything more than what it really was, a rationalization for a decision made on entirely different grounds, Battle and the rest of the black leadership devoted all their efforts to Coleman Young and denied they were the least bit guilty of disloyalty to the union.

The struggle that was waged within the union between the white leadership that supported Ravitz and the black leadership that assisted Young opened old wounds and left new scars. Not only was race pitted against race, but the political lines of an earlier day were remembered and redrawn. Coleman Young was once more the Stalinist, and his opponents were once again the Trotskyite socialists who had helped Walter Reuther eradicate the influence of the communists, which for them was identical with the influence of the Soviet Union, from the American labor movement. Black against white,

Stalinist against Trotskyite—all this was troubling enough. But another division that developed would not disappear with the end of an election. Ravitz was a Jew, and Coleman Young was a black. The union leaders who were for Young were all black; the union leaders who were for Ravitz were all white, and in the mind of many blacks, were led by Jews. Ken Morris, regional director of Region 1-B, and Sam Fishman, director of the Michigan CAP, were both Jews, and though Fishman was not a voting member of the executive board, both had played, in the opinion of the black leadership at least, a major part in the decision to endorse Ravitz instead of Young. Blacks and Jews, with a common history of tragedy and oppression, looked at each other and saw not allies but danger.

The primary campaign of Coleman Young was based on a powerful organization created by Robert Millender. It was composed of four elements, the three most important of which were entirely black. There would no doubt be white liberals who would vote for Young or any other black candidate simply because it was the liberal thing to do. The number was difficult to predict, and the group was hard to organize outside the established liberal associations. White members of the National Association for the Advancement of Colored People (NAACP) or the American Civil Liberties Union (ACLU) or the Americans for Democratic Action (ADA) might be expected to contribute time or money to Coleman Young, but the election of Detroit's first black mayor would have to be the result of an unprecedented political organization in the black community. The black Democratic establishment made up of elected public officials and officials from the First and Thirteenth Congressional District committees formed one part of that organization. Another part was supplied by black leaders in the trade union movement. The third, and in some ways the most effective because the most far-reaching, was composed of the black churches. Hundreds of black Baptist churches, some with as few as several dozen members, formed the framework of the black community's social structure. While middle-class suburban whites had countless organizations to join and nearly limitless opportunities to associate with others, a history of discrimination and deprivation had permitted blacks few alternatives to church as a place not only of worship but of collective effort. The church was a community, and the minister was its representative. The neighborhood church—and in Detroit a block or two could be a neighborhood—was the single existing unit of organization. Working through an umbrella organization, the Council of Black Baptist Ministers, Millender used the churches as the centers of a grass roots effort to register black voters, especially the newly enfranchised young voter who was from eighteen to twenty-one years old. On election day he used the churches to get them to the polls.[15] The Reverend Albert Cleage, who used the white man's own definition of the black ancestry requisite to be called black to demonstrate that

Christ could not possibly have been white,[16] added the formidable assistance of Detroit's most energetically political church, the Shrine of the Black Madonna.

The primary was no contest. Ravitz finished third, and Coleman Young, who had finished second, prepared to face John Nichols in the November election. As one party activist put it, Young "had beaten the shit out of the UAW in the primary. He never forgot that he had won the primary without them and they never forgot it either." In the general election, Young had the support of the union, and he had it on his own terms. He did not have to make any promise or meet any test; the UAW was not going to endorse Nichols or give even the appearance of neutrality in a contest between a black Democrat and a white reactionary commissioner of police. Some party leaders who looked to the establishment of a broad labor base for a reconstructed Democratic party were concerned. They seemed to "fear that the ability to build a labor-based coalition would be diminished by the emergence of a black mayor who was Stalinist, racist, who would take positions antithetical to the broad constituency. Coleman would have greater allegiance to the black community than to the labor movement." No one, however, who held a leadership position in the state Democratic party had any desire to see Nichols win or any interest in a public statement of regret about the choice available. With labor and the Democratic party firmly or at least formally behind him, Coleman Young went after John Nichols and the police.

Though he described himself as a politician and claimed that "the next mayor must understand political processes to be effective,"[17] Young seemed to have no interest in normal political practices. Instead of appealing to the broadest possible constituency by avoiding anything conceivably controversial, he appeared deliberately to divide Detroit on the basis of race. On the Sunday evening before the election both candidates appeared on the "Lou Gordon Show," where Young claimed that relations between the police and the black community had deteriorated because some black prisoners had been mistreated by white police. He vowed that under his administration the police would be compelled to treat "all people, black and white equally."[18] Gordon, who had made his reputation by asking questions without consideration for either the comfort of the guest or any reasonable standard of good taste, demanded that the black candidate for mayor explain his association with Haywood Brown and the Black Panther party. Young's response was scarcely a repudiation of the Black Panthers: "Young said he sometimes associates with the Black Panthers because he feels they are shifting away from their militant ways to what he considers more constructive programs. He cited Bobby Seale's running for mayor in California as an indication of that shift away from militancy."[19]

On the same Sunday that Young attacked the behavior of the Detroit police and applauded the activities of Bobby Seale and the Black Panthers, the *Detroit News* published its last poll before the election. Young was ahead among "likely" voters by 5 percent, and among "all" voters by 12 percent. Among those most likely to vote, 48 percent were for Young, 43 percent for Nichols, and 9 percent still undecided.[20] Young was ahead, the race was close, and the undecided seemed to hold the outcome in their hands. Despite his rhetoric, which was considerably more militant than anything Richard Austin had uttered four years earlier, and despite his campaign, which was designed to appeal almost exclusively to a black majority that might not really exist, the *News* poll gave Young the same 18 percent of the white vote Austin had received in 1969. Whether there was a black majority or not, the percentage of black voters had unquestionably increased over those four years. If Young held the same white vote as Austin, there could be little doubt what the outcome would be. That the Jewish vote split 67 percent for Nichols and 33 percent undecided was probably a result of a statistically insufficient sample and not a harbinger of any racially motivated opposition.[21]

On November 6, Coleman Young became the first black mayor of Detroit by a margin of victory very close to what had been Richard Austin's margin of defeat. Young received 231,786 votes to John Nichols's 217,479.[22] Unlike Austin, however, Young received not 18 percent but only 9 percent of the white vote. Young took 92 percent of the black vote, while Nichols obtained 91 percent of the white vote. Robert Pisor, political writer for the *Detroit News,* accurately analyzed the outcome:

> In every previous Detroit election, such a voting pattern would have resulted in a comfortable victory for the white candidate, simply because as late as 1969 whites held a 60-40 voting edge. Yesterday, however, the same pattern produced Detroit's first black mayor and put four blacks on the nine-member City Council.[23]

Black voters outnumbered white voters "by about 228,800 to 220,000." Four years earlier, "white voters outnumbered black voters in the mayoral race by 308,700 to 209,800."[24]

The UAW had supported Ravitz in the primary in the belief that in a general election against Coleman Young a white reactionary would be elected mayor by a white constituency. Robert Millender had really argued that implicitly the UAW was right; white voters would elect a white reactionary instead of a black to public office. Millender, however, believed the UAW was wrong about the continued existence of a white majority in the electorate, and he had been right. Detroit had a black majority, and Millender had been able to mobilize and organize it on behalf of a black candidate for mayor. White voters had not elected Richard Austin in 1969, and they did not elect

Coleman Young in 1973. Detroit had become the first city in America, and Michigan the first state, to elect two black congressmen, but that had happened only after the creation of two predominantly black congressional districts. Detroit had now become the largest city in the nation to elect a black mayor, but that had happened only after Detroit itself had become black. With a black constituency, black politicians had little need of white voters.

What Millender and the white leadership of the UAW agreed on was at least as important for the future of Michigan politics and the Michigan Democratic party as what they had disagreed on. The union's fear of what white voters were likely to do in a contest between a white and a black candidate was clearly connected with its analysis of what had happened a year earlier. Nineteen seventy-two had not only been an electoral disaster; for many of those directly involved it had been personally traumatic. A coalition carefully conceived and maintained for the better part of two generations had been blown apart. In massive numbers white blue-collar workers had rejected what for many of them was the party of their birth in response to their fear that busing might bring blacks to their suburban neighborhoods, or far worse, compel their children to attend black schools in the ghetto. White candidates of both parties deserted principle and sometimes abandoned decency to disassociate themselves from what white voters believed was compulsory integration. White candidates did not need to be told that their election depended on white voters.

When Morley Winograd was elected state party chairman three months after the worst Democratic defeat in this century, labor gave him its support in the knowledge that he would help them help the party recapture the blue-collar suburban ring. Tom Gray had taken an extreme position in advocating positions deliberately antagonistic to blacks, but everyone understood that the party could not afford to be identified, as John Bruff had put it, "only with the young, the poor and the black." What white politicians understood, black politicians were more than willing to use. If white candidates had to appeal to the fears and even the hatred of a white majority in the suburbs of Detroit, black politicians could certainly use the same tactics to attract the energetic support of a black majority in the city. If it was acceptable and even necessary for Frank Kelley, the attorney general of the State of Michigan, to issue a press release announcing that he was immediately leaving the Democratic national convention in the summer of 1972 to take personal charge of the appeal of Judge Roth's busing order,[25] Coleman Young could scarcely be criticized when he made a comparable promise as Detroit's newly elected mayor: "I plan to push the pushers off the streets and I mean the ones in blue uniforms and shiny buttons as well as the ones in the Superfly outfits."[26]

Although the election of Coleman Young would seem to have increased the prospects of racial division within the Democratic party, there were instead, at least for a time, increased possibilities for moderation. Young had been elected mayor of Detroit; his appeal to a black constituency within the city limits of Detroit had nothing directly to do with the white residents of the surrounding suburbs. Moreover, his demonstrated ability to turn out a large black vote would make even the most calculating Democratic strategist pause before suggesting anything that would deliberately sacrifice substantial portions of it. Not only the hope of a larger black vote but the fear of political embarrassment improved the prospects for accommodation. Before the election of Coleman Young there was no single spokesman for the black community. Before the election of Coleman Young there had not been the same need to worry about black political reaction that there was now that an authoritative and powerful black spokesman had come into existence. Young might be able to deliver a larger black vote than Democratic candidates for governor and other statewide offices had ever seen. He was clearly able to make a great deal of trouble, and all of it in public, if the Democratic party ignored the interests of his new constituency. With a little luck and a great deal of planning, the election of a black mayor in 1973 might actually help to elect a Democratic governor in 1974.

Notes

1. Morley Winograd, interview with author, August 22, 1982.

2. Bernard M. Ryan, interview with author, July 7, 1982.

3. Bruce Miller, interview with author, August 29, 1982.

4. Morley Winograd, interview with author, August 22, 1982.

5. *Detroit News,* February 5, 1973.

6. Bernard M. Ryan, interview with author, July 7, 1982; Morley Winograd, interview with author, August 22, 1982.

7. Tacitus *Histories* 1.56.

8. Each of the congressional district delegations was divided between members and alternates. Each member and alternate was then placed in the appropriate category. The lists were mimeographed and distributed to those who needed the information to canvass the districts they were assigned to watch over.

9. Burton was also a UAW staff member, but his loyalties were more to the black caucus than to the union's citizenship department.

10. *Detroit Free Press,* February 12, 1973.

11. Kirk Cheyfitz, "The Survivor," *Monthly Detroit,* February, 1981.

12. *Young v. Detroit City Clerk,* 389 Mich. 333 (1973).

13. Quoted in Cheyfitz, "The Survivor."

14. Battle's argument was supplied by Kirk Cheyfitz from notes he had taken as part of his biographical work on Coleman Young. Kirk Cheyfitz, interview with author, October 7, 1982.

15. Bernard M. Ryan, interview with author, July 7, 1982.

16. See Herbert Storing, ed., *What Country Have I?: Political Writings by Black Americans* (New York: St. Martin's Press, 1970).

17. *Detroit News,* October 28, 1973.

18. *Detroit News,* November 5, 1972.

19. Ibid.

20. *Detroit News,* November 4, 1973.

21. Ibid.

22. *Detroit News,* November 7, 1973.

23. Robert L. Pisor, "Strength of Black Vote Gave Young His Historic Victory," *Detroit News,* November 7, 1973.

24. Ibid.

25. Office of Attorney General Frank Kelley, press release, 9.00 P.M., July 10, 1972. The full text of the release read:

Attorney General Frank J. Kelley will interrupt his stay at the Democratic National Convention in Florida to fly home to Michigan tonight to take personal charge of the state's legal actions in regard to today's decision by Judge Roth. . . . Kelley will arrive in Detroit in the early morning hours and proceed to Lansing where he will meet early tomorrow morning with members of his staff. An announcement of the state's actions is expected later in the morning.

26. *Detroit News,* November 7, 1973.

PART 2

The Union, the Party, and the Electorate

CHAPTER 4

1974 and the
Politics of Integrity

In 1972 the Democratic party adopted rules designed to replace the old coalition of the New Deal with a new coalition of the new politics. The New Deal had appealed to the economically disadvantaged with the promise of a redistribution of wealth that would guarantee that no one would be without what was minimally necessary to provide the daily essentials of life. The new politics promised to provide almost unlimited opportunity for the expression of even the most idiosyncratic individuality. The New Deal had confronted the Great Depression and the fact of economic scarcity, and if more through expediency and experimentation than through conscious and deliberate prearrangement, gave government the responsibility for the management of the national economy.[1] The new politics, having witnessed between 1960 and 1972 the longest single peacetime period of sustained economic growth in American history, decided that the economic problem had been solved, and that politics need no longer be confined to the details of distribution. Just as Marx had foreseen the day in which material abundance would make it possible for each individual to become all the things of which the entire human species was capable,[2] the theorists of the new left believed that industrial capitalism had progressed to the point where no additional effort was required to supply adequately the economic needs of the population. Politics could now be directed to the removal of the last remaining limitations on human development. While government managed the economy, and the economy continued its regular provision of goods and services, government would now also protect the right of each citizen to pursue freely what some designated personal morality and others dismissed as private pleasure. In what came to be called post-industrial society, a stage that Martin Heidigger thought had been reached in the America of the 1930s and that he thought meant not only the end of history, as Marx believed, but the end of humanity,[3] the free enjoyment of each would be the free enjoyment of all. Public morality would be the sum total of the multitude of different private values. Abortion would be available on demand, because no one could judge what any individual woman should do with her body, and amnesty would be conferred on whoever chose not to carry arms, because no one could judge what any man should do with his. Acid or any other mind-altering drug would not be denied to consenting adults, because reality was a matter of subjective preference.

It was not only the left that acted on the assumption that economic scarcity was a problem already permanently solved. Though it was primarily responding to the left, the right reacted as if politics was mainly a struggle between definitions of morality. What the left proclaimed as the historically inevitable enhancement of the individual, the right attacked as an outrageous attempt to undermine the time-honored values of family and country. Abortion was a repudiation of life and a reflection of an increasing inability to place sex in the service of love. Amnesty was a rejection of the basic principle, without which no nation could possibly survive, that a citizen unwilling to die for his country had no country to die for. Acid, and all the other degrading chemical substances with which an entire generation seemed intent on escaping a reality it had neither made nor taken the trouble to understand, could secure approval only from those for whom private fantasy was more important than personal responsibility and public duty. The left looked at the right and saw a huge amorphous mass of stupidity, intolerance, and blatant prejudice. The right looked at the left and saw an effeminate, self-proclaimed elite who accompanied their demands for a radical egalitarianism with pretentions of moral superiority that only made more glaring their moral bankruptcy.[4]

Those in the labor movement and elsewhere who blamed the electoral disaster of 1972 on the new left and its temporary domination of the Democratic party were as little interested in the comparative moral claims of right and left as they were in any extended analysis of the relationship between morality and politics. It seemed almost self-evident that the basic issues of politics, as well as the basis of a successful Democratic coalition, must be economic. On one level, this was nothing more than the common sense judgment that prudence demands concentration on what unites the divergent elements of any political coalition. At another level, it was a reflection of the Marxist, and therewith socialist, doctrine that economics is primary, and both politics and morality derivative. At any level, no one wanted to fight the next campaign on what were called social, but what were really moral, questions. But when, however, the defeat of 1972 was followed by a victory of nearly equal proportions two years later, no one doubted that it was precisely because of a moral issue. Yet few believed, then or later, that it was failure to understand that moral issue adequately that led to a mistaken reliance on an economic proposal and the loss of the greatest prize labor and the Democratic party had sought to win.

Perhaps because a good many people assume that politics is theft and most politicians thieves, there was, despite Lawrence O'Brien's claims of outrage and George McGovern's charges of criminal conduct, no discernible hesitation among the American electorate to vote for Richard Nixon after a break-in occurred at the Watergate offices of the Democratic National Committee. If politicians are expected to act badly, however, presidents and other high public officials are not. A politician running for public office is permitted to behave according to the rules ascribed by Hobbes to the state of nature; a politician elected to office is required to conduct himself in compliance with standards befitting the ministry. No one much cared that the offices of one political party were burglarized or that the other party was widely suspected of complicity in the act. So long as the politicians limited their depredations to each other, the public might follow the story as a minor amusement but would never consider it noteworthy, much less notorious. But once public officials became involved in an attempt to conceal what had really taken place, the line between politics and government had been crossed, and the tolerance shown the inconsequential mischief of party hacks was replaced with a rigid morality that refused to excuse any infraction of law or ethics. What the Nixon campaign did in 1972 would not have surprised any of the millions of voters who believe in the inherent corruption of politics. What the Nixon campaign did was one thing; what Richard Nixon did as president was something else again.

Almost exactly one year after Richard Nixon was elected to a second term as president of the United States through the electoral annihilation of George McGovern and the Democratic party, Michigan Senator Philip A. Hart asked Nixon to "resign with grace." Hart was the fourth member of the United States Senate to call for the president's resignation. In Hart's judgment Nixon no longer had credibility and could no longer govern. If Nixon chose not to resign, Hart would not rule out the possibility of impeachment: "If reasonable grounds were found and the only alternatives were to impeach or sweep under the rug, I would hope it wouldn't be swept under the rug." There appeared to be reasonable grounds for impeachment: "I've read where the President used police powers for activities not authorized by law. I've read where he decided that a tap be placed on his brother's telephone. I don't know whether this is solid evidence but both would appear to be federal crimes." Impeachment would of course be an ordeal, and it was not something Hart looked forward to with enthusiasm: "If the President should resign with grace it might be the very best way to get us out of this situation."[5] While Hart thought Nixon should resign and might be impeached if he did not, Michigan's other senator, Republican Robert Griffin, continued to insist that Nixon could still recover and serve out his term.[6] Nixon thought so too, and as a measure of insurance, appointed Gerald Ford vice-president when Spiro Agnew was forced to resign. Surely no one would want Nixon out now.

Gerald Ford in the presidency was a prospect too ludicrous for comment. Nixon was safe.

Grand Rapids is the second largest city in Michigan and, in good times, one of the most prosperous communities in the upper Midwest. For years it was known for its furniture, which was solidly and uniformly middle class, and its politics, which, personified by its congressman of a quarter century, House minority leader Gerald Ford, were solidly Republican. Grand Rapids was also, to the general view, uncommonly religious. Many of its citizens were Dutch, and many of the Dutch were Calvinists for whom religion, like life altogether, was a series of unending obligations and unyielding struggles against temptation. In Grand Rapids life was routine, religious, regular, rigid, and dull. Or so at least it appeared to those whose knowledge of the city was based primarily on their observation of the House minority leader, who gave every evidence of being routine, religious, regular, rigid, and dull. Any town that had elected Gerald Ford for twelve successive terms, often by enormous margins, clearly lacked the imagination to do anything except continue to elect Republican congressmen. The special election called to fill the unexpired term of former Congressman and now Vice-President Gerald Ford would be interesting only to those who were curious about which Republican would next hold the seat. The Republican party thought so, and state senate majority leader Robert VanderLaan thought so. Owen Bieber, of UAW Region 1-D, and John Annulis, director of the Kent County UAW-CAP, were not so sure. Neither was Richard VanderVeen.

The constituency that kept Gerald Ford in Congress for a quarter of a century had contained a Republican majority, but it was a majority that had steadily diminished from nearly three-fourths at the beginning of his congressional career, to barely half at its end. In twenty-five years Grand Rapids had changed, even if Gerald Ford had not. As the city grew larger, its population became more diverse and substantially more Democratic. It was not population changes alone, however, that caused the erosion of Republican strength. Beginning with his election in 1950 as chairman of the Kent County CIO-PAC (Political Action Committee), John Annulis of the UAW worked full time to build a competitive Democratic party in the county. In the first few years of his chairmanship, Annulis developed the first voter identification program in Michigan. Labor now knew not only that 75 percent of the UAW members and 63 percent of all union members in Kent County were Democrats, but who they were and where they lived. Through the regular review of voter registration and identification lists the union developed and maintained in the county one of the best political intelligence systems anywhere in the state.[7] This system, along with a vigorous political education campaign within the union, added to the natural results of an expanding and progressively more diverse population to bring about an increase in the Democratic vote from 29.4 percent in 1946 to 46.2 percent in 1964.[8] From a Republican stronghold where "only or mainly union leadership or personnel would openly admit to being Democrat," Kent County had become by 1968 the source of one of the largest Democratic votes in the state.[9] In the 1970 gubernatorial campaign, Levin received 51,800 Kent County votes, the fifth largest county total he collected.[10] That same year the base Democratic vote in Kent County was approximately 45 percent.[11] Phil Hart did far better than Sander Levin and exceeded the base party vote by a comfortable margin. Hart, running against Lenore Romney, carried 60.5 percent of the Fifth District vote.[12] The Fifth District was not Democratic, nor was it even what is normally considered marginal. It was still Republican, but not nearly so Republican as those who had grown used to the presence of Gerald Ford as the Republican candidate believed.[13] Labor, especially John Annulis and Owen Bieber, considered the special election to replace Ford worth the bother of a full-fledged fight.

By normal calculations the Democratic candidate in a contest to replace Gerald Ford should have been a moderate or even a conservative who could convince the voters of Grand Rapids that a change of parties did not in any important respect mean a change of policy. Richard VanderVeen, however, became the Democratic nominee without even bothering to deny he was a liberal Democrat who had no intention of following in the footsteps of his now famous predecessor. VanderVeen was not only a liberal Democrat, he was also a man who had already run for three different offices and been defeated in each attempt. In 1960 he had been asked to run for lieutenant governor by a number of prominent state Democrats on the theory that the party slate in November would be strengthened by the presence of a Democratic candidate from the western region of the state. VanderVeen ran, but was defeated in the primary election by T. John Lesinski, who cared nothing at all for someone else's view of the requirements of a balanced ticket. VanderVeen had to watch silently as Lesinski won election and became lieutenant governor. Phil Hart had gone to the United States Senate from that position, and John Swainson had become governor; Lesinski would leave it to become the chief judge of the newly created state court of appeals in 1963. VanderVeen could look forward to nothing of the sort. With statewide office apparently beyond his grasp, he tried his hand at more local politics. He ran once for Congress against Gerald Ford in 1958, and like everyone else who tried it, was beaten decisively. He ran for mayor of East Grand Rapids, but even there he was rejected. There seemed to be nothing in the future for Richard VanderVeen but the continued practice of law. Political defeat, however, had not extinguished political ambition, and beneath what even the *Grand Rapids Press* described as a "soft-spoken and unassuming" demeanor,[14] VanderVeen was much more ambitious than anyone really knew.

The special election was characterized by brevity and notoriety. Unlike a normal congressional campaign, which can sometimes last a year or longer in the case of a particularly eager and intent challenger, the race in Grand Rapids to replace Gerald Ford lasted barely six weeks. Because it was a special election, it was the only congressional contest taking place not only in the state but in the nation. Because it was an election to fill the vacancy created by Nixon's appointment of Ford to the vice-presidency, it attracted even greater attention. For political activists, there was no place else to go; for the political reporters of both the print and the electronic media, there was nothing else to cover. For members of the Democratic party, it was an opportunity to do something to demonstrate declining support for the president. VanderVeen might not be able to win, but any reduction of the normal Republican margin of victory could be used to claim a Nixon defeat.

As a result, money was no longer the scarce commodity it had been for Democratic congressional candidates in the Fifth District. VanderVeen actually outspent his Republican opponent more than three-to-one. "For the first time on record, Democrats spent more money than Republicans for a congressional race in this district—reportedly about $70,000 to the Republican's $20,000."[15] Of that $70,000, $18,000 was donated by labor.[16] VanderVeen used a considerable portion of the money to purchase the services of a Boston political consulting firm no one at the time had really heard of. Martilla and Associates came into Grand Rapids and took over the VanderVeen campaign. The campaign director appointed by Martilla, Tom Vallely, quickly discovered that the UAW was the campaign's organizational key and that to get along with the UAW it was necessary to get along with both John Annulis and his deputy, Scotty McPhail. Annulis, however, was not the easiest person to get along with. Two years earlier, he had developed a hatred for the McGovern campaign workers who came into Grand Rapids even before he met them. It was enough that "they drove up here in their Volkswagens." Annulis got along with Vallely, however, and not only because he drove a car made by UAW members. Annulis wanted desperately to elect a Democratic congressman, and Vallely had no intention of telling Annulis or anyone else in the UAW how to operate its voter identification or its get-out-the-vote program.

The UAW provided most of the political organization, but VanderVeen and the Martilla professionals produced what was probably decisive for the outcome. Grand Rapids, understandably, was enormously proud of Gerald Ford. It did not, however, feel especially indebted to Richard Nixon. Even though the city had changed a great deal in the twenty-five years Ford served in Congress, it was still a place in which the basic virtues were held in high regard. Nixon may have appointed Gerald Ford to the vice-presidency, but that could scarcely efface or even mitigate the president's responsibility for

Watergate. Moreover, as VanderVeen shrewdly understood, Nixon's appointment of Ford meant that only Nixon stood between a son of Grand Rapids and the presidency itself. VanderVeen fashioned an appeal that was a remarkable combination of high principle and crass self-interest. The Democratic candidate for Congress declared that the election was "a referendum on the moral bankruptcy of Richard Nixon,"[17] and then, in a move that surprised nearly everyone and completely confounded the Republican candidate, announced that in his judgment "The President of the United States should be Gerald Ford."[18]

The same simple message was run in newspaper ads and repeated by the candidate whenever and wherever possible. Impeachment of Richard Nixon, though clearly suggested, was never expressly demanded. Through this single expedient, VanderVeen became the best friend of Gerald Ford, while his Republican opponent, Robert VanderLaan, who could not quite bring himself to abandon a Republican president, could only reply that Ford was a great man and Nixon a good president. The special election was turned into a public referendum on whether Nixon should stay in office or whether the sins of Watergate should be expiated by a Ford presidency. On February 18, the voters of the Fifth District of Michigan surprised the nation and stunned the White House by electing Richard VanderVeen to what nearly everyone had assumed was one of the most Republican seats in Congress. It was not even very close. VanderVeen collected 53,008 votes, or 50.9 percent of the total, while VanderLaan received 46,159 votes, or only 44.3 percent.[19] Nearly all of the remaining votes went to a candidate of the conservative American Independent party. Not only did VanderVeen carry Grand Rapids, he "missed carrying the suburban and rural areas, which Ford won two to one in 1972, by only about 300 votes."[20]

VanderVeen's election was viewed as an event with national significance. House Speaker Carl Albert seized upon it to declare that "the Democrats are going to sweep the nation this year."[21] The Republican national chairman, George Bush, seemed to suggest something very similar when he remarked, "Candidly, this is a seat we felt confident we would hold in spite of the national problem."[22] The Michigan Republican party chairman, William McLaughlin, was more candid still, and more to the point: "Watergate killed us."[23] Phil Hart thought McLaughlin was exactly right. Speaking to 325 people attending a Ninth Congressional District Democratic gathering in Muskegon two days after VanderVeen's election, Hart had no doubt about the meaning of what had happened. VanderVeen had posed the question " 'How do you vote on Richard Nixon?' The people voted no. I don't see how Republicans can escape that conclusion. . . . For Republicans to break a lifelong habit and vote Democratic has to say something." The Grand Rapids election had sent Washington a clear message that there is "a deep loss of faith in President Nixon."[24] Douglas Frost, one of Martilla's operatives, saw no reason not to exploit this loss of faith. Democrats, in his opinion, should go after Nixon directly. "Front said he felt this tactic would be effective in almost any part of the country."[25] On the other side of Michigan, a Democratic candidate in another special election to fill a congressional vacancy did not need to be told twice what to do to win.

On the last day of January, barely two weeks before the Fifth District special election, Eighth District Congressman James Harvey resigned from the Congress to accept appointment to the federal bench. The resignation had been anticipated. The Republican congressman had been nominated months earlier, and it was only a question of time before the Senate would confirm his appointment. J. Robert Traxler, Democratic state representative from Bay City, was so certain a vacancy would occur that he had begun his own campaign for the office in the summer. Traxler easily won the Democratic primary on March 19, capturing 84 percent of the vote in a three-way race.[26] On the Republican side, Harvey's administrative assistant, James Sparling, showed strength of his own, defeating three opponents with 61.2 percent of the total.[27] Traxler and Sparling had very little time to enjoy their victories. The general election was less than a month away. On April 16, voters from the Eighth Congressional District would become the second Michigan electorate in sixty days to have a chance to affect the political and presidential fortunes of Richard Nixon.

The Eighth District had elected a Democrat to the Congress only twice in the twentieth century, and had not done it at all since 1932. Harvey had carried the district in 1972 with 60 percent of the vote, and in light of the fact that Gerald Ford that year had won with 61 percent of the vote, the district appeared solidly Republican. Or at least it appeared so on the surface. Nineteen seventy-two had been as good a year as Republican candidates were ever likely to see; 60 percent was not all that impressive. Moreover, the 60 percent had been won by a moderate Republican incumbent who had never angered anyone. Even more interesting to potential Democratic challengers was a fact that the 1972 election tended to obscure. The Eighth District had been reapportioned, and the Democratic legislature that did the reapportionment placed both Saginaw, which had a large black population among its 92,000 inhabitants, and Bay City, which had a large Polish population among its 49,000 residents, within the district. Even though they were immediately adjacent to each other, this was the first time the two cities had ever been put in the same congressional district.[28]

J. Robert Traxler was the political creature of Tony Bielawski, the undisputed boss of the Bay County Democratic Party, who decided not only who would be a precinct delegate but who would be a candidate for public office. Traxler had paid his dues. After two years as an assistant county prosecutor, he had been picked by the county chairman to run for the state house of representatives in a reapportioned Bay City district in 1962. The new district and Tony Bielawski's old machine sent Traxler to the legislature and kept him there for six terms. After election to his second term in 1964, Traxler found himself part of the first Democratic majority in the state house of representatives in nearly thirty years. He had seniority over all the new first-term legislators elected in the Johnson landslide, and he was one of the very few elected before 1964 who had a college education. At the age of thirty-four, J. Robert Traxler became one of the youngest majority leaders in the country. Traxler, however, loved politics and disdained legislation. Except for legislative pay raises, for which he seemed willing to trade his vote on almost any issue, Traxler appeared to have no serious interest in the Democratic legislative program or the details of the legislative process. When Joseph Kowalski, who had been Speaker of the House until 1966, when the Republicans elected 55 of the 110 House members and then obtained one Democratic defector to organize the house, died, Traxler was passed over by his colleagues, and William Ryan of Detroit was chosen the new Democratic leader. If he was disappointed he did not show it. Neither victory nor defeat served to spur either the energies or the ambitions of J. Robert Traxler. He seemed perfectly content to remain one of the most committed practitioners of one of the oldest forms of political conduct. Traxler seemed destined to remain the quintessential glad-handing, back-slapping, ward-heeling politician. But then, just as he had been in the right place at the right time in 1965 and had become majority leader in the state house, he found himself with an opportunity to run for Congress without having even to sacrifice his seat in the state legislature. If he lost in the April campaign for Congress he could still run in the August primary for nomination to yet another term as a state representative.

J. Robert Traxler believed that what voters wanted more than anything else were public officials who gave them a feeling of warm assurance. He decided that his name might appear too formal to inspire immediate intimacy, and lest he lose the vote of even a single constituent, he took the requisite steps to have his name appear on the ballot as simply "Bob Traxler." A candidate willing to change his name for a vote had no hesitation about asking that the election be decided on a basis that had nothing whatever to do with his own or his opponent's qualifications. Bob Traxler urged everyone to view the special election as "a referendum on Nixon's policies and moral leadership."[29] According to the Democratic candidate, nothing less than the future of America was at stake in this single contest for a solitary seat in the House of Representatives: "If Republicans win here, Richard Nixon will come out on the front steps of the White House and blow a trumpet. He'll shout 'All is well,' and then retire, and we won't see him again for three more years."[30]

The attempt to make the election a referendum on Richard Nixon received enormous assistance from of all people the Republican candidate. On April 1, James M. Sparling announced that he had invited the president to visit the district. Sparling, who according to a Market Opinion Research poll released March 30 trailed Traxler by seven points, insisted that he had not invited the president to campaign for him but, rather, to see for himself what was going on in the country: "I just think he should get out of the White House, where he is isolated, and face the people."[31] Nixon, who hadn't really had any good news since the night he defeated George McGovern, was at this point in his steadily declining fortunes desperate for anything that offered the slightest shred of hope that he might somehow survive the spectre of Watergate. The president of the United States accepted Sparling's invitation to spend three hours on April 10 traveling by automobile between some of the smallest towns in one of the most rural parts of outstate Michigan.

When Nixon arrived in the Eighth District, he was confined to a schedule that deliberately avoided appearances in Saginaw and Bay City,[32] the only cities of any size in the district, and limited in his public remarks to a discussion of the deficiencies of the Democratic candidate. During the three-hour motorcade that wound its way through fifty miles of the thumb area of the state, Nixon spoke "before large and generally friendly crowds," where he "emphasized two of Sparling's themes against Traxler: allegedly poor attendance in the state house and reliance on organized labor for support." The embattled president insisted that "Sparling isn't going to miss scores and scores of votes when it counts." Moreover, and this was a line Nixon had doubtless employed thousands of times at thousands of Republican rallies in every state and nearly every congressional district in the country, Sparling was "a man who will not be controlled by big labor." From one stop to the next the presidential motorcade traveled down two-lane country roads, and neither the Secret Service escort nor the presidential seal itself could mask the loneliness of the journey or the futility of the task. Not once did Richard Nixon mention Watergate, and his silence seemed to scream the name. After he left, the Republican chairman, William McLaughlin, who two months earlier had analyzed the loss of Gerald Ford's home district by saying simply, "Watergate killed us," described the president's visit as "fabulous—nothing but a plus. . . . It's got to help us in the campaign." If McLaughlin was satisfied so was Bob Traxler: "Nixon and his record are the campaign's only issues."[33]

Though he had probably said it because he had been told it was an issue on which the Democrat was vulnerable, Nixon's charge that Traxler was controlled by big labor lacked only the corollary that Traxler was a willing subject to be entirely accurate. The special election in the Eighth District had become even more of a national event than the earlier election in the Fifth. While most observers had assumed a Republican victory in Grand Rapids,

VanderVeen's stunning upset, combined with the increasing revelations of
White House involvement in the Watergate cover-up, made the contest in the
Eighth one that was expected to go against Richard Nixon and the Republican
party. If VanderVeen had lost in February, it would not have done much to
improve the prospects of the president and his party. If Traxler were to lose in
April, it might appear to be a sign of support for a president unfairly treated,
and it would certainly be treated that way by Republican and White House
spokesmen. Though Traxler had engaged in considerable exaggeration when
he suggested a Republican victory would save the Nixon presidency, it could
have provided a temporary delay in the process of destruction. The race in the
Eighth District took on an importance out of all proportion to the value of a
single seat in the House. Labor became so involved in the Traxler campaign
that it sometimes seemed that the AFL-CIO executive council had for some
unknown reason decided to hold an April meeting in Saginaw, Michigan,
instead of Bar Harbor, Florida. The list of unions that at one time or another
sent ranking officials at the national level to the Eighth District read like the
roll call of a meeting presided over by George Meany. The International
Association of Machinists, the United Transportation Union, the Amalgamated Clothing Workers, the Retail Clerks, the Interaonal Brotherhood of
Electrical Workers, the Communication Workers of America, and the Amalgamated Meat Cutters, all had a presence and all participated in this one effort
to place one more nail in the political coffin of Richard Nixon. They were not
alone. The National Educational Association had people all over the district as
part of its attempt to establish itself as a political force. None of these unions,
however, not alone, and not even in combination, came close to what was
done by the UAW. With Sam Fishman taking personal command of the
union's effort in the district, the UAW supplied the largest single share of the
money Traxler received from organized labor, and he received a great deal.
Five days before the April 16 election, the Traxler campaign reported labor
contributions of $27,000. Moreover, "Democratic sources estimated the final
labor figure would exceed $50,000."[34] This was only part of what was
actually done. The UAW alone furnished Traxler with campaign workers
from among the 43,000 active and 6,000 retired UAW members living in the
district. William Dodd, the national political director of the UAW, who was
also on hand, publicly admitted that many of the union's retirees "worked
eight-hour to ten-hour days in the Traxler campaign."[35]

    With union money and union manpower, Traxler was able to defeat
James Sparling 59,918 to 56,575 and become the first Democrat elected to
Congress from the Eighth District in more than forty years. Nixon's visit had
not helped Sparling, even in the areas in which he campaigned. Congressman
Harvey had received 73 percent of the vote in the thumb area of the district in
1972; Sparling got only 60 percent.[36] With the help of Tony Bielawski's

efficient organization, Traxler more than offset his three-to-two loss in the thumb by carrying the Bay City area by more than two-to-one.[37] The Democratic victory led Gerald Ford to express the fear that the party of the opposition might obtain "an overwhelming majority, which leads to further legislative dictatorship."[38] No one seemed to take seriously this rather awkward attempt to suggest that the Congress was a greater threat to liberty than the Nixon White House. Nor did any Democrat permit it to deflect attention from what was now obvious even to the most unrepentant Republican supporter of the president. Nixon, and Nixon alone, was the issue. Robert Strauss, the national Democratic chairman, said that the primary issue in the Eighth District election had been what he called "the Nixon leadership," and that that issue "would be the Democratic campaign theme in the fall."[39] Richard Nixon was no longer safe.

Robert Strauss had been wrong. It was not "the Nixon leadership," but the Nixon legacy, that would be the dominant issue and the major Democratic advantage in the fall campaign. Through the spring and summer of 1974 disclosures of new improprieties in the White House followed each other with increasing rapidity. Each new disclosure brought closer what growing numbers of Americans believed was the inevitable demise of the Nixon presidency. By the beginning of August it was no longer a question of whether Nixon would leave office before the expiration of his term, but whether he would leave through resignation or impeachment. On August 8, Senator Philip Hart rose on the floor of the United States Senate and raised a question that would have a greater and more immediate relevance than he imagined.

> During the past several days many statements urging resignation by President Nixon or a rapid impeachment and trial of the President by Congress have been made by people from every political quarter. With this discussion has come speculation that removal of the President from office would be accompanied by a form of pardon or immunity from prosecution by Congress, the succeeding President, special prosecutor or by Mr. Nixon himself.

> It is ironic to see such an immunity discussed for Mr. Nixon when we have yet to act in the more obvious case of those men who, compelled by their conscience, chose not to fight in the war in Southeast Asia.

> An amnesty would for these men be consistent with an American tradition of forgetting the deeds of the past when they were acts of conscience. Such a claim has not and cannot be made by Mr. Nixon in light of recent events.

> I urge my colleagues to consider whether we are to place the one person with more power than any other in the land in a position above the law for alleged acts of political expediency and abuse of power, while at the same time we continue

to punish and exile other Americans who acted out of conscience in refusing to participate in that tragic war. I think that we should not.[40]

That evening Richard Nixon, in a nationally televised address, announced his resignation. Hart immediately issued a statement in which he praised the president's decision and repeated his call for equal treatment before the law:

It is never easy or pleasant to see a man compelled by events to leave an assignment. It was not easy tonight to watch the President.

His plea that we seek, under Jerry Ford, to focus on problems other than Watergate was absolutely right.

As for Nixon, the citizen, I would expect he would agree he should be treated as any other citizen. And, on the issue of whether certain conduct was bad judgement or violations of law, he would want the courts to decide.

In sum, I think it was a graceful speech and a noble act which should benefit the nation.[41]

Hart was not at all satisfied with what he had said and, a few days later, wrote a last-minute addition to a constituent newsletter in which he set forth what he believed every American now knew. "We know," he said, "that the system works—it has just been demonstrated. We know that the people will respond to our new President—they always have in times of stress and national need." The country also understood, Hart was convinced, that the new president provided the perfect contrast to the qualities that had just driven Nixon from the White House. "We know that we are fortunate to have a man taking over as President that even his harshest critics describe as scrupulously honest and whom I know to be a truthful, decent man." The honesty of Gerald Ford, however, was not enough. There was more to the requirements of governance than an unwillingness to deceive. "We know, too, that simply changing the President will not solve the problems of the nation." Hart had not said anything with which anyone could possibly disagree. The system had apparently worked; the House and the Senate had both conducted themselves with more decorum and greater intelligence than many thought possible; Nixon had left office, and so far as the world could see, a vigilant press and an outraged public had caught and punished wrongdoing in the highest place of all. The American public would no doubt respond with sincere enthusiasm and even affection to the unassuming former congressman from Grand Rapids. Nor would anyone deny that the problems faced by the Great Republic would not simply dissolve in the presence of Gerald Ford's affable goodwill. There was ground for disagreement, however, when Hart went on to add that "we all sense the new determination—the desire to put history behind us and to set about attacking those problems.''[42] Watergate provided a once-in-a-lifetime political opportunity, and a party that had been instructing the electorate for fully fifty years on the importance of never forgetting that Herbert Hoover had caused the Great Depression was not about to let go of what Richard Nixon had given it. Phil Hart might be interested in the fundamental economic and social problems of the country; Democratic candidates for Congress were obsessed with the overriding importance of their own elections.

There was one Democratic congressional candidate, however, who was not intent on making Watergate a permanent trademark of the Republican party, and who agreed with Hart that the present problems of the country deserved more attention than the past delinquencies of the former president. Though Paul Todd was the only Democrat who had managed to be elected to Congress from the Third District since his own grandfather had done it two generations earlier, the reaction of professional politicians and the political operatives of the UAW and the AFL-CIO to his refusal to exploit Watergate for all it was worth was of the sort usually reserved for the most stupid rank amateur. Precisely because Todd appeared to have a reasonable chance of recapturing the seat he had won in 1964 and lost in 1966, his unwillingness to attack the incumbent Republican, Garry Brown, seemed almost indecent. For those to whom the fortunes of the Democratic party defined the highest standards of morality, Todd was guilty of the worst possible indiscretion. His conduct was especially reprehensible because Brown, as a member of the House Banking Committee, had been linked, if only tangentially, with activities connected with Watergate. Paul Todd, however, was not a typical candidate for Congress. While most candidates are willing to do anything necessary to win, approaching politics with the same vigor and much the same mentality as they would an athletic contest, Todd almost seemed to run out of a sense of public duty that was accompanied by a private wish not to serve. It was no accident that Phil Hart and Paul Todd thoroughly enjoyed each other's company.

Todd had agreed to run in 1974 with some reluctance, and only after the insistent urging of Michigan AFL-CIO president Bill Marshall. On the novel theory that Watergate ought to serve as a warning against excess of every sort, Todd proclaimed a self-imposed spending limitation of $40,000. On the unusual, not to say unique, principle that the voters of a district could probably make up their minds about their own representative in Congress without the distractions and distortions created by imported political consultants, Todd banned their use in his own campaign. On the remarkable assumption that if law breaking by public officials was a vice, attempts by political candidates to attach guilt by association was no virtue, Todd declared that any attempt to smear Garry Brown with the taint of Watergate was dirty politics at its worst.

Finally, and this alone was enough to drive the leadership of labor and the Democratic party to utter distraction, Todd, who on this issue disagreed with Phil Hart, recommended that Watergate be put to rest once and for all with a pardon of Richard Nixon. When, ten days later, Gerald Ford did exactly that, Paul Todd was the only Democratic candidate in Michigan and perhaps in the country who not only agreed with the president but said so.[43]

On Tuesday, September 10, 1974, two days after Gerald Ford had returned from Sunday services and pardoned Richard Nixon, Phil Hart spoke in the Senate. The "initial euphoria of self-congratulation on the way 'our system worked' " had "given way to more sober analysis." In the month between the Nixon resignation and the Nixon pardon, Hart had come to recognize that, as he put it, "The nightmare of Watergate may be over; the reality of Watergate cannot be so quickly relegated to history." The system would work only if permitted to *finish* its work. "If we would be true to the system we now applaud, there is unfinished Watergate business on our national agenda." The senator did not mean the kind of business those who were so upset with Paul Todd had in mind. The work that needed to be done had nothing to do with political or partisan advantage.

> One task is to fashion safeguards, within the limits of human frailty, against future abuses of the public trust. We must restore the executive-legislative balance, protect privacy and dissent, and insure the independent pursuit of justice in sensitive criminal investigations.

> But the most immediate requirement for restoring full confidence in our system of justice is to complete the investigation and resolution of charges arising from Watergate or in other alleged offenses involving the President and his associates. The precipitous pardon of Richard Nixon immensely complicates this task.[44]

While others attacked first Nixon and then the pardon without the slightest hesitation about the accuracy of their charges or the propriety of the penalties they demanded, Hart examined his conscience before coming to any conclusion.

> Like many others, I have spent time during the past few weeks considering how the ends of justice could best be served in regard to Richard Nixon. It is not a question easily approached with detachment. The nagging doubt remains that one's efforts to strip away personal bias, to set aside outrage over the protracted coverup and the abuses gradually revealed, have not been successful.

> Yet no American sought a pound of flesh, even when the need to remove the President from office grew increasingly compelling. Nor is there any blood-lust for vengeance in this Chamber now. In our quieter moments, all my colleagues know that. No one who witnessed Richard Nixon's last hours in office is un-

mindful of his anguish. And beyond the claims of compassion, there is some
national interest in a merciful amnesia.[45]

Nevertheless, Hart did not agree with those who argued that Nixon had
suffered enough, that "his fall from the highest office in the land leaves a
permanent stigma qualitatively different" from anything sustained by any of
those who faced fines or imprisonment for their participation in either the
break-in or the cover-up. "The Founding Fathers clearly decided that a President's removal from office was not so harsh a punishment that he should face
no further prosecution, regardless of his transgressions. The Constitution
expressly provides for both removal and then prosecution."[46] Hart wanted
justice, and justice required that nothing—not compassion and not even the
beneficial results that would follow a final forgetting of the whole ignoble
episode—stand in the way of the unfettered workings of the American
Constitution.

While Phil Hart sought to direct public attention to the detrimental effect the
pardon would have on constitutional government, the campaign of Richard
VanderVeen was wondering what effect it would have on the crucial question
of whether Gerald Ford's home town would give its new Democratic congressman a full term in office. After the special election in February, Grand
Rapids Republicans were in a state of shock; VanderVeen was a member of
Congress, at least for the next ten months; and John Martilla of Martilla and
Associates was an enormous success and in demand by candidates all over the
country. Though he had acquired a national reputation through the Vander-
Veen victory, Martilla did not permit sentiment to affect business. Martilla
agreed to run the new congressman's campaign for a full term, but, unlike the
special election, he would do it from a distance and through an intermediary.
During the special election Martilla and his associates had been able to devote
all their time and attention to the only campaign taking place anywhere. With
dozens of campaigns to run in the fall, Martilla hired people to direct the day-
to-day operations while the Boston firm took care of polling, media advertis-
ing, and campaign strategy. To run VanderVeen's campaign Martilla selected
a young graduate of the Harvard Law School who had never met Richard
VanderVeen and had never been to Grand Rapids. It was an uncommonly
intelligent choice.

Ken Levine had several friends from Harvard who were working in the
Martilla firm. Though Levine was practicing law in New York with the
prestigious firm of Paul, Weiss, Rifkind, Wharton and Garrison, he was
finding the life of a junior associate somewhat less than exciting. The tedium
of the law was especially difficult to bear after the intense and important part
he had played in the 1972 presidential campaign. Working directly for Anne

Wexler, Levine, still in his early twenties, had been a regional director of the Democratic National Committee's voter registration program. In the strange world of the McGovern campaign he had become the de facto chairman of the black registration campaign in Philadelphia and had barely escaped imprisonment when Richard Nixon visited the city and Mayor Frank Rizzo, never a stickler for civil liberties, directed the police to pick up and detain anyone visibly involved with the Democratic registration program. Levine missed politics and despised the abstract legalisms of a Wall Street law firm. He called one of his friends from Harvard who was with Martilla to see if there might be something he could do in the coming election. When he was asked if he might be interested in running a congressional campaign in Grand Rapids, Levine said it would depend mainly on the candidate. Martilla arranged a meeting.

When Levine met VanderVeen in the congressman's Washington office, the only thing he knew they had in common was the Harvard Law School and membership in the Democratic party. When he discovered that VanderVeen was not only an apparently thoughtful, decent human being, but a liberal Democrat, Levine was impressed. That the first Grand Rapids Democratic congressman in living memory should be, in Levine's assessment, "very liberal" on abortion and school busing, issues that drove conservatives and a great many moderates into a frenzy, seemed as close to political courage as it was reasonable to expect. Levine no longer had any hesitation. He agreed to become VanderVeen's campaign manager, and in June flew into Grand Rapids for the first time in his life.

Levine's first trip to the Fifth District (and only his second trip to Michigan) was not the beginning of VanderVeen's reelection campaign. In a real sense the congressman had "never really stopped campaigning since his February victory, returning home nearly every week and remaining as highly visible as possible."[47] VanderVeen was willing to spend as much time as necessary to hold on to the first public office he had been able to win. Levine, however, knew that more than the energy and dedication of the candidate would be necessary. He had not been involved in the special election, and he had never even been to Grand Rapids; but he knew from an undergraduate course at Cornell University that labor ran the Democratic party in Grand Rapids and he knew from the Martilla people, who had established good relations with the UAW, and from Arnie Miller, who had been brought into Michigan in 1972 by McGovern and thrown out by Sam Fishman, whom it was important to know. What neither he nor Martilla knew for certain were the issues that would be decisive in November. To find out, they devised a benchmark poll containing 160 different questions. While Levine poured over the returns, looking for the most significant and potentially most advantageous issues, VanderVeen was only interested in whether he was ahead.[48] It was a question that, to say the least, was premature. The primary election was still two months away, and the Republican nomination was not going to be given again to Robert VanderLaan.

The Republican party had been embarrassed by its loss of what presumably had become a safe congressional seat. The easiest explanation, and the one that was therefore immediately embraced, was the one that was really no explanation at all. VanderVeen's victory was simply a matter of chance that constituted what could only be a temporary departure from the logic of politics and the natural laws of human behavior. VanderLaan's failure was not a failing of the Republican party, but was instead distinctly personal. In the accepted tradition of political parties, an unexpected loss was made the responsibility of an unexpectedly inept candidate. It was therefore not entirely surprising that the Republican party "organization dumped VanderLaan, who had expressed interest in running again, and replaced him with Paul Goebel, a popular Kent County commissioner with a reputation as a strong campaigner."[49] With the support of the party organization, Goebel defeated several other candidates in the August primary and immediately began the campaign to recapture a seat that was rightfully Republican. It was a campaign that seemed to have everything in its favor. If the special election had been made into a referendum on whether the morally suspect Richard Nixon or the upright Gerald Ford should sit in the White House, the Nixon resignation, coming within days of Goebel's nomination, appeared to deprive VanderVeen and the Democrats of what had been their only important issue. Without any effort on his own part, the new Republican candidate had removed a major problem and received what was seen as a potentially decisive advantage. The citizens of Grand Rapids no longer faced the duty of voting against Richard Nixon; they now had the opportunity of voting for President Ford. The executive director of the Michigan Republican party put it succinctly: "What better way to pay tribute to President Ford than to elect a Republican to his old House seat?"[50] The brevity of Richard VanderVeen's congressional career seemed likely to approach historic proportions.

A month after Paul Goebel won the Republican nomination for Congress, the citizens of Grand Rapids were not in a mood to give Gerald Ford anything, much less a tribute that involved something so important as the election of their member of Congress. When Gerald Ford pardoned Richard Nixon, and Ford's press secretary, who was also a native of Grand Rapids, resigned in protest, no one in the Fifth District was heard to complain that Jerry terHorst had abandoned their president. TerHorst himself best described the reaction in Grand Rapids when he wrote, a month later, that "the Nixon pardon drove this staunchly moralistic community up the wall."[51] VanderVeen's strategy in the special election had succeeded not simply because the suggestion that Gerald Ford should be president appealed to home town pride, but because it demonstrated a recognition that Richard Nixon had brought dishonor to the presidency. After only a summer in Grand Rapids, Ken Levine already had a feeling for the kind of community Grand Rapids was: "people there have a basic sense of fairness about them. Grand Rapids was what the rest of the country had been twenty years earlier."[52] That sense of fairness was unleashed with a vengeance. "Ford was subjected to intense criticism in the local press."[53] No one approved of what the city's favorite public official had done. Almost no one. Demonstrating a singular lack of understanding of the kind of constituency he was dealing with, Paul Goebel "initially backed Ford's decision," and as if to show that nothing Ford did could possibly be wrong in principle or detrimental in Grand Rapids, he "even suggested there should be Watergate pardons for other Nixon aides."[54] When it became clear even to Goebel that the prevalent belief in Grand Rapids was not "our President right or wrong," the Republican candidate, having already departed from prudence, dismissed principle. For the duration of the campaign he did everything possible to avoid discussion of the Nixon pardon and to avoid even the mention of pardons for anyone else. Clemency was something he now wanted more to receive than to bestow.

With a far surer grasp of what was expedient, the Democratic incumbent managed to oppose the pardon without appearing to dislike the president. Just as in February he had obtained the approval of those who thought it would be an honor to Grand Rapids to have Ford in the White House, without incurring the disfavor of those who might have thought a demand for Nixon's resignation or impeachment unfairly premature, so now VanderVeen expressed his disapproval of the pardon and said nothing about the president.[55] Through his silence VanderVeen said what nearly everyone in Grand Rapids thought: Gerald Ford had acted in error, but—and this was a distinction intuitively understood and of immense political significance—his error was the consequence of a character that was not sufficiently severe. It was an error that could be forgiven even if it could never quite be condoned. Unlike Nixon, Ford had done nothing wrong; he had simply let his goodwill interfere with his good judgment. In the first major instance in which an advantage went to one candidate over the other because of their own abilities, VanderVeen had clearly triumphed. But there was still nearly two months to go before the election. By then the pardon and Goebel's damaging reaction to it might well be forgotten or surpassed by other events or other issues.

With a month to go, the election, at least according to the Republicans, was almost too close to call. Goebel released a poll conducted by Market Opinion Research that showed him trailing VanderVeen by only 5 points, 45 to 40, with 15 percent of the electorate still undecided. This was announced on October 17. Three days earlier, VanderVeen "had said, on the basis of polls taken by his own organization, he could predict flatly that he will be reelected."[56] VanderVeen was willing to state categorically that victory was inevitable, but he would not provide any supporting documentation. The *Grand Rapids Press* reported that "He wouldn't then, and wouldn't after Goebel's poll was released, reveal exactly what his polls showed or how many persons were questioned."[57] According to the polling that was done for his campaign at the beginning of October, VanderVeen had a 10-point lead. Ken Levine, however, thought it was really much closer. Because there were a great many undecideds, and because most of the undecideds were found among independents who indicated by margins of two- and three-to-one that they were going to vote for Milliken, the Republican candidate for governor, Levine estimated that VanderVeen actually led by only 51 to 49. In other words, Levine thought the race was even closer than Goebel did.[58] A week after Goebel announced his poll, VanderVeen issued a statement in which he released what his poll showed, but not the poll itself. According to the congressman, the poll, conducted by Martilla and Associates, had him comfortably ahead, 51–31.[59] Not everyone believed it.

Whether VanderVeen was ahead by two points, five points, or even twenty points, Goebel was behind, and he knew it. With only two weeks remaining before the election, the Republican candidate decided to go on the attack. On Monday, October 21, the Goebel campaign ran a full-page ad in the *Grand Rapids Press* entitled: "A Congressman's Real Record Is How He Votes . . . Not What He Says." The ad was an attempt to attach VanderVeen to the labor movement, which presumably did not have anything like majority support in Grand Rapids and its environs. "During his campaign for Congress in February," the Goebel ad informed the reader, "Mr. VanderVeen promised to represent all of the people in the 5th District and not just the special interest groups." The ad had not been run for the purpose of extolling the incumbent's virtues or praising his ability to keep a promise: "Why is it then that in the last seven months he voted in favor of every single one of the ten national Labor bills presented to the Congress? . . ." Among the ten votes identified as being in favor of labor was one against H.R. 7824, a bill to reduce legal services for the poor. Goebel might have had a rather broad notion of what a labor bill was, but he had no difficulty accompanying his charge that VanderVeen was not supporting the interest of all the people of Grand Rapids with a complaint that the congressman had voted not only for labor, but "against every one of the eight bills advanced by the U.S. Chamber of Commerce." One of the bills the Chamber of Commerce thought necessary for the preservation of the republic was H.R. 12859, aimed at reducing federal aid to mass transit. What was good for big business was obviously Goebel's definition of the public interest. VanderVeen's voting record demonstrated unmistakably that he was "a representative of Big Labor, which is definitely a special interest group. . . ." Goebel also queried whether it was

"not just a coincidence that Big Labor is by far and away the major contributor to his campaign for re-election or are they just making sure they retain
THEIR representative in the Congress?"[60]

The evening of the day this ad appeared in the *Grand Rapids Press*,
Goebel repeated the allegation almost verbatim during a debate with Vander-
Veen at the local YMCA. When his opponent told the audience of 150 that he
represented "organized labor, not the Fifth District in Congress," Vander-
Veen was wounded more than Goebel or anyone else could have known.
Labor had been the congressman's major single source of financial assistance
and was playing a role in his reelection bid that was more substantial than
anyone knew. But the congressman had lost too many times and been disappointed too often not to feel entitled to recognition for what had been an
unexpected and a major political victory. No one had tried to blame labor for
his defeat in 1958; he had been perfectly capable of losing without improper
assistance. More importantly, Richard VanderVeen was about the last member of Congress anyone could ever seriously accuse of doing someone else's
bidding. He had voted the way Goebel said he did, but he had cast the votes
on his own. The fact was that he agreed with the labor position on those
issues; he was not owned by labor or anyone else. Most Democratic candidates for Congress are used to the accusation Goebel made against Vander-
Veen, just as most Republican candidates are at one time or another called the
captive of big business. Most candidates simply return the favor and ignore
the attack. VanderVeen, however, seemed to want something more than his
own clear conscience; he seemed to be almost as much interested in his
reputation for independence as he was in his own integrity. Instead of explaining why the votes enumerated in the ad were in his judgment in the best
interest of the Fifth District, VanderVeen replied as if he had been personally
attacked: "I certainly am no lackey for labor."[61] He would make that clear
beyond any possibility of doubt on election night.

Goebel had gone on the attack and he had available a very formidable
weapon. The charge that a Democratic congressman voted with labor and not
with business may have been shocking to the Republican party; it was doubtful that many who had voted for VanderVeen in February were either surprised or distressed. The announcement that Grand Rapids would have a
chance to welcome home the president of the United States, who was coming
back to help his party reclaim his old seat in the House, seemed much more
likely to injure the Democratic incumbent. When Ford accepted Goebel's
invitation, the local paper appeared only to state the obvious when it said,
"The President is not expected to go anywhere here without Goebel at his
side, although it is conceded that VanderVeen will be a chief greeter when Air
Force One arrives at Kent County Airport."[62] Ford was coming to campaign
for Goebel, but the incumbent congressman could properly great the president

upon his arrival in the district VanderVeen now represented. At first, however, VanderVeen was not all that eager to do it. Nevertheless, at Levine's insistence, he told the *Grand Rapids Press*, "I certainly plan to be there."[63]

When Air Force One touched down at Kent County Airport and taxied to a stop, Congressman VanderVeen was there to shake President Ford's hand and welcome him home to Grand Rapids. Paul Goebel was nowhere to be seen. VanderVeen and Goebel had not been the only ones who wanted to welcome Gerald Ford home. Whatever they thought about the pardon, thousands of Ford's friends, both those who knew him and those who had never seen him in person, wanted to be there when the president arrived. Faced with an enormous traffic jam and absolutely no chance of getting to the airport on time if they waited for the traffic to clear, Ken Levine ordered the driver of VanderVeen's car to get out of the obstructed lane and to drive instead on the wrong side of the road. Apparently there was no one in the Goebel campaign who was willing or resourceful enough to violate the traffic laws. VanderVeen stood with the president while the news photographers and the television cameras took their pictures, one of which would be displayed prominently in the next edition of the *Grand Rapids Press*, while Paul Goebel barely made it to the airport before the president left. Worse yet, Goebel's failure to be there on time received almost as much attention as VanderVeen's well-publicized handshake with Gerald Ford. The *Grand Rapids Press* reported:

> One who missed the greeting was Paul W. Goebel, Jr. The main reason for Ford's visit was to boost Goebel's chances in next Tuesday's election. But Goebel was stuck in the traffic jam outside the airport entrance and the President was already off the plane before the candidate reached the landing area. Then he had to convince a damp and suspicious Secret Service man that being "Paul Goebel" was adequate credential to pass through security.[64]

Goebel was having a difficult time. Having missed entirely all the coverage he might have received at the president's arrival, he barely had time to recover his composure and listen attentively as Grand Rapids's favorite citizen asked "everyone of you to help in any way you can to elect Paul Goebel so I can have the good help I need in Washington."[65] The president refrained from expressing any hope that if elected Goebel might manage to arrive in Washington before the Congress convened.

VanderVeen had won the special election by insisting that Gerald Ford, not Richard Nixon, should be president of the United States. In the contest for a full term he had refused to criticize Ford even after the new president pardoned Nixon. He had been the first person to greet Ford upon his arrival in Grand Rapids and lost no opportunity to tie himself publicly not to labor, or even to the Democratic party, but to the Republican president. Polling data "clearly showed that the people of the 5th district liked Dick VanderVeen but not the Democrats."[66] This, in combination with the fact that most of those undecided in the congressional race were independents who favored Milliken in the gubernatorial contest, led Levine to use a strategy that shunned all connection with any of the other Democratic candidates, including especially Sander Levin, the Democratic candidate for governor. Not only did Vander-Veen ignore other Democratic candidates, he almost never mentioned his party affiliation. None of this was nearly so unusual, however, as his method of appealing both to the independents who supported Milliken and to everyone who approved of Gerald Ford. Refusing to run with the gubernatorial candidate of his own party, VanderVeen decided to run with the Republican candidate instead. One political ad produced by the VanderVeen campaign on the subject of public employment ended with the statement that Ford and Milliken both supported the same concept that VanderVeen was advocating. The Levin campaign was furious, because the ad ended with the statement "good men agree."[67] While VanderVeen let everyone know that he was running in the "Ford-Milliken tradition,"[68] he did not hesitate to have Phil Hart sign a fund-raising letter sent to potential out-of-state contributors drawn from a list supplied by one of the country's most generous liberal contributors, Stewart Mott. Nor did a candidacy in the "Ford-Milliken tradition," nor even his annoyed insistence that he was not their "lackey," prevent him from accepting the assistance of organized labor. Had he refused labor's support, more than half his campaign resources would have disappeared. He was not labor's lackey, but the election of Richard VanderVeen to the Congress of the United States without the massive help of the UAW was an impossibility.

John Annulis was upset about VanderVeen's association with Milliken and Ford in his media campaign. But he did not really believe that electing a Democratic governor was more important than electing a Democratic congressman to a full term. Annulis, and many other UAW leaders in the area, had spent a generation building for the time when it would become possible to defeat the Republicans and the business interests they represented. Vander-Veen, who had practiced corporate law in Grand Rapids for twenty-five years, could get money from people like Robert Pew, president of the Steelcase Corporation and a member of the family that owned Sun Oil, people who did not normally contribute to candidates of the Democratic party; but labor still provided the largest single source of financial assistance for his campaign. As of October 14, VanderVeen had spent $59,525 and had been given $19,000 by the UAW.[69] By the end of the campaign, VanderVeen had raised and spent slightly more than $160,000. Labor had contributed $45,000, of which more than $21,000 came directly from the UAW.[70] Though impressive by themselves, these figures seriously underplay the contribution of the UAW. They do not, for example, reflect the value or the actual cost of the letter the union sent to each of its active and retired members urging them to vote for Vander-Veen; nor do they take account of the thousands of telephone calls the union made to its members reminding them to vote and whom to vote for.

Perhaps the UAW's most significant contribution to the reelection campaign took place on election day itself. Ken Levine had made frequent and public mention of what, as he well understood, was a politically effective fact: the VanderVeen campaign had 3,000 volunteer workers and could lay claim to broad popular support. There was, of course, something inspiring about the willingness of so many citizens to give up their time to work as volunteers in a congressional campaign, but this useful statement was also slightly misleading. For purposes of Levine's list, a volunteer was anyone who had ever expressed a willingness to do anything at all for even the smallest amount of time. A signature on a card and a check mark in a box labeled "phone calling" was enough to constitute enrollment as a soldier in an army of volunteers grown to 3,000 strong. Out of the 3,000 willing to do something, the campaign was able to put 500 volunteers on the street on election day to help with a get-out-the-vote effort. Each of these volunteers worked two or three hours. The UAW effort made this seem almost insignificant.

Levine had grown increasingly nervous as election day approached and he was still unsuccessful in his attempts to find out exactly what the union was going to do. When he would ask, Scotty McPhail would just look at him, smile, and say, "We do election day like you've never seen." Levine would smile back, and reply: "I hope so, because if you don't we've had it." McPhail was right. Levine had never seen anything like it. The UAW, using a system all its own, determined the precincts that needed the greatest effort and put 500 of their own people into them. The union's 500, however, did not work two or three hours and then quit, congratulating themselves on their important contribution to Democratic victory and civic virtue. Instead, each of the UAW workers spent thirteen straight hours, from 7:00 in the morning, when the polls opened, until 8:00 in the evening, when the polls closed, getting out the Democratic vote. The UAW's effort was well organized and extremely efficient, and it depended not only on the dedication of its members but on the union's ability to pay them for what they did. Campaign contributions come in many forms.

Richard VanderVeen ran almost as if he had been endorsed by a Republican president and a Republican governor. Unlike most candidates who in fact had that support in 1974, VanderVeen also had the formidable and almost fanatical support of the UAW. In addition, he had what should have given pause to those who regarded Grand Rapids as a solidly Republican community whose selection of a Democratic successor to Gerald Ford was a temporary political aberration, the endorsement of the *Grand Rapids Press,* a paper that had been owned by that most Republican of senators, Arthur Vandenberg, and that had never failed to endorse the congressional candidacies of Gerald Ford. When the *Grand Rapids Press* endorsed VanderVeen within a week of the election it observed: "We are told that Mr. Goebel should be elected because Jerry Ford wants him. That simply is not good enough, and we hold the President in no less esteem and respect than we did in supporting his candidacy for 12 terms."[71] Paul Goebel had nothing to match this. He had completely misunderstood the public reaction to the pardon. He had managed somehow to miss the arrival of the president of the United States. He had accused his opponent of being the captive of labor and showed himself the prisoner of business. He had nothing like the volunteer organization of the incumbent, and none of the business enterprises with which he felt so comfortable could take the first step toward approaching the political power and expertise of the UAW. He did have the endorsement of Gerald Ford to advance his candidacy, but that endorsement, as the *Grand Rapids Press* argued and as the electorate now decided, was simply not enough. VanderVeen defeated Goebel by almost 10 percentage points, 52.3 percent to 43.9 percent.[72]

After the polls were closed and the outcome was apparent, Richard VanderVeen walked into the Eastern Avenue Hall in Grand Rapids at 10:35 P.M. and proclaimed to his campaign workers: "This Congressional seat belongs to the public." And then, according to the *Grand Rapids Press,* he said something that seemed strange coming from a candidate who had attached himself so closely to the president: "We're looking forward to the day when I can be greeted as the congressman from the Fifth District and not as the congressman who succeeded Jerry Ford."[73] This was not what he was supposed to have said that evening, and it barely covers what he really said. Several days earlier, Ken Levine, though apprehensive to the very end, had been reasonably confident of victory. Barney Rush, director of organization for the campaign, was something of a polling wizard, and just two days before the election he had managed to complete a poll that showed VanderVeen to be securely ahead. On the morning of the election, Levine, along with David Frank, wrote VanderVeen's victory speech. In it, the congressman was to say such things as "the only reason I won is because so many friends have given me so much help," "the Fifth district wants honest, decent government," and "I had little to do with the result." In short, it was a magnanimous speech in which VanderVeen gave credit to everyone and took none for himself. This was not only a respectable thing to do; it fit perfectly the public perception of the kind of man Dick VanderVeen was. Levine, who credited Frank with most of the work on it, considered it one of the best victory speeches he had ever seen. He was somewhat concerned when Mike Serpe, who in addition to his duties as a scheduler and advance man served as VanderVeen's driver, told him that he thought VanderVeen was working on a victory speech of his own. This sort of thing had happened before. A week before the election, for example, VanderVeen said he was tired of shaking hands at plant gates; he wanted to talk about issues and he would not appear at the factory scheduled for the next morning. Levine told him that nothing was more important than to bring out the largest possible Democratic vote: "The more plant gates you hit, the more people are motivated to vote. This is not the time to do a big policy speech." VanderVeen promised to be ready in the morning. He did as he had promised, and Levine fully expected that he would again do as he was asked. Levine briefed VanderVeen on the speech that had been prepared for him and instructed Serpe to take the congressman to the Eastern Avenue Hall when it looked like the election had been won.

When VanderVeen entered, the hall was filled with campaign volunteers who were already celebrating victory. It did not, however, contain any of the hundreds of UAW members who had been working since dawn. VanderVeen had personally decided that there would not be room enough for everyone; therefore the UAW was celebrating a few miles away, in the auditorium of the headquarters of UAW Region 1-D. VanderVeen was scheduled to appear first at the Eastern Avenue Hall and then at the UAW auditorium, and when he had finished thanking all of those who had taken an active part in his election effort, he would then appear at each of the local television stations. He had his speech and his schedule. He ignored both. When the unassuming, dignified Richard VanderVeen stood before the crowd jamming Eastern Avenue Hall, victory suddenly became an intoxicant. The congressman did not bother to thank anyone. Instead, he took advantage of the moment to let loose all the pent-up frustrations of two decades of thwarted ambition: "Everybody said I couldn't win but I did it. I won. I didn't need any help from anybody. I took on the President of the United States and I won." It was as if the real Richard VanderVeen had just broken free from the restraints Martilla and Associates had kept on him for almost a year. Levine could not believe it: "The guy was deranged." Incredulity quickly yielded to outrage. As soon as VanderVeen was finished Levine told him they were going immediately to the UAW's celebration. VanderVeen replied that he wanted a meeting, and the two of them went into the only place that afforded any privacy, a coat closet. In the dim glow of a single lightbulb, the two of them stood there, barely able to hear each other over the noise of the hall. VanderVeen announced with a distinct air of defiance that he was not going to the UAW, he was going to the television stations: "I'm going on TV. You can come with me if you want, but I'm going on TV." Levine told him, "Dick, 500 UAW members have busted their asses since 6:00 this morning. You wouldn't be a congressman without the UAW. You owe it to them to be there. They've been calling for an hour. They're waiting for you." VanderVeen was not moved. "Let them wait. I'm tired of everybody talking about the UAW and about Jerry Ford. From now on they'll be talking about Dick VanderVeen." Levine, who at this point could not stand it anymore, looked at VanderVeen and said, "Somebody has to go to the UAW and if you won't, I will, and you can go to the TV stations."[74]

Levine walked out of the closet, and while VanderVeen appeared on television, his campaign manager spoke to several hundred union members and on behalf of the candidate thanked them for making Dick VanderVeen a member of Congress. It was 11:15, and the hundreds who had waited for their candidate were too exhausted to stay any longer. Only about a dozen people were still there at half-past midnight when Richard VanderVeen, having spoken of his victory on television, showed up. Five years later John Annulis retired from the UAW, and at his retirement dinner everyone agreed that the greatest political victory in UAW Region 1-D, not only during Annulis's long years of service to the union but in their lifetimes, was the election of Dick VanderVeen in 1974. Ken Levine flew in from Washington, D.C. to be there. VanderVeen did not attend.

Notes

1. The reluctance with which FDR moved the federal government into the business of economic management is carefully described in Herbert Stein, *The Fiscal Revolution in America* (Chicago: University of Chicago Press, 1969).

2. Karl Marx, "On the Jewish Question," in *Karl Marx: Early Writings,* T. B. Bottomore ed. and trans. (New York: McGraw Hill, 1964).

3. Martin Heidegger, *An Introduction to Metaphysics,* trans. Ralph Manneim (Garden City, N.Y.: Anchor Books, 1961).

4. Irving Kristol, *Two Cheers for Capitalism* (New York: Basic Books, 1978).

5. *Jackson Citizen-Patriot,* November 15, 1973.

6. Ibid.

7. Michigan Democratic Party, Field Report, September 12, 1969.

8. Ibid.

9. Ibid.

10. State of Michigan, *Official Canvass of Votes 1970,* p. 4.

11. This represents the percentage of the vote received by the Democratic candidates for the State Board of Education. State of Michigan, *Official Canvass of Votes 1970,* p. 55.

12. *Congressional Quarterly Weekly Report,* February 9, 1974, p. 301.

13. *Congressional Quarterly,* for example, described it as "One of the hardest Congressional districts in the country for a Democratic to capture. . . ." Ibid.

14. *Grand Rapids Press,* October 31, 1974.

15. *Congressional Quarterly Weekly Report,* February 23, 1974, p. 493.

16. *Congressional Quarterly Weekly Report,* June 8, 1974, p. 1476.

17. *Congressional Quarterly Weekly Report,* February 9, 1974, p. 301.
18. *Congressional Quarterly Weekly Report,* October 12, 1974, p. 2761.
19. *Congressional Quarterly Weekly Report,* February 23, 1974, p. 493.
20. Ibid.
21. Ibid.
22. Ibid.
23. *Congressional Quarterly Weekly Report,* October 19, 1974, p. 2934.
24. *Muskegon Chronicle,* February 21, 1974.
25. *Congressional Quarterly Weekly Report,* February 23, 1974, p. 493.
26. *Congressional Quarterly Weekly Report,* March 23, 1974, p. 732.
27. Ibid.
28. Michael Barone, Grant Ujifusa, and Douglas Matthews, *The Almanac of American Politics 1978* (New York: E. P. Dutton, 1977), p. 417.
29. Quoted in *Congressional Quarterly Weekly Report,* April 20, 1974, p. 985.
30. *Congressional Quarterly Weekly Report,* April 6, 1974, p. 881.
31. Ibid.
32. Barone, Ujitusa, and Matthews, *Almanac of American Politics 1978,* p. 417.
33. *Congressional Quarterly Weekly Report,* April 13, 1974, p. 945.
34. *Congressional Quarterly Weekly Report,* June 8, 1974, p. 1476.
35. Ibid.
36. *Congressional Quarterly Weekly Report,* April 20, 1974, p. 985.
37. Barone, Ujitusa, and Matthews, *Almanac of American Politics 1978,* p. 417.
38. *Congressional Quarterly Weekly Report,* April 20, 1974, p. 985.
39. Ibid.
40. Floor statement of Philip A. Hart, August 8, 1974.
41. Comment of Philip A. Hart on Nixon resignation speech, August 8, 1974.
42. Philip A. Hart, "Washington Memo," August, 1974.
43. Dudley W. Buffa, special assistant to Philip A. Hart, memo to Sidney H. Woolner, administrative assistant to Philip A. Hart, September 17, 1974.
44. Remarks of Senator Philip A. Hart concerning pardon granted former president Nixon, September 10, 1974. See also, *Congressional Record* 120, no. 135, Tuesday, September 10, 1974.
45. Ibid.
46. Ibid.
47. *Congressional Quarterly Weekly Report,* October 12, 1974, p. 2761.
48. Ken Levine, interview with author, September 10, 1982.
49. *Congressional Quarterly Weekly Report,* October 19, 1974, p. 2934.
50. Ibid.
51. Jerald terHorst, *Grand Rapids Press,* October 25, 1974.
52. Ken Levine, interview with author, September 10, 1982.
53. *Congressional Quarterly Weekly Report,* October 19, 1974, p. 2934.
54. Jerald terHorst, *Grand Rapids Press,* October 25, 1974.
55. *Congressional Quarterly Weekly Report,* October 19, 1974, p. 2934.
56. *Grand Rapids Press,* October 17, 1974.
57. Ibid.
58. Dudley W. Buffa, memo to Sidney H. Woolner, October 8, 1974.

59. *Grand Rapids Press,* October 23, 1974.
60. *Grand Rapids Press,* October 21, 1974.
61. *Grand Rapids Press,* October 22, 1974.
62. *Grand Rapids Press,* October 17, 1974.
63. Ibid.
64. *Grand Rapids Press,* October 30, 1974.
65. Ibid.
66. Ken Levine, interview with author, September 10, 1982.
67. Dudley W. Buffa, memo to Sidney H. Woolner, October 10, 1974.
68. Ken Levine, interview with author, September 10, 1982.
69. *Grand Rapids Press,* October 28, 1974.
70. Ken Levine, interview with author, September 10, 1982.
71. *Grand Rapids Press,* October 31, 1974.
72. *Grand Rapids Press,* November 6, 1974.
73. Ibid.
74. Ken Levine, interview with author, September 10, 1982.

CHAPTER 5

1974 and the Politics of Deception

When Richard VanderVeen defeated Robert VanderLaan in a special election to fill the unexpired term of Gerald Ford, Republicans were stunned and most Democrats surprised. When VanderVeen was elected to a full term in November, Republicans were disappointed, Democrats were pleased, and no one was greatly astonished. The unraveling tale of Watergate; the growing demand for impeachment; the first resignation of an American president; the decision to pardon Richard Nixon—this combination of events, any one of which would have caused serious problems for the Republican party, created an expectation that the 1974 election would produce a Democratic victory as great as the one the Republicans had achieved just two years earlier. The prospect of a major alteration in the balance of political power might excite Democratic and depress Republican politicians, but among the general public politics and politicians were viewed with indifference and even contempt. "Even Grand Rapids, which has a son in the White House faces election time with a shrug. 'They've all lost a lot of confidence in their leaders, but especially Republicans,' said a longtime Western Michigan political observer."[1] The electorate seemed to be divided between those who wanted to punish the Republican party and those who were unwilling to vote Democratic and so would simply not vote at all.

Those who anticipated a decisive Democratic victory were not disappointed. Michigan's nineteen-member congressional delegation had been divided twelve-to-seven in favor of the Republicans following the 1972 election. After the 1974 election the delegation was still divided twelve-to-seven, but the advantage was with the Democrats. VanderVeen accounted for one of the new Democratic seats, and Bob Traxler, who had also come to the Congress in a special election, accounted for another. After the special election, Traxler lost no opportunity to let his new constituents know what he was doing for them. The Sunday after his April election he was a guest on a nationally televised news panel, where he turned every question about the national relevance of his victory in the special election into a discussion of the close relationship that existed between him and the citizens of the Eighth District. As Traxler later put it: "We looked at that program as if it was a closed circuit broadcast back to the district." Television was a rare and therefore unreliable means of communicating with his constituency, but as a member of Congress, even if the most recent one, Traxler had available free and unlimited use of the United States Postal Service. During the half year of the unexpired term he had been elected to fill, Congressman Traxler sent more than a million pieces of mail into the Eighth District. This extraordinary use, or abuse, of the franking privilege was something the congressman apparently considered normal practice for a member of Congress intent on reelection. He found it mildly amusing and a matter of some satisfaction that "we decided maybe we had overdone it when one woman complained she had received three different mailings on the same day."

Traxler and VanderVeen, the two most recent additions to the list of incumbents seeking reelection, won by smaller margins than any of the other Michigan Democratic congressmen. In the suburbs of Detroit, the Democratic incumbents recaptured the overwhelming majorities they had traditionally enjoyed before 1972. William Ford in the Fifteenth and John Dingell in the Sixteenth both received 79 percent of the vote cast. Two years earlier Ford had won with 66 percent and Dingell with 68 percent of the vote. In the Fourteenth District, Lucien Nedzi, who had been reelected with 55 percent of the vote in 1972, was returned to Congress with 72 percent of the vote. More importantly, Nedzi did not have any significant opposition in the Democratic primary. In 1972 he had won the nomination with less than a majority; had he faced only one opponent instead of three, he might not have won at all. In the Twelfth District, James O'Hara improved his margin by a full 21 points, from 51 percent to 72.1 percent of the vote. With busing replaced by Watergate as the main issue, the citizens of Macomb County, like the citizens of Michigan as a whole, were more interested in the integrity of public officials than in the extent and sincerity of those officials' opposition to the compulsory integration of the races.[2]

The Seventeenth District followed the other Democratic suburban districts with an increased margin of victory, but unlike the others, it had no Democratic incumbent. When Martha Griffiths decided not to run for another term, five candidates sought the Democratic nomination. Patrick McDonald, "a member of the Detroit Board of Education who was trying to make a lifelong political career out of opposition to busing," appeared to have a reasonable chance of success at the outset.[3] So also did Robert E. Fitzpatrick, chairman of the Wayne County Board of Commissioners, who had retained the services of the same John Martilla who had assisted in the Fifth District special election.[4] A third candidate, Joseph Levin, had the advantage of a well-known name and a very large amount of money, while Kathleen Strauss had a loyal, if not a very broad-based, following among consumer activists. The fifth candidate, William Brodhead, had his position as a member of the state house of representatives and the support of the Liberal Conference, an organization that had been "formed in the late sixties to oppose the Vietnam War within the Democratic Party."[5] Brodhead had something more, the support of the AFL-CIO, which made "an unusually early endorsement . . . in an attempt to head off McDonald,"[6] and the support of the UAW, which distrusted McDonald and despised Fitzpatrick. As a member of the Detroit School Board, McDonald had demonstrated through his repeated opposition to busing a far greater concern with his own political ambitions than with the need to reconcile the races in a racially divided city. On the other hand, Fitzpatrick had lost whatever hope he might ever have had for UAW support in 1971 when he not only ran for chairman of the county commission against George Killeen, who was backed by the union, but, the most grievous sin of all, had won.[7] With the UAW, the AFL-CIO, and the Liberal Conference behind him, Brodhead was clearly "the favorite of labor and the Democratic organization in the district."[8] Nevertheless, he very nearly lost, defeating Patrick McDonald by only 256 votes.[9] He had nothing like the same difficulty in the general election. Martha Griffiths had carried the district with 66 percent of the vote in 1972. In his first election as the Democratic candidate for Congress, Bill Brodhead carried the district with 75.5 percent of the vote.[10]

In 1974 every Democratic incumbent in Michigan was reelected to Congress, and both Democrats who had been elected to fill unexpired terms in special elections were given full two-year terms. In two districts in which Republicans had been elected in 1972, the Sixth and the Eighteenth, voters also elected Democrats. In the Sixth, M. Robert Carr, a former assistant state attorney general, had run surprisingly well in 1972 against Congressman Charles Chamberlain, losing by only 2,457 votes.[11] The congressman had not been seriously challenged for years, and it was not an experience he found either invigorating or worth repeating. Within a year Chamberlain announced his decision not to seek reelection, and M. Robert Carr, who like J. Robert Traxler made certain his name appeared on the ballot as just plain "Bob," considered his own election a foregone conclusion. In this judgment he was not entirely alone. He had come closer than any other Democratic challenger to a Republican incumbent Congressman in 1972, and it seemed only logical that the replacement of that year's so-called social issues by the question of Watergate as the major preoccupation of the electorate would easily supply the single additional percentage point necessary to elect him. Carr, moreover, was running not only against Watergate but against a candidate who had neither the advantages of incumbency nor the benefit of long and frequent exposure to the public. When Clifford Taylor, a thirty-one-year-old former assistant Ingham County prosecutor, announced his candidacy for the Republican nomination in the Sixth Congressional District he was known by less than 1 percent of the electorate. When he somehow managed to win the Republican primary by defeating the director of the state department of licensing and regulation, William Ballenger, who was both more widely known and more lavishly financed,[12] Taylor became the first Sixth District Republican congressional candidate in decades who was known by a smaller percentage of the electorate than his Democratic opponent. Victory in the Republican primary had been improbable; victory in November seemed impossible.

Some of the advantages enjoyed by Carr were more apparent than real. Although 1974 was almost everywhere a better year for Democratic congressional candidates than 1972, it was not immediately clear whether it would be so in the Sixth District. That Carr had come as close as he had to Chamberlain was at least partly attributable to the fact that 1972 was the first election in which the age of eligibility had been lowered from twenty-one to eighteen. Thousands of students at Michigan State University had been able to vote for the first time. The novelty of the opportunity and the enthusiasm with which many of them embraced the McGovern candidacy would both be absent. Carr had another potential problem. He had campaigned vigorously and with effect against the Republican incumbent in 1972. Chamberlain had secured repeated reelections and driven a whole series of Democratic opponents to the edge of madness by doing almost nothing in the Congress and nearly everything conceivable in the district. Carr had neatly formulated the sum and substance of Congressman Chamberlain when he said in 1972: "If I get elected, I may not get re-elected because the voters will know about me. I won't go to Washington and rest on my franking privileges."[13] He promised to "report my views and my votes," and vowed that he would "debate my opponent in the campaign." He had no intention of becoming another Charles Chamberlain, hanging on to an office he was afraid to use: "Chamberlain and others seem to believe strongly in the idea that you can't get hurt by the speech you never make or by the vote your constituents never know about."[14] Carr had made Chamberlain the issue and he had very nearly won. Two years later Chamberlain was not a candidate, and Clifford Taylor had never held public office. Carr had nothing to attack. Worse yet, because he had come so close in 1972, and because he had never hesitated to suggest that he had caused Chamberlain to choose retirement rather than face certain defeat in 1974, Carr looked to himself and to the world as if he already held the office. Taylor was more than willing to treat Carr as an incumbent and to make him the central subject of debate.

Though he had attacked Chamberlain in 1972 without apparent reluctance, Carr seemed unable to understand how Taylor could attack him.

When the Republican candidate ran newspaper ads quoting Carr's own statements to support Taylor's charges of inconsistency or incompetence, he accused Taylor of dirty politics but did not dispute the accuracy or the context of the quotations. When the *Lansing State Journal* offered to arrange a television debate between the candidates, H. Bernard Schroeder, Carr's campaign manager, rejected it on the curious ground that the paper had endorsed Chamberlain in 1972: "I just don't think the Journal would be interested in seeing Bob Carr going to Congress." Carr agreed: "I think the State Journal's impartiality is questionable." On behalf of the Carr campaign, Schroeder made it clear that the endorsement of Chamberlain had been not only an indication of bias against Carr, but a violation of high principle. "The Carr campaign . . . believes a newspaper's responsibility is to refrain from any endorsement, Schroeder said."[15] A Republican opponent's attack on Bob Carr and a newspaper's endorsement of a Republican incumbent were equally improper.

Taylor's attacks and Carr's continuing refusal to engage in the debates he had called for and promised two years earlier took their toll. As the campaign entered the final few weeks Taylor was closing what had been a substantial gap in public support. The closer he got, the more effective he became. No one had expected him to win the Republican primary, and no one had expected him to have much of a chance in the general election. He had defied the odds in August and now seemed to have at least an even chance of winning in November. Carr had begun with a degree of confidence that was overweening; he approached the end almost immobilized by confusion and uncertainty. Though the UAW had contributed more than $20,000 to his campaign, and though labor as a whole had supplied more than half the money raised,[16] he had placed himself deeply in debt. Carr, whose arrogant manner had discouraged more than one potential volunteer, nearly broke down as he explained to Phil Hart that if he did not win he would have to spend the rest of his life paying back what he owed. When Donald Riegle, still a member of Congress, came into the district during the last week of the campaign, he found Carr barely able to function. At the age of thirty-one, M. Robert Carr had of his own free will gambled his future on the outcome of a single election for a single seat in the Congress of the United States. He came closer to losing it than he had to winning it in 1972. Carr defeated Clifford Taylor by less than a thousand votes, 73,956 to 73,309.[17] With 50.3 percent of the vote, Carr recovered his composure and looked forward to the long and successful political career he had never doubted would one day be his.

While Bob Carr was trying to become the first Democrat elected to Congress from the Sixth District in almost two decades, another former assistant attorney general was attempting to become a Democratic congressman from a district that had been designed for that very purpose. In 1972, the

newly created Eighteenth District had been captured by Robert Huber, a
Republican for whom it was a point of honor never to permit anyone to be on
his political right. Huber's victory was everywhere understood to be the
consequence of the busing issue and of his own almost violent opposition to
busing in any form or for any purpose. No one appreciated more thoroughly
the connection between busing and Huber's claim on the loyalty of the district
constituency than James J. Blanchard, whose ambition for a seat in the Congress of the United States had apparently existed since the day, nearly fourteen years earlier, when he decided he was not likely to become president. As
a freshman at Michigan State University in 1960, Blanchard had a rather
unusual reaction to the election of John F. Kennedy: "I remember after
Kennedy was elected taking a look in the mirror one morning and saying,
'Nope, you'll never do it. If you want to be president, you've got to look like
him, talk like him, act like him, have money like him.' It would be enough, I
decided, to be United States Congressman from Ferndale, Michigan."[18]
After receiving his law degree from the University of Minnesota, Blanchard
returned to Michigan and was hired by the office of the state attorney general.
During the 1970 gubernatorial campaign he worked in the Levin campaign as
outstate field coordinator, and in 1972 he was involved in Frank Kelley's
campaign for the United States Senate. Within weeks of the 1972 election,
while most other Democrats were recovering from defeat or the closest brush
with it they had ever experienced, Blanchard was taking the first steps toward
a 1974 congressional candidacy. He met privately with a Republican acquaintance who had played a prominent part in Robert Griffin's campaign and
obtained demographic information about the Eighteenth District.

Though he considered Adlai Stevenson "his earliest political idol,"[19]
and though he had been involved in the "dump Johnson" movement in 1964,
Blanchard had no interest in running against the ultraconservative Robert
Huber for the sake of defending the cause of liberalism: "I decided that even
though I was against busing . . . that there was no way I could out-bus
Huber."[20] It is not clear what he would have done had he thought there was a
way he could, as he put it, "out-bus" the incumbent. Blanchard's approach
to the busing issue, like his approach to the question of a candidacy, had
nothing to do with matters of public policy. Busing was Huber's issue, and so
long as it remained the leading issue in the district, Huber was unbeatable.
Blanchard scarcely underestimated the hold busing had on the emotions of the
electorate of the Eighteenth District. Even though busing had been replaced
by Watergate as early as 1973 as the major subject of public discussion and
debate; even though the problem of race seemed almost everywhere to have
been suddenly swept aside by the problem of morality; even though corruption seemed to have replaced prejudice as the major means of reaching and
influencing the public mind, or at least the public instinct, Blanchard held

back. He held back until he was convinced the United States Supreme Court would strike down the school desegregation order of United States District Court Judge Stephen Roth. Though he had not participated in the attorney general's preparation of the brief filed in *Milliken v. Bradley*, Blanchard was in the audience when Frank Kelley argued the case before the Supreme Court in February, 1974. Eight years later Blanchard remembered having remarkable powers of observation and foresight on that occasion: "I watched the court. I watched Kelley . . . and I left saying to myself that the court would overturn the busing decision—that it would not be an issue if I ran against Huber."[21] Five months later, on July 25, the Supreme Court, by a vote of five-to-four, a margin that underlines the predictive powers of a thirty-two-year-old assistant state attorney general, held that multidistrict busing was a remedy that could be ordered by a federal court only where there had been a finding that all the districts involved had been responsible for the segregation to be remedied. The lower court was ordered to devise a remedy that involved only the Detroit city schools.[22] The suburbs and the political aspirations of James J. Blanchard were apparently protected against the prospect of racial integration in the public schools.

Blanchard's ability to read the mind of the Supreme Court may have been unique, but his ambition to become the Democratic candidate for Congress from the Eighteenth District was not. When he declared his candidacy he had to run not against Robert Huber but against several other candidates for the Democratic nomination. Of the eleven candidates in the field,[23] two, Macomb County treasurer Adam Nowakowski, and Hazel Park school superintendent Wilfred Webb, seemed most likely to present serious opposition. Blanchard, however, "was the only candidate not so mesmerized by the 1972 race as to stress the busing issue. . . ."[24] While the others proclaimed their unequaled ability to prevent busing, Blanchard concentrated on a more effective, if a more prosaic, strategy.

> "I borrowed $30,000 from my relatives and raised $10,000 in small contributions. We targeted every expenditure to the people most likely to vote—from precise placement of billboards to literature drops. I walked door-to-door for nine months and nailed those likely voters two and three times."[25]

Perseverance had its reward. Blanchard won the primary with 33.8 percent of the vote,[26] defeating both Wilfred Webb, who followed with 30.5 percent, and Adam Nowakowski, who finished third with 24 percent.[27]

The picture of a young candidate for Congress drawing on his own and his family's resources to wage a lonely nine-month battle to capture a nomination against better-known, if less able, opponents is not entirely accurate. The leadership of the Oakland County Democratic party and the most powerful officials of UAW Region 1-B had all expected reapportionment to permit them finally to elect a Democrat to Congress from Oakland County. John Dewan, the CAP coordinator in Region 1-B, was never really kidding when he would laughingly remark that he was going to elect a Democratic congressman before he retired. In the winter of 1974 Dewan had a good idea that his ambition would be realized before the end of the year, and that Jim Blanchard would be the Democratic candidate who would do it. Betty Howe, who had been chosen by the union to succeed Morley Winograd as chairman of the Oakland County Democratic committee, understood that the reputation of party leaders depended on increasing the number of successful Democratic candidates for public office. Neither Nowakowski nor Webb was nearly so attractive a candidate to offer in the general election as a young, well-educated, and personable assistant attorney general. Though the party organization clung to its formal position of neutrality, and though the UAW did not make a formal endorsement in the primary, Blanchard was nevertheless the beneficiary of all the informal assistance that the experience of the union leadership and the shrewd intelligence of Betty Howe could provide. Jim Blanchard went into the general election as the candidate of the Democratic party and with the endorsement of the UAW. In a very real sense he had become the candidate of both much earlier.

With the Supreme Court's decision in *Milliken v. Bradley* and the apparent removal of busing as an issue of overriding importance in the Eighteenth District, Robert Huber faced the unfortunate necessity of asking a predominantly Democratic constituency to support the ultraconservative policies of a Republican congressman. With busing no longer available to divert Democratic voters from their normal and traditional loyalties, reelection of the incumbent seemed unlikely. With Richard Nixon and the spectacle of Watergate creating an unprecedented degree of apathy and even antagonism among Republican voters, Huber's continued tenure in office appeared impossible. Though strictly speaking he was the challenger, Blanchard correctly assumed that his nomination was tantamount to election unless he committed a major blunder. The only mistake that could conceivably deny him what he referred to as "my life's goal"[28] was that of somehow permitting busing to once again become an issue. Unlike his major opposition in the primary, he did not call attention to busing by repeated and vigorous statements about it, but he calmly explained his opposition whenever the question came up. In what a number of union officials thought a master stroke, Blanchard filled the district with billboards on which his small son gazed up at him as if to say, as John Dewan put it, "I know you wouldn't bus me, Daddy."

The Blanchard campaign, along with the party and labor leadership in Oakland County, was so convinced that only busing could prevent the election of a Democratic congressman that nothing that might prevent the reemergence of the issue seemed inappropriate. On the interesting theory that Phil Hart was associated in the public mind exclusively with busing, and that any association with Hart would therefore cause some unspecified but no doubt decisive segment of the electorate to vote against the Democratic candidate for Congress, the senior senator from Michigan was not invited to campaign in the district. Fear of Phil Hart went much further, and the absence of political tact went much deeper. Bernard Winograd, brother of the Democratic state chairman and an officer of the Oakland County Democratic committee, asked, or rather demanded, that Phil Hart stay out of not only the district but all of Oakland County for the duration of the campaign. When Hart, or rather his assistant acting on his behalf, accepted an invitation to speak at a fund-raising dinner for the Democratic candidate in the county's other congressional district, the Nineteenth, the Oakland County Democratic organization suggested that perhaps he did not understand that the candidate had no chance of winning whatsoever. It was incredible that anyone, least of all someone involved with the Oakland County Democratic party, should believe that Phil Hart did not know that the area in which he had lived and begun his own political career was the safest Republican seat in Michigan, or that this was in any way relevant. No one can remember the time or cite the instance when Phil Hart supported a candidate or took a position on an issue based on an assessment of the likely outcome. He did not even permit personal mistreatment to influence his decision to assist those candidates he believed would improve the quality of the Congress. When the Blanchard campaign, with a really remarkable degree of self-importance, asked Hart to be the featured guest and the major attraction at a fund-raising event at the home of former deputy attorney general Leon Cohan, which, it was explained as if to avoid the suspicion of hypocrisy, was not in the district, the senator did not hesitate to accept.

In the end Blanchard's caution seemed excessive. The result was not even close. Nineteen seventy-two and the election of Robert Huber seemed a strange aberration. No longer distracted by the intrusion of social issues that, if susceptible to exploitation, seemed beyond solution, Democrats returned to their party and left no uncertainty about the real nature of the political composition of the Eighteenth District. Blanchard became the "Congressman from Ferndale" by a margin of three-to-two, receiving 63,331 votes (60.6 percent) to Huber's 41,179 votes (39.4 percent).[29] It is doubtful whether anyone but the candidate and his family was more pleased about the defeat of Robert Huber than Phil Hart, who considered the newly elected Democratic congressman a "bright young man with considerable promise." But then Hart, as someone later wrote, "was the kind of man who would strain to interpret a colleague's motives as decent, but never seemed to have to strain to make his own noble."[30]

While Blanchard and Carr were expending their resources and their energies in the exhausting struggle to become freshmen members of Congress, Donald W. Riegle, Jr., was barely concerned with his own congressional race. Elected in 1966 in an astonishing upset of John Mackie, the Democratic congressman and former state highway commissioner, Riegle quickly established himself as a candidly ambitious Republican for whom the presidency was the ultimate and inevitable political prize. Reelected by a wide margin in 1968, Riegle was eager to run for the Senate in 1970 against Phil Hart. When George Romney's wife, Lenore, received the endorsement of the Republican state central committee, Riegle was deprived of what he was almost alone in believing was an opportunity to advance, rather than to end, his political career. Compelled to run again for Congress, Riegle persuaded the leadership of UAW Region 1-C that no Democrat could possibly improve on his record of support for the legislation that labor favored. Pat Patterson, the union's regional director, had come to appreciate the regularity with which the young Republican congressman had solicited his views on legislation pending in the Congress and did nothing to resist the growing support for Riegle among the membership. For the first time anyone could remember, the UAW endorsed a Republican congressman for reelection, and Riegle demolished his Democratic opponent in November.

Riegle's increasing support within the UAW and his ever-larger margins of victory in what was a predominantly Democratic district were accompanied by his growing disenchantment with the Republican leadership. Having attacked Phil Hart in 1970 for waiting too long to oppose the war in Vietnam, Riegle joined a small group of Republican dissidents whose opposition to the war took the form of a challenge to the renomination of Richard Nixon.[31] After the insurgent candidacy of Congressman Pete McCloskey came to its barely noticed end, Riegle was rumored to be considering a change of parties. Though he insisted that "I don't want to switch parties—I really don't," he refused to rule out the possibility. He would say nothing more definitive than "I'm running for Congress again this year as a Republican. Beyond that, I just don't know."[32] Riegle was once again easily reelected, but three months into his fourth term he announced his decision to renounce his affiliation with the Republican party. In the early spring of 1973, Phil Hart introduced the newest Democratic congressman to the Democratic state central committee. The next year, when the Republican leadership that had appeared an insurmountable obstacle to his future ambitions had been discredited and destroyed by Watergate, Riegle was no longer in a position to be among those who could begin to rebuild and restore a more progressive Republican party. He was instead simply another number in the long list of Democrats elected to Congress. With Riegle's removal from the Republican and addition to the Democratic column, the Michigan Democratic party was able to claim twelve of Michigan's nineteen congressional seats after the 1974 election; that was the largest number of Democratic congressman the state had elected since 1966.[33] The leadership of the UAW and the Michigan Democratic party would have preferred to have been able to claim the governorship.

A few weeks after Sander Levin lost to Governor William Milliken by 44,000 votes in the 1970 election, Sam Fishman, who had a sometimes uncanny grasp of the psychological price paid by candidates for high office, remarked that Levin would have been better off had he been defeated decisively: "When you lose by this small a margin you're never going to be able to stop thinking about all the things that could have been done differently so you could have won." Fishman was undoubtedly correct. In only six years, Sander Levin, with degrees from the University of Chicago, Columbia, and the Harvard Law School, had gained election to the state senate, been chosen to lead the state Democratic party, and won the Democratic gubernatorial nomination in a contest with Zolton Ferency, who had been the party's candidate four years earlier. The magnitude of the accomplishment, and the brevity of time within which it was achieved, might easily have led even the most cautious of men to assume that the future would follow the past and provide new opportunities for greater importance and larger fame. Expectations of an easy and inevitable political advance, like the youthful assumption of personal indestructibility, gave way to the harsh lessons of experience. The promising public career of Sander Levin was brought to a halt by a defeat that, because it was so narrow, could be explained in almost any number of ways, and therefore in the most fundamental sense simply defied explanation. Levin could do nothing to change the outcome of the 1970 election; he could only look forward to 1974 and hope that he would be given a second chance. He was not yet forty years of age.

At an earlier age even than Sander Levin had been compelled to face the fact of his own political mortality, Jerome Cavanagh had witnessed the rapidity with which those seemingly favored by fortune become the playthings of fate. Running for mayor of Detroit in 1961 against incumbent Louis Miriani, Cavanagh's chances were generally estimated to be somewhat less than none at all. When he managed to pull off the greatest upset in the political history of the city, there seemed no limit to how far this young Irish Catholic could go. Reelected to a second term in 1965, the question was no longer whether Cavanagh would seek higher office but whether he would become a candidate for governor or for the United States Senate. Perhaps because George Romney held what appeared to be a vise grip on the governor's office, or perhaps because that other famous Irish Catholic politician, John F. Kennedy, had been in the Senate, Cavanagh decided he had no real interest in the Democratic gubernatorial nomination. While Zolton Ferency entered upon what was to be the first in a long series of gubernatorial campaigns and the last in which he would receive the nomination, Jerome Cavanagh became a candidate for the Democratic nomination for the Senate. He was not alone. Standing between the mayor of Detroit and the Democratic nomination was the formidable figure of G. Mennen Williams. Eighteen years earlier, Williams had pulled off an upset of his own by defeating incumbent Kim Sigler to become governor of Michigan. He had been the same age Cavanagh was now, and at thirty-seven had become known, at least for a time, as the boy wonder of Michigan. Cavanagh looked forward to the same recognition. Williams was heavily favored and widely supported within the party organization and the labor movement. Cavanagh had been in this situation when he first became mayor, but Louis Miriani was not G. Mennen Williams. Cavanagh was beaten handily, and after Williams was defeated by Republican Robert Griffin in November, was blamed for the loss of the Senate seat that had been held by Patrick McNamara. Five years after the beginning of a career that was filled with promise, Jerome Cavanagh had lost a Democratic primary, and of greater significance for his future prospects, had antagonized the large number of party members and union officers for whom opposition to G. Mennen Williams was the worst sort of disloyalty.

A year after his defeat in the senatorial primary, Cavanagh received another major blow to his ambitions. The Detroit riot of 1967 left forty-three people dead, whole sections of the city in ruins, and the political careers of the mayor of Detroit and the governor of Michigan in serious jeopardy. When federal troops were brought in, George Romney supposedly accused Cavanagh of ruining his political future. The mayor in turn remarked that he also had once had political ambitions. After an almost embarrassing candidacy for the Republican presidential nomination, Romney left Lansing in 1969 to become secretary of the Department of Housing and Urban Development in the new Nixon administration. Later that same year, Cavanagh watched as Richard Austin and Roman Gribbs fought for the right to succeed him as mayor of Detroit. When Gribbs took office, Cavanagh returned to private life and soon moved out of the city altogether. Barely forty, Jerome Cavanagh seemed to have no future in public life. Still, even in Ann Arbor, where he settled, and where, at least in Democratic circles, wisdom is sometimes regarded as the special competence of the young, his retirement seemed premature. Five years later, Cavanagh decided that the Democratic nomination for governor was no longer as unattractive as it had been eight years earlier. But what could have been his for the asking in 1966 he could not gain in 1974 without once again entering a Democratic primary in which someone else was favored by both the labor movement and the party organization.

Cavanagh had lost to Williams in the 1966 senatorial primary, and Sander Levin had lost to William Milliken in the 1970 gubernatorial election. For both candidates 1974 was in all probability the last chance to rescue their political careers. Levin began his second gubernatorial campaign in the fall of 1973. For ten months he walked door-to-door in the Detroit suburbs, trying to increase his following among the very voters who had rejected his candidacy in 1970. He had lost the election in the suburbs, but he had also been hurt throughout the state by "his image as a dull, colorless, and unexciting candidate—'Levin could deplore the beheading of little children and make it sound like he was reading a PTA press release,' one Democrat is reported to have complained."[34] The criticism, if unfair, was widespread; Levin at his best was mediocre on his feet. He was not and would never be a great or even a very good speaker, but he had a clear mind, and he tried to show energy and generate excitement by attacking the governor and his administration. Like many other good students who have entered politics, Levin prided himself on his ability to master the most complex issues of public importance and paid too little attention to the problem of gaining the interest of the public. Having previously lost the governorship at least in part because of a failure to capture the public imagination, Levin now thought he had a means by which to win the hearts and minds of the electorate. He decided that the major target in his attack on the Republican administration would be "state utility regulation. . . . He is blaming many problems and rate rises on Milliken's appointees to the state regulatory boards."[35] Charisma was a quality that seemed forever beyond both the reach and the understanding of Sander Levin.

Although no one felt intense attachment to Levin as a political figure, neither did anyone dislike him with great emotion. The same could not be said for Cavanagh. Both those who were attracted to him and those who hated him did so with feeling. Few felt as strongly about him as Neil Staebler, and Staebler was neither an ally nor a friend. The former state Democratic chairman viewed Cavanagh's gubernatorial candidacy with neither approval nor disinterest. Staebler had not forgotten that Cavanagh had run against G. Mennen Williams in 1966; nor had he forgotten what many others had never known, that this was the same Jerome Cavanagh who as a young man had helped George Fitzgerald and the Teamsters in their effort to use fraudulent petitions to elect precinct delegates opposed to the new coalition of liberals and labor that Williams led and Staebler had done so much to organize. Cavanagh's past record of opposition to what Staebler understood to be the best interests of what he regarded as the most democratic political organization in America would have been enough for him to favor Levin. But Staebler was now convinced that Cavanagh's political sins were accompanied by a more serious form of misbehavior. Louis J. Rome, former executive director of the Michigan Commission on Crime, Delinquency, and Criminal Administration, alleged "that Cavanagh had underworld connections when he served as mayor." Cavanagh filed suit for $15 million against Rome and

Staebler, "who allegedly held conversations with Rome on the subject."[36] Staebler, who was not amused, sued Cavanagh for a comparable amount.

Cavanagh was never able to mount a serious threat to Levin. His campaign had barely begun when it was interrupted first by the discovery that he had cancer, and then by surgery to treat it. Not long after he was able to return to an active campaign schedule, the allegations of criminal connections began to surface. At the end of July Cavanagh still had not been able to concentrate fully on the campaign. During the last week of campaigning, Cavanagh greeted a bar owner in Grand Blanc, just outside Flint, with "Hi, I'm Jerry Cavanagh, candidate for mayor."[37] Perhaps the former boy wonder of Detroit politics already knew that this second attempt to win a state Democratic primary was likely to be his last. The UAW, which had endorsed Levin in the 1970 primary to make certain the nomination did not go to Zolton Ferency, remained neutral in 1974. The union believed that Levin did not need an endorsement to win the primary, but he might need those who had supported Cavanagh to win the general; a labor endorsement might cause unnecessary and potentially harmful antagonism. Labor stayed out of it, and Levin defeated Cavanagh by more than two-to-one, 441,515 to 199,178.[38] It was a victory in which, as the headline of the *Detroit News* put it, "Levin proves he is not a 'loser.' "[39] It was a defeat that demonstrated the continuing validity of the political principle that getting even is always a good idea. Well into the early morning of election night, one Gerald Murphy, who described himself as one of the "old Cavanagh crowd," remarked:

> Jerry made his mistake when he tried to take on Soapy Williams in the 1966 Senate primary. I told Jerry not to do it because Soapy was the champ, the guy who rebuilt the party. No one could beat him. But Jerry insisted on bucking the tide. He alienated the party people.[40]

With the nomination in hand, Levin entered his second race against William Milliken with what the *Detroit News* considered "advantages he did not have in 1970." A major advantage was supposedly a better, because more experienced and larger, political organization.[41] In this the *News* fell prey to what an ancient writer held to be a common error: "the public forms inflated ideas of what it cannot see for itself."[42] A more effective, because more tightly controlled, political organization would be employed on Levin's behalf, but it was not under his direction. Almost immediately after the primary election, the Levin campaign became the Democratic party campaign. When he was state party chairman during the 1968 campaign, Levin had himself insisted that all statewide campaigns be coordinated through the state party organization. This had provided the institutional framework within which Levin could employ his considerable abilities to exercise personal control.

What Levin had done then, Morley Winograd would do now, and because he had already taken steps to establish greater dominance over the party organization than Levin had ever imagined possible, he would do it with a firmer hand and a more certain effect.

When Levin first ran for governor, his own party had inflicted upon him a blow from which it is fair to say he never fully recovered. At the August convention of the state Democratic party following Levin's victory over Zolton Ferency in the primary, resolutions in support of abortion and amnesty were adopted that almost seemed designed by Republican strategists. What some believed to be a secret compulsion for self-immolation became even more pronounced two years later, when nearly every device that could possibly alienate the American electorate was employed with devastating effect by the liberal wing of the Democratic party. Morley Winograd had not become chairman of the party to preside over the continued deterioration of its organization or to watch with indifference another in a seemingly endless string of failed gubernatorial candidacies. The 1974 Democratic state convention was so different from the August conventions of 1970 and 1972 as to invite the suspicion that it was being held by another party. Resolutions that might damage the prospects of Democratic candidates for public office were not even debated, much less adopted. Nominations for the state board of education and the governing boards of the three major universities were decided in advance by the party leadership and what had by now become the dominant power within it, the labor movement. At 11 P.M. on Saturday evening, the unity caucus met and ratified what had been done. On Sunday the convention assembled and routinely did as it had been told. If Levin lost again, it would be impossible to blame it on any embarrassment occasioned by an indiscretion of the Democratic party.

More than anything else, Sander Levin wanted to become governor. That, however, was both the beginning and the end of political certainty in the matter. It was astonishing how little had really been decided during the four years since his last campaign. As late as the second week in September, with less than two months remaining before the election, Morley Winograd privately "agreed that the Levin campaign doesn't know where it is going."[43] Sam Fishman asked Levin to provide a statement of the central theme of the campaign. When Levin appeared to be at something of a loss, Fishman, trying to be helpful, reformulated the question. What, he asked, are the reasons people should vote for you instead of Milliken? Levin's response was that he offered "new leadership," a phrase that did very little to define the campaign or to differentiate it from a thousand others. Sander Levin, perhaps the best-educated man running for governor that year anywhere in the country, really had no idea about, because he had really given no thought to, what he would do if he became governor. Confident in his capacity to confront successfully whatever problem he might face, he had apparently spent the four years since his defeat pondering not the duties of the office but the difficulties of the election. This was a supposition impossible to doubt when, later in the same meeting, Levin remarked what a great improvement it was over 1970 to have the services of political consultant David Garth, who could "tell us what the issues are and what we should do about them." The new leadership seemed more like a new willingness to follow wherever public opinion might lead.

Levin was not alone in looking to others to discover what he should say or do. Milliken had his own political consultant who had his own ideas about how to appeal to public opinion. John Deardorff advised the governor not to emphasize, as he had in 1970, the accomplishments of his administration or even the major issues confronting the state. Deardorff wanted Milliken to talk instead about his own background, experience, education—in other words, about Milliken the person rather than Milliken the governor. Watergate had clearly increased public concern about the integrity of public officials, and Deardorff was only adopting a point of view readily available in the writings of Plato and Aristotle when he suggested that character was the most reliable guarantee of future conduct: "During one term, a governor or senator will have to confront issues that nobody can predict at the moment. There ought to be more attention paid to the guy's background, rather than to how he will vote on abortion."[44] Deardorff apparently found no irony in the implicit suggestion that the question of character might be used to avoid dealing directly with a political issue that generated intense public reaction.

Deardorff's suggested strategy was given more precise form as the Milliken campaign analyzed data from public opinion polls. The director of the Milliken campaign, James Barnes, "noted that polls have shown that people, as a result of the Watergate scandal, are looking for open, forthright, candid candidates." This, of course, was to suggest that before Watergate people were not looking for candidates who were open, forthright, and candid. Barnes believed he had found something even more important, something that could be used to great advantage. "According to the polls," he confided, "it is more important that the candidate be forthright with the people than for him to agree with them on all of the issues."[45] The application of science to politics, in the form of public opinion polls that were accurate within a few percentage points, yielded the remarkable conclusion that people prefer not to be lied to. Though the director of the Milliken campaign professed to find this of more than passing interest, he quickly protested that the governor's own forthrightness was of course not based on any sort of calculation derived from a scientific sampling of public opinion.[46] Milliken had John Deardorff, and Levin had David Garth, to help them determine what they should say and even how they should say it. The Milliken campaign had polling data indicating that at least the impression of integrity was an important political attribute. The Levin campaign's polling data led to a rather different conclusion.

The polling data that generated some of the most important decisions in the gubernatorial campaign was supplied not by the Levin campaign but by the state Democratic party. Through an ingenious scheme of financial interdependence, Morley Winograd had made certain that the gubernatorial campaign could not operate independently of the state party. Instead of the normal arrangement in which the party supplied direct financial assistance to a campaign, Winograd invented a division of labor under which some of the most essential campaign functions were carried out by the party itself. While the Levin campaign budget of $620,750[47] was devoted almost exclusively to media, the state party's campaign budget of $138,350[48] provided for the costs of political organization. The party, not the Levin campaign, had the responsibility for office rent and equipment, telephones, and the get-out-the vote effort. The party, not the Levin campaign, allocated $25,000 for polling.[49] The party, not the Levin campaign, would decide the type and the frequency of any polling that might be done.

With Levin dependent on the party for an essential part of his own campaign, it was not difficult for Winograd, who was fully supported by the UAW, to assert the authority of the state party organization. The authority was assured by the way it was employed. Almost immediately after the August state convention, Winograd began a series of weekly meetings that continued until the election. At eight o'clock every Monday morning, the chairman called to order a meeting of the party, labor, the congressional delegation, the state legislative leadership, and the statewide campaigns. Winograd, Sam Fishman of the UAW, and Bill Marshall of the AFL-CIO were almost always there. Phil Hart never attended, but he always sent a representative. John Dingell came once, and Paul Donahue, assistant to Congressman Lucien Nedzi, occasionally attended. Frank Kelley, the attorney general, and Richard Austin, the secretary of state, both seeking reelection but facing only nominal opposition, participated several times. The Levin campaign was almost always represented by its manager, Laird Harris. Levin personally attended three or four meetings. These Monday morning gatherings were ostensibly for the purpose of providing the broadest possible participation in the conduct of the Democratic campaign. In reality they were a device for communicating information and approving decisions that had already been made. There were occasions, however, when serious problems were discussed. Levin, for example, expressed disappointment and a certain degree of incredulity about polling information Winograd had just disclosed that showed him running poorly in western Wayne County. He claimed not to understand how he could have spent so much time in an area and apparently not been able to make any appreciable progress. Winograd thought he knew the reason.

During the second week in September, a poll commissioned by the state party had been conducted among Michigan voters. The results themselves were less interesting than the process the poll set in motion. Those who had been interviewed for the poll were contacted five more times during the remainder of the campaign. The changes in their collective attitudes and opinions signaled whether Levin's strategy and tactics needed to be altered in any way. In the past the party had rarely used even one poll, much less a system for tracking the changes taking place among the electorate. Winograd had seen the need and originated the idea, but labor was also enthusiastic. After the 1970 election, Sam Fishman had complained that the state senate seat that included most of Lansing could have been won if the UAW had contributed more money, which it would have done had it known how close the race really was. Now, for the first time, everyone could know not only who was leading in the gubernatorial contest, a service already provided by the *Detroit News,* but the specific issues and groups that held the key to victory. This was seen as such a crucial part of the campaign that even Libby Maynard, vice-chairman of the state party, was pressed into service as one of the volunteers who made the telephone calls in the tracking polls.

Nothing was more important than generating information through modern polling techniques, and nothing seemed more self-explanatory than the information the party obtained. Levin was losing the election to Milliken, and he was losing it in western Wayne County. That conclusion, however, could as easily have been supplied by someone like Congressman John Dingell's assistant, Charles Prather, who seemed to have been invented by Damon Runyon to make incredibly accurate political predictions on the basis of a single conversation in a working-class bar. But what not even the most experienced politician could have known, and what Winograd now knew, was the percentage of the voters of western Wayne County who felt a particular way about a particular issue. This information could provide the basis for a political strategy that appealed to the electorate by embracing the position it already held.

Among the residents of western Wayne County two positions were held by massive majorities. Seventy percent were in favor of Proposition C, which had been placed on the ballot by Citizen's Lobby, an organization headed by Douglas Ross, to eliminate the sales tax on food and drugs. Seventy-five percent opposed additional taxes of any sort, whether new ones or increases in existing ones. The governor's race seemed likely to be decided in the suburban communities of western Wayne County, and there was now no room for differing opinions about what the voters who lived there really wanted. They wanted passage of Proposition C, and they most emphatically did not want any new taxes to take the place of those Proposition C would repeal. Winograd was barely able to restrain his enthusiasm when he announced these findings at the regular Monday morning leadership meeting six weeks before the election and then added that Sandy Levin had finally agreed both to support Proposition C and to promise not to increase taxes to make up for the revenues that would be lost. No one asked how the revenue would be made up; the decision had already been made. After the meeting broke up, one of those present mentioned privately to John Bruff that "Levin just lost by five points. No one is going to believe him."

Among those who heard Levin for the first time publicly couple advocacy of the repeal of the sales tax on food and drugs with an insistence that no other taxes be increased was none other than William Milliken. The governor could scarcely believe his ears. The two gubernatorial candidates were engaged in a debate on the Michigan State University public broadcasting station, WKAR, when the Democratic challenger stated his support of ballot Proposal C, and then, when asked how he would make up for the revenues lost through repeal, asserted that it could be done entirely by "cutting fat" from the governor's budget.[50] Sensing an opportunity, Milliken insisted that repeal would cost the state $200 million a year, and that this could not possibly be made up without either drastic reductions in state spending or substantial increases in the state income tax. Looking directly at Levin, Milliken said, "You can't have it both ways."[51] Levin, however, refused to qualify his initial answer and instead repeated his insistence that the 4 percent sales tax on food and the 2 percent sales tax on drugs could be terminated without subjecting the people of Michigan to more taxation or fewer governmental services.

Though the numbers who actually heard the exchange between Milliken and Levin could not have been more than a miniscule fraction of the electorate, it became the single most important, and perhaps even the decisive, event of the campaign. The two candidates might both be "seen as well-intentioned, hard-working public servants, identical in their blandness,"[52] but there was now an issue that provided a clear contrast between them. Levin was for Proposal C and Milliken was against it. The news media was not slow to inform the public that there was in fact a basic difference between the candidates for the state's highest office. Reporter Robert Longstaff wrote, "Levin supports it and says the loss of $200 million in revenue can be made up by trimming the budget. Milliken takes what is generally conceded to be the unpopular position; he opposes repeal and says it is unrealistic of Levin to avoid talk of an income-tax increase to make up the loss."[53] There was more than a little irony in the fact that each side was elated at what had taken place in the WKAR debate and convinced that the opposition had committed a blunder of major proportions. On the same day as the debate Morley Winograd offered the judgment that at one stroke Sander Levin had put the governor in the politically impossible position of arguing that tax repeal must lead to tax increase. Milliken was finished. For their part, members of the Milliken campaign were convinced that Sander Levin had just supplied the rope that would both hang himself and rescue a drowning man. In their judgment, Milliken had been losing the election until Levin made the incredible mistake of insisting that $200 million in lost revenue out of a budget of only $3 billion could somehow be made up by means of more efficient management. Even after the election, the fact that Levin's position was the result of a calculation based on an analysis of polling data seemed to them too absurd to be taken seriously.[54]

Whatever the Republicans might believe, Levin and the Democrats found nothing to regret about their decision. Two weeks after his first debate with the governor, Levin was insisting with even greater assurance that Proposal C should be adopted and no new taxation enacted.

> The sales tax on food and medicine hurts low and middle income families the most because they are taxes added onto the cost of inflation. Every time a housewife passes through the supermarket checkout, and pays that 4% tax on food, she is paying a surcharge on inflation. Although my Republican opponent, William Milliken, says we can't afford to cut these taxes and still balance the state budget, I insist that we can and must.[55]

The question, of course, was how? While Levin continued to insist that it could be done through greater efficiency in government, the expressions of disbelief—not only by the governor and other Republicans but by a number of Democrats, including William Copeland, chairman of the Ways and Means Committee of the state house of representatives—encouraged a greater specificity. Levin announced he would achieve the requisite reduction in expenditures by limiting out-of-state travel; by reducing the staff of the governor; by revising the budget system to require annual justifications of each expenditure; by trimming millions of dollars of waste, including $77.6 million a federal audit had claimed could be saved on welfare alone; and by recovering $59.4 million the state auditor had said could be saved by cutting waste and collecting revenues due the state.[56] Having decided on political grounds to favor repeal and oppose taxation, Levin had now at least managed to marshal what might almost pass for a factual basis to support his position.

Though the Milliken campaign was convinced that Levin had accidentally stumbled into an untenable position, the governor did not hesitate to accuse his Democratic opponent of an egregious and deliberate act of deceit. On October 29, Milliken and Levin appeared before 1,100 people at the Detroit Economic Club in the last formal debate of the campaign. "Levin continued to dangle before the voters the prospect of the sales tax repeal without a compensating increase in other taxes. . . ." Belying his reputation as a mild-mannered man somehow above, or at least outside, the vindictiveness that tends to characterize political contests, Milliken "charged Levin

with political ambition, deception, distortion and demagoguery.'' The governor, who, it must be remembered, had a poll of his own showing that the
voters wanted public officials with integrity, did everything he could to portray Sander Levin as a man who had none. ''Somewhere along the line,''
Milliken asserted, ''he decided to hitch his ambition to Proposal C. He made
a cold, calculated political decision in order to get the best of both worlds. His
approach is promise them everything, give them reality after the election, that
is deception . . . distortion.'' If it was not certain after this onslaught which
candidate was the most accomplished practitioner of demagoguery, neither
was it clear which of them had the greater claim to integrity. Instead of
responding in kind, Levin replied without apparent anger, ''This campaign
began on a basis of the issues; the race began to get close; problems under-
mined the Governor's position and the Milliken campaign shifted to a personal attack. It will reflect more on him than on me.''[57]

Although the audience at the Economic Club had ''interrupted Milliken
with applause four times, loudest when he accused Levin of demogoguery,''[58] the very savagery of the governor's attack seemed to betray an uncertainty about the outcome of an election that was less than a week away. He
had cause for concern. On October 6, the *Detroit News* had published its first
poll, and although it showed Milliken ahead among both ''all voters'' and
''likely voters,'' his lead among those in the latter category was only 5
percentage points. Four years earlier the first *News* poll had shown Milliken
ahead among ''likely voters'' by 6 percentage points, and that election, as the
News reminded its readers, ''ended in a virtual dead heat which required
nearly two days to determine a winner.''[59] Four years earlier, in other words,
Milliken had begun with a larger lead and almost lost. When the *Detroit News*
published its second poll two weeks later, on October 20, Milliken had
increased his lead among likely voters by a single percentage point, from 5 to
6. Eleven percent of the electorate, however, were still undecided.[60] In the
final regularly scheduled poll, the *News* reported on November 3 that Milliken's lead among likely voters had been reduced from 6 to 4 percentage
points. The Governor now led by only 45 to 41, and 12 percent of the
electorate had not yet made up their minds whether to vote for the Republican
incumbent or the Democratic challenger. This was the largest percentage of
undecided voters this late in a campaign in the twenty-five year history of the
Detroit News poll.[61] By the time this poll was published, however, no one,
including the *News,* believed it was any longer accurate. Between the time the
survey was conducted and the time the results were tabulated, Milliken found
himself compelled to decide whether his running mate would hurt him more
by leaving the Republican ticket or staying on it.

Milliken and the Republican party understood as well as Morley
Winograd and the UAW that the suburban vote was the key to victory in the

gubernatorial or any other statewide contest in Michigan. When the lieutenant governor, James Brickley, discovered that his job was boring and that he might grow old waiting for the chance to move from the second to the first position in state government, he decided not to run for a second term. Milliken's new running mate was a state representative from Oakland County who had also served on the zoning board of appeal and on the city commission of Troy, one of the most affluent communities in the most affluent county in the state. When the name of James Damman began to be heard as that of a prospective running mate for Milliken, the Oakland County Democratic chairman, Betty Howe, wrote the governor a letter "asking that he investigate reports about the state lawmaker."[62] Damman reportedly had "received 80 percent of his campaign contributions in his successful bid for the state legislature from land developers." Moreover, Oakland County records "show that Damman had personal business dealings with many of his financial backers and voted for several of their plans while serving on the zoning board of appeals and the city commission of Troy from 1967–70."[63] Howe, who had once been a reporter for a local newspaper, had done her work with an extraordinary attention to detail. The governor, however, ignored her request and would apparently have ignored the matter altogether had Howe not made certain that reporters from the *Detroit Free Press* were given enough information to whet their appetite for more. In the year of Watergate the public might want public officials with the old virtues of integrity and honesty, but every enterprising and ambitious reporter prayed for corruption to uncover and deception to disclose.

When the *Free Press* broke the story about the relationship between Damman and land developers in Troy it pulled no punches. Damman was described as someone who had been involved in "subterfuge, profiteering, and abuse of power," someone who had used inside information as a city commissioner to profit in a land investment partnership.[64] The allegations against Damman were so serious and the political consequences to Milliken so potentially devastating, that the governor immediately opened up the possibility that Damman would be asked to leave the ticket. Milliken, "his re-election effort wounded by allegations against his running mate, said Thursday night it is possible he will ask James Damman to quit the Republican ticket." The governor, however, was quick to add that this would happen only if "there was a whole new series of information coming in, but I don't see it coming." Nevertheless, on the next day, which was the last Friday before the election, Milliken canceled all campaign appearances and spent eleven hours conferring "with top aides." That evening he stated he had "found no reason to disavow or dump running mate James J. Damman."[65] On neither that day nor the next, however, did the governor announce any final decision. On Sunday, newspapers around the state headlined Milliken's decision to keep Damman on the ticket. Though privately convinced that Damman was a "stupid politician,"[66] the governor publicly declared, "On the basis of my personal examination of this matter in the past two days, which has been intensive, I am of the opinion that the conclusions reached by the Free Press are not justified by the facts."[67] Two hours later, Levin declared: "I would have got him [Damman] off the ticket."[68] The *Detroit Free Press,* in what some Democratic leaders suspected was nothing short of a conspiracy with the governor's office, did not agree. On the editorial page of its Sunday edition, the *Free Press* in effect recanted. "We do not know," the editorial writers wrote in words that seemed designed to protect against the possibility of litigation, "of facts that in light of the information turned up by the Governor's lawyers, would show Mr. Damman guilty of 'subterfuge, profiteering and abuse of power.'"[69] The *Free Press* announced that it no longer sought Damman's removal from the Republican ticket, and then, in an accompanying editorial, did everything it could to complete its apologies for any inconvenience the governor might have been caused by repeating its endorsement of William Milliken for another term.

Damman was safe, at least for one election; the *Free Press* was sorry; but everyone knew Milliken was hurt. On Monday, the *Detroit News* published a special poll taken to measure the extent of the damage. Among likely voters Milliken led by only 3 percentage points, 46.5 to 43.5, with 8.6 percent undecided. Among all voters, however, Levin led, 45.2 to 43.1 percent.[70] Given the normal margin of error, the race seemed too close to call. Milliken and Levin returned to what each thought was his own source of advantage. The Levin campaign ran newspaper ads on the day before the election stating: "Sander Levin Favors Eliminating the Sales Tax on Food and Medicine. Governor Milliken Opposes Removal of These Unfair Taxes."[71] Milliken, in the last face-to-face encounter with his opponent, looked at Levin on the "Lou Gordon Show" and questioned "your credibility, your sense of responsibility," on tax issues,[72] and called Levin's position on Proposal C "insincere and impractical."[73]

The 1974 election was a triumph for the Democratic party around the nation and throughout Michigan. All of the incumbent congressmen, including two who had been elected during the same year in special elections, were reelected. Two Democratic challengers defeated Republican congressmen, and one Republican changed parties. In the state legislature, Democrats captured 24 of 38 seats in the state senate and 66 of 110 seats in the state house. For "the first time in a decade, Democrats will control both chambers in the Michigan legislature when it convenes in January."[74] Democrats easily won the elections for seats on the three university boards and the state board of education. It was the worst year for the Republican party since the Goldwater debacle of 1964. Richard Nixon and Watergate hung over every Republican candidate like an incubus. Democrats won almost everything in sight by doing nothing more than being the only available alternative to the party that had been led by the first president ever to resign from office. Democrats won almost everything, but they did not win what Michigan Democrats wanted most of all. They did not win the governorship; they did not even come close. Milliken defeated Levin by a margin substantially greater than the 44,000 votes that had separated them in 1970. This time Milliken received 1,333,693 votes, or 51.6 percent, to Levin's 1,221,293 votes, or 47.3 percent.[75] Despite all the effort Levin had devoted to winning the favor of suburban voters, and despite his deliberate attempt to associate himself with Proposal C (which passed by an overwhelming majority)—despite all this, Milliken ran better in the suburbs than he had in 1970. In Warren, for example, Milliken increased his vote from 21,196 to 22,590, while Levin's vote declined from 29,406 to 24,880.[76] In an editorial, the *Grand Rapids Press* explained why it thought Milliken had won. The governor's victory "was grounded on integrity and sincerity. The Governor never minced words about his opposition to the popular food tax repeal, and he never dodged the possibility that the state might be forced into increasing other taxes soon."[77]

Notes

1. *Grand Rapids Press*, October 16, 1974.
2. Voting statistics from: Michael Barone, Grant Ujifusa, and Douglas Matthews, *The Almanac of American Politics 1978* (New York: E. P. Dutton, 1977), pp. 497–506; *Congressional Quarterly Weekly Report*, November 9, 1974, p. 3087.
3. Barone, Ujifusa, and Matthews, *Almanac of American Politics 1978*, p. 433.
4. *Congressional Quarterly Weekly Report*, July 27, 1974, p. 1961.
5. Barone, Ujifusa, and Matthews, *Almanac of American Politics 1978*, p. 433.
6. *Congressional Quarterly Weekly Report*, July 27, 1974, p. 1961.
7. *Detroit Free Press*, August 8, 1982.
8. Barone, Ujifusa, and Matthews, *Almanac of American Politics 1978*, p. 433.
9. Ibid.
10. *Congressional Quarterly Weekly Report*, November 9, 1974, p. 3087.
11. State of Michigan, *Official Canvass of Votes 1972*, p. 68.
12. *Lansing State Journal*, September 15, 1974.
13. *Lansing State Journal*, October 16, 1974.
14. Ibid.
15. Ibid.
16. *Lansing State Journal*, October 17, 1974.
17. State of Michigan, *Official Canvass of Votes 1974*, p. 86.
18. Hillel Levin, "The Next Deal: Jim Blanchard," *Monthly Detroit*, September, 1982, p. 58.
19. Ibid., p. 54.
20. Ibid., p. 58

21. Ibid., p. 120.

22. *Milliken v. Bradley,* 418 U.S. 717 (1974). The decision was written by Chief Justice Burger. Justices Douglas, Brennan, Marshall, and White dissented.

23. Levin, "The Next Deal," p. 120.

24. Barone, Ujifusa, and Matthews, *Almanac of American Politics 1978,* p. 433.

25. Levin, "The Next Deal," p. 120.

26. Barone, Ujifusa, and Matthews, *Almanac of American Politics 1978,* p. 433.

27. *Congressional Quarterly Weekly Report,* August 10, 1974, p. 2140. The numerical vote count was: Blanchard, 16,356; Nowakowski, 11,614; Webb, 14,815.

28. Levin, "The Next Deal," p. 120.

29. *Congressional Quarterly Weekly Report,* November 9, 1974, p. 3087.

30. Barone, Ujifusa, and Matthews, *Almanac of American Politics 1978,* p. 399.

31. Donald W. Riegle, Jr., *O Congress* (Garden City, N.Y.: Doubleday and Co., 1972).

32. *Lansing State Journal,* August 2, 1972.

33. *Detroit News,* November 6, 1974.

34. *Congressional Quarterly Weekly Report,* July 27, 1974, p. 1961.

35. Ibid.

36. Ibid.

37. *Detroit News,* July 29, 1974.

38. *Congressional Quarterly Weekly Report,* August 10, 1974, p. 2140.

39. *Detroit News,* August 7, 1974.

40. Ibid.

41. *Detroit News,* August 7, 1974.

42. Tacitus *Histories* 2.83.

43. Dudley W. Buffa, memo to Sidney H. Woolner, September 11, 1974.

44. *Congressional Quarterly Weekly Report,* May 4, 1974, p. 1105.

45. *Grand Rapids Press,* October 20, 1974.

46. Ibid.

47. "Levin for Governor budget," October, 1974.

48. Michigan Democratic Party, "Democratic Party Campaign Budget," (internal document, October, 1974).

49. Ibid.

50. *Detroit News,* November 6, 1974.

51. Joyce Braithwaite, letter to author, December 12, 1982.

52. *Grand Rapids Press,* October 16, 1974.

53. Robert Longstaff, *Grand Rapids Press,* October 20, 1974.

54. Two months after the 1974 election, Philip Van Dam, special assistant to United States Senator Robert Griffin, who had taken a leave of absence to work full-time in the Milliken campaign, thought it impossible that Levin could purposely have taken the position he did.

55. *Michigan AFL-CIO News,* October 17, 1974.

56. Ibid.

57. *Grand Rapids Press,* October 30, 1974.

58. Ibid.

59. *Detroit News,* October 6, 1974.
60. *Detroit News,* October 20, 1974.
61. *Detroit News,* November 3, 1974.
62. *Grand Rapids Press,* October 22, 1974.
63. Ibid.
64. Quoted in *Detroit News,* November 3, 1974.
65. *Grand Rapids Press,* November 2, 1974.
66. Philip Van Dam, interview with author, January, 1975.
67. *Grand Rapids Press,* November 3, 1974.
68. *Detroit News,* November 3, 1974.
69. *Detroit Free Press,* November 3, 1974.
70. *Detroit News,* November 4, 1974.
71. *Grand Rapids Press,* November 4, 1974.
72. Ibid.
73. *Detroit News,* November 4, 1974.
74. *Detroit News,* November 6, 1974.
75. *Congressional Quarterly Weekly Report,* November 9, 1974, p. 3087.
76. *Detroit Free Press,* November 6, 1974.
77. *Grand Rapids Press,* November 7, 1974.

CHAPTER 6

The Year of the Long Shot, 1976

In 1972, Richard Nixon destroyed George McGovern, and the Democratic party seemed on the verge of destroying itself. Two years later, the Michigan Republican party watched with incredulity as two supposedly safe Republican congressional seats were lost to the Democrats in special elections. In the general election the results were even worse. From a majority of twelve among the nineteen-member congressional delegation, Republicans fell to a minority of only seven. On the state level, they found themselves for the first time in a decade facing Democratic majorities in both houses of the legislature. The governing boards of the three major universities, as well as the state board of education, were all controlled by the Democratic party. The offices of secretary of state and the attorney general remained in Democratic hands, and only two of the seven state supreme court justices had been nominated in a Republican state convention.

Despite the extensive losses sustained by the state Republican party in 1974, Michigan Democrats were far from jubilant. It was all well and good to add a few more votes to what had already been a substantial Democratic majority in the United States House of Representatives; it was a source of some satisfaction to now control both houses of the state legislature instead of only one; it was obviously important to reelect Richard Austin as secretary of state and Frank Kelley as attorney general; and it was undoubtedly a significant achievement to elect Democrats to local offices in counties where that had almost never happened before. But William Milliken still sat in the governor's office, and for the first time in American history, a Michigan Republican occupied the White House. With the 1974 election over, and every active politician's attention immediately directed to 1976, the advantage seemed actually to lie with the Republicans. A Republican president could be expected to pay special attention to the economic and political needs of his home state, and a Republican governor could be expected to do everything he could to avoid the political embarrassment that would follow the failure to deliver Michigan to Gerald Ford. For a time, however, there was a

danger that William Milliken would find himself unable to deliver Michigan
to Gerald Ford even in a Republican primary.

In 1972, over the vigorous opposition of the UAW, the Democratic state
central committee had decided by a majority of only a single vote to endorse
the principle of a Michigan presidential primary. The youthful supporters of
George McGovern saw a primary as a means by which both to remove
political decisions from the self-interest of the politicians and to return power
directly to the people. A number of Democratic leaders and almost the entire
leadership of the UAW and the AFL-CIO, on the other hand, believed that a
presidential primary would grievously reduce the ability of political parties to
influence the selection of their own nominees. This, it was feared, would be
particularly true in Michigan, where there was no party registration and where
anyone, Democrat, Republican, or independent, could vote in any primary he
or she wished. With no real contest for the Republican nomination, the only
issue was who would face Richard Nixon in the general election, and that, of
course, was to give a powerful incentive to Republican and independent
participation in the Democratic primary. Labor's point of view did not prevail
either in the state central committee or in the state legislature. With the
Republican governor giving full expression to his own belief that a presidential primary would help cleanse the political process of the corruption of party
politics, Michigan adopted a presidential primary. When George Wallace,
and not George McGovern, carried 52 percent of the vote in the Democratic
primary in May, labor was not surprised. And neither William Milliken nor
any other member of the Republican leadership seemed the least bit distressed
about the discomfort experienced by a Democratic party that after decades of
devotion to civil rights now found itself obligated by state law to support the
candidacy of George Corley Wallace.

In 1976, as in 1972, the president was a Republican and a candidate.
Unlike Nixon, however, Ford faced a serious contest for the nomination.
Though Ford had been associated with nearly every conservative cause possible to imagine during his quarter century of service in the Congress, Ronald
Reagan still commanded the primary allegiance of conservatives in the country. Despite his apparent affability, the former California governor did not
hesitate to challenge a president of his own party once he decided he might
have a chance to win. A major part of the Reagan strategy was to win "open"
primaries that permitted conservative Democrats to cross over and vote in the
Republican contest. . . ."[1]

[The] Michigan primary on May 18 loomed as a potential disaster for the President. Ford's home state's primary voting system was a particular invitation to
crossovers; unlike some states where voters had to declare publicly in which

party primary they wished to participate in order to obtain the proper ballot, Michiganders had complete anonymity.[2]

There was a real danger "that great numbers of the 809,000 Wallace voters of 1972 would invade the Republican primary—or return to it—to vote for Reagan."[3]

Governor Milliken insisted that "The President can't afford to lose Michigan. And he won't."[4] But his ability to keep that promise was much less than what it would have been if, instead of supporting, he had opposed the presidential primary bill four years earlier. Michigan's Republican state central committee, along with those of Ohio, Pennsylvania, and New York, had "responded almost at once with endorsements" when Ford declared his candidacy,[5] but the party organization no longer had the power or the authority to determine the membership or the political loyalties of the Michigan delegation to the national convention. Because of Michigan's Republican governor, Michigan's Republican president would have to expend both time and money to campaign for the eighty-four convention votes of his own home state. The Wallace phenomenon was proving to be a force that could not be confined to the politically pleasant pastime of making life miserable for the Democratic party.

If the leadership of the Michigan Republican party had ever really believed that the Wallace constituency was entirely or even mainly composed of voters who would only vote Democratic, Ronald Reagan did not share their perception. From the very beginning of his Michigan campaign, Reagan said all the things Wallace supporters wanted to hear. He called busing to achieve racial balance in the public schools a "failed social experiment," and therewith not only repeated the Wallace position but ingeniously recalled the populist attack against "pointy headed bureaucrats" and the evils of liberal social engineering. On the ban against school prayer he did little more than paraphrase Wallace when he remarked: "I've told people if we get government out of the classroom, we might get God back in."[6] There was little if anything George Wallace had said in 1972 that Ronald Reagan did not repeat in 1976. That he did so with a manner more unassuming and urbane than Wallace's might lessen the animosity of moderates; it did nothing to loosen the attachment of conservatives.

Reagan's appeal to the Wallace constituency produced more than the ordinary number of political ironies. William Milliken discovered that the only clear result of his professed desire to place the selection of a presidential nominee somehow above politics was to place himself in a position where he could feel compelled to utter such statesmanlike remarks as the promise that Michigan would be "the state where the celluloid candidacy of Ronald Reagan will be exposed."[7] William McLaughlin, the Republican state chairman, who had not disagreed with the governor's support of the presidential primary bill, claimed that what had then been a matter of high principle now provided an opportunity for a dangerous expediency. In a statement that raised the political practice of insincerity almost to the level of an art form, the Republican chairman, who had not objected when George Wallace appealed for Republican votes in 1972, said he was "completely shocked at Governor Reagan's blatant appeal for Democrats to give him the presidential nomination of the Republican Party."[8] To make certain that no one could possibly think that the Michigan Republican party, led by Governor Milliken and chairman McLaughlin, could possibly object to anything on narrowly political grounds, McLaughlin invoked the sanctity of the American two-party system: "By encouraging Democrats to create mischief in our primary, he severely damages our vital two-party system."[9] Then, as if that were not enough, McLaughlin advanced the precise argument the UAW had used four years earlier in its unsuccessful effort to block the presidential primary.

> It is and must remain the prerogative of a political party to choose its own candidates. That prerogative no longer exists when one party has control of the decision-making process in both parties. . . . This tactic makes a mockery out of our party's nominating process and seriously threatens the destruction of the Republican Party.[10]

William McLaughlin was now in complete agreement with Sam Fishman and Bill Marshall. It was of far greater importance to McLaughlin that, as it turned out, he was not in agreement with either the governor or the president.

Strict adherence to the doctrine of the separation of the parties was a principled position that the Republican chairman had adopted on eminently practical considerations. The leadership of the Michigan Republican party was unanimous in its support of Gerald Ford and united in its determination to repel the candidacy of Ronald Reagan. If Reagan was making an appeal to Democratic voters, then it was only sensible to find or invent some ground on which to attack him for pursuing his own advantage. The tactic of the chairman, however, did not receive the endorsement or the support of Michigan's two most powerful elected Republican officials. Both Governor Milliken and Senator Robert Griffin, each of whom was very good at grasping the essentials of a political situation, realized what McLaughlin seems somehow to have forgotten: that Michigan Republicans were successful only when they were able to attract the support of Democrats and independents. They had no principled objections to employing in a primary the same weapons they had learned to use with such effect in general elections. Not only Milliken and Griffin but "the President, himself, began to appeal directly to Democrats and independents to crossover and vote for Ford, not Reagan."[11] Campaigning in

Detroit, Ford did not hesitate to announce, "I want every person registered in the state to vote for me, whether they call themselves Democrats, Republicans, or independents."[12] The president also "appealed unabashedly for special treatment as a native son."[13] During the final weekend of the Michigan campaign, Ford whistlestopped on a train between Flint and Niles, "plaintively asking the home folks not to forget one of their own."[14] Rising above the consistent application of principle, William McLaughlin failed to reprimand the president for this shameless appeal for Democratic help to determine the outcome of the Republican primary.

With each candidate and nearly every Republican public official appealing to everyone to vote in the Republican primary whether they considered themselves members of the party or not; with Michigan voters given their first, and depending on the result, possibly their last opportunity to cast a ballot for the state's first president; and with civic pride and partisan advantage working in almost natural harmony, the turnout was beyond anything Michigan had ever seen. More than twice the number of people who had ever voted in any statewide Republican primary voted in the Republican presidential primary. Nearly a million of the state's 4.6 million registered voters marked ballots for either Gerald Ford or Ronald Reagan. When it was over and the tabulation complete, Ford had 65 percent of the vote and Reagan only 34 percent.[15] Of the eighty-four convention votes to which Michigan was entitled, Ford had won fifty-five and Reagan twenty-nine. It seemed an impressive victory for the president, but Michigan was Ford's home state, and a substantial winning margin did little more than meet the expectations of the media and the public. Ford had won fifty-five more votes toward the number necessary to secure the nomination. Reagan, however, had twenty-nine when without the presidential primary William Milliken had been so eager and labor so unwilling to hold in 1972, he might not have had any at all.

While Gerald Ford easily defeated Ronald Reagan in the Republican primary, Jimmy Carter, who three weeks earlier had enjoyed a lead of more than two-to-one over Congressman Morris Udall, did not do nearly so well. This was far less interesting and in the long run far less important than the fact that the success or failure of Jimmy Carter in the spring of 1976 should have any significance at all. Less than a year before, in the summer of 1975, Carter had arrived in Detroit and had had a very difficult time seeing anyone. When he walked into the office of Mayor Coleman Young, the mayor was unavailable, and Malcolm Dade, who handled political matters in city hall, hastily gathered a few people together to avoid embarrassing the former Georgia governor. For similar reasons, the editorial staff of the *Detroit Free Press* quickly brought together a few writers to conduct an interview with the visiting candidate for the presidency. Carter, it was clear, had absolutely no chance of ever becoming a serious candidate for the Democratic nomination. A year earlier, however, he had done something in Michigan that perhaps more than anything else eventually brought him the nomination and the presidency.

In the early spring of 1974 the Wayne County Democratic committee was planning its annual fund raising dinner, the Wayne County Soiree. Several nationally known Democrats had been invited to speak at the dinner, but none of them had been able to accept. When no one could think of anyone else to ask, Bernard Ryan, a member of the state party's field staff whose responsibilities included much of Wayne County, mentioned a new name. Jimmy Carter, former governor of Georgia and now in charge of the Democratic National Committee's congressional campaign committee, was supposed to be "willing to go anywhere." More out of desperation than from any feeling of enthusiasm, Ryan was told to find out if Carter would speak at the gathering. Ryan reached a Carter aide by the name of Hamilton Jordan, who accepted the invitation on the spot. "As soon as I said the Wayne County Democratic Committee, Jordan said: 'That's where Detroit is isn't it?' When I told him that was where it was all right, Jordan said, 'We'll do it.' He didn't say he'd get back to me. He didn't say he had to confirm it with Carter. It was Detroit and they wanted it."[16] Carter spoke at the Wayne County Soiree, but his speech did nothing to improve his prospects, and no one who sat in the audience that evening had any reason to expect more of him after he had finished than they had before he began. Leonard Woodcock, however, was not in the audience. He was sitting right next to Carter on the dais, and they talked throughout the dinner. The next morning, Jimmy Carter and Leonard Woodcock met for breakfast.

Though Robert Strauss, Democratic national chairman, did not regard the chairmanship of the 1974 congressional campaign committee as anything very important when he offered it, Carter used it to advantage. "In Washington, Carter worked with Bill Dodd, political director of the United Auto Workers, and Mike Miller, political director of the Communication Workers. It was the Georgian's first chance to get a good feel for the union leaders who are so important to any Democrat who wants to win in the northern industrial states."[17] No other union leader, however, did as much for Carter as Leonard Woodcock. The president of the UAW was reported to have seen "another Kennedy in Carter,"[18] but in fact he saw something more. Woodcock once explained to Danny Sain, UAW political coordinator in Region 1-C, that "I was for John Kennedy with my heart and I was for Lyndon Johnson with my head. With Jimmy Carter it's both my heart and my head." Though only Woodcock himself knows precisely when he decided to support Carter for the Democratic nomination, it was undoubtedly very early, much before any public declaration was ever made. In the Iowa caucuses in January, 1976,

Carter scored his first victory, one without which his campaign, which depended entirely on winning early to establish the candidate as a serious contender, might not have been able to continue. The UAW, which had not endorsed any candidate, "played an important role" in Carter's success.[19] It was in Florida, however, that Leonard Woodcock and the UAW helped Jimmy Carter establish himself not simply as a respectable candidate but as the Democratic front-runner.

Shortly after the 1976 presidential election, Jody Powell, reflecting on the Florida primary, remarked:

> One of the major things that we had going for us against George Wallace in Florida was that Jimmy Carter was a Southerner also, and we could profit from that by convincing people that Carter was a Southerner with a real chance to win the nomination. . . . Our win in New Hampshire had a greater impact, I think, on Southern voters than it did on the rest of the country.[20]

According to Jimmy Carter, George Wallace "had told Floridians that a vote for him would 'send a message to Washington.' A vote for me, I told them, would send a President there."[21] Carter's greatest advantage in Florida, however, especially in relation to the larger purpose of winning the nomination, was the very presence of George Wallace. Southerners might be persuaded that Carter was a southerner who could win; liberal Democrats did not need to be persuaded that Wallace was a southerner who must lose. Carter understood this liberal antipathy to Wallace and exploited it for everything it was worth. It proved to be worth a great deal. "Using the argument that he alone could eliminate Wallace, Carter . . . persuaded some of the major candidates to stay out of the state. . . ."[22] Mo Udall was one of the candidates who stayed out. Udall's "liberal supporters came to him and said the Carter people had convinced them it was essential to beat Wallace, and they would probably wind up being Udall delegates anyway."[23] Udall did not object. The strategy would save him time and money without any damage to his own prospects: "I didn't think that the party was really going to nominate Jimmy Carter. If Carter could be used as an engine to destroy Wallace, well, then, fine."[24] Udall would soon learn that instead of his using Carter to eliminate Wallace, Carter had used Wallace to eliminate him.

Employing almost Machiavellian ingenuity, Carter had convinced several Democratic candidates, including Udall, to let him perform the supreme service of ending the Wallace threat early in the campaign. Though there is reason to believe that Leonard Woodcock had already decided to do everything he could to advance the Carter candidacy, nearly everyone at the time believed Woodcock was helping Carter in Florida only for the temporary purpose of defeating George Wallace. Elizabeth Drew, for example, reported that "Woodcock's effort is for the purpose not of electing Carter but of defeating Wallace—reducing Wallace as a threat in Indiana and Michigan."[25] Woodcock himself did nothing to discredit the theory. When he "showed up at a dinner party Carter attended in St. Petersburg Woodcock emphasized to reporters that he was not making any endorsements at the time. Not yet. But he also spoke very warmly, very openly, about Carter."[26] He did much more. He campaigned actively for Carter throughout Florida, and more importantly, organized the large number of UAW retirees who lived there into a formidable campaign apparatus for Jimmy Carter.

With the support of Leonard Woodcock and the UAW and with the financial assistance of those liberals like Max Palevsky who had been led to believe that supporting him was the way to destroy George Wallace,[27] Jimmy Carter won the Florida primary and seemed to demonstrate that Iowa and New Hampshire had been a sign more of strength than of luck. Late in the evening of the primary voting day, Leonard Woodcock sat in a Florida motel room with several of the leaders of his union, among them Buddy Battle, director of UAW Region 1-A. Battle was the only black regional director, and his region, which included most of Detroit, contained much of the union's black membership. Though Coleman Young would later earn the reputation as the first major black public figure in the North to endorse Jimmy Carter and would as a consequence receive the gratitude, and Detroit the generosity, of President Carter, the mayor's boyhood friend, Buddy Battle, became the first northern black with any substantial power to move toward Carter when he told Woodcock that "I can live with the guy."[28] None of the other UAW leaders present expressed dissatisfaction with Woodcock's obvious enchantment with Jimmy Carter. Mo Udall might continue to believe that while Carter had "been masterful at getting Leonard Woodcock to endorse him 'just for Florida,' "[29] the UAW president was not yet fully committed; but in fact it was no longer a question of what the UAW was going to do, but of when it was going to do it.

In a real sense the May 18 Michigan presidential primary campaign began on Saturday, April 10, when Michigan Democrats held their annual Jefferson-Jackson Day Dinner. The candidates for the Democratic nomination had been invited to attend and address the dinner, and three of them, Jimmy Carter, George Wallace, and Mo Udall, had accepted. When Carter arrived in Detroit that afternoon he was met at the airport by Leonard Woodcock and the mayor of Detroit. Coleman Young had been convinced by his close friend and assistant, Bill Beckham, that Carter was going to win the Democratic nomination and would very likely be the next president of the United States. Young, whom Beckham described even in private as a "political genius," did not need to be told of the advantages available to those who walk early with winners. Woodcock reportedly informed Carter that to be completely acceptable to organized labor he would have to endorse rather than oppose the principle of national health insurance, a concept that Walter Reuther had made almost a cornerstone of the UAW's social agenda; then he accompanied Carter to a rally at UAW Local 174. Carter, using a line that he recited more and more frequently as his candidacy came closer to its ultimate objective and that he never accompanied with a smile, informed his audience that he "did not intend to lose."[30] Although Woodcock "said he wouldn't announce his support for a Democratic presidential candidate until more primaries are held, his attendance clearly indicated he is leaning toward support of Carter. He admitted he is 'very sympathetic' toward him."[31]

Woodcock's feelings about Jimmy Carter were not shared by all of organized labor, or even, interestingly enough, by everyone in the UAW. At almost the same time that Woodcock was standing beside Jimmy Carter at Local 174, Bill Marshall, president of the Michigan AFL-CIO, Tom Turner, president of the Metropolitan Detroit AFL-CIO council, and Paul Treska, director of the United Transportation Union, along with Ken Bannon, a UAW vice-president, endorsed the presidential candidacy of Senator Henry Jackson. Douglas Fraser, UAW vice-president and CAP director, who had failed by only a single vote to become the union's president upon the death of Walter Reuther and who everyone understood would assume the presidency upon the retirement of Leonard Woodcock, was not inclined to support Carter, Jackson, or any other of the declared candidates. Clinging to liberalism while nearly everyone else was looking for something else, Fraser was "urging" the last of the unrepentant New Deal liberals, Hubert Humphrey, "to begin actively campaigning for the nomination."[32] With Woodcock and Fraser in apparent disagreement, UAW-CAP, the political arm of the union, "refused to endorse anyone for the May 18th primary."[33]

On the evening of the Jefferson-Jackson Day Dinner, when the Secret Service finished their normal "sweep" of the place where in this instance three presidential candidates were going to appear, the doors of Cobo Hall were opened, and the 2,500 Democrats who had paid fifty dollars apiece for the privilege of eating a barely digestible meal while listening to a series of speeches that were likely to be barely audible in a room that was more fit to be an airplane hangar than the site of a public forum, began to file in. Phil Hart found his friend, Congressman Lucien Nedzi, and the two of them headed for a holding area where the dignitaries who were to sit at the head table gathered to await their entrance. While Jimmy Carter presented himself, at least to northern Democratic liberals, as the latest and most successful of the enlightened governors of the New South, the transformation of race relations was most clearly exemplified that evening when Phil Hart took his seat on the dais immediately to the right of George Wallace. Hart, who had served as floor manager in the Senate for the Voting Rights Act of 1965, a bill that more than anything else had enfranchised the black population of the southern states, and Wallace, who had gained national attention by his defiance of the federal government's imposition of desegregation, treated each other as if they were veterans of an ancient war in which the memory of the battle was more vivid than the causes of the conflict. Hart believed Wallace to be utterly sincere when he remarked that during his few days of local campaigning he had sensed that race relations were more on edge in Detroit than in the cities of the South. The senator thought that the observation was interesting and that it just might be true.

The struggle for civil rights in the South, like the Civil War itself, had been a conflict in which the lines were drawn with clarity and precision. Phil Hart and millions of Americans had insisted that black citizens be accorded nothing more and nothing less than the same legal protection for their constitutional rights as white citizens. George Wallace and millions of Americans, including most white southerners, declared that the segregation of the races was the rightful prerogative of the southern states. Hart had won and Wallace had lost. The equality of the races was now embedded in federal statute and enshrined as an unbreakable principle of constitutional law. The question of race, however, as George Wallace himself had shown by his shrewd exploitation of the busing issue in the Michigan presidential primary in 1972, was still a reality in American politics. In 1976, race and region again played a part in a presidential primary, but this time they were surrounded by irony and enveloped in ambiguity. One of the earliest of the ironies was the very fact that on the dais were another liberal Democratic member of the Congress and another former southern governor, and the latter, not the former, had the endorsement of the first black mayor of Detroit.

Jimmy Carter had the support of Coleman Young, but while the candidates spoke, Morris Udall had the attention of the audience. Carter's speech was a repetition of what had by now become his routine promise of a ''government as good as our people.'' The speech was uninspiring, and Carter gave it in a high-pitched, sing-song fashion that made it almost completely unintelligible. At one table near the very front of the hall, several members of the congressional staff debated whether if Carter were elected he would become the first American president to require the regular services of a speech therapist. This was clearly cruel, but it also clearly illustrated the growing belief that Carter, who had no obvious qualifications for the position, was very close to achieving what only a few months earlier had been a ludicrous impossibility, the Democratic nomination for the presidency. Udall, who understood as well as anyone how formidable Carter had become, began his speech by confessing that he had arrived in Michigan depressed because

Coleman Young and Leonard Woodcock and a number of others had indicated support or sympathy for the Carter candidacy. But then, Udall continued, his spirits lifted and his hopes soared when he noticed as he entered
the city limits that the sign on the boundary read: "Welcome to Motown."

After the laughter subsided, Udall, with a thoughtfulness that was both
rare and intelligent, remarked that the current system of selecting nominees
for the presidency was all wrong. Instead of demanding that candidates demonstrate their ability to convince others to support them, "we should simply
look around the country and find the most qualified person there is and then
insist they represent our party. If we did that, there is no question but that the
Democratic nominee for President would be Phil Hart." With an imposing
manner and a voice that could be heard as clearly at the back of the room as at
the front, Udall devoted the rest of his speech to a firm defense of Democratic
liberalism. It was a speech that in another time might have been given by
Hubert Humphrey to an audience of Michigan Democrats who loved and
believed every word of it. Udall struck a chord, but it seemed to be one more
of memory than of excitement. Still, his was clearly the dominant performance of the evening, and had the Michigan primary been decided on the
basis of the candidates' abilities to address an audience, Udall would have
won an overwhelming victory. It was not the rhetorical abilities of the candidates, however, that would be decisive on May 18.

Walking out of Cobo Hall after the dinner, Phil Hart was still impressed
with how well Udall had spoken in defense of liberalism. Almost as if he were
a little angry with himself, he said: "I don't know why I haven't endorsed
him." When his assistant replied, "Well, then, why don't you?" Hart answered, "I probably should." Within a week Hart had done precisely that. It
was not, however, the endorsement of the Democratic senator but that of the
president of the United Automobile Workers of America that carried with it
the power of the most formidable political organization in Michigan. On May
7, Leonard Woodcock finally announced formally his endorsement of Jimmy
Carter for the Democratic nomination. Henry Jackson had dropped out of the
race, and Hubert Humphrey had decided not to get into it. The choice had
narrowed to Morris Udall and Jimmy Carter. That made it easier for Woodcock to obtain the agreement of those, like Ken Bannon and Douglas Fraser,
who had not shared his initial enthusiasm for Carter, but it had nothing to do
with Woodcock's own decision. When he made his endorsement, Woodcock
revealed what those within the inner circles of the UAW leadership had
known for months: "I had made up my mind a long time ago to be for
Governor Carter."[34]

The Michigan presidential primary had become essentially a two-man
race. George Wallace was entered, but after Florida he was no longer considered a serious threat to repeat or even come close to what he had done in 1972.

Carter had done what he had promised northern liberals he could do if left alone to confront George Wallace in the South. With Wallace almost certain to run a very poor third, Mo Udall was the only remaining source of potential trouble, and Udall did not appear to have any chance at all. Udall did have the endorsement of Phil Hart and John Conyers, but Carter, who had appealed to the peculiar American identification of honesty with innocence by insisting that he "scorn[ed] organization support and endorsements," had "the endorsements and backing of Leonard Woodcock, of Henry Ford II, and of Mayor Coleman Young."[35] Though Woodcock, Young, and Ford "represented constituencies that at times would barely speak to one another,"[36] and their combined support was therefore considered formidable, Carter also had an even more solid source of strength in Michigan.

When Jimmy Carter first began thinking seriously about running for the presidency, Peter Bourne, a psychiatrist and one of his advisors, wrote a lengthy memo in which he analyzed the American psyche and predicted that in 1976 the people would want nothing so much as a candidate who represented the simplicity and honesty that seemed to have characterized the country before the apparent complexity of present day problems and the obvious corruption of the recent administration of Richard Nixon.[37] This analysis led directly to Carter's almost unprecedented and sometimes embarrassing emphasis on personal honesty and the basic goodness of the public. It also led to something else, something that was more subtle, and in Michigan at least, probably more effective. Jody Powell understood what it was.

> I think people draw an artificial distinction between what's an issue and what's a non-issue. . . . People all over the land were looking for something they thought they had known once and somehow had lost touch with. I think that pine trees and home towns said something even to people who had never seen a small town.[38]

In Michigan, Jimmy Carter represented home in more than a symbolic sense. Most blacks who lived in Michigan had been born in the South, like Coleman Young, or had been born to parents who had migrated to the North in search of a better life. Blacks, who for obvious reasons did not support George Wallace in 1972, felt a kinship with Carter that could not be explained by any of the usual political indices. Carter was a white Baptist, and many of Detroit's blacks belonged to black Baptist churches; both were southern Baptists and both had been a victim of the South's "peculiar institution." For northern blacks the legacy of slavery had not been extirpated by civil rights laws and economic opportunity. They had been forced to flee their American origins, and if they had found some small measure of freedom in the North, they had been forced to pay the price of a people twice uprooted. For southern white politicians, especially one like Carter who had played with the race question but never quite exploited it like a Lester Maddox or a George Wallace, there was a long legacy of national disdain. The South suffered the indignities of sectional inferiority. Blacks had been deprived of freedom, and whites had been deprived of respect. Black and white together shared in the sense of common defeat. Jimmy Carter represented the promise that the years of victimization had had a value; they had made possible the redemption of Lincoln's promise of a "new birth of freedom." The candidacy of Jimmy Carter meant that the South had finally changed and that northern blacks could look back on their southern home without further fear.

It was a tribute both to the new improvement in race relations and to the political sophistication of Jimmy Carter that the "mystic chords of memory"[39] that tie both a people and a culture together attracted not only black but southern white residents of Michigan as well. Southern whites were the second largest ethnic group in Michigan, and the southern home they remembered had nothing in it of racial equality. Carter, like George Wallace, had been a southern governor, and while Wallace's record on race relations had been decidedly in favor of white supremacy, Carter's had not been clearly or consistently in support of racial equality. Remer Tyson, the political reporter for the *Detroit Free Press,* had worked for Carl Sanders when Carter defeated him for the Democratic nomination for governor in 1970 and had not forgotten that Carter had won by appealing to "the red-neck vote."[40] Reg Murphy, editor of the *Atlanta Constitution,* agreed. He contended that "Carter beat Sanders . . . with a blatant appeal to the Ax-Handle King's [Lester Maddox] white racist constituency."[41] Carter had even gone so far as to state that he would consult frequently with Alabama Governor George Wallace.[42] Carter had of course hung a portrait of Martin Luther King, Jr., in the state Capitol building, but that, according to Murphy, "was cosmetic, the kind of calculated gesture Jimmy Carter is skilled at making whenever he wants to cover up some ugly political truth about himself."[43] Carter's record on race relations was sufficiently ambiguous to permit both blacks and whites to see in him the representation of what home was supposed to be. The Carter campaign, while it appealed for the black vote through Coleman Young, assumed that "a healthy share of" the "1972 Wallace voters would go for Carter."[44]

With such important endorsements and such a substantial base in the electorate, "Carter and his strategists felt good about Michigan."[45] Carter assumed "he had the Michigan primary against Udall well in hand,"[46] and, according to Jody Powell, "everybody thought Carter ought to go into Maryland, and so we did it."[47] The decision to leave Michigan in the hands of the established political organizations of Coleman Young and Leonard Woodcock so that Carter could go to Maryland and call California Governor Jerry Brown an opportunist because he had associated himself with established political organizations was based on more than feelings and assumptions. Three weeks before the May 18 primary, Carter was leading Udall, fifty-two percentages points to nineteen. The Udall campaign "just assumed we were going to lose and lose badly."[48] That Udall was even in it at that point was only because "we also thought we just might be able to hang on to the end—because if we did, and if the convention was truly an open convention, we thought Mo just might be able to end up as Vice-President."[49] Still, while Udall was behind in the poll by a considerable margin, Peter Hart, who was polling for him, noticed that of the 52 percent who indicated a preference for Carter, only 21 percent expressed strong support, while 31 percent were "weak" in their support. Moreover, "almost half of his weak supporters agreed that he was fuzzy on the issues and that he was all things to all people."[50]

Morris Udall had believed at least as early as the Florida primary that Carter had received support from a great many people who did not believe he had any chance to gain the nomination, much less the presidency. Liberals, according to Udall, had "felt it was nice to have a fresh voice, and wasn't it great that you had a reasonable, sensible, Southern Governor in the contest. But they weren't really looking at him closely and saying, 'Do I want this man to be President. . . .'" Once Carter had become the leading contender for the Democratic nomination, however, all of a sudden "they're all saying, who is he and what does he stand for?"[51] Peter Hart's polling data indicated clearly that what liberals had begun to ask was a question on which Jimmy Carter seemed vulnerable with the electorate as a whole. Though Udall at first rejected the suggestion of a negative campaign, he relented once he realized there was really no other way to win. When Peter Hart and the leadership of the Udall campaign "met to discuss Michigan there was a definite decision that both media and candidate would go negative because it was the only way left."[52] As he campaigned across Michigan, Udall began to employ what he called "Udall's Quick Carter Quiz," "a checklist . . . asking questions about where Carter stood on welfare reform, right-to-work, and the reduction of specific federal agencies."[53] They were difficult questions to answer. On each of the issues Udall raised, Carter had, at some point in his political career and even at some time in his campaign for the presidency, made utterly contradictory statements. The same tactic was used with devastating effect in a television commercial in which actor Cliff Robertson read Carter's conflicting statements while a cartoon figure of Carter rotated, showing in constant alteration the famous smile and the then not so well-known Carter frown. The Carter campaign viewed the use of Carter's own words as a personal attack and the expression of political desperation.

Udall had become increasingly resentful of Carter's ability to attract support of widely divergent constituencies through the use of apparently inconsistent statements on matters of major importance. The congressman was even more annoyed with liberals who failed to recognize that there was only one liberal candidate left, and that it was not Carter. On May 13, Udall, while campaigning in Saginaw, accused both Leonard Woodcock and Coleman Young of deserting the principles of liberalism for the pursuit of power. "I don't see how Young can turn his back on me," Udall complained. "He and the UAW just want to win."[54] Coleman Young certainly wanted to win, and he proceeded to give Udall something he could really complain about. The day after Udall charged Young with forgetting his past political beliefs, Young charged Udall with not having sufficiently rejected his past religious affiliations. Speaking to a gathering of Detroit's black Baptist ministers, a group that formed the basis of the most extensive political network in the city, Young sought to use the religion of the two candidates to divide them on the basis of race: "I am asking you to make a choice between a man from Georgia who fights to let you in his church, and a man from Arizona whose church won't even let you in the back door."[55] Udall was a Mormon who years earlier had publicly broken with that church's belief that its priesthood and heaven were both open only to whites. Udall demanded an apology, but Young, who had succeeded in reminding the black community that Udall was a Mormon from the distant West, while Jimmy Carter was a Baptist from the South, refused.

The campaign had become far more bitter and vindictive than anyone had imagined it would, and far closer than anyone had thought possible. On the Sunday before the election, Detroit's most controversial and most widely followed television commentator and newspaper columnist, Lou Gordon, endorsed Morris Udall—or more accurately, attacked Jimmy Carter. After citing several of the most damaging accusations of Robert Shrum, who had recently resigned as a Carter speech-writer because of what he considered the political and moral hypocrisy of the candidate, Gordon went after Carter with a vengeance. According to him, Carter was guilty of "a degree of manipulation and deception" unlike anything encountered in any previous political campaign. "I have been around politics and politicians for 30 years and I have never known anyone who fooled so many people for so long with a smile and guile." Gordon could remember someone to compare Carter with, however, and it was not a comparison that many others had yet begun to make. "There is too much of Richard Nixon in Carter and frankly that is frightening."[56]

While the public was being entertained with what had suddenly become a spirited exchange of bitter attacks on the credibility of the candidates, the UAW was engaged in a campaign to convince its own membership to support the candidacy of Jimmy Carter, a campaign made unusually intense by the absence of a formal endorsement. When Leonard Woodcock publicly threw his support to Carter on May 7, it was taken as tantamount to an endorsement by the 1.3 million-member union over which he presided. In this instance, however, Woodcock dispensed with the procedure by which any political endorsement had first to be recommended by the executive board and then ratified by a convention of CAP delegates. Deprived of the opportunity even to cast a ballot, much less express an opinion, on the question of which candidate the union should support, some elected leaders of a few locals scattered throughout the state were resentful. Most, however, hid any reservations they might have had and operated as if nothing out of the ordinary had been done. The UAW had perhaps the most thoroughly democratic procedures for its own internal governance of any union in the country, but when the single most powerful member of the union chose not to employ them, dissent was far from vigorous.

Had there been a formal endorsement by the UAW, the lives of the union's political operatives would have been considerably easier in the spring of 1976. A formal endorsement would have placed the prestige of the union on the line, but because every member of the union could be said to share in that prestige, though some obviously shared larger portions than others, failure would have been felt by the institution as a whole, and in a manner of speaking, distributed among the membership. Once Leonard Woodcock made a personal, as distinguished from an institutional, endorsement, failure would also be personal. Woodcock, the scholarly, self-assured president of the UAW, who could have easily passed as the scholarly, self-assured president of Harvard University, never did anything casually, and his endorsement of Carter was one of the most serious commitments he had ever made. The political staff of the union understood that and all the ramifications that followed from it. Though the procedure for the selection of UAW officials is very democratic, the relationship between the elected officials and their appointed staff is not. In keeping with the UAW's long tradition of obeisance to the forms of equality, Woodcock and Sam Fishman called each other by their given names, but the real nature of the relationship was revealed when a visitor remarked to Fishman that he was having a difficult time making up his mind who to support in the May primary. Fishman, with a look of detached bemusement, replied: "I don't have that problem. Leonard made up my mind for me." Political operatives further down the line found themselves too exhausted for either detachment or bemusement. In Region 1-E, one of regional director Bard Young's staff assistants paused in his labors only long enough to complain about the pressure he was working under: "Leonard really wants this one and my ass is on the line." He understood, as did every other union operative, that if Carter lost, Woodcock would be embarrassed, and he might find himself exchanging a position of political influence for a return to the tedium and anonymity of life on the assembly line.

Jimmy Carter had decided to concentrate his own efforts in Maryland instead of Michigan because of his belief that he could rely on the efforts of Coleman Young and Leonard Woodcock. Neither had held anything back. Young had mobilized the black Baptist ministers and much of the black community. Woodcock had marshaled his political cadres and mustered the resources of the union to turn out a Carter vote among the membership of the UAW. On election day, however, Hamilton Jordan was no longer confident of victory: "I don't like it. I just don't like it. . . . It's slipping away. It's that damn crossover."[57] In a poll conducted Sunday evening, Pat Cadell had detected an interesting and ominous phenomenon. Democrats were deciding to vote in the Ford-Reagan primary, and most of the crossover was coming from those who had previously expressed their preference for Jimmy Carter. "Sunday night," according to Cadell, "it all came apart. We'd lost eight percent in crossovers. I really hit the panic button. Soon ten points of our twenty-point lead was gone in a matter of twelve hours."[58] If the trend continued the race would be even twenty-four hours later on the Monday evening before the election. When Monday evening arrived, Cadell began to believe Carter might actually lose. It was "the worst night of the campaign."[59]

Jimmy Carter's remarkable climb from obscurity to the presidency has sometimes been compared for sheer improbability to Harry Truman's miraculous victory in 1948, an upset enshrined for the ages in the day-after photo of a grinning Truman holding up the morning edition of the *Chicago Tribune,* which announced the election of Thomas Dewey. Truman had gone to bed a certain loser and awakened in the morning to the news of his reelection. After he left the presidency, Truman spoke in Michigan at a Jefferson-Jackson Day Dinner. Tom Quimby was then the Democratic national committeeman and was given what to him was the distinct honor of looking after Truman during his short stay. When it came time to say good-bye, Quimby remarked with great courtesy, "Mr. President, it has been an honor for me to be with you. I have always admired you and especially your ability to reach a decision and not to look back. I have never forgotten the way everyone counted you out in 1948 and you just went to bed election night and did not even know you had been re-elected until the next morning." Truman looked at Quimby for a moment as they stood alone in his hotel suite and then smiled slightly and said, "Well, you know, I'm an old man, and old men have to get up in the middle of the night to take a leak." Truman had known the result before he awoke in the morning.

Jimmy Carter claimed that on the night of May 18 he had acted much as Truman supposedly had: "I never thought I was going to lose in Michigan all through the night. . . . I went to bed fairly early when I was ahead, and when I woke I knew I'd won."[60] Carter, who was not nearly as old in 1976 as Truman had been in 1948, apparently did not have any need to awaken in the middle of the night. But the truth about Harry Truman was somewhat different from the legend, and the truth about Jimmy Carter was rather different from his claim.

According to a reporter who was with him at the time, on the night of the election:

> Carter sat in his suite watching the returns. He sat slumped in a chair, staring at the television, his face mirroring concern, frustration and disappointment. But when he went downstairs to greet his supporters in the hotel ballroom and to be interviewed by reporters, he was smiling, apparently happy and confident and very much turned on.
>
> He told reporters about how his delegate totals had climbed significantly that night. . . . He smiled, he waved, he shook hands, and then he rode the elevator upstairs and went to bed, an unhappy winner.[61]

Whether he had gone to bed confident, disappointed, or simply puzzled, when he woke up, Jimmy Carter had lost in Maryland and won in Michigan, 306,352 to 304,213,[62] a margin so small that the Udall campaign treated it as a victory. David Olmstead, the chairman of the Michigan Carter campaign, only added to the impression of failure by claiming that he had warned Atlanta weeks earlier of what might happen and that his warning had been ignored. Olmstead was not heard from again. Carter had nearly lost and had only won because of the margin he had rolled up outside the metropolitan area. In Detroit and its suburbs, he carried only the two black congressional districts, the First and the Thirteenth. Udall defeated him in every other district in southeastern Michigan. Two years later Coleman Young would explain Carter's failure to do better by pointing to a picture on the wall behind his desk in which Carter stood with the mayor, Leonard Woodcock, Henry Ford, and Chrysler president John Riccardo. For Coleman Young it was obvious: "Hell, which one do you hate?" There might have been a racial backlash by some white voters who were either not from the South or were too prejudiced against blacks to support a southern white who was not. The new face of Jimmy Carter might have become too familiar. Udall might have caught Carter in enough inconsistencies and contradictions to create distrust in the mind of the electorate. All of this might have been true, but the outcome was more than anything else based upon "the low Democratic turnout. . . ."[63] Half of those who had voted for George Wallace in the 1972 Democratic primary voted in the Republican primary. "Those that stayed in the Democratic column," according to the *New York Times*, "voted heavily for Mr. Carter, suggesting that he may have done much better had the Wallace people not been permitted to wander."[64]

Carter might have done better had half the Wallace vote not crossed over, or crossed back, to the Republican primary. That Carter won at all, however, was the result of the endorsements of Leonard Woodcock and Coleman Young. While, as the *Times* noted, "a large percentage of the auto workers' membership in Michigan is composed of white Southerners and blacks, groups that have strongly supported Mr. Carter elsewhere,'' and he might therefore "conceivably had done as well without Mr. Woodcock,'' he did remarkably well with him. "Mr. Carter got almost two-thirds of the UAW votes, which comprised an astonishing 30 percent of the total, while losing among other union members."[65] Among black voters, two-thirds voted for Carter, while only one-third supported Mo Udall. Leonard Woodcock and Coleman Young were both entitled to the gratitude of Jimmy Carter.

In the early spring of 1975, Senator Henry Jackson, then one of the leading candidates for the Democratic presidential nomination, held a press conference in Troy to announce that attorney general Frank Kelley would serve as chairman of his Michigan campaign committee. After the press conference, John Bruff and Sam Fishman, both of whom were sympathetic to the Jackson candidacy, had dinner together. Fishman, Bruff, and the other members of the small group that had helped elect Morley Winograd chairman of the state party had continued to meet regularly to plan party strategy and coordinate political tactics. In recent weeks they had begun to discuss possible candidates for the Democratic nomination to succeed Phil Hart, should Hart decide not to seek a fourth term in the Senate. Though Bruff liked Hart, and Fishman had an almost unbounded affection for him, neither one of them really wanted him to run again. Within the political leadership of the UAW, and among those Democratic party officials who like Bruff had been through the ravages of the busing controversy of 1972, the working assumption was that a Hart candidacy would probably fail and would almost certainly jeopardize the chances of other Democratic candidates who were on the same ticket. A number of potential candidates had come under review, but Bruff thought the most formidable one would be the secretary of state, Richard Austin. Though busing had driven large numbers of the residents of Bruff's Macomb County into a frenzy, and though Bruff had, largely for that reason, expressed in no uncertain terms his hope that Phil Hart not run again, the fact that Austin was black did not diminish his enthusiasm in the least. In the case of his closest friend, Jim O'Hara had been right in 1972 when he suggested it was possible to oppose busing and be utterly blind to color.

Sam Fishman and John Bruff were not the only ones who were actively engaged in exploring senatorial possibilities. Between November, 1974 and June, 1975, nearly every Democrat who hoped one day to sit in the Senate visited Phil Hart and encouraged him to run for a fourth term. Then, with differing degrees of hesitation, they would add that if, however, he should decide not to run again, they themselves might want to consider seeking the position. Hart would hear them out, thank them for their suggestion that he stay, and, using almost precisely the same words each time, tell them that he would not feel at all offended if they began to spend time getting around the state to become better known. Some took the words to mean what they said, while others read into them their own private ambitions. Congressman Donald Riegle, for example, claimed later that the senator had told him he had decided not to run. Hart viewed Riegle's claim with the contempt it deserved. Riegle, however, did not go so far as Congressman Richard VanderVeen of Grand Rapids, who, within days of his conversation with Hart, began to tell others that not only was the senator not going to seek reelection, but that he, Richard VanderVeen, was Hart's own choice to succeed him.

While some professed to know what Hart was going to do, and others speculated about the consequences that would likely follow either of the choices he might make, the senator kept his counsel.[66] Unlike some of the leaders of the party and the UAW, he had no doubts about his ability to win a fourth term. His reservations were instead about whether he could carry out the responsibilities of the office for another six years. He would be seventy years old at the end of another term, and as he put it, "I feel fine now, but at my age you really can't assume that you're going to be able to function fully a few years from now. I've seen too many people carried out of this place." Despite those reservations, it was not at all clear what his decision was finally going to be. It was not even clear when he announced that he had made it. At a press conference held just before the annual Oakland County Phil Hart Day Dinner in April, he replied to a reporter's question about his future plans by saying he knew what he was going to do but was not yet prepared to reveal what it was. It was a mark of the respect he commanded that none of the reporters present pressed him to do so. After the dinner, however, his own special assistant, who had heard enough intimations and drawn enough inferences about what Hart was going to do to have contracted an advanced case of severe schizophrenia, could no longer contain himself: "Tonight you tell them you've made up your mind and you know what you're going to do. I can't help it. What is it? Are you going to run or not?" Hart managed to base his refusal to answer on his concern for the continued honesty of his assistant: "If I don't tell you then you won't have to lie when someone asks you what I'm going to do. You can say you don't know and mean it." The logic was impeccable, and the cheerfulness in the smile on the face of Philip Hart unforgettable.

On June 5, 1975, Philip Hart placed a brief statement in the *Congressional Record.* It began simply, "Mr. President, I would like to announce that I will not seek re-election." He went on to give a brief explanation.

> At difficult moments, politicians have a tendency to fall back on tried and true sayings, but at least on some occasions, such sayings are right on target.
>
> At this moment in my life, that is true of these words: "Eternal vigilance is the price of liberty."
>
> Those words imply that frustrations will be encountered, and no one should enter

politics who does not expect and is not willing to accept frustrations as part of the job.

Those words make clear the continuing effort which should be made by a person who would be elected to public office, and no one should run for office unless he believes that he will have the energy and stamina to be fully vigilant for the entire term sought.

And, finally, those words emphasize that no one institution is all important, and that the guard should be changed with some regularity.[67]

For Phil Hart, "the time has come to change at least this part of the guard." Two months after this announcement the senator was informed he had cancer. He would die in the last week of what he had decided would be his last term.

For a time it seemed that every able bodied Democrat in Michigan was at least thinking about becoming a candidate for the United States Senate. But when the deadline finally came for filing for a place on the primary ballot, there were only four candidates. One of them, James Elsman, was given no chance of winning the nomination, though he would damage the prospects of one of the others. Each of the other three had impressive credentials, and, at the beginning, each of them could entertain a rational expectation of success. Of the three, two— James G. O'Hara and Donald W. Riegle, Jr.—served in the House of Representatives and thus had had the best possible preparation for a seat in the Senate. The third, Richard Austin, was Michigan's secretary of state, a position that provided the sort of administrative experience that was almost perfectly worthless in the Congress. However, the office had a statewide constituency, and that gave Austin an enormous advantage in name recognition alone. While O'Hara and Riegle were well known in their respective districts, there were nineteen congressional districts in the state, and only Austin was well known in all of them. When the race for the Democratic nomination to succeed Phil Hart in the Senate began, almost everyone not directly associated with the campaigns of Riegle and O'Hara assumed that Austin was certain to become the first black nominated by the Democratic party for the United States Senate in the history of the republic. Though rigorously neutral in the primary, Phil Hart privately assumed the same thing and wondered how Washington would react to a black senator who, unlike the Republican Edward Brooke, was more interested in the legislation of the Congress than the social life of Georgetown. "Austin," as the senator put it, "could do a lot of good here." Only a major mistake or the active intervention of organized labor seemed likely to deprive Austin of the opportunity to run in the general election in November.

If labor was going to support anyone in the Senate primary, it did not seem possible it could be anyone other than Jim O'Hara. For eighteen years O'Hara had represented labor's interests in the Congress and had become one of the most accomplished legislators in the House. In the last public appearance Phil Hart ever made, he remarked, "there have been few men and women through these halls who have had that quality which constitutes my definition of 'craftsman' in the field of honing legislation Jim O'Hara has."[68] O'Hara had decided to give up a long career in the House for the chance to begin a new one in the Senate at least in part because he had become convinced that he would have no real future if he stayed where he was. He had tried a few years earlier to win a leadership position with the Democratic majority and had failed. The Senate offered new hope, and hope is of all things the most difficult to resist.[69] With his distinguished record, his long and close association with organized labor, and his position as a suburban Democratic congressman who represented a blue-collar constituency, O'Hara could expect that those to whom he had given service would now give him support. He did obtain the formal endorsement of the state AFL-CIO, though that was more the work of Al Barkan in Washington than of Bill Marshall in Lansing; and he did receive most of the $218,000 he was able to raise from trade union contributions;[70] but he did not receive the one thing that might have made a difference, the endorsement of the UAW.

When Leonard Woodcock endorsed Jimmy Carter in the Michigan presidential primary, the only other candidates for the Democratic nomination who had had any serious support among the members of the UAW executive board, Hubert Humphrey and Henry Jackson, had either withdrawn from the race or decided not to enter it. Had there been a competing candidate with support on the executive board, Woodcock might still have endorsed Carter and might still have been able to carry the union and its political apparatus with him, but the task would have been more difficult and more unpleasant. Thus the absence of any candidate who both appealed to their political principles and had a reasonable chance of capturing the nomination made the executive board more willing to support Woodcock's choice; but there was also a very good reason for them to go along with it. As Coleman Young had understood, the Democratic nomination was almost certain to go to Jimmy Carter, and the individuals and institutions that supported him early would have the largest claims on his future allegiance. Both the personal conviction of Leonard Woodcock and the self-interest of the union favored endorsement in the presidential primary. Neither the personal preferences of the members of the UAW executive board nor the union's interest supported endorsement in the Senate primary.

Though each of them had acquired their own positions through a majority vote, there was an understanding among the regional directors who served on the governing board of Michigan CAP that an endorsement of a candidate running for statewide office could only be made if there was unanimous agreement among them. This gave to each of them the power effectively to veto an endorsement that all the others might wish to make. It was a power that protected a director from the awkward situation that would be created if he found himself compelled to oppose a candidate who came from his own region. Endorsement in a contested primary presented the possibility of problems easily avoided by a policy of neutrality. If this was to the advantage of the regional directors, it was not in any way damaging to the interests of the union. A candidate for the presidency who obtained the Democratic nomination without the active assistance of the UAW might be able to ignore the demands of the union, but the Democratic nominee for a Senate seat from Michigan could not. A Democratic candidate for the U.S. Senate or any other statewide office needed the UAW if he were to have any chance at all of defeating the Republican candidate in the general election. From the point of view of sheer self-interest, the union, with a few exceptions, the most important of which was its endorsement of Sander Levin in the 1970 gubernatorial primary, generally found very little to be gained by getting involved in a party primary.

The normal reluctance of the UAW to take sides in a Democratic primary was compounded and intensified in 1976 by the question of race. Although some black labor leaders, like Tom Turner of the Metropolitan Detroit AFL-CIO, privately tried to think of ways to persuade Richard Austin not to become a candidate; and although some white Democrats wondered whether black UAW leaders like Marc Stepp and Buddy Battle, who were both more closely aligned with the mayor of Detroit than with the secretary of state, really wanted Coleman Young to become only the second-ranking black public official in Michigan, no black UAW leader had any interest in publicly opposing a black candidate for the United States Senate. Nor was the UAW as a whole eager to find itself the major source of opposition to the nomination of the secretary of state, who, it must be remembered, was not only black, but the overwhelming favorite to win the Democratic primary. Moreover, no union official, black or white, wanted a repetition of the internal difficulties of just a few years before, when the union had endorsed Mel Ravitz and the black leadership had campaigned for Coleman Young.

There were obvious reasons not to endorse one of Austin's opponents, but there were also reasons not to endorse him. Although some of the party and labor leadership feared that Austin would win the primary and then, because of his race, lose the general, that was not the reason the UAW adopted a position of formal neutrality. It was instead because Jim O'Hara and Donald Riegle each had at least one regional director who would refuse to support and could thus prevent an endorsement of either of the other candidates. From the point of view of the union as an institution it was just as well: whoever won would require the help, and therewith place themselves in the debt, of the UAW.

The union's policy of neutrality was not rigorously followed in every region. Nowhere was violation more flagrant than in Region 1-C, where Don

Ellis, the regional director, did everything he possibly could to help Riegle. Acting as if the UAW had announced its endorsement rather than its neutrality, Region 1-C actually contributed $5,000 directly to the Riegle campaign. Ellis would undoubtedly have given more, but that amount was the maximum contribution permitted by federal law. While Region 1-C blatantly ignored the decision of the international, several union retirees who had recently served on the staff of the UAW-CAP quietly appeared on the campaign payroll of Jim O'Hara. Salome Williams, who had retired from her position as Sam Fishman's secretary, became O'Hara's scheduler, and Russ Leach, who had been a political operative in the union for years, worked as a field organizer. Not everyone was prepared to ignore or forget O'Hara's long association with labor or his innumerable legislative contributions to the welfare of the American working class.

Without the endorsement of the UAW, O'Hara had very little chance to overtake Richard Austin, no matter what individual members of the union might do. O'Hara was one of the most effective legislators in the Congress and one of the least inspiring candidates for statewide office. The attention to detail that marked his work in the House doomed his candidacy for the Senate. James O'Hara was brilliant within an organization and thoroughly unable to generate the public enthusiasm required to build a political organization of his own.

If O'Hara seemed too prosaic a figure to attract broad support or even widespread attention, the other congressman in the race, Donald Riegle, appeared too compulsively demagogic to threaten seriously the large lead Austin already enjoyed. Riegle, who presented himself as the most egalitarian of liberals while he was in the process of seeking to deprive a black Democrat of the Senate nomination, attacked Austin directly, not on the ground of race, but on that of age. Without the slightest compunction or the least hesitation, Riegle "stressed his youth and activism and criticized Austin for attempting to begin a Senate career at age 63."[71] With a zeal that was almost indistinguishable from fanaticism, Riegle, who had wanted to run against Phil Hart in 1970, ran against Austin by telling every Democratic voter he could corner that "what this country and state need in the Senate is a fighter—and one young enough to stay there for awhile."[72] His remarkable energy was expended not only in attacks on Austin, but on raising more money than anyone ever before had for a statewide Democratic primary. While O'Hara raised $218,000, Riegle had more than $300,000 to spend on his Senate campaign, much of it from sources outside Michigan, including, for example, three $5,000 contributions from dairy interests.[73] He spent it as fast as he raised it; at one point he "was buying television advertising at the rate of about $25,000 a week. . . ."[74] There was never enough. At the Democratic national convention in New York, Riegle cornered delegates and tried to convince them that their financial contribution to his campaign would make the difference between victory and defeat.

Because of his persistence and because he had begun years earlier to cultivate potential contributors in, among other places, southern California, Riegle was able to outspend Austin by more than $170,000.[75] No one had really expected him to raise that much money, but then no one seriously thought it would do him much good. With only two weeks remaining before the primary election, Richard Austin, according to the *Detroit News*, enjoyed a substantial and seemingly safe twenty-seven-point lead.[76]

The *News* poll gave 44 percent of the vote to Austin, with 17 percent for Riegle and only 12 percent for O'Hara. That was a large lead for Riegle to overcome, but it was smaller than the one he had faced earlier in the summer. Riegle, however, had had less to do with the reduction than had a candidate with no chance whatever to finish higher than last. James Elsman was a practicing attorney who had run unsuccessfully for Congress and had now decided to seek defeat in a larger arena. Elsman was known within party circles not only for his willingness to lose but for the unusual lack of grace with which he did it. In 1976 he appeared less interested in winning himself than in somehow making certain no one else did. Whenever there was a joint appearance of all the Democratic candidates, Elsman could be counted on to attack O'Hara for his labor support and Riegle for the special interests that were contributing to his campaign. The most vicious and devastating attacks, however, were reserved for Richard Austin. "Elsman accused Austin of coercing managers of the branch offices, some of whom held their offices as Democratic Party patronage, to make contributions to the Austin campaign."[77] This was hardly a major revelation. In Michigan, the managers of the branch offices "routinely have turned back part of their incomes to the party or the secretary of state as the price of holding office."[78] More precisely, branch managers who were appointed by the secretary of state returned 10 percent of their net proceeds to the secretary, who in turn split it evenly with the state Democratic party, an arrangement that brought the party between $65,000 and $75,000 each year.[79] Austin, however, and there was irony sufficient for a political lifetime in this, had been trying to end the arrangement for some time. He had begun "phasing this practice out during his term, and more than half the offices," were "now under civil service."[80] An even larger number would have been transformed from patronage to civil service positions had it not been for both the reluctance of the fee managers to have their incomes reduced and the resistance of their state legislators to have one of their most reliable sources of campaign contributions eliminated.

Elsman's accusation might have been passed over as the empty outrage of an embittered man had not the Austin campaign engaged in a questionable practice and then employed a dubious strategy. It was an open secret within the Democratic party that whether Richard Austin knew it or not, his deputy, Walter Elliott, held meetings with the branch managers and assigned to each of them the amount he or she would be expected to contribute to the campaign. The branch managers were placed in an unenviable position. They were being told that they must contribute to a campaign which, if successful, would cost them what in many cases were jobs more remunerative than anything else they were likely to find. If Austin won, he would go to the Senate, and the next secretary of state would be appointed by a Republican governor. To say the least, it was doubtful they would be asked to stay on in their patronage positions. Not only were they being told, in effect, to buy themselves into unemployment, the price was expensive. The federal election law limited individual contributions to a candidate for federal office to $1,000, but as was explained to them with great patience and clarity, the law permitted everyone, including the husband or wife or even the children of each branch manager, to contribute that much. Those branch managers who found themselves faced with an assessment of more than $1,000 were made to understand that federal law should be no hindrance to their compliance.

With all the fee managers involved it was impossible to keep the meetings a secret. Those who supported other candidates in the Senate primary did not hesitate to use to advantage the information supplied by a disgruntled or indiscreet branch manager. The press was soon demanding that the Austin campaign make a full disclosure of all its financial dealings. In reply, Austin "called for an audit by the IRS, the Michigan Revenue Department, and the Fair Campaign Practices Commission," but he refused "to allow reporters to examine the records."[81] The press reacted in the way anyone, including the Austin campaign, could have predicted they would. Remer Tyson of the *Detroit Free Press* regarded Austin's refusal to let him examine the records as a personal affront. He explained to an assistant of Senator Philip Hart that he would now go after the story until he found something. The "something" was not difficult to find. By examining campaign finance reports, the *Detroit News* was able to demonstrate an interesting pattern of campaign contributions among the branch managers. According to the *News*, "Austin appointees, their spouses and relatives account for more than $50,000 of the $130,000 he had raised. . . ." In "at least 15 instances, spouses or relatives of Austin appointees contributed amounts up to $1,000."[82] When added to the appointee's contribution, more than the $1,000 permitted an individual contributor was received. The *News* correctly pointed out that there was nothing illegal about what it nevertheless described as "double-dipping."[83]

More damaging than the reports of campaign contributions by the branch managers and their relatives; more damaging than the disclosure that the fee system had generated nearly a million dollars in patronage for the secretary of state and the Democratic party;[84] more damaging than any suggestion that politics, as the famous Mr. Dooley had once remarked, "ain't beanbag," was a present the branch managers gave Richard Austin. Lou Gordon, who had been outraged by Austin's refusal to appear on his show with the other candidates, reveled in revenge when he recounted what others had already revealed, that Austin had received a $2,850 air-conditioning system for his home. Austin claimed he had not known anything about it and that when he did find out, "it had already been installed when I arrived home. I was embarrassed and raised hell about it." But, as Austin put it, "what can you do? This is the kind of gift that can't be returned." He claimed that he did not have the money to reimburse the managers, but Gordon reported that Austin made up to $57,000 a year as secretary of state.[85] Gordon predicted that Riegle would win.

A week before the election, the Riegle campaign announced that the Austin lead had been cut to only 3 percentage points. Austin, according to the Riegle poll, was supported by only 32 percent of the electorate, while Riegle had increased his following to 29 percent.[86] There was already a widespread suspicion that Riegle invented whatever polling data he needed, and his "opponents doubted the results" of this latest poll.[87] Austin had undoubtedly been harmed by the adverse publicity of the previous few weeks, but few people saw anything more than illusion or deception when Riegle predicted on the day before the election "a major upset in the making."[88] Everyone believed him, however, when, less than six hours after the polls closed, he said in his suite at the Pontchartrain Hotel, "I think it is clear that we've won."[89]

Few Democrats had expected Riegle to win, and no one had expected him to win by a substantial margin. He received, however, fully 43.6 percent of the vote, while Austin received only 28.8 percent. O'Hara was close behind with 23.2 percent, while for all his trouble Elsman finished a dismal fourth with only 4.4 percent.[90] Riegle had done well throughout the state. He carried his own county, Genesee, by a margin of four-to-one, and defeated Austin by margins of two-to-one in Saginaw and Washtenaw counties and by a margin of three-to-one in Bay County. In Wayne County, supposedly the stronghold of Austin support, Riegle lost narrowly, amassing 98,000 votes to Austin's 100,000.[91] While Austin had little to say after the primary, and O'Hara "blamed his defeat on misleading polls and media failure to adequately cover the campaign," Riegle "interpreted his victory to mean 'that what the people are saying is they want a fighter for constructive change in the U.S. Senate. I'm that fighter.' "[92] The fall campaign would give him more opportunity to prove it than he could possibly have imagined.

The victory of Donald Riegle in the Democratic Senate primary destroyed the political career of James G. O'Hara and seriously disrupted plans for the complete restoration of the old Democratic coalition. Had O'Hara won the nomination, those within the labor movement and the party leadership who believed the party had to recapture the allegiance of the white working class by supporting a liberal economic policy and a conservative social policy would have had their theory confirmed and their power increased. O'Hara, however, had lost, and the Democratic nomination belonged to a candidate who had actually sought to distinguish himself from O'Hara on the ground of their disagreement on the question of affirmative action for women. Riegle had played to the liberal wing of the Democratic party while O'Hara had deliberately practiced what he called the "old politics." While O'Hara accumulated the endorsements of trade unions, Riegle appealed directly to the electorate through the mass media. The most liberal of the three candidates for the nomination had won, and contrary to the central assumption of those who advocated the restoration of the old Democratic coalition, the liberal Democrat entered the general election as the decided favorite in a race with a moderate Republican.

During the primary campaign, Riegle, "the most accomplished media stroker, once became so agitated that he barked to a reporter that he had done everything to get press attention short of 'pulling down my pants in front of city hall.' "[93] It was not necessary to do anything so extraordinary to receive attention in the general election. Like Jimmy Carter's emergence from political obscurity to capture the presidential nomination, Riegle's remarkable victory in the primary supplied nearly instant fame. In September, instead of facing an opponent with a seemingly insurmountable lead, Riegle found himself leading the Republican candidate, Congressman Marvin Esch, by nineteen points. With the presidential campaign operating with public funding, Riegle did not have to compete with Carter for private contributions and therefore did not have to fear being buried under an avalanche of Republican money. With the full support of organized labor and the Democratic party, both of which were intent on keeping a seat that had been Democratic since Phil Hart took it away from an incumbent Republican senator eighteen years before, Riegle appeared certain to be elected in November. Even a drop in his lead from nineteen points to seven in October seemed no more ominous than the expected reduction in the margin as the election approached. Then, on Sunday, October 17, the bottom fell out.

The *Detroit News,* in a story with the lurid headline "Riegle Tapes Reveal Talks with Girl Friend," reported its acquisition of tape recordings of private phone conversations between Riegle and a young woman. "Representative Donald W. Riegle, Jr., D-Mich., in 1969 was involved with a worker in his congressional office in a torrid and tape-recorded extra-marital affair on Capitol Hill which he once described as more important that a 'lousy subcommittee hearing.' "[94] Not content with making a private matter public, the *News* provided lengthy extracts from the tape-recorded conversations. Though there is in the classical theory of democracy a clear connection between private

restraint and public responsibility, the *Detroit News* had as little understanding of that principle as it had of the basic essentials of journalistic propriety.
The intention was clearly to embarrass Riegle and thereby assist Marvin Esch.
Former Republican governor George Romney, who had actively campaigned
for Riegle when he first ran for Congress in 1966, joined in the effort by
advising the citizens of Michigan to consider the alleged affair before voting.
Though he offered no information that might satisfy a curiosity as eager to
learn about the Republican as the Democratic candidate for the Senate,
Romney suggested that when deciding between them, the public "ought to
take a look at their private life and their public life."[95]

When the *News* broke its story on what almost immediately became
known as the "Riegle tapes," Democrats generally viewed it as a new low in
the long history of political partiality in the editorial policy of the paper. That
the *News* had been unfair and unprincipled, however, did not change the
effect of its action; no one believed for a minute that it had not seriously and
perhaps fatally damaged Riegle's candidacy. After winning the nomination
because of apparent improprieties committed by Richard Austin and his campaign, Riegle, in what some saw as a kind of rough justice, seemed likely to
lose the election because of his own indiscretions. Riegle had been hurt, but
Esch had not yet won. The *Detroit News* and the Republican candidate soon
learned that it was impossible to put Riegle on the defensive. Instead of
offering meek apologies and timid explanations, Riegle reacted by attacking
the *News* for what he called "the most vicious and distorted campaign directed at anybody in politics that I've witnessed."[96] Moreover, if the *News*
was going to assist Esch by attacking him, Riegle made certain that his own
attacks on the *News* would also fall on his opponent. Though he admitted he
had no evidence of it whatsoever, Riegle, nothing daunted, charged that the
Detroit News and Marvin Esch had entered into a conspiracy to discredit him
and his candidacy.[97] The contest to succeed the single most respected member
of the United States Senate had become the least ennobling campaign anyone
could remember. Character assassination had become the common idiom of
political discourse.

On the last weekend of the 1976 campaign, no one could be certain that
Marvin Esch might not defeat Donald Riegle or that Gerald Ford might not
overtake Jimmy Carter. On the evening before the election, with everything
still in doubt, Jimmy Carter and Donald Riegle both made the last appearances
of their exhausting, dark horse campaigns in the Industrial Mutual Association
Auditorium (IMA) in Flint, Michigan. Though he really came to Flint because
it seemed the most strategic location from which to win over a large undecided
vote that could give him Ford's home state, Carter had in fact promised to
return to the city when he had campaigned there during the primary. To those
who believed in him and the promises he made, his presence seemed to bring

his strange, compelling campaign full circle. Riegle had also come full circle. He had begun his political career by upsetting a heavily favored Democratic incumbent in his first campaign for Congress. Now, only twelve years later, the former Republican congressman was returning home to make his last appeal for support in his campaign to become a Democratic member of the United States Senate. When Carter and Riegle appeared in the IMA auditorium that evening, thousands who could not get in stood in the streets and listened in the night as loudspeakers brought them the words of first Riegle and then Carter. Weeks later, Morley Winograd would say that "there was never a more exciting or enthusiastic finish to a campaign in Michigan."[98] In the excitement and enthusiasm all doubts about the outcome vanished, and everyone knew what was going to happen. The next day, when Donald Riegle was elected to the Senate and Jimmy Carter was elected president of the United States, it seemed almost anticlimactic.

Notes

1. Jules Witcover, *Marathon* (New York: Viking Press, 1977), p. 422.
2. Ibid.
3. Ibid.
4. Ibid., p. 423.
5. Ibid.
6. Quoted in ibid.
7. Quoted in ibid.
8. Ibid.
9. Ibid.
10. Ibid., pp. 423–24.
11. Ibid., p. 424.
12. Quoted in ibid.
13. Ibid.
14. Ibid.
15. State of Michigan, *Official Canvass of Votes 1976*, p. 7.
16. Bernard M. Ryan, interview with author, October 16, 1982.
17. Martin Schram, *Running for President: A Journal of the Carter Campaign* (New York: Simon and Schuster, 1977), pp. 69–70.
18. Kandy Stroud, *How Jimmy Won: The Victory Campaign from Plains to the White House* (New York: William Morrow and Co., 1977), p. 423.
19. Laurence H. Shoup, *The Carter Presidency and Beyond: Power and Politics in the 1980's* (Palo Alto, Calif.: Ramparts Press, 1980), p. 61.
20. Jonathan Moore and Janet Fraser, eds., *Campaign for President: 1976 in Retrospect* (Cambridge, Mass.: Ballinger Publishing Co., 1977), p. 88.
21. Jimmy Carter, *Keeping Faith: Memoirs of a President* (New York: Bantam Books, 1982), p. 22.
22. Stroud, *How Jimmy Won*, p. 265.

23. Witcover, *Marathon,* p. 258.
24. Quoted in ibid., p. 258.
25. Elizabeth Drew, *American Journal: The Events of 1976* (New York: Random House, 1976), pp. 75–76.
26. Schram, *Running for President,* p. 94.
27. Stroud, *How Jimmy Won,* p. 265. The same argument helped raise $25,000 from Democratic liberals in Beverly Hills, for Carter in the Florida primary. Bert Coffey, interview with author, December 23, 1982.
28. Transcript of tape recording of meeting of black political caucus, February, 1978.
29. Quoted in Drew, *American Journal,* p. 148; see also Stroud, *How Jimmy Won,* p. 258.
30. *Detroit News,* April 11, 1976. At the Democratic national convention, Carter used this same line when he spoke to the California delegation. He did not smile when he did so.
31. Ibid.
32. Ibid.
33. Ibid.
34. Quoted in *Atlanta Constitution,* May 8, 1976.
35. Drew, *American Journal,* p. 179.
36. Schram, *Running for President,* p. 162.
37. Drew, *American Journal,* p. 103.
38. Moore and Fraser, eds., *Campaign for President,* p. 90.
39. Abraham Lincoln, Second Inaugural Speech, March 4, 1865.
40. Tyson described his involvement in Georgia politics the same evening Senator Henry Jackson held a press conference in Troy, Michigan to announce the formation of his Michigan committee as part of his campaign for the Democratic presidential nomination.
41. Vic Gold, *PR as in President* (Garden City, N.Y.: Doubleday and Co., 1977), p. 15.
42. James Wooten, *Dasher: The Root and Rising of Jimmy Carter* (New York: Summit Books, 1978), p. 294.
43. Gold, *PR As In President,* p. 16.
44. Witcover, *Marathon,* p. 337.
45. Schram, *Running for President,* p. 162.
46. Witcover, *Marathon,* p. 337.
47. Moore and Fraser, eds., *Campaign for President,* p. 100.
48. Schram, *Running for President,* p. 164.
49. Ibid.
50. Moore and Fraser, eds., *Campaign for President,* p. 104.
51. Quoted in Stroud, *How Jimmy Won,* p. 258.
52. Moore and Fraser, eds., *Campaign for President,* p. 104.
53. Schram, *Running for President,* p. 164.
54. *Detroit News,* May 14, 1976.
55. *Detroit News,* May 16, 1976; see also Schram, *Running for President,* p. 164.

56. *Detroit News,* May 16, 1976.

57. Schram, *Running for President,* p. 165.

58. Quoted in ibid.

59. Ibid., p. 166.

60. Quoted in ibid., p. 167.

61. Ibid.

62. *Detroit News,* May 19, 1976.

63. *New York Times,* May 20, 1976.

64. Ibid.

65. *New York Times,* May 19, 1976.

66. When the senator had not announced his decision by the end of May, "some Democrats anxious to make a run for Hart's seat" were reported as "getting a little edgy while Hart keeps his options open by his public silence." *Lansing State Journal,* June 1, 1975.

67. Office of Philip A. Hart, press release, June 5, 1975.

68. Remarks of Philip A. Hart at reception given by the Michigan delegation to honor him and Congressman James G. O'Hara, Cannon House Office Building Caucus Room, September 26, 1976.

69. "The natural flights of the human mind are not from pleasure to pleasure, but from hope to hope." Samuel Johnson, "The Rambler," in *Works of Samuel Johnson,* vol. 3 (New Haven: Yale University Press, 1969), p. 10.

70. *Detroit News,* August 2, 1976.

71. *Congressional Quarterly Weekly Report,* August 7, 1976, p. 2155.

72. *Detroit News,* August 4, 1976.

73. *Detroit News,* August 1, 1976.

74. *Detroit News,* August 4, 1976.

75. Ibid.

76. *Detroit News,* July 20, 1976.

77. *Congressional Quarterly Weekly Report,* July 24, 1976, p. 2008.

78. Ibid.

79. Bernard M. Ryan, interview with author, November 12, 1982.

80. *Congressional Quarterly Weekly Report,* July 24, 1976, p. 2008.

81. Ibid.

82. *Detroit News,* August 1, 1976.

83. Ibid.

84. Ibid.

85. Ibid.

86. *Congressional Quarterly Weekly Report,* August 7, 1976, p. 2155.

87. Ibid.

88. *Detroit News,* August 4, 1976.

89. Ibid.

90. *Congressional Quarterly Weekly Report,* August 7, 1976, p. 2156.

91. Ibid.

92. *Detroit News,* August 4, 1976.

93. *Detroit News,* August 2, 1976.

94. *Detroit News,* October 17, 1976.
95. *Detroit News,* October 18, 1976.
96. *Detroit News,* October 17, 1976.
97. *Detroit News,* October 18, 1976.
98. *Michigan Democrat,* December, 1976.

CHAPTER 7

The Creation of a
Gubernatorial Candidate, 1978

Within four years of the election of Morley Winograd to his first term as chairman, the Michigan Democratic party had achieved a substantial improvement in the political balance of power. There were now Democratic majorities in the congressional delegation and in both houses of the state legislature. Secretary of State Richard Austin and Attorney General Frank Kelley were both reelected, and they "broke modern records for Democratic statewide officeholders, capturing 70 percent of the vote."[1] Democrats outnumbered Republicans on the state supreme court and on all of the elected state educational boards. Donald Riegle had been elected to the United States Senate, and thus the Democratic party continued to hold the seat Phil Hart had first won in 1958. Though Jimmy Carter had lost Michigan to Gerald Ford, he had won the presidency and brought to a close eight years of Republican control of the national administration. As he sought a third consecutive term as chairman of the state party, Winograd could claim with considerable justification that "In the four years since my first election, our Party has made significant gains. . . ."[2]

The increase in the number of Democrats elected to important positions of public authority had been accompanied by a steady increase in the power of the state chairman. Two years after a fight for the chairmanship that had taken two ballots and had pitted him against many Democratic liberals, most of the outstate county committees, and much of the black leadership, Morley Winograd ran for a second term unopposed. The coalition of liberals, blacks, and outstate activists that had formed to challenge him in 1973 not only acquiesced but actively supported him in 1975. Of the four co-chairmen of his 1975 campaign, three represented constituencies that had favored Robert Mitchell in 1973. State Senator David S. Holmes, Jr., chaired the black caucus and now co-chaired the Winograd reelection committee. Francis D. Brouillette was a member of the Eleventh district committee and had failed by less than a single percentage point to become a Democratic congressman from the most northern district in Michigan. Richard W. Bailey taught English at the University of Michigan and was a quintessential Democratic liberal. Betty Burch, chairman of the Sixteenth District, was the only one of the four co-chairmen who had supported Winograd in 1973 and the only one who could be said to represent the interest and the influence of organized labor.

With an unusual ability to make new friends of old enemies, Winograd had coopted, and, at least for the moment, thereby destroyed, the source of both past and potential opposition. With a shrewd understanding of the use of symbolic gestures, Winograd arranged to have Richard Austin, who had refused even to meet with him before his first nomination for the office, place his name in nomination for a second term. No one in politics is quite so grateful as someone who has failed to support a victorious candidate and is given a second chance. Austin nominated Winograd with a speech that could have been used to nominate an incumbent president. "Morley Winograd has demonstrated his conviction that a healthy party system presenting reasonable alternatives to the voters is vital to responsive government. The hallmarks of his administration have been involvement and unity." Austin seemed almost to suggest that the alternative to Winograd was economic disaster and political chaos: "As we face the challenges of the cluttered and fuzzy economic scene; as we face the crisis in leadership in government; as we face the need to attract and involve more people in the political process, I urge that we close ranks behind proven party leadership." With "full confidence and great pride," Richard Austin evidenced his new loyalty: "I nominate and earnestly urge the re-election of Chairman of the Michigan Democratic Party, Morley Winograd."[3]

When Winograd sought a third term two years later, his campaign was led not by 4 co-chairmen, but by a committee of 125 prominent Democrats from every level of public and party office and from every district and county in the state. Austin, Kelley, Coleman Young, the senate majority leader, the Speaker of the House, almost the entire Democratic congressional delegation, everyone who had run for the Democratic nomination for the U.S. Senate in 1976, and everyone except Zolton Ferency who was likely to run for the Democratic nomination for governor in 1978 lent his name to a candidacy that everyone supported and no one opposed. On February 8, the chairman announced that his name would be placed in nomination at the Democratic state convention in Detroit by the newly elected senator, Donald W. Riegle.[4] Winograd professed to be "very pleased to have Senator Riegle's support in my bid for a third term as Democratic State Chairman." With the self-assurance of a candidate who cannot lose, he added, in obvious understatement, "The overall support I have received for my candidacy is quite satisfying."[5] No one opposed him for reelection, no one spoke against him from the floor of the convention, and no one cast a single ballot against him. Morley

Winograd was elected to a third term on February 13 "by acclamation of more than 1,000 delegates at the two-day convention at Cobo Hall."[6]

Winograd and his allies in the labor movement had subjected the Michigan Democratic party to an unprecedented degree of control. Although Democratic candidates had been unusually successful under this arrangement, Republicans continued to hold the governorship, and the sixteen-year-long failure to capture the state's highest office threatened not only to limit the party's progress but to reverse it. In a document prepared to begin the planning for the party's effort in the 1978 campaign, the state chairman acknowledged that even without a Democratic governor, the party had "been able to mount vigorous campaigns and accomplish major policy objectives." The ability to do this, however, had been dependent on "the strong and enthusiastic support of the heart of the Democratic coalition-organized labor and minorities," a dependence that in turn had created a widespread belief that the party was organized to serve the needs and advance the interests of labor and minorities alone. According to Winograd, "the absence of a public presence by a Democratic executive has reinforced a perception by the electorate that that is all we stand for or care about." There was only one way to convince the electorate that the party, which was now firmly under the control of the UAW, represented a broader constituency than that of labor and minorities: "In order to correct this perception, it is absolutely critical that we win the Governorship in 1978."[7]

If the election of a Democratic governor was necessary to improve the public's perception of the party, it was essential for the continued maintenance of the existing party organization. The governor's office, in Winograd's judgment, was

> not only crucial in order to change the public's misconception of our party but also to reinvigorate our party with new support and supporters. Many dedicated people have devoted more time than is justifiable to continuing our party's efforts. Many of them however are nearing the limits of their patience or interest. If the party is to avoid being captured by those who might move into the vacuum created by the departure of our 'party regulars,' we need the excitement of running a government from the Governor's office to keep the faithful faithful.[8]

Winograd and his allies had taken control of the party in 1973 to move it away from the new politics of McCarthy and McGovern and toward the political center. Four years later, the party stood in danger of being recaptured by the liberal left unless it elected a Democratic governor. In politics, moderation was one virtue that was not its own reward.

Though planning for the gubernatorial campaign had begun immediately after the 1976 election, the events that would have the greatest effect on the

1978 campaign had their origins in the election returns of 1974. In that year, Sander Levin had been defeated by the incumbent Republican governor, William Milliken, for the second time. Levin had actually lost ground between his first and his second campaign, not only to his Republican opponent but in relation to the rest of the Democratic ticket. In 1970, Levin had fallen behind the base Democratic vote, as measured by the vote for the state board of education, in precisely those industrial counties that were the traditional source of Democratic strength. In 1974 he fell behind further still. According to a post-election analysis conducted by the state party, "Levin trailed the Board in Macomb by 16.6% or 2.9% more than in 1970; in Genesee by 14.28% or 10.48% more than in '70; Ingham 13.92% or 7.32% more; . . . Bay by 11.87% or 4.27% more; Oakland by 10.68% or 7.19% more."[9] In Wayne County, Levin trailed the board by the same 12.6 percent as he had four years earlier.[10]

A substantial number of people who had voted for Democratic candidates on most of the ballot had obviously decided to vote for the Republican candidate for governor. It was one thing to determine that ticket splitters existed; it was another to find out who they were and why they had voted as they did. The author of the party's statistical analysis of the 1974 election was prepared to offer some general observations. There were two elements of the Democratic coalition that were quite "volatile." Though Catholics had been "a major part of the coalition," their attachment to the party had eroded "especially when elections have included sensitive Catholic issues as parochiaid and abortion." The other group from which defection was most likely was what could be called the Wallace constituency, "the middle class in service occupations, the barber, sanitation worker, the hair dresser," people who were "more gut oriented voters," and who were "conservative in their social views and family oriented." The Catholics and the service workers had begun to feel alienated from the Democratic party with "the large influx of college professors, authors, the avant-garde, the liberal, issue-oriented Yankee and the rational technocrat" into the party. The only thing that could keep the coalition together was "economics; an economics of relief to the middle class taxpayers, aiding the lower class and socking it to the corporate rich."[11]

The statistical analysis did both too little and too much. It did too little because it completely ignored the impact on the electorate of Levin's inability to explain adequately how he could honestly promise not to increase taxes while supporting repeal of the sales tax on food and medicine. It did too much because it suggested that by itself a single-minded insistence on some populist program of economic class warfare could hold a coalition of diverse and often discordant elements tightly together.[12] However, it did succeed in confirming the view that was now prevalent within the party and labor leadership. Those

Democrats most willing to split their ticket and vote for a Republican at the top, whether they were Catholics who were concerned with abortion or Protestants who were opposed to school busing, were social conservatives. Any Democratic candidate who was going to have a realistic chance of becoming governor would have to be able to keep the support of these nominally Democratic and indisputably conservative voters.

The 1974 election seemed to prove that Sander Levin was not the candidate who could keep the loyalty or win the support of white working-class suburban Democrats. That was not the only lesson it offered, however. Levin had failed by a larger margin than he had in 1970. Perhaps he would have failed in any event, but it was clear that he would have done better if he had been able to match the amount of money spent by the Milliken campaign. Like every other Democratic candidate who had attempted to defeat an incumbent Republican governor, he had been badly outspent. The Milliken campaign was able to spend well over a million dollars, while Levin had less than three quarters of that amount. Of the three things Morley Winograd believed necessary if the Democratic party was ever going to elect a Governor, organization, money, and an attractive candidate, the Republicans had been matched in 1974 in only the first category. Not only did the party have to find a candidate who could appeal to Democrats of every description, but it somehow had to find a way to cancel the financial advantage typically enjoyed by the Republicans. For a time it appeared that both problems might be solved with a single solution.

On October 30, 1964, less than a week before that year's presidential election, Lyndon Baines Johnson arrived at Detroit Metropolitan Airport and announced to the thousands who had come to see just how much bigger than life he really was that "I want all of you to go to the polls early, stay late, and vote for Phil Hart all day long."[13] Caught up in the exuberance of the moment, the president of the United States had suggested publicly in Michigan what some suspected he had demanded privately in Texas in order to survive several remarkably close encounters with defeat. Though no one voted for Phil Hart or any other Democrat more than once on election day, it must have seemed to Republicans that Johnson's advice had been followed literally. For the first time since the second election of Franklin Delano Roosevelt, there were Democratic majorities in both houses of the state legislature. With both reapportionment under the new constitutional principle of "one man, one vote" and Johnson's enormous margin of victory over Barry Goldwater working against them, the Republican contingents in the state house and the senate were a shadow of their former selves. Democrats held 73 of the 110 house seats, 23 of the 38 seats in the senate, and seemed to have established a dominance that threatened to reduce the Republicans to a permanent minority. Two years later what had been reasonable expectations seemed nothing more than arrogant assumptions. After the 1966 election there was once again a Republican majority in the senate and a Republican speaker in the house.

Although the Democrats recaptured control of the house in 1968 and held it through each of the succeeding elections, they did not win majority power when the next senate election was held in 1970. In 1974, however, the Democratic party, assisted as it had been in 1964 by a new apportionment of legislative districts, finally won a majority in the senate to match its control in the house. It had not been easy. The UAW alone had contributed $17,000 to the campaign of John Otterbacher so that he might win a senate district deliberately drawn to make possible the election of a Democratic candidate from Grand Rapids. Otterbacher's victory was typical. Districts were drawn to the Democrats' advantage, and labor supplied the largest single source of the money and manpower for the Democratic candidates who ran in them. Otterbacher in Grand Rapids, Anthony Derezinski in Muskegon, Earl Nelson in Lansing, Gary Corbin in Flint, and Kerry Kammer in Oakland County were all elected to the state senate from districts that were more Democratic after reapportionment than they had been before. If reapportionment created new Democratic districts, it also rearranged old ones. On the east side of Detroit, two Democratic members of the state house gave up their seats to contest with each other the right to sit in a senate seat that had been occupied by a man who had once been one of Jimmy Hoffa's closest friends.

William Fitzgerald had first been elected to the state legislature to fill the vacancy created by the death of his father, William Fitzgerald, Sr. The son, who had graduated from Western Michigan University and gone on to become a lawyer, was better qualified for the office than the father, but he owed his election more to the name he had been given than to any degree he had earned. While William Fitzgerald, Jr., served in the house, his uncle, George Fitzgerald, who had for years been general counsel to the Teamsters and personal lawyer to Jimmy Hoffa, served in the state senate. When the uncle, whose health had been failing for some time, announced he would not seek another term, the nephew decided to quit the family tradition in the house in order to follow it in the senate. Fitzgerald won the nomination. With the nomination in hand, he turned his attention not to the general election, where the Democratic candidate had no chance whatever to lose, but to the possibility of becoming majority leader in the Michigan state senate.

While it would be unthinkable for a newly elected member of the United States Senate to so much as suggest himself for consideration as majority leader, it was not nearly so outrageous an idea for a new member of the state senate. More than a third of the Democratic members of the senate would, like Fitzgerald, be entering their first term, and Fitzgerald had already served with many of them in the state house. The new members might prefer to be led by one of their own rather than by one of those with greater seniority. This potential advantage proved superfluous. Those who were returning to the senate were far more interested in what they regarded as the source of real, as opposed to the symbols of apparent, power. Democratic senators reelected to a Democratic-controlled senate wanted the chairmanships of important committees, not the empty formalities of the majority leadership. Fitzgerald had no serious opposition for the position, but he did have a very serious ally. While neither Morley Winograd nor the UAW had as yet given much thought to whether Bill Fitzgerald should or should not be elected majority leader by the Democratic caucus, Jerry Coomes and the Catholic Conference had. With Bill Ryan Speaker of the House and Bill Fitzgerald majority leader in the senate, both houses of the legislature would be under at least the nominal direction of Catholic legislators, and the Catholic Conference would be in a powerful strategic position to thwart any attempt to pass legislation it opposed. This was eminently logical, but some thought at the time that Coomes and the Catholic Conference were looking less to what the selection of Bill Fitzgerald as majority leader might mean for legislation than to what it might do for the prospects of electing a Catholic governor.

Though none of the returning members of the senate wanted the position for themselves, nearly all of them wanted something in exchange for their support. Fitzgerald had assumed from the beginning that he could ''broker the position as majority leader,''[14] and he demonstrated the validity of that assumption by promising to each Democratic senator whatever it took to obtain his vote. Nothing was too important to be withheld, and committee chairmanships were guaranteed to members who had yet to serve a single day in the state senate. Nothing was too ludicrous or undignified to be considered, and the aspirant to the leadership of the senate agreed with apparent enthusiasm when Basil Brown, who had served in the senate longer than anyone, facetiously agreed to surrender his vote if Fitzgerald promised to water his plants at regular intervals. Through a series of such private arrangements, Fitzgerald acquired substantial support among the Democratic membership of the newly elected state senate. The UAW, which had not taken an active part in the matter during the fall, had no objection to Fitzgerald, but it did have serious concerns about the chairmanship of the Senate Appropriations Committee. State Senator Bill Huffman of Madison Heights wanted it, but the UAW preferred Senator Jerome Hart of Saginaw. With the support of labor and the many private commitments he had received in exchange for private promises, William Fitzgerald, with the vote of all but three or four of the twenty-four members of the Democratic party, was formally selected majority leader of the senate. In one of his first official acts, the new majority leader named Jerome Hart chairman of the Senate Appropriations Committee.

Bill Fitzgerald viewed his new position not as the culmination of his career, but as the means by which to advance his ambitions. He wanted to be governor, and almost as soon as he assumed his new office he set about to win the future allegiance of labor. If Fitzgerald did not want to remain very long in the senate, neither did the UAW intend to rest content with Democratic majorities in the legislature. Fitzgerald and the UAW both wanted a Democratic governor in 1978, even if the union was not yet quite so certain as Fitzgerald who that Democrat ought to be. The UAW had little difficulty convincing the majority leader that what both of them wanted required the adoption of Morley Winograd's scheme to eliminate the Republican financial advantage in gubernatorial elections. Winograd had simply suggested that the state do what the federal government had recently done. At one stroke, the Congress, in the Campaign Spending Reform Act of 1974, had removed both the influence of private money in the election of the president and the possibility that one candidate might outspend the other. Equal amounts of public money would be given the candidates of the two major parties in the presidential campaign of 1976. Winograd and the UAW could think of no reason why precisely the same arrangement should not be employed in the gubernatorial campaign of 1978. Neither could Bill Fitzgerald. Neither, oddly enough, could Bill Milliken.

Whether it was sheer coincidence, or whether Milliken wanted to enter his own reelection campaign as a Republican who favored the kind of reform then being urged in reaction to the excesses of the Nixon administration, the governor had advocated public financing in his state of the state address in January, 1974.[15] Whatever his motivations might have been, it would have been difficult for him now to oppose what he had claimed to support. With Democratic majorities in both the house and the senate, with the Democratic party and the UAW doing everything possible on its behalf, and with a Republican governor who had already publicly proposed it, Michigan became the first state in the union to pass a law providing public funding in the election of its governor. What the legislature had passed and the governor had signed was struck down by the state supreme court. The court had no constitutional objections to public financing of gubernatorial campaigns; it objected instead to other provisions of the act that established reporting requirements and expenditure limitations on lobbyists. The legislature redrafted the bill, leaving out what the supreme court had found unconstitutional, and passed it again. This time the court did not object.

Fitzgerald had played a major role in the effort to pass the law that would give the next Democratic candidate for governor financial resources equal to those of his Republican opponent. But while that seemed to increase his chances in the future, it also created a threat to his present position. At the insistence of some of the newer and more reform-minded members of the senate, the law had included limitations on the activities of legislative lobbyists and a requirement that they fully disclose their expenditures. Those measures had been opposed by a number of other Democratic senators who had served in the senate for some time and grown used to the ways of the world and the favors of friends. For them, majority power meant nothing so much as new opportunities for self-indulgence. State Senator Joe Mack, for example, did not even bother to wait for the election of a majority leader to have his senate office completely redone by an interior decorator. The considerable expense this entailed had not been authorized by anyone, but Mack, nothing daunted, had the bill paid with public funds. Another Democratic state senator, Arthur Cartwright of Detroit, was caught charging the senate for expenses he had never incurred and submitting receipts that had never existed. As the majority leader's principal assistant described it, "These guys wanted to take, take, take. Fitz tried to keep them happy without letting them steal the store. They wanted everything."[16] The one thing they did not want was the kind of reform that would subject to public scrutiny every kindness a friendly and humane lobbyist tried to perform for them. Fitzgerald, who had obtained their votes for majority leader by engaging in the same kind of personal exchange they identified with the nature of politics, seemed to them to have betrayed their trust by taking the side of labor and the state party on the issue of reform—and trust, after all, is a standard that even thieves insist upon.

The suspicion that Fitzgerald was no longer one of them ripened into certainty as the majority leader yielded to the pressure of the UAW and began to turn down their endless requests for more money with which to increase staff or enlarge and enrich their surroundings. Through its own lavish expenditures on itself, the state senate had established itself in the public mind as the proper object, rather than a possible source, of political and governmental reform. Fitzgerald had little difficulty choosing between becoming a good old boy in the senate and continuing his quest for the state's highest office. Many of the senior members of the senate had even less trouble choosing between curtailment of the constant increase in the symbols of their own importance and the removal of the majority leader. In this they were not only assisted, but largely led, by a senator who was moved less by a desire to avenge the denial of favors than by an ambition to deny Fitzgerald an office both men wanted.

In 1970, Patrick McCollough had been elected to the state senate from Dearborn largely, if not exclusively, on the strength of a last name that had been made famous and respectable by his mother, Lucille McCollough, who had served in the state house of representatives since 1954. Perhaps because both of them owed their public careers to their names rather than to their own unassisted efforts, Fitzgerald and McCollough seemed incapable of contemplating even the possibility of political failure. Fitzgerald had become majority leader and had begun immediately to use his position to build a base of support around the state. McCollough wanted to deprive his potential adversary for the gubernatorial nomination of this advantage, and if possible, secure the advantage for himself. When Fitzgerald began to move toward the more reform-minded members of the senate, McCollough began moving closer to those members for whom reform was indistinguishable from personal hardship. During all of the machinations that were involved as he sought to undermine the majority leader's support, McCollough had a powerful ally who had once served in the state house, but never in the state senate.

After leaving the house, James Karoub had become a lobbyist whose rumored associations and arrangements could be described in the words an ancient historian had used on a larger figure: "For Lucius Vitellius, despite his . . . reputation, did get things done. . . ."[17] Karoub had been the leading public spokesman among legislative lobbyists in opposition to the disclosure requirements of the reform bill of 1975. He protested that it was a serious and unconstitutional infringement of the First Amendment right freely to petition government for a redress of grievances; he was accused of trying to protect an enormously lucrative business from a public examination that by exposing the source might destroy the strength of its success. Fitzgerald had opposed him on the matter of reform, but that was not why Karoub preferred McCollough, who had himself been one of the sponsors of the legislation. Karoub's major competitor for clients was Jerry Coomes, who at one time had headed the Catholic Conference and had been instrumental in the selection of Fitzgerald as majority leader. With his close relations with not only Fitzgerald but Bill Ryan, Coomes could legitimately claim to have the best access to the leaders of each of the houses of the legislature. This was an arrangement that could conceivably threaten to reduce the long and profitable client list of James Karoub. Patrick McCollough, who wanted to be governor, and James Karoub, who wanted to influence the legislature in order to sell his influence, were in complete agreement that Fitzgerald had to go.[18] They did not agree that McCollough was the logical replacement.

When McCollough began his campaign to discredit Fitzgerald, he approached perhaps the most influential and certainly the most artful of the devotees of the old politics in the senate, Bill Huffman of Madison Heights. Huffman was a friend of Karoub, but he would not become involved in a conspiracy against Fitzgerald simply for the sake of Patrick McCollough. What he would not do for McCollough, however, he was perfectly willing to do if, as a result, his old friend, state Senator William Faust, became the next majority leader. Faust became the first choice of those determined to force the removal of William Fitzgerald. McCollough preferred himself to Faust, but he preferred Faust, or anybody else for that matter, to Fitzgerald.

While McCollough was intriguing against Fitzgerald, and Karoub was intriguing against almost everybody, the majority leader remained supremely confident of his ability to withstand a challenge from anybody. The UAW, which viewed the matter as a question of whether the state senate would be controlled by Bill Fitzgerald or Jimmy Karoub, lobbied heavily for Fitzgerald. The MEA, which was in the process of trying to establish itself as a political power, claimed that it would deliver the vote of Lansing Senator Earl Nelson.[19] Senator Daniel Cooper of Oak Park told Fitzgerald he was for him. But then so did Bill Huffman, and with enough conviction that the evening before the vote was to be taken Fitzgerald remarked that "if Huffman isn't for me I don't deserve to be majority leader."[20] Huffman was not, and Fitzgerald, whether he deserved it or not, was replaced. Senators Cooper and Nelson both attended the victory party of the new senate majority leader, William Faust. The party was held and paid for by James Karoub, who had demonstrated that on this occasion at least, he—not the UAW or the Michigan Democratic party or Jerry Coomes or the Catholic Conference—held the reins of power in the senate. Having become majority leader by agreeing to the demands of those to whom private advantage was everything and the public interest nothing, William Fitzgerald now found that his ambition for higher office had somehow made him a martyr to reform. It might not be a bad way to run for governor.

William Fitzgerald had been removed as majority leader by a vote of his Democratic colleagues in the senate, but that was a defeat that did little to diminish his prospects in the Democratic gubernatorial primary. For two years Fitzgerald had used the title of majority leader to travel the state and establish his credentials with party activists in every county and district. With the primary only eighteen months away, the former representative of the political establishment could now continue his unofficial campaign for the governorship as the new voice of reform. As majority leader he had been able to become better known than a single senator without a leadership position; as the majority leader who had been deposed by the senate's old guard, those who had begun to hear of him began to think better of him. This was true among the members of the Democratic party active in the county and district organizations; it was also true within the leadership of both the UAW and the state Democratic party.

The party and the union had begun to have serious reservations about the political reliability and public responsibility of several of the senior Democratic state senators almost from the beginning of the 1975 session. By February, 1977, matters had reached the point of an open break. At the Democratic convention that elected Morley Winograd to his third term, delegates adopted a resolution calling for an end to the seniority system in the state senate.[21] No one, least of all the Democratic senators, needed to be told who would be harmed and who likely be helped by the termination of a system in which political longevity was both the criterion and the justification for power. The

UAW had played a principal part in designing the party resolution, but it spoke in its own name to announce that state senators Daniel Cooper, Thomas Guastello, Joe Mack, and Arthur Cartwright might find themselves with union-endorsed opposition in the next election. UAW legislative director Frank Garrison left little room for doubt that the union was serious: "We've decided we're going to face this question of the Senate square on. It's the oldtimers with the long seniority who cause all the chaos and forget where the hell they came from."[22] That was only the beginning. It was not long before Senator Guastello (who, it may be noted, had made a career out of opposing his congressman, James G. O'Hara and O'Hara's closest political ally, John Bruff, on political matters in Macomb County) was summoned to Solidarity House. On the chance that Guastello and several others who were invited with him might mistakenly believe they were dealing with a few political operatives and not the full force of the second largest trade union in America, they were met by the UAW's "top brass, including President Douglas Fraser." Guastello was presented "with a list of 19 bills—ranging from consumer rights to environmental protection to political reform—on which the Senator lined up against the union."[23]

The leadership of the UAW genuinely believed that Democratic senators like Thomas Guastello had deserted the principles of the Democratic party and opposed the best interests of the union membership. That was more than enough to set in motion plans for their political destruction. The vote to remove William Fitzgerald as majority leader, however, signified more than a difference of opinion or a dispute over personalities. The union was completely convinced that James Karoub and many of the senators with whom he had the greatest influence were guilty of the worst forms of corruption. The UAW, despite its preoccupation with the forms of democracy, had very little tolerance for dissent from its own political position in any case. And when, as here, the union confronted adversaries it considered to be motivated more by personal venality than political opinion, the lines were clearly drawn, with those who were for the union on one side and those who were against it on the other. There was no middle ground. On the question of the retention of the majority leader, the UAW had not only been opposed by people it had come to despise, it had been defeated. The union would not forget either its friends or its enemies. Patrick McCollough had set out to deprive a potential rival of an advantage; he had instead driven William Fitzgerald and the UAW closer together.

Before any Democratic candidate formally declared his intention to enter the gubernatorial primary, the leadership of the UAW passed from Leonard Woodcock, who became the first American ambassador to the People's Republic of China, to Walter Reuther's designated successor, Douglas Fraser.

The elevation of Fraser was accompanied by the selection of Irving Bluestone to succeed the new president as chairman of the union's political organization, UAW-CAP. Bluestone was endowed with a remarkable intelligence surpassed by no one in either the union or the auto industry. Although his manner was not as cold as Robert McNamara's, he conveyed the same impression of controlled efficiency that McNamara had. Intelligence is attracted to itself, and in his new position of responsibility for the UAW's political interests, Bluestone quickly discerned that few legislators and none of the prospective Democratic candidates for governor could rival the Speaker of the House in either knowledge or judgment. Bobby Crim had risen from the relative obscurity of teaching in a public school to become the most powerful Democrat, and the second most powerful man, in state government. For a time he had seriously thought of relinquishing his position in the house to run for governor in 1974. Bluestone suggested he do more than consider it for 1978. Crim was agreeable, but only on a condition. The speaker was willing to campaign for the governorship, but he was not interested in campaigning for the nomination. He would run, but only if the UAW persuaded the other Democratic candidates to step aside. Even if Bluestone had been willing to attempt, the UAW no longer possessed the means to produce, this result. The public financing of gubernatorial elections that the UAW and the Democratic party had so ardently embraced as a method to eliminate the Republican financial advantage in the general election had also reduced the union's influence with potential candidates for the nomination. With public money now available to candidates in the primary, a UAW promise to either give or withhold financial assistance had lost much of its meaning and nearly all of its force. As Sam Fishman later explained it, "with public funding there was no way we could possibly get any of the other guys out of it." In 1974 Crim had made his decision to run dependent on more money than anyone was able to guarantee. In 1978 he conditioned it on an act of political power no longer possible to accomplish. In 1978, as in 1974, Bobby Crim decided that because the risks could not be removed, he would not become a candidate for governor.

In the end, four candidates entered the Democratic gubernatorial primary, and only one of them, Zolton Ferency, was well known at the beginning. In this instance, fame was not an unmitigated advantage. More people knew of Zolton Ferency than knew of any of the others or perhaps even of all of them together, but most of those who had heard of him had already opposed him on the three previous occasions when he had run for governor. With declining political appeal, he had lost to George Romney in 1966, lost the Democratic nomination to Sander Levin in 1970, and then, as if to place defeat under the protection of principle, deserted his old party to form and lead a new one (the Human Rights party) to a 1 percent share of the gubernatorial vote in 1974. Lured by the possibility of using public money to reach a wider audience and convinced that he would have a better chance to capture the nomination than someone who had never before run for statewide office, Ferency now abandoned the party he had founded and used. Masking betrayal as cleverness, he deflected attention from his own apostasy by ridiculing the faith of others. Calling himself a born again Democrat,[24] Ferency began his third campaign for the Democratic nomination and his fourth campaign for governor.

The provision of matching funds in the gubernatorial primary permitted Zolton Ferency to spend more than he had ever been able to before, but it also provided the means by which the other candidates, Fitzgerald, McCollough, and William Ralls, could become serious contenders for the nomination. By raising $50,000 in contributions of $100 or less, each of them received $100,000 from the state treasury and a guarantee that every subsequent dollar donation in private money would be matched by $2 in public funds until the candidate had reached a total limit of $1 million with which to finance his primary campaign. No one could know what might happen in a contest between candidates each of whom might end up spending more than the total amount spent on the Democratic candidate for governor in the general election of 1974. William Ralls, for example, had spent the better part of his five years as the only Democrat on the three-member Public Service Commission voting against utility rate increases and speaking against utility mismanagement. He entered the race for the Democratic nomination a relative unknown, but a few hundred thousand dollars expended on an intelligent media effort could bring both a candidate and his record to public attention. Patrick McCollough had served in the state senate since 1970, and William Fitzgerald since 1974, but neither of them entered the gubernatorial primary recognized by more than a few percent of the Michigan electorate. Public money, however, could do more for a candidacy than public service, except at the highest and most visible level, ever could.

Three of the four candidates for the Democratic nomination began in almost equal anonymity, with approximately equal chances to acquire enormous resources. Fitzgerald, nevertheless, began in a better position than either McCollough or Ralls. The state party was, as always, formally neutral, but the leadership's actual preference for Fitzgerald was evidenced by the degree to which party activists joined his campaign. The private encouragement of the leadership, and the open assistance of those county- and district-level Democrats who followed wherever the leadership led, helped build an organization that gave credence to the claim that Fitzgerald would win. Those interested in associating with the Democratic nominee whoever he might turn out to be increasingly contributed to Fitzgerald. It soon became apparent that Fitzgerald had the advantage in both money and organization. Of the four candidates, the former majority leader was expected to "come the closest to

receiving the $660,000 maximum allowed'' in public money. Fitzgerald
"raised the most money in small contributions and fielded the best organization, and he has hired Washington consultants to do his polling and media
work."[25] When to all of this was added his Irish Catholic name, the support
of much of Detroit's political establishment, and the endorsement of such
legislative leaders as the Speaker of the House, it seemed that Fitzgerald could
not be stopped by anyone except perhaps the UAW.

The UAW had no desire to stop him. He had been their faithful political
ally; the others had not. William Ralls had never opposed the union, but
neither had he ever been in a position where that had really been a possibility.
Moreover, Ralls lost whatever advantage his obvious intelligence might have
given him with the leadership of the union by his imprudent and repeated
insistence that he would win the nomination because he was smarter than the
other candidates. McCollough, on the other hand, had not only opposed the
union, but had led the opposition on the question of whether William
Fitzgerald should remain the majority leader in the senate. McCollough compounded his difficulties, not, like Ralls, through too great a concern that his
intelligence be recognized, but by too little regard for his reputation for
honesty. Steve Yokich, director of UAW Region 1, refused to have anything
to do with him after McCollough claimed he had raised through contributions,
when he in fact had borrowed, the money used to package a campaign tabloid
in the Sunday Detroit papers at the beginning of his candidacy. However,
neither the intellectual pretensions of Bill Ralls nor the prevarications of
Patrick McCollough came close to producing the disdain and distrust with
which the political leadership of the UAW viewed the latest candidacy of
Zolton Ferency. Sam Fishman had managed Ferency's first campaign for
governor and had been responsible for getting him the union's support when
he then ran for another term as state chairman of the Democratic party. That,
however, had been a long time ago. During the ten years that had elapsed,
Ferency had grown embittered as one defeat had followed another, and more
and more frequently he used his famous wit to revile those who at one time
had supported, but now opposed, his ambitions. In 1966 Zolton Ferency had
campaigned against George Romney and big business. In 1978 he spent his
anger on Sam Fishman and organized labor. Ferency charged that labor had
lost its liberalism. Labor thought Ferency had lost his reason.

No other gubernatorial candidate—not Ralls, not McCollough, and most
emphatically not Ferency—had a greater claim on the gratitude or a better
hold on the loyalty of the UAW than Bill Fitzgerald. Nevertheless, the union
remained neutral throughout the gubernatorial primary. Fitzgerald wanted it
that way. Convinced that he could win the primary without a union endorsement, Fitzgerald feared it would be not only superfluous in the primary, but
harmful in the general. The endorsement of the UAW in the primary, he

reasoned, might brand him as the candidate of labor and inhibit his ability to appeal to the broad constituency necessary to carry a general election against a popular incumbent governor. Sam Fishman shared Fitzgerald's opinion that he would win the primary and had no reason to insist on an endorsement that had in the past been difficult to arrange, even under the best of circumstances.

With the UAW content to watch with formal impartiality, the four candidates for the Democratic nomination were left to their own devices. Zolton Ferency, whose strange political career had now covered more than two decades, found himself at age fifty-six once more the self-proclaimed guardian of the left. Though all three of his opponents were twenty years his junior, Ferency stood on its head the famous dictum of Winston Churchill that "anyone under 40 who is not a liberal doesn't have a heart; anyone over 40 who is not a conservative doesn't have a head." As if to prove their cautious maturity and their fitness to assume the highest responsibilities of public authority, McCollough, Ralls, and Fitzgerald gave "at least qualified support to the Headlee amendment, which would tie the growth of property taxes to the rate of inflation."[26] Only Ferency openly opposed the amendment, which was unintelligible when it was proposed and thoroughly useless after it was adopted. What might have passed for political courage in another candidate was dismissed as only the latest manifestation of Ferency's refusal to recognize or comply with political reality. The suspicion was already growing that Zolton Ferency cared far less about winning the Democratic nomination than he did about retaining the allegiance and the adulation of the left wing of the Democratic party.

After the election of John F. Kennedy, young men of ambition who had never been to Massachusetts began to speak of the need to sacrifice personal interests for the national interest in voices that made them sound as if they had been born and bred in Boston. With the ascendancy of Lyndon Baines Johnson, the clipped cadence of the New England Brahmin yielded to the slower and more indirect speech of the shrewd and suspicious son of the country. Aspiring young candidates for political careers now began to detect and declaim upon the advantages and even the virtues of a politics rooted in a clear understanding of the imperatives of self-interest. All of us lead our lives and think our thoughts according to patterns that owe their origins to others. Much of this is done from habit and without conscious effort. But while nearly everyone takes their bearings from what is customary, politicians, especially those who harbor the greatest ambitions, take theirs from what has proven successful. Somewhere deep inside his subconscious—or, if an older tradition be preferred, his soul—Zolton Ferency had a picture or a pattern of an agitator able to move enormous masses of the downtrodden to decisive action on behalf of a final resolution of the eternal human problem. Patrick Mc-

Collough had modeled himself after a more prosaic vision and a more contemporary example.

Jimmy Carter, whose own insistence that he would never lie to the American people was identical to the line used in Fletcher Knebel's book *Dark Horse,* a book Carter read before he became a candidate, had spoken of things not normally mentioned in political campaigns. With what could just as easily have been the deep and honest conviction of a believer or the masterful artifice of a hypocrite, Carter had given as much expression to his concern with love and goodness as to any of the more traditional questions of public policy. He had made his own apparent sincerity the basis for an appeal to people who had never before been politically active. Patrick McCollough had been one of the first public officials in Michigan actively to support Carter, and now, two years later, he made a concerted effort to repeat Carter's success by emulating his example. McCollough assembled an organization made up of many of the same people who had been drawn into politics by Jimmy Carter in 1976. Though he had been around politics all his life and though he lived in the birthplace of the automobile industry, McCollough campaigned, as Carter had before him, as if he were a rural innocent who could somehow defeat the forces of corruption. Wherever he spoke and whatever else he said, McCollough always emphasized his early support of Jimmy Carter and explained it as the natural result of Carter's honesty and sincerity. In a voice that strained to sound sincere, McCollough volunteered to undertake in Michigan the same program of honest government Jimmy Carter was giving the country. Both those who believed and those who suspected the sincerity of Jimmy Carter were able to accept Patrick McCollough as a product of the same mold.

McCollough might contrive to be sincere, but as a two-term member of the state senate he could not hope to represent himself, as Jimmy Carter had, as an outsider who could reform government precisely because he had never been corrupted by participation in it. The fourth candidate for the Democratic nomination tried to do so. Though he had served on the Public Service Commission, which was a part of the government, Bill Ralls could point to an almost unblemished record of opposition to commission decisions to permit rate increases for public utilities. With two Republicans consistently voting together on the three-member commission, Ralls had been a permanent minority and could therefore act without the restraints of governmental responsibility. Lacking the power to determine what the utility rates would be, he attacked every increase as unwarranted. Through unceasing dissent, Ralls presented himself as a citizen whose desire to protect the consumer from the avarice of the utilities was frustrated by the cowardice or corruption of the Republican politicians who governed the commission. His gubernatorial campaign was based almost entirely on the argument that when he gained command of the executive branch of state government, he (who had never before run for public office) could block the power of the utilities and remove the influence of the politicians. Like Jimmy Carter, Ralls sought political power by means of a campaign directed against politics and politicians.

Whether because they followed the pattern of Jimmy Carter with too little or too much fidelity, Patrick McCollough and Bill Ralls both failed by a wide margin to realize the ambition they shared. McCollough, though he attracted some support among blue-collar voters in parts of both western Wayne County and Macomb County, finished last in the four-man race with 105,239 votes, or 17.4 percent of the total. Ralls did only slightly better. With scattered support in Oakland County and in the thumb area, he received 108,758 votes, or 18 percent. Zolton Ferency alone managed to present a serious challenge to Fitzgerald, and Ferency ended the campaign having added little if anything to the support with which he had begun. He held the allegiance of the left wing and failed to attract anyone else. "He ran well in his usual bases of support, carrying the university towns of Ann Arbor and East Lansing, liberal suburbs in Oakland County, and black wards in inner-city Detroit."[27] Ferency received 155,803 votes, or 25.7 percent of the total. This might have been enough had Ralls and McCollough each taken a quarter of the total, or if there had been more candidates in the race. But there were only four candidates, and neither Ralls nor McCollough had come close to a 25 percent share of the total vote cast. Instead of winning by a small margin, Ferency finished a distant second. Bill Fitzgerald. with strong support "in the heavily Catholic industrial cities outside Detroit" and among blue-collar Catholics in Macomb County, carried 38.9 percent of the vote and became the Democratic candidate for governor.[28] The party now had a Catholic candidate with which to reclaim the suburban Catholic vote.

Notes

1. Morley Winograd, Report to Democratic State Central Committee, December 14, 1974.
2. Morley Winograd, letter to party leaders, January 3, 1977.
3. Speech of Richard H. Austin nominating Morley A. Winograd for party chairman, Detroit, January 26, 1975.
4. Re-elect Winograd Committee, press release, February 8, 1977.
5. Ibid.
6. *Royal Oak Tribune,* February 14, 1977.
7. Morley Winograd, "Campaign Plan, '78 Election," June, 1977, p. 2.
8. Ibid.
9. Al Flory, "A Statistical Analysis of the 1974 Election," n.d., p. 7.
10. Ibid.

11. Ibid., p. 9.

12. The determination of the author of the statistical analysis to discover economics as the source of every important conflict is evidenced in remarkable fashion by his disclosure of the real causes of the American Civil War: "Contrary to what many people have come to believe, the Civil War was not as much a war between the slave-freeing Yankee North and the slave-owning South as a war between these Anglo-Saxons of the North, the true Yankees and the Anglo-Saxons of the South, over the control of the U.S. economic system." Anyone who could so easily dismiss the distinction between slavery and freedom in order to demonstrate the primacy of an economic theory of causation was not likely to expend much energy or thought measuring the effect on the electorate of a candidate's willful and deliberate decision to lie. Ibid., p. 10.

13. *Public Papers of Lyndon B. Johnson 1963–64*, vol. 2 (Washington, D.C.: U.S. Government Printing Office, 1965), p. 1530.

14. Wally Long, interview with author, August 24, 1982.

15. State of the State Address, Governor William Milliken, January 10, 1974.

16. Wally Long, interview with author, August 24, 1982.

17. Tacitus *Histories* 3.77.

18. The conspiracy was hardly a secret. Governor Milliken noticed McCollough and Karoub talking together outside his office and remarked with a knowing smile, "If the two of you are together something must be up." Larry Tokarski, interview with author, August 20, 1982.

19. Morley Winograd, interview with author, August 22, 1982.

20. Wally Long, interview with author, August 24, 1982.

21. *Royal Oak Daily Tribune*, February 14, 1977.

22. Ibid.

23. *Detroit Free Press*, October 16, 1978.

24. *Congressional Quarterly Weekly Report*, July 29, 1978, p. 1938.

25. Ibid.

26. Ibid.

27. *Congressional Quarterly Weekly Report*, August 12, 1978, p. 2111.

28. Ibid.

CHAPTER 8

Winners and Losers, 1978

From the time of the resignation of Richard Nixon to the inauguration of Jimmy Carter, Michigan Republicans held the presidency, the governorship, and one of the state's two seats in the United States Senate. This combination of political power had seldom been seen in American history and had never before been experienced in Michigan. It was not to last. In the 1976 election, Gerald Ford's attempt to keep by election what he had gained by appointment failed by a narrow margin. Within months of Ford's defeat, Senator Robert Griffin sustained a loss of his own, when Howard Baker prevailed by a single vote in the contest to become minority leader of the Senate. Ford's loss had deprived Griffin of influence in the executive branch; his own defeat limited his influence in the legislature. Until November he had been able to look forward to a position of national importance; after January he could foresee a career of declining significance in the Senate. The death of his friend and fellow senator, Phil Hart, only intensified his dissatisfaction. In April, Robert Griffin announced that he would not be a candidate for reelection in 1978. He was, as he put it, tired of the Senate.

Ford had been defeated and Griffin would not run. Only William Milliken was left, and no one was certain whether he would run for another term or, now that it was open, seek the Senate seat Griffin had held since 1966. There was even the possibility that the governor would decide not to run for anything at all. The single certainty concerning the future of William Milliken was that if he did not choose to retire he would be almost impossible to defeat. As late as June, 1977, Morley Winograd argued that the Democratic party should concentrate its efforts on whichever office Milliken did not seek. Though the election of a Democratic governor was "our first priority," it could not, according to the Democratic chairman, "be our sole objective. If Governor Milliken should decide to run for re-election, the [Peter] Hart survey and everyone's intuition tells us he would be a formidable candidate indeed." This required that "reasonable people . . . think of a fall-back position. This secondary goal should be the election of a Democratic U.S. Senator." If, however, Milliken "should decide to run for the Senate, our chances of obtaining this victory become rather remote.'' But in that event Democratic ''chances for electing a Governor increase dramatically.'' Indeed, ''should such a decision by the Governor occur,'' the Democratic interest in the senate seat ''decreases markedly in importance—almost to the point of abandonment.''[1] It was not hard to determine what Winograd hoped Milliken would do.

None of the four candidates for the Democratic gubernatorial nomination had waited to see whether the governor would seek reelection before committing themselves to a contest in which the value of victory appeared to depend largely on what Milliken did. After nearly a decade in office, the governor had no reason to reach an early decision. The Democratic hopefuls had no such luxury. To have any chance of winning the party primary, they had to begin without any certain knowledge of whom they might face in the general election. The candidates for the Democratic senatorial nomination faced a similar dilemma. Several of the candidates in what would eventually become a six-man race had begun their campaigns when no one doubted that Robert Griffin would seek a third term in the Senate. State Senator John Otterbacher had run briefly in the 1976 Senate primary and then withdrawn in favor of Donald Riegle. Whether or not the 1976 effort was deliberately designed to set the stage for a more serious attempt in 1978, Otterbacher had never really stopped campaigning. He expected to run against Griffin, and he at least was convinced he would win. Philip Power, who had been born to great wealth and owned a chain of suburban newspapers, had made it clear that he would spend whatever amount of money was necessary to acquire the right to spend even more money in a campaign against the Republican incumbent. Richard VanderVeen had yielded to those who believed he had a duty to hold the House seat he had won in 1974 instead of seeking the Senate nomination in 1976. He had not run for the Senate, but he had not won reelection to the House. Out of the House, he eagerly sought admission to the Senate. These were not the only Democrats who were ready to seek their party's nomination against Robert Griffin, but Otterbacher was the earliest, Power easily the wealthiest, and VanderVeen the only one anyone had ever really heard about. The field appeared likely to be both large and unknown.

The absence of any well-known Democratic candidate seemed to underscore the belief that Griffin, who had beaten first G. Mennen Williams and then Frank Kelley, would be difficult to defeat. Kelley, who had not run for the Senate in 1976, when he could have done so without giving up his position as attorney general and without facing a Republican incumbent, was not likely to run in 1978, when he would have to do both. Richard Austin had run in 1976 and had lost the Democratic primary in a campaign that had raised questions about his integrity. He was not about to risk a repetition of the experience. Most of the other potential candidates who possessed both the political credibility and the requisite level of public recognition were members of the congressional delegation. Those who had served in the House the longest, however, had acquired too much influence, and in some cases at least, had become too addicted to life in the Congress, to risk ending their political careers. Those who were recent arrivals found it too early to hazard promising futures on the doubtful outcome of a statewide race against a Republican incumbent. There was only one exception. William Ford had contemplated a Senate campaign for several years, and had his close friend Jim O'Hara not run in 1976, might well have sought the nomination to succeed Phil Hart. A number of prominent Democratic leaders, including Morley Winograd, expected Ford to become a candidate in 1978. Ford, however, was cautious; he was not going to run unless he was certain he would win. But when Robert Griffin announced he would not seek reelection the only remaining uncertainty seemed to be whether Bill Ford would be the only formidable candidate who would now enter the Democratic primary.

Griffin's decision to retire did attract additional candidates to the Democratic primary, but none of them were of the sort to discourage others by their presence. Another state senator, Anthony Derezinski, and even a state representative, Paul Rosenbaum, could discover nothing in themselves that suffered in comparison with the others, and decided that as the field grew larger the percentage of the vote needed to win would inevitably grow smaller. As the only candidate with a Polish name, Derezinski convinced himself that an appeal to an ethnic constituency might be sufficient to win the nomination. As chairman of the House Judiciary Committee, Rosenbaum had found that speeches denouncing crime and criminals were met with nearly violent enthusiasm by the all-white audiences of Democratic clubs in western Wayne County. With a confidence in his own abilities so strong as to suggest that for him self-love held the status of a religious principle, Rosenbaum expected to use the law-and-order issue in 1978 with at least as much effect as George Wallace had used it in the Michigan presidential primary of 1972.

None of the Democratic candidates could possibly have caused Bill Ford the least delay or the slightest discomfort if he had decided to run. It was not the presence of competition but the absence of a UAW commitment that kept the congressman out of the race. Ford was willing to run, but he wanted the union to guarantee in advance that it would endorse his candidacy. He had enough influence with labor to obtain a private meeting of the UAW executive board to discuss his candidacy and his conditions, but not enough to get everything he required. When the UAW decided that it could not promise an endorsement in advance of a candidacy, Ford had no trouble abandoning the risks of a Senate campaign for the certainty of continued service in the House. It began to look as if the Democratic candidate for the United States Senate might be either a defeated member of Congress or a political neophyte whose only claim on the attention of the public or the allegiance of the party was his enormous wealth.

There was, however, one other potential candidate who could enter the Senate primary with the benefit of a well-known name. Carl Levin had achieved a reputation as president of the Detroit Common Council and was known throughout the city. But were he to become a statewide candidate, his principal advantage would not be his accomplishments in Detroit. His brother Sander had twice been the Democratic candidate for governor, and his cousin Charles had been elected to the state supreme court. Since 1970, millions of dollars had been spent to make the Levin name known to Michigan voters. Phil Power would have to spend a substantial portion of his substantial fortune just to match the expenditures that had already been made, and that Carl Levin, in a manner of speaking, stood to inherit. If Levin ran, he would be the front-runner the day he announced. For months rumors persisted that Levin might become a candidate, but he had still not announced any decision when the Republicans once again surprised the public and disrupted the plans of the Democratic party.

When William Milliken ended months of speculation by disclosing his intention to seek yet another term as governor, Democratic gubernatorial candidates were privately disappointed, but Republicans who wanted to run for the Senate were nearly ecstatic. L. Brooks Patterson, whose ambition was sufficiently broad to encompass any office higher than that of a county prosecutor, had already announced his determination to seek whichever office Milliken did not. He immediately announced his candidacy for the Republican nomination for the Senate. He was not alone. Lieutenant Governor James Damman had been replaced as Milliken's running mate by former lieutenant governor James Brickley, and viewing his dismissal not as a disgrace but as an opportunity, became a candidate to replace Robert Griffin. The most formidable candidate, however, and the clear favorite for the nomination, was a wealthy congressman from the Upper Peninsula, Philip Ruppe.

Each of the major Republican candidates had his strengths, but none of them could replace what the Republican ticket had lost with the retirement of an incumbent senator. That problem was soon solved. Milliken had persuaded James Brickley to leave the presidency of Eastern Michigan University to run again for lieutenant governor (a position Brickley had described when he left it four years earlier as "boring") in order to eliminate a repetition of the embarrassment Damman had caused in 1974. The governor now persuaded Robert Griffin to repudiate his decision to retire and run again for the Senate. The announcement that Griffin had ended his retirement before it had even begun was followed almost immediately by a quiet and dignified statement in which Damman withdrew from the Republican Senate primary. Congressman Philip Ruppe was too outraged to be quiet, while L. Brooks Patterson had never known how to be dignified. Ruppe protested against the back-room dealings of the Milliken administration, withdrew from the race, and placing in the sharpest contrast what had been done to him and what he would do to others, refused to run for reelection to the Congress because other candidates had entered the primary in reliance on his announcement that he was running for the Senate. Ruppe was able to combine righteous indignation with self-respect. Patterson could not. Bearing witness to the warning of Procopius that "men who are wronged are likely to become desperate,"[2] the Oakland County prosecutor condemned Milliken and Griffin and refused to quit. L. Brooks Patterson would win the Republican nomination for the Senate or make certain that Robert Griffin entered the general election with as many wounds as he could possibly inflict.

While all of the Republican candidates except Patterson were driven out of the race by the reemergence of Robert Griffin, Carl Levin followed the senator's declaration with one of his own. With his own private poll showing him with nearly 40 percent of the Democratic vote, Levin, the last candidate to enter, began with an enormous lead. Within the leadership of the Democratic party, Levin was thought to have as much chance of losing the primary, as he had of winning the general, election. Carl Levin was considered a liberal, and even worse for his prospects as a statewide candidate, a liberal who held the second highest office in the city of Detroit. There was little doubt that this was a combination perfectly lethal to a Democratic candidacy in 1978. In the polling that Peter Hart had done for the state party in 1977, voters were given a number of issues and provided with the contrasting positions taken by two hypothetical candidates, Smith, who was slightly left of center, and Jones, who was slightly right of center. The results were devastating.

> No ideological or partisan descriptions were given of either candidate or their position. The voters were asked to place themselves and the Democratic and Republican parties on a scale in relationship to these two candidates' positions. The voters placed themselves, on the average, slightly to the conservative or Jones side, a score of 45, and the Democratic Party thirteen points away on the liberal side with a 58. The Republican Party ended up with a 44, only one point away from being in perfect harmony with the voter. What is worse, the perceived differences were greatest on those issues which have been most traditionally associated with the Democratic Party such as aid to Detroit and unemployment compensation benefits.[3]

In a two-way race between the slightly conservative Jones and the somewhat liberal Smith, Jones won fifty-three to thirty-five, and carried ticket-splitters fifty-six to twenty-nine. Jones even won among regular Democrats, forty-seven to forty-three.[4] After a close examination of the Hart poll, Libby Maynard, vice-chairman of the Michigan Democratic party and long-time friend of the Levin family, concluded that Carl Levin had absolutely no chance to be elected to the United States Senate in 1978.

Each of the other Democratic candidates embraced with enthusiasm the assumption that Levin could not defeat Griffin and held himself out as the only nominee who did not share this fatal disability. Paul Rosenbaum, for example, who was running somewhere "to the right even of the Republican incumbent,"[5] did not hesitate to promise that his appeal to conservative Democrats, an appeal made in a rhetorical style he modestly described as brilliant, would be supported by a campaign treasury of no less than $600,000. That this was nearly twice what Donald Riegle, after a decade in Congress, had been able to raise for his own Senate primary two years earlier did nothing to diminish the conviction or dispel the illusions of the two-term state representative. Rosenbaum believed he could raise the money needed to make himself known and never doubted that once he was known he would be impossible to defeat. John Otterbacher and Anthony Derezinski, the two other young state legislators in the race, were equally insistent that their belief in themselves must inevitably be shared by others. Otterbacher, a clinical psychologist, sought to impress audiences with his youthful sincerity and fervid dedication to work. Every speech was substantially the same and always began with a recitation of the number of miles he had driven campaigning "in 82 of the 83 counties" of Michigan. Otterbacher alone could defeat Robert Griffin, because he had demonstrated the greatest dedication to the task. Derezinski, on the other hand, was the only Democrat who could defeat Griffin, because as the only Catholic and the only Polish candidate in the race, he alone could retain the allegiance of the largest ethnic group and one of the most important religious groups of the old Democratic coalition. Rosenbaum, Otterbacher, and Derezinski had all fallen victim to a common human failing. It was as Thucydides had written more than two thousand years ago: "the usual thing among men is that when they want something they will, without any reflection, leave that to hope, while they will employ the full force of reason in rejecting what they find unpalatable."[6]

The three state legislators were not the only ones unwilling to bring to bear on their own candidacies the analytical abilities with which they demonstrated the futility of the campaigns of their opponents. Richard VanderVeen, referring for obvious reasons not to his 1976 defeat but to his victory in 1974, when he won the Grand Rapids congressional seat formerly held by Gerald Ford, argued that in 1978 the Democratic party needed a candidate who had already proven he could win a race he was supposed to lose. VanderVeen sought to broaden his appeal within the party by a tactic almost guaranteed to narrow his appeal within the general electorate. Already established as a prominent political figure in western Michigan, VanderVeen, from motives similar in nature to those that led both Robert Carr and J. Robert Traxler to change their names on the ballot, changed his residency. The former congressman from Grand Rapids became the newest senatorial candidate from Detroit. In this fashion VanderVeen sought to combine strength in western Michigan with support from black voters in Detroit who, he believed, would be attracted by his liberalism and captivated by his willingness to live among them. Mayor Coleman Young, who had called Levin a "son of a bitch" for opposing a pay raise he wanted and a "prick" for no particular reason at all, remained formally neutral but made certain that at least some of his appointees—for example, Patti Knox—did what they could to enhance the otherwise dim prospects of Richard VanderVeen.

Neither the former congressman, however, nor any of the three state legislators really offered a serious challenge to Carl Levin. There were only two possible sources of opposition that might have any chance at all of denying Levin the nomination. One was the candidacy of Philip Power; the other was the organized force of organized labor. At the beginning of his campaign for the Democratic senatorial nomination, Power gave every indication that he intended and expected to buy it. While other candidates made promises to raise several hundred thousand dollars and were not believed, Power spoke of a million-dollar campaign and was never doubted. He let it be known at every opportunity that he would spend at least that much, and that as other candidates discovered he meant what he said they would withdraw from a contest for which they lacked the resources necessary to compete. This was not without effect. Democrats who had repeatedly blamed defeat on their inability to match the money of Republicans decided Power could not be stopped. A number of prominent party leaders, like Gene Kuthy of Oakland County, argued that Power should not be stopped in the primary precisely because he was the first candidate in memory who would be able to outspend the Republican candidate in the general election. If public office was subject to purchase, it was better that a Democrat instead of a Republican was the highest bidder. Power did nothing to discourage this line of thought. Though it was his first campaign for public office, it was very far from his first experience in the exploitation of great wealth. As if to suggest that his opponents in the Democratic primary faced not only his own considerable fortune, estimated at between $9 and $18 million, but almost the entire capital accumulation of the Western world, or at least the Fortune 500, Power casually remarked to Sam Fishman that he could easily raise half a million dollars simply by calling five hundred friends who would each contribute and not miss for a moment the $1,000 maximum permitted by federal law. Fishman, whose knowledge of politics and indifference to personal finance both approached legendary proportions, could not believe it but had no reason to dispute it.

In the realm of strategy, perhaps the most artful undertaking, as such disparate characters as Willie Sutton and T. E. Lawrence both understood, is to make the greatest strength of an opponent the source of his greatest weakness. Sutton, who robbed banks for a living because, as he put it, that was where the money was, was frequently imprisoned and often escaped. It was the easiest where it was supposed to be the most difficult; the authorities, having assumed impregnability, discarded vigilance.[7] T. E. Lawrence, or Lawrence of Arabia, waged guerilla war against the Turkish armed forces in Arabia during the First World War by refusing to challenge their control over their major military bases. What the Turk kept, the Turk had to supply with material that could then not be used elsewhere. Lawrence simply let the Turkish force imprison itself in its own fortifications while he led the Arab Revolt around them.[8] Power, like the Turkish army, was vulnerable in his strength. He had decided to capture the nomination by the ostentatious display and the lavish expenditure of what for a Democratic primary was an unprecedented amount of money. It was not difficult to invent the means by which to turn his own money against him, but it proved impossible to find more than one candidate intelligent enough to grasp and employ it. Though six Senate candidates ended up on the primary ballot in August, several others had begun, but for various reasons been unable to continue. Early in the campaign one of these sent all the other candidates a telegram calling for agreement on a spending limitation of $300,000, an amount which, as the telegram pointed out, was comparable to what had been spent by the winning candidate in the Democratic Senate primary in 1976.

Power was caught unaware by the call for a voluntary spending limitation, and for a time his campaign was thrown into confusion. If he agreed to spend only $300,000, his principal advantage and major qualification for the nomination would disappear. If he alone refused to agree to the limit, he would appear intent on buying a seat in the Senate, an impression that might have less appeal to the public than it had had with the party leadership. Power, however, received a reprieve from the consequences of this dilemma. While Carl Levin agreed to the limitation, all the other candidates, whether because they believed they would raise as much money as Donald Riegle had or because they had convinced themselves Philip Power could not, refused. Power could now spend whatever he wished. He proceeded to spend more than $800,000 of his own money, even before the campaign entered its last month. Almost all of it was spent on a media campaign to make him well known.[9] Although no one was driven out of the contest by Power's willingness to spend enormous amounts of money, he continued to spend it. Most of what he spent was his to give. If he ever made the five hundred phone calls he had told Sam Fishman would be sufficient to raise $500,000, the results must have been disappointing. He did call Henry Ford, but Ford gave him only $500. In the latter stages of the campaign Power made most of his calls to reporters to complain that their frequent stories about his expenditures made it difficult to solicit contributions. It is not easy, after all, for a multimillionaire to convince others that he needs contributions or would be grateful if he received them.

Power had almost unlimited resources with which to advance an otherwise rather limited candidacy. Unable to generate enthusiasm among active Democrats or much interest on the part of the public, his candidacy took on the predictability of a lavish but dull commercial promotion. Levin, who once claimed to have decided to enter the race precisely to prevent Power from buying the nomination, did not complain about the money Power spent, nor did he give the slightest suggestion that he believed it might affect the outcome. Power, as Levin well knew, would have to spend several times the amount he had so confidently asserted would be sufficient to give him victory in order to match the money that had been spent publicizing the Levin name in the last several statewide elections. Even then he would still be far short of compensating fully for the value of the free publicity given the Levins during their years of public service and political campaigning. Money alone was not likely to deny the nomination to Carl Levin.

Power and his money seemed unlikely to defeat Levin, and labor appeared unwilling even to try. In January, Irving Bluestone had confided to one of the candidates that the UAW had to adopt a more formal approach to Democratic primaries. In too many elections, he complained, the leadership of the union discussed the different Democratic candidates with wholly inadequate information. Frequently, only a few members of the union's executive board had any direct acquaintance with the candidates they were being asked to consider. The chairman of UAW-CAP promised that in this election things would be different. This time there would be some arrangement by which all of the candidates would be brought before the regional directors and vice-presidents who made up the governing body of Michigan CAP. It did not happen. Bluestone did establish a formal screening committee, and each of the Michigan regional directors was made a member of it. But when the first candidate for the Democratic senatorial nomination took his seat in the second-floor room of Solidarity House at 8 A.M. on the day on which all of the candidates were to be given an hour to answer questions and state their opinions, not a single regional director was present. All of them had sent in their place their political coordinators. Sam Fishman presided over what was indistinguishable from the many meetings of CAP coordinators he had called in the past.

The first candidate had little chance of winning the nomination with the endorsement of the UAW and none whatsoever without it. With an appreciation of his own self-interest, he suggested at the end of his presentation that the union should make an endorsement in the Democratic primary and that if it endorsed another candidate he would willingly withdraw and support the candidate of the UAW. The suggestion that a candidate for the Democratic nomination ought to bow to the wishes of the UAW was scarcely courageous, but it was, under the circumstances, realistic. It was also a reasonably effective tactic. Each of the other Democratic candidates was asked in turn whether they would also withdraw if the union endorsed someone else. Each of the others, except for Richard VanderVeen, insisted that nothing could get him out of a race he was destined to win. The UAW was not pleased.

Despite its displeasure the union did nothing. Sam Fishman had believed for some time that the union should become directly involved in Democratic primaries, and Douglas Fraser and Irving Bluestone both agreed with this proposition as an abstract statement of policy; but none of them had the slightest interest in committing the power and prestige of the UAW to any candidate who could not establish a credible campaign on his own. The massive resources of Philip Power and the well-known name of Carl Levin had effectively deprived the other candidates of any except an outside chance at the nomination; none of them could be considered for a union endorsement. Only Power and Levin were left. Though Bard Young, director of UAW Region 1-E, thought it might be possible "to educate" Philip Power and though Steve Yokich, director of Region 1, preferred Power over Levin for personal reasons, the UAW never seriously considered endorsing Levin's main opponent. The UAW never actually decided the question of endorsement at all. Through informal discussions it became apparent that there was no sentiment for an endorsement, and as a result, the matter was never taken up for a formal decision. The structural procedures envisioned by Irving Bluestone had been a chimera. For all its concern with public issues and all its extensive political operations, the UAW continued to be an organization in which, as someone closely involved put it, "there has not been a serious political discussion in a meeting of the executive board in 10 years."

The UAW was neutral, and after inviting all the candidates to address a meeting of its executive council, so was the Michigan AFL-CIO. The MEA president, Keith Geiger, seemed to believe that perhaps Power was owed something for the support his suburban newspapers had given teachers during recent strikes, but that organization also refrained from giving an endorsement. The Teamsters, with their usual indifference to democratic procedures, invited none of the candidates to appear before them and endorsed Paul Rosenbaum. The Teamsters, who always had a reason for what they did, kept to their practice of refusing to disclose what it was. It was not, however, difficult to guess. Rosenbaum was still chairman of the House Judiciary Committee and had not hesitated to exploit that position for political advantage. He had assured several party leaders that he alone would have a statewide campaign apparatus in place because he alone could command the attention and direct the efforts of every state and local judge. He had even gone so far as to threaten to use his chairmanship of the Judiciary Committee to prevent passage of legislation recommended by T. John Lesinski as part of a major reform of the Wayne County court system unless Lesinski, the former lieutenant governor and former chief judge of the Michigan court of appeals, endorsed his senatorial candidacy. With an artistic display of profanity, Lesinski described the various biological impossibilities that Rosenbaum and his demand could engage in. The Teamsters were undoubtedly easier to deal with.

While labor, with the exception of the Teamsters, remained neutral, the state's two major newspapers, the *Detroit News* and the *Detroit Free Press,* each endorsed a candidate. Whether because of an editorial bias against publishers or a reluctance to find the owner of some of their suburban competitors in the Senate, neither one endorsed Philip Power. Nor did either one endorse Levin, the president of the Detroit Common Council. Instead, the *Free Press* threw its support to former congressman Richard VanderVeen, who was presumably the most experienced and the most confessedly liberal of the Democratic candidates. The *News,* on the other hand, endorsed state senator Anthony Derezinski, who appeared more attuned to the cautious conservatism of that paper than did any of the others. The editorial recommendations of the *News* and the *Free Press* had as little effect on the outcome as did the endorsement of the Teamsters.

With the UAW and the AFL-CIO neutral, and with the two Detroit papers split between two of the lesser challengers, Carl Levin had only to withstand the frenzied spending of Philip Power to win the Democratic nomination for the United States Senate. It did not prove difficult. Levin crushed his most formidable opponent by a margin of two-to-one. He ended the primary campaign with almost exactly the level of popular support with which he had begun. His poll before he entered showed him with nearly 40 percent of the Democratic vote; he received 39.6 percent. Power set a new American record for money spent by a candidate on himself in a Senate primary (one million dollars), and received all of 114,113 votes, or only 20 percent of the total. Levin carried half of the vote in Wayne and Oakland counties and more than a third of the vote in Macomb. Power carried only four counties in the state, and his home county of Washtenaw was not among them. Richard VanderVeen finished a distant third, with 14.6 percent of the vote. The former congressman carried twelve counties "in the Dutch country around his Grand Rapids home," but despite the endorsement of the *Free Press,* ran fourth in

Wayne County, with only 9 percent of the county vote. Anthony Derezinski ran fourth, with 9.3 percent of the vote. His appeal to a Polish constituency and his endorsement by the *News* combined to give him barely one-fifth of Levin's vote in Wayne County. John Otterbacher ended what was nearly a three-year quest for a Senate nomination with 8.4 percent of the vote and a fifth-place finish. Paul Rosenbaum, who had raised less than a quarter of the money he had claimed he would, finished dead last, with a dismal 8.1 percent of the total vote cast.[10]

Fourteen months before William Fitzgerald and Carl Levin won the Democratic nominations for governor and United States Senator, Morley Winograd had analyzed Peter Hart's polling data and concluded that William Milliken would be almost impossible to defeat, while Carl Levin could not possibly win. Now that Milliken was again the Republican candidate for governor and Levin the Democratic candidate for the Senate, there seemed to be a real danger that both positions would remain in the control of the Republican party. This would have the most serious consequences for the future of the Democratic party. "Failure to win either state-wide election in 1978," Winograd had written in 1977, "would recreate the 'loser's' image our 1976 victory began to destroy. The effect on party morale would be devastating. A major decline in support and supporters would almost inevitably occur."[11] The certainty of that defeat, however, was no longer as apparent as it had been a year earlier. Winograd had anticipated that possibility when he warned that it was impossible to "foresee all of the events that will inevitably alter the political landscape before we reach November of 1978."[12]

Nothing had altered the political landscape of Michigan more to the apparent advantage of the Republican party than the political resurrection of Robert Griffin. It was difficult to imagine that the senator who had defeated G. Mennen Williams and Frank Kelley in his first two Senate campaigns would be very seriously tested by Carl Levin in his third. But Griffin had made a major mistake. When he reached his decision not to run for a third term, the Republican senator explained, quite honestly, that he had grown tired of the Senate. Having announced his decision to retire, Griffin approached his last year in what was to be his last term without the same attention to those matters that are of little importance in the Senate but that can be of major political importance to the electorate. Freed from the constraints of political necessity, Griffin no longer cared about attending sessions of the Senate solely for the sake of appearance. When he changed his mind about running again, he could do nothing to change the record of roll-call votes he had missed. Sensing an opportunity, L. Brooks Patterson did everything he could to make Griffin's apparent lack of interest in the job a principal issue of the primary campaign. Patterson went so far as to stand on a sidewalk in

Detroit and offer $216 to any passerby who "knew the significance of that figure in his race against Griffin. Only three people knew it was the number of roll call votes Griffin missed in the 1977 session."[13] A far greater number knew how many roll-call votes Griffin had missed after they had read about what Patterson had done.

The Levin campaign took over where Patterson left off. Though the Democratic and Republican candidates for the Senate had fundamentally different attitudes on a number of major public questions, there was little substantive debate. Though labor endorsed Levin and business made large financial contributions to Griffin,[14] there was no serious discussion of the relation that ought to exist between labor and business or between either of them and government. Instead, the 1978 Senate campaign turned on the issue of whether Robert Griffin really wanted the job, a question an observer might have thought adequately answered by the fact he was a candidate for it. Levin, however, purported not to be convinced. At every opportunity he reminded Griffin that he had said he was tired of the Senate. This was invariably followed by a recitation of Griffin's record of absenteeism. It was something of an understatement to report, as the *Detroit News* did, that "Griffin's failure to answer 216 roll calls in the Senate in 1977 has been a focus of Levin's campaign."[15] Levin actually seemed to suggest that each roll-call vote was equivalent to a full day's work in the Senate, making every absence an inexcusable dereliction of duty. As if to make certain that no one failed to follow the logic of this to its inescapable conclusion, Levin put it plainly: "If any one of us missed 216 days of work in a year, we'd be fired."[16] The steady attacks of L. Brooks Patterson and Carl Levin had a cumulative effect on the reputation and the prospects of Robert Griffin. With only a month remaining before the November election, the *Detroit Free Press* published a poll in which Michigan's senior senator was running a full five points behind Carl Levin.[17]

The gubernatorial race was a different story. It had not taken long after the 1974 election for the leadership of the Democratic party to conclude that the second successive failure of Sander Levin to defeat William Milliken demonstrated nothing so much as the deficiencies of the candidate. In a year in which Democrats were everywhere triumphant, the victory of a Republican governor pointed to his opponent's serious inability either to appeal to the electorate or to take advantage of obvious political opportunity. It soon became an article of faith that nearly anyone except Sander Levin could have defeated William Milliken. There was, of course, no way ever to know whether anyone else could have won in 1974. But it was possible to identify the voters Levin had failed to attract. He had lost the very voters he and everyone else had known he had to win. He had not been able to win the support of the white, Catholic, blue-collar suburban voters who had defected from their normal Democratic allegiances in 1970. This was maddening to the Democratic leadership. In 1970, Milliken had made substantial inroads into the Catholic, blue-collar, suburban constituency because of a ballot proposal to provide public money for parochial schools. In 1974, public assistance to parochial schools had not played any part in the campaign. The major issue had instead been taxation, and on that issue Levin had taken precisely the position that corresponded with what the polls showed was the point of view of an overwhelming majority. Nevertheless, Catholic blue-collar voters had deserted Levin in even larger numbers than they had before.

In 1978, William Milliken, though still formidable, did not seem quite so unbeatable as he had in the spring of 1977 when Morley Winograd drafted his campaign plan. Milliken had been governor since 1969, and especially since the PBB incident (considered in some circles the worst case of toxic substance contamination in American history), had begun to suffer some erosion of his popularity. He seemed more vulnerable than he had been before, and the Democratic candidate appeared strongest precisely where the Republicans had previously been able to take advantage of weakness. Unlike Sander Levin, William Fitzgerald was an Irish Catholic. Unlike William Milliken, Fitzgerald was personally and publicly opposed to abortion. The Democratic candidate seemed almost to have been invented for the purpose of reclaiming the allegiance and the votes of the Catholic working class. On paper, as Morley Winograd looked at it, Bill Fitzgerald seemed like a very good candidate indeed.[18]

Fitzgerald understood both the major strength and the potential weakness of the Republican governor. Milliken's strength was his ability to portray himself as a decent man who was above the petty bickering of partisan politics. This, as Peter Hart's polling had shown, was especially attractive to ticket-splitters, who tended to view themselves as above partisan affiliation.[19] The governor's weakness, in Fitzgerald's judgment at least, was the record of his Republican administration. Fitzgerald tried to separate the private person from the public official. He admitted that Milliken had "charm, sensitivity and grace" while charging that the governor's "popularity has masked ineptitude in office."[20] Fitzgerald accused Milliken of incompetence in each of three areas where he believed the administration had no adequate defense. He attacked the Milliken administration for failing to attract new business to the state or even to prevent old business from leaving; he denounced the governor's refusal to alter a tax structure that was unfair to both the middle and the lower classes; and he condemned the long period of government inaction that had followed the first discovery of cattle feed contaminated with the deadly chemical PBB. Fitzgerald wanted to concentrate attention on the Republican administration; William Milliken did not.

William Milliken's reputation for polite civility was so well established that he could escape rebuke when he practiced what in nearly any other candidate would rightfully have been condemned as intemperance, if not brutality. In their debate at the Detroit Economic Club at the end of the 1974 campaign, the governor had subjected Sander Levin to a savage personal attack that was passed off as an honest display of outraged virtue. At the beginning of the 1978 campaign, the governor did it again. Speaking before the Republican state convention, Milliken "abandoned his 'nice guy' image and blasted Fitzgerald, calling him unfit to govern."[21] Reminding his audience that Fitzgerald had been replaced as majority leader in the state senate, he asked a question that was as irrelevant as it was effective: "If you can't lead 38 people how can you really lead more than nine million people?"[22] Though other Republicans carried the attack against Fitzgerald through much of the campaign, Milliken did not abandon the field. In the middle of October, the governor was still insisting that the real issue in the campaign was the character of his Democratic opponent.

> I think the principle issue is one of leadership. . . . I'm prepared fully to defend my record. . . . On the other hand, Senator Fitzgerald's record is clearly an issue in this campaign. . . . The fact that he introduced and passed three bills. The fact that he was absent 2,800 times in the course of this legislative session. The fact that he served and then was replaced as majority leader.[23]

There did not seem to be any limit to what the governor could say with impunity.

That Milliken was engaging in this sort of personal attack in the middle of October suggested that he was not entirely confident about the outcome of the election, and his fear appeared to have some justification. The *Detroit News* had only a few days earlier published a poll in which the governor's lead among likely voters had fallen to 4 percent. Fitzgerald had gained ground at a rate that permitted him to claim that if he was slightly behind when the poll was conducted, he must have gone ahead by the time the poll was published: "I think it's clear that we've overtaken him and neutralized his entire race."[24] Fitzgerald did nothing to dispel the appearance of growing confidence when he went on to accuse the governor of refusing to debate "because I'd eat him alive, that's why."[25] Yet even while the Democratic candidate was exhibiting this remarkable self-assurance, he knew that the prospects of victory were far more remote than the public opinion polls published by the state's most Republican paper suggested.

The declining popularity of William Milliken, chronicled by Democratic party polls since 1977, had never reached the point where the governor was unpopular with a majority of the Michigan electorate. Democratic victory depended on an increase in the governor's unpopularity, but a series of tracking polls begun after the primary election gave the Democratic party no hint of any change in the level of support he enjoyed.[26] While the *Detroit News* published polls that appeared to show a narrowing margin until, two weeks before the election, each of the candidates was favored by 44 percent of the likely voters, the survey data assembled for the Democratic party suggested that Fitzgerald was in serious difficulty. Milliken was still much too popular, and Fitzgerald had not succeeded in attracting the support of sufficient numbers of what had been regarded as his natural constituency. It seemed astonishing to the party and labor leadership, but the governor was still supported by a substantial proportion of Catholic voters.

Though some might have doubted that Catholic voters would support a candidate simply because they shared his religion, and though some members of the party leadership might have remembered that in a 1974 poll another Irish Catholic, Phil Hart, had received his lowest rating from Italian Catholics, Fitzgerald's failure was explained on the basis of what might be called an insufficient Catholicism. Fitzgerald himself advanced the theory. If Catholics were not supporting him, it must be because that although they knew he was Catholic, they did not know how good a Catholic he really was. Fitzgerald had not only an explanation but a remedy. Pope John Paul I had just died. If Fitzgerald could become a member of the official delegation sent by the United States to the Pope's funeral, no Catholic could doubt the sincerity or the depth of his religious convictions. Why attendance at an event at which some of the leading participants were Protestants would lead Catholics to this conclusion was never discussed. Fitzgerald's suggestion—which, it must be remembered, did offer a solution to the problem that had plagued not only this, but the two preceding gubernatorial campaigns as well—was taken up with alacrity. Sam Fishman and Morley Winograd enthusiastically endorsed it,[27] and Winograd immediately took steps to arrange it. He called the office of Hamilton Jordan at the White House and explained to an assistant what was needed. Jordan's assistant replied, ''We want to do everything we can to help.'' William Fitzgerald became a member of the official delegation of the United States of America at the funeral of His Holiness, Pope John Paul I. At the close of the 1978 campaign, Jimmy Carter spoke at a Democratic rally in Flint, and in a voice that seemed to express amazement at what he had done, remarked that he had such high regard for Bill Fitzgerald that he had included him in the ''small delegation I sent to Rome to represent me and our government at the funeral of the Pope. I chose Bill Fitzgerald and just a few others.''[28]

While Fitzgerald could think of no better way to improve his standing with Michigan Catholics than to accompany the president's mother to Rome, the means by which to undermine the governor's standing with the Michigan electorate was closer to home. Of all the failings Fitzgerald ascribed to the Milliken administration, none had created a greater public outcry or a more

legitimate cause for concern than the PBB disaster. Though Patrick Mc-
Collough had attempted to exploit the issue during the Democratic primary,
Fitzgerald had stayed away from it on the ground that it was a subject with
which he was not sufficiently familiar. Milliken, however, appeared to be
more vulnerable on this issue than any other, and Fitzgerald's earlier reluctance yielded to the present opportunity. He charged that the PBB problem
was "clearly leadership and management default. . . . Adequate testing
wasn't done by the Public Health Department. . . . The Department of Agri-
culture did not move decisively to contain the problem and remove the meat
and the dairy products from our food chain. There was too much indecision,
inaction and drift in this administration's handling of that problem."[29]
Fitzgerald went further still. In early October, his "campaign aired and then
withdrew a radio ad that implied, at least, that PBB was responsible for a
number of human ailments, including loss of hair and memory, blindness,
liver cancer, and 'the brain developing outside the head.' "[30] Milliken characterized the ad as "a new low in Michigan politics," and broadened his own
attack to accuse Fitzgerald of "a totally irresponsible campaign. He is over-
stating his case, distorting and exaggerating the issues and pandering to emotions and to fears."[31]

The emotions and fears engendered by the PBB issue were not limited to
those to whom Fitzgerald appealed for support. On October 18, the *Detroit
Free Press* reported that the episode of the "Lou Grant" television program
to be broadcast on Monday, November 6, the day before the election, would
tell a story about PBB.[32] The next day, October 19, the *Free Press* informed
its readers that the show would be delayed until after the election: "The
move, which will affect the entire network, came because CBS didn't want to
risk affecting the outcome of the Michigan's governor's race, in which PBB
has been a major issue."[33] If it seemed odd that CBS or any other television
network would consider the possible consequences for the politics of a single
state in its programming decisions, curiosity turned to suspicion when the
Free Press went on to report that "Channel 2, which carries the 'Lou Grant'
show in the Detroit area, asked the network Wednesday to move the episode.
Program manager, Jim Major, said the station would have acted on its own to
change the show date from November 6 if CBS had not."[34] Having spent
years calling for the deregulation of broadcasting, or at the very least, the
repeal of the fairness doctrine, television demonstrated precisely how far it
could be trusted never to permit political considerations to color its selection
of what the public really has a right to know.

A campaign in which neither side had done anything that could be
offered as a model of civic responsibility degenerated at the end to acts of
desperation. Fitzgerald held Milliken personally responsible for every misfor-
tune that had befallen the state and began to use the language of ridicule,

referring to the governor as "poor, bungling, Billy." The UAW, which could not contribute any direct assistance to the publicly funded campaign of the Democratic gubernatorial candidate, used Fitzgerald's new-found phrase and described Milliken as "Poor Bungling Billy" in "tens of thousands of brochures" distributed among its own membership.[35] If the personal assault on the governor had any effect, it was mainly to discredit Fitzgerald. Frank Angelo, perhaps the most respected journalist in Detroit, was so disturbed by what was taking place that on October 30 he told the readers of his column in the *Detroit Free Press* that "it is my intention in the next few hundred words to do something that I have never done before, and am not likely to do again: make an unequivocal political endorsement." Milliken, in Angelo's judgment, "deserves to be re-elected, and handily, on the basis of his total record as a public official, as governor, and as a human being. Beyond that, I am compelled to add that no one deserves to be elected governor on the basis of the campaign conducted by William Fitzgerald."[36]

While Fitzgerald attacked the Milliken administration at what were supposedly its weakest points, the Milliken campaign sought to deprive Fitzgerald of at least some of the support of the two most reliable components of the Democratic coalition, labor and blacks. With only a few days remaining before the election, 180,000 tabloids announcing labor support for Milliken were distributed to industrial workers in Detroit. The tabloid prominently displayed a picture of the governor along with several AFL-CIO leaders, including Si Chapple, administrative assistant to Bill Marshall, president of the Michigan AFL-CIO; Stan Arnold of the Building Trades; and Herman Shelton of the Communication Workers. Marshall was outraged over the use of the photo and the implication that leaders of his organization supported the reelection of the Republican governor. Outrage spread throughout both labor and the higher echelons of the Democratic party as the story of the tabloid's origins began to unravel. On October 25, according to the *Detroit Free Press*, plans for the tabloid had been made "when Milliken met with Michigan's top Teamster, Robert Holmes, and AFL-CIO officials who included Tom Turner, president of the Metropolitan Detroit AFL-CIO."[37]

The leaders of the Democratic party were as little surprised that Milliken would agree to meet with the head of the Teamsters in Bobby Holmes's Detroit office as they were at the absence of any comment about it by the editorial writers of the Detroit papers. But they were surprised to hear that Tom Turner was involved. Turner immediately denied any connection with the effort to assist the Milliken campaign: "I met with the governor to talk about the country's deficit."[38] He did not bother to explain why the governor of Michigan, two weeks before a gubernatorial election, would journey to Detroit to discuss a national economic problem with several local labor leaders. Not only did Turner claim he was "not there to map strategy for that paper," he insisted that the "Democratic Party knows where I stand. I support Fitzgerald."[39] Turner sought to distance himself as far as possible from even the suggestion that he had played a part in the Milliken labor tabloid by describing it as similar to the "political dirty tricks" of the Richard Nixon era.[40] Turner was not the only one denying any responsibility for the tabloid. Joyce Braithwaite, director of the Milliken campaign, disclaimed any connection between the tabloid and the Milliken campaign organization: "This publication was initiated by, executed by, prepared by and paid for by labor—for distribution within labor. The Milliken campaign did not suggest, control, or direct it, but we most certainly did welcome it."[41] Years later, she was much more specific: "The fact is that a number of labor leaders, including Tom Turner, initiated an effort to have a campaign tabloid that would be circulated among labor organizations on behalf of the Governor."[42]

If the labor tabloid had been the invention of the Teamsters, as Tom Turner seemed to imply, and if Joyce Braithwaite had been correct in her assertion that it was intended solely for "distribution within labor," then logically it would have been distributed to Teamsters throughout the state, or at least throughout the whole metropolitan area. In fact, the tabloid was distributed only in Detroit and mainly among blacks. If this, despite his protests, pointed to the involvement of Tom Turner, there was another consideration that suggested he was not the only black leader who had given assistance to the governor. That was the sheer volume of tabloids distributed. It would have been nothing short of a secular miracle if Turner, even with the help of his entire organization, had been able to distribute 180,000 tabloids in the last few days of the campaign. The Fitzgerald campaign thought it knew who besides Turner was responsible.

Four years earlier, when Sander Levin began his second attempt to become governor, the *Detroit News* had suggested he would have a more solid base of support in Detroit than he had had in 1970, when "Milliken all but neutralized then Mayor Roman S. Gribbs by pumping much needed state money into Detroit."[43] In 1974 Levin would have the "active support" of Detroit Mayor Coleman Young, who "could greatly increase Levin's support among black voters."[44] Levin did receive Young's endorsement, but he did not obtain any larger share of the black vote. In 1978, Fitzgerald did not even get the endorsement. The mayor of Detroit and the governor of Michigan had developed a close working relationship that was so beneficial to the city that the mayor's assistant Malcolm Dade remarked privately during the 1976 presidential campaign that "it would be hard to find a Democrat who would do more for Detroit than Milliken has." Coleman Young had obtained a substantial increase in federal assistance for the city through his support for Jimmy Carter, and he was not about to risk a decrease in state assistance by giving his support to William Fitzgerald. Young was vice-chairman of the

Democratic National Committee, and he dutifully endorsed the Democratic ticket. But he was first and foremost mayor of Detroit, and he carefully refrained from ever endorsing Fitzgerald by name. Though Malcolm Dade claimed that "Fitz never sought support in the city,"[45] Fitzgerald in fact sought repeatedly to arrange a meeting with the mayor, but Young would not even return the phone calls of his own party's candidate for governor.[46]

Whatever may have been the extent of Young's assistance to the Milliken campaign, whether he "never campaigned for Milliken but never denied Milliken had made commitments to the city,"[47] the effect of the mayor's failure to help Fitzgerald seemed apparent. Milliken did not carry the city of Detroit and he did not even come close to carrying the black vote. He did, however, increase his share of the city's vote from 22 percent in 1974 to 34 percent in 1978 and in a great many black precincts "his support, which had been negligible in the past, jumped to 20 or 25 percent."[48] With what was described as "largely the result of unexpectedly strong support in metropolitan Detroit," Milliken administered to William Fitzgerald a defeat that was staggering in its proportions. The governor did not carry Detroit, but he became the first Republican gubernatorial candidate to carry Wayne County since 1946. He carried Macomb and Oakland counties as well, and therewith swept the three counties that made up the heart of Democratic strength in the state. In addition to the tri-county metropolitan area, Milliken carried every industrial county in Michigan. Fitzgerald was able to win majorities only in the rural counties of the north, in which allegiance to the Republican party had been replaced by fear of the effects of PBB contamination.

It was a Milliken victory, but it was not entirely a Democratic defeat. Fitzgerald was beaten decisively, but Carl Levin won the Senate seat Robert Griffin had held for the Republicans for twelve years. Milliken had managed to make Fitzgerald the issue through the constant repetition of the Democratic candidate's record of absenteeism in the legislature. The tactic had not received enthusiastic approval within the campaign organization of Robert Griffin, as the senator tried unsuccessfully to deflect attention from his own record of roll calls missed and sessions not attended. Milliken and Levin had both waged campaigns that concentrated more on the alleged deficiencies of their opponents than on their own proposed contributions to public policy. Both had attacked, and both had been rewarded. That was one lesson of the 1978 campaign. There was another. Morley Winograd had probably been entirely correct when he had suggested in the spring of 1977 that whatever office Milliken sought Milliken would almost certainly get. The governor was as formidable a political figure as there was in the country. But if the prospects of a Fitzgerald victory had never been very good, they had certainly not been enhanced by the defection of fully a quarter of the black vote of Detroit. Coleman Young seemed to want to have it both ways. The mayor of Detroit wanted to exercise a powerful influence within the Democratic party, but at the same time he apparently did not hesitate to help a Republican who was willing to help him. The black leadership could not be relied on by the leadership of the Democratic party. This was not the first time Morley Winograd had come to this conclusion, and it would not be the last.

Notes

1. Morley Winograd, "Campaign Plan, '78 Election," June, 1977, p. 3.
2. Procopius, *Secret History*, trans. Richard Atwater (Ann Arbor: University of Michigan Press, 1963), p. 35.
3. Winograd, "Campaign Plan, '78 Election."
4. Ibid.
5. *Congressional Quarterly Weekly Report*, July 29, 1978, p. 1938.
6. Thucydides *Peloponnesian War* 4.108.
7. Willie Sutton, *Where The Money Was* (New York: Viking Press, 1976).
8. T. E. Lawrence, *Seven Pillars of Wisdom, a Triumph* (Garden City, N.Y.: Doubleday, Doran & Co., 1935); B. H. Liddell-Hart, *T. E. Lawrence in Arabia and After* (London: Jonathan Cape, 1965).
9. *Congressional Quarterly Weekly Report*, July 29, 1978, p. 1937.
10. *Congressional Quarterly Weekly Report*, August 12, 1978, pp. 2111–12.
11. Morley Winograd, "Campaign Plan, '78 Election," p. 3.
12. Ibid., p. 2.
13. *Congressional Quarterly Weekly Report*, July 29, 1978, p. 1938.
14. Levin received $5,000 from AFL-CIO COPE (Committee on Political Education) and $10,000 from the UAW. Griffin, for example, was given $3,000 by Amoco PAC, $5,000 by the Automobile and Truck Dealers Election Action Committee. *Congressional Quarterly Weekly Report*, November 11, 1978, p. 3262.
15. *Detroit News*, October 20, 1978.
16. Quoted in *Congressional Quarterly Weekly Report*, October 14, 1978, p. 2847.
17. Ibid.
18. Morley Winograd, interview with author, August 22, 1982. See also *Congressional Quarterly Weekly Report*, October 14, 1978, p. 2848.
19. "Ticket-splitters not only consider themselves independent, they also don't like political parties or partisanship." Winograd, "Campaign Plan, '78 Election" p. 6.
20. *Congressional Quarterly Weekly Report*, October 14, 1978, p. 2848.
21. Ibid.
22. Quoted in ibid.
23. *Detroit Free Press*, October 19, 1978.
24. *Detroit Free Press*, October 17, 1978.
25. Ibid.
26. Wally Long, interview with author, August 24, 1982.
27. Morley Winograd, interview with author, February 8, 1983.
28. Quoted in *Detroit Free Press*, November 3, 1978.

29. *Detroit Free Press,* October 19, 1978.
30. *Detroit Free Press,* October 29, 1978.
31. Ibid.
32. *Detroit Free Press,* October 18, 1978.
33. *Detroit Free Press,* October 19, 1978.
34. Ibid.
35. *Detroit Free Press,* October 29, 1978.
36. *Detroit Free Press,* October 30, 1978.
37. *Detroit Free Press,* November 4, 1978.
38. Ibid.
39. Ibid.
40. *Detroit Free Press,* November 5, 1978.
41. Ibid.
42. Joyce Braithwaite, executive assistant to Governor William G. Milliken, letter to author, December 14, 1982.
43. *Detroit News,* August 7, 1974.
44. Ibid.
45. Malcolm Dade, interview with author, August 22, 1982.
46. Wally Long, interview with author, August 24, 1982.
47. Malcolm Dade. interview with author, August 22, 1982.
48. *Detroit Free Press,* November 8, 1978.

PART 3
Division and Victory

CHAPTER 9

Black and White, Jew and Gentile

The Michigan Democratic party had emerged from the 1978 election divided between the white leadership of the party and the black leadership of Detroit. It was not a new division. Morley Winograd had campaigned for the chairmanship in 1973 on a promise to move the party back to the political center, and that, according to Winograd, required the rejection of any kind of quotas for representation within the party. The quota system adopted by the Democratic party in 1972, by which equal opportunity was effectively replaced with the promise of equality of result, had contributed, many believed, to electoral disaster. What Winograd proposed to give up, however, minority groups, whose power had been increased by the 1972 rules, wanted to keep. Blacks were especially reluctant to exchange a guarantee of proportional representation on the governing bodies of the Democratic party for the opportunity to compete for the votes of a white majority. Black resistance was intensified, moreover, by the suspicion that the abandonment of quotas would inevitably lead to the denial of the assistance necessary to overcome the effects of past injustice. The whole theory of affirmative action was based on the premise that without compensatory treatment for those who had been disadvantaged by discrimination, equality of opportunity would simply perpetuate a system of inequality. Affirmative action, however, if it was to mean anything, had to lead to something. As the only thing it could possibly lead to, if there really was an honest belief in racial equality, was the presence of blacks in every area of American life in proportion to their percentage of the population, the fastest way to achieve it was to require it. Affirmative action, unless it was a mask for continued racism, was indistinguishable from a system of racial quotas.

What seemed a sensible solution to blacks was a symbol of persecution to Jews. While blacks saw quotas as a means of increasing opportunity, Jews remembered them as a device by which they had been deprived of their liberty, their livelihood, and ultimately their lives. Blacks could thus expect no help from Jews in any attempt to establish a system of representation based on racial quotas. In Michigan, the absence of Jewish help, in the judgment of the black leadership, constituted an enormous obstacle. The black leadership in Detroit was convinced that the Michigan Democratic party was completely under Jewish control. In private they complained that not only were the party chairman, Morley Winograd, and the party's principal fund raiser, Stuart Hertzberg, Jews, but so also were the director of the UAW's political arm, Sam Fishman, and, after Douglas Fraser moved up to the presidency of the union, the vice-president in charge of UAW-CAP, Irving Bluestone. For the black leadership, Jewish domination of the Michigan Democratic party and of the political arm of the trade union that controlled it was beyond dispute.

The black leadership wanted to reduce Jewish influence in the party and hoped eventually to remove Morley Winograd from the chairmanship. Those who supported Winograd believed that any move by the black leadership against him would likely take the form of support for a candidacy by Michael Berry. If Berry ran for the chairmanship and was elected with the help of black Democrats, not only would the chairmanship of the state party go from a Jew to an Arab, but the position of Sam Fishman as director of the UAW's political activities would be placed at risk. While Winograd was chairman, Coleman Young might complain about him to Douglas Fraser, but Sam Fishman could report that Winograd worked well with the union. If Michael Berry became chairman, Coleman Young could complain to Fraser about Sam Fishman, and Berry could report that Fishman was an obstacle to decent relations between labor and the party. All of this was of course speculation and suspicion, but no one doubted and the black leadership did not deny its displeasure with Winograd and distrust of Fishman.

The election of Jimmy Carter appeared to offer Coleman Young and the black leadership a rare opportunity. When Carter became president he moved quickly to take control of the Democratic National Committee. The committee dutifully elected Carter's nominee, Ken Curtis, as national chairman, and Carter's choice, Coleman Young, as vice-chairman of the national Democratic party. Neither Morley Winograd nor Sam Fishman had been consulted beforehand. Nor were they consulted by the Carter White House about the large number of positions in the new administration given to the friends and associates of the mayor of Detroit. On matters of both patronage and politics, Jimmy Carter looked to Coleman Young and not to the UAW or the Michigan Democratic party. Winograd was so disturbed that he wrote a memo to the White House warning that the president needed to develop a public alliance with someone in the white community to balance his well-known relationship with Coleman Young. He suggested Bobby Crim, the Democratic Speaker of the House, as a logical choice. The memo and the suggestion were both ignored.[1] As the president's closest ally in Michigan and, as vice-chairman of the national Democratic party, Coleman Young now had much more power than he had ever had before with which to attempt to acquire greater influence in the state party. He would, moreover, have the assistance of much of the black leadership within the UAW. Marc Stepp, who had become a vice-president upon the death of Nelson "Jack" Edwards, and Buddy Battle, director of UAW Region 1-A, could almost always be counted upon to represent the mayor's point of view within the councils of the union.

One of the first indications that the black leadership felt a new assertiveness was their decision to boycott meetings of the unity caucus. Although the caucus had been used for three years to give the party leadership complete control over the state central committee, blacks had continued to participate in its proceedings long after its real purpose had become apparent. In the winter of 1977, however, blacks from the First and Thirteenth districts let it be known that they would no longer attend meetings of a body they regarded as hostile to their interests and antagonistic to the mayor. This did little to damage the ability of the unity caucus to dominate and direct the state central committee. The only difference was that now the delegates from the First and Thirteenth districts voted against the position of the caucus at central committee meetings with as much reliability as the other delegates, including blacks from districts outside the Detroit metropolitan area, voted for it. The First and Thirteenth would continue to follow the lead of Coleman Young, but by itself their opposition could not present any serious threat to the continued control of Morley Winograd and his allies in the labor movement. It was rather more difficult to manage the problems created by a black vice-president of the UAW.

In April, 1977, William Ralls informed Morley Winograd of his decision to resign from the Michigan Public Service Commission in order to campaign for the Democratic nomination for governor.[2] Ralls was the only Democrat on the three-member commission, and because state law required that no more than two members be of the same political party, his replacement would also have to be a Democrat. Winograd contacted his Republican counterpart, William McLaughlin, and asked him to find out the form in which the governor would prefer to receive the recommendations of the Democratic party. Several weeks later, in the early part of May, McLaughlin told Winograd that the governor wanted any suggestions to be in writing. On May 16, at a regular meeting of the party officers, potential candidates were discussed and a decision made not to recommend any one of them over any of the others. As Winograd later explained to Douglas Fraser:

> It was the unanimous opinion of those present that since we did not know whether or not we would have any real input into the selection, we should begin by sending the Governor a list of all those people who had applied through us

who were Democrats and seek further information from the Governor's office
before doing anything else.³

Two days later, the chairman of the Michigan Democratic party followed his
instructions and wrote to the Republican governor.

Though the governor had no choice but to name a Democrat to replace
Ralls, there was no legal remedy available to the Democratic party if the
governor named someone whose Democratic credentials were unsupported by
any history of party activity. What the law omitted, politics supplied. Winograd artfully reminded the governor that "By statute, this position must be
filled by gubernatorial appointment with advice and consent of the Senate
and, in this instance, the position must be filled by a Democrat." There was
no need to remind the governor that the senate was controlled by a Democratic
majority. After describing the importance of "the regulation of the utility
industry" to the future prosperity of the state and expressing the desire of the
Michigan Democratic party "to be as helpful as possible in the course of your
decision-making process," Winograd listed the names of the nine Democrats
who had indicated their interest in serving on the Public Service Commission
and confirmed that all of them were "active Democrats." The chairman's
letter ended with a polite but unmistakable warning:

> In short, because of the sensitivity of the position and the importance of it to the
> State of Michigan, I am indicating to you the desire on the part of the leadership
> of our Party to work on a cooperative basis to arrive at a decision which, when
> forwarded to the Michigan Senate and announced to the general public, will be
> received without controversy."⁴

Five days later Winograd wrote again to the governor, this time to add the
name of John F. McEwan of River Rouge, to the list of candidates.⁵ McEwan
had been added, as Winograd later explained, after Marc Stepp had expressed
an "interest in having his name forwarded."⁶

The governor did not bother to respond to Winograd's letter for nearly a
month and then only expressed his appreciation for the list of names and gave
his assurance that these "candidates will be given every consideration at the
time the appointment is made."⁷ This seemed to confirm what the leadership
of the Democratic party suspected: "Our attitude on this whole subject had
been conditioned by past actions of the Governor in attempting to circumvent
the State Senate in their constitutional and statutory role of confirming certain
Gubernatorial appointments." Perhaps the most blatant example of this had
been Milliken's attempt "to stack the Workmen's Compensation Appeal
Board with anti-labor types, during a Senate recess, so that the sixty days for
rejection would expire without their action." Milliken's letter betrayed an

intention to again circumvent the spirit of the law: "He did not tell us whom he was considering as we had requested. He had not asked a representative to contact us. He planned to ignore us and conduct his review in secret." In a June press conference the governor had "specifically declined to even answer reporter's questions about his search."[8]

Less than two weeks after the governor assured the state Democratic chairman that the list of Democratic candidates would "be given every consideration," he appointed a black attorney, Willa Mae King, to the vacancy on the Public Service Commission. Morley Winograd had never heard of her. On Wednesday, July 6, when he learned of the appointment from the media, Winograd began to telephone the Democratic black leadership "to find out more about Mrs. King. I called Marc Stepp and Buddy Battle first. Buddy at first indicated she was a Republican and then corrected himself saying she had done some things on behalf of some Democratic candidates locally."[9] Stepp told Winograd that he knew King and would have her call. She never did. After speaking with the two most important black UAW leaders, Winograd contacted Malcolm Dade in the Detroit mayor's office and the Democratic chairmen of the two black congressional districts, Freddie Burton in the Thirteenth and Hubert Holley in the First.

> Malcolm Dade said he would find out the Mayor's opinion but in his own mind, while she had been active on behalf of the Mayor and on behalf of some other local Democrats, he would not characterize her as a Democrat. He also said that those kind of appointments made Governor Milliken hard to beat. Freddie Burton told me the Thirteenth District had endorsed her when she ran for judge but he was unsure of her political affiliation. Hubert Holley told me that despite 'labor pressure' the First District had not endorsed her and he didn't know her. George Gore later informed me that the specific reason for not endorsing her was her Republican background. Among other comments I received voluntarily once the stories broke, was the information that she had been seen at fundraisers for Republican candidates like Marvin Esch.[10]

Though Mrs. King's Democratic credentials appeared to be of dubious validity, Winograd tried to direct the attention of the media instead to the governor's refusal to follow in practice the "sunshine" laws he supported in theory. Because of Milliken's failure to conduct the appointment process in full view of the public, "his appointment would have to be reviewed thoroughly by the State Senate in order to bring the person's credentials, background, and ability before the public."[11] Winograd withheld comment on the question of the nominee's political activity and partisan affiliation. "I indicated my lack of knowledge of Mrs. King's earlier interest in the appointment, or her Democratic credentials."[12] When the press asked whether he thought King was a closet Republican, Winograd replied that he "didn't know her well enough to say whether she was or was not such a person."[13] While the *Detroit Free Press* provided a reasonably accurate account of what Winograd had said,[14] the *Detroit News* reported that Winograd had actually called King a "closet Republican."[15] Marc Stepp was offended. Despite his own recommendation of another candidate, John McEwan, for the position, Stepp owed a political debt to King for help she had given him in his own UAW election.[16] He did not hesitate to repay it, first by privately promoting King[17] and then by publicly condemning the state Democratic chairman. The *Michigan Chronicle,* Detroit's black newspaper, quoted the UAW vice-president as saying "Morley Winograd's smart-aleck type remarks are probably the reason Democrats can't elect a governor in Michigan."[18]

Morley Winograd was not amused. He immediately wrote to Stepp to set the record straight: "I was surprised and very disappointed to read your reported remarks in the Michigan Chronicle concerning my 'smart-aleck type' statements. I am at a loss as to what would have provoked such a comment from someone who is not only a fellow party officer but a Vice-President of the UAW and someone whom I consider to be a friend."[19] Winograd then detailed the series of events that had followed the resignation of Bill Ralls from the Public Service Commission down to the appointment of Willa Mae King. At the end of his letter he expressed the hope that Stepp would "agree your reported statements were mistaken and unwarranted. I know how it is possible for the press to distort one's meaning. . . . I hope this letter will help eliminate any misunderstanding on your part about my role in this matter." In a postscript, Winograd added, "Given these clarifications, I would appreciate it if you could suggest how we might correct the current misinformation the readers of the Michigan Chronicle now have and which misunderstanding might hurt our Democratic effort in 1978."[20] Stepp's only response to this lengthy explanation was to suggest that Winograd write a letter to the *Michigan Chronicle.* Six months later, he would have much more to say, and none of it would be favorable to the chairman of the Michigan Democratic party.

In 1964, the Democratic national convention, under the direction of Lyndon Johnson, arranged a compromise under which the all-white regular Mississippi delegation was seated along with two black delegates from the Mississippi Freedom Democratic party. There was more involved in that event, however, than merely a symbolic break in the color line. The convention declared that beginning in 1968 no delegation would be seated from any state where the vote was denied on the basis of race or color. "Until then," according to Theodore H. White, "the great American parties had been patchworks of diverse delegations, each state choosing its delegates by its own rules. . . . Now, however, for the first time, a national party imposed binding rules."[21] Four years later, in

1968, the power that had been used to prohibit the exclusion of anyone on the basis of race was extended ostensibly to guarantee "that all Democratic voters get 'full, meaningful, and timely opportunity to participate in the selection of delegates' to the next convention."[22] This required a major reworking of the rules of the party. The task was beyond the competence of a convention and was entrusted to a commission chaired first by George McGovern and then by Donald Fraser. The McGovern-Fraser Commission constructed a set of rules that ensured participation by imposing what were in effect quotas for minorities and women. These rules helped facilitate the nomination of George McGovern and, in the judgment of some, the election of Richard Nixon. The McGovern Commission was followed by another commission, chaired by Barbara Mikulski, which, it was hoped, would subject the McGovern reforms to a needed reformation. The Mikulski Commission, however, failed to make any fundamental alteration in the basic premise of its predecessor. Women and minorities were still to be guaranteed representation in at least rough approximation to their proportion of the population. The third commission established to reform or at least rework the rules of the national Democratic party was formally called the Commission on Presidential Nomination and Party Structure. It was chaired by Morley Winograd of Michigan.

On January 20, 1978, the Winograd Commission held its final meeting and prepared its final list of proposals for the consideration of the Democratic National Committee. Though the commission made several recommendations to alter the system of presidential primaries, from the abbreviation of the period during which they take place to a requirement that candidates receive an increasing share of the vote to remain in contention for the nomination, its most controversial suggestion concerned the principle of affirmative action. The Winograd Commission unanimously recommended the addition of two paragraphs to the existing affirmative action rules. The first paragraph read:

> With respect to women, blacks, hispanics, and Native Americans, each state party shall develop and submit affirmative action programs for these groups including not only outreach activities such as recruitment, education and training, but also remedial action to overcome the effects of past discrimination.[23]

While this appeared to continue the commitment to affirmative action, the second suggested paragraph seemed to undermine the first by applying the principle to any group, whether the victims of discrimination or not, that did not have adequate representation in the party. It read:

> With respect to groups such as ethnics, youth, persons over 65 years of age, workers, persons with a high school education or less, physically handicapped, and other groups significantly underrepresented in our party affairs, each state

party shall develop and submit party outreach programs for such groups identified in their plans, including recruitment, education and training, in order to
achieve full participation by such groups in the delegate selection process and at
all levels of party affairs.[24]

The only real difference between the two paragraphs was that the groups
referred to in the first would continue to be subject to ''remedial action to
overcome the effects of past discrimination.'' In an earlier draft, the Winograd Commission had made no such distinction between the groups that were
to be given preferential treatment and had, moreover, listed ''women,'' ''minorities,'' and several other groups without mentioning blacks.

In Michigan, the black leadership was alarmed. Three weeks after the
Winograd Commission held its final meeting, the Michigan Democratic black
caucus held a three-day retreat at the Hospitality Inn in Lansing. State Senator
David S. Holmes, chairman of the caucus, warned in his opening address that
the work of the Winograd Commission was a threat to the affirmative action
program adopted by the 1976 Democratic National Convention. It would
mean, he claimed, ''a battle for survival.''[25] A special session of the black
caucus was devoted to a discussion of the Winograd Commission report and
its implications for black participation in the Democratic party. With Coleman
Young and Marc Stepp serving as moderators, the caucus listened to Morris
Cooper, a black staff member of the Winograd Commission, explain what the
commission had proposed. As soon as Cooper finished reading the two paragraphs that were to be added to the affirmative action rules, a member of the
caucus interrupted:

Hold it right there. That's the nitty-gritty when they try to put the shaft to the
brother. Before now, since during the '50s in this state . . . we've sent 20%
blacks to all conventions. Black folks. Now that 20% will be deleted—listen to
me brother. I want you to read how they're gonna try to shaft black folks.[26]

Cooper reread the two paragraphs. This time another member of the caucus
commented on what seemed, at least to the black caucus, the obvious intention of the white leadership of the Winograd Commission:

It's clear that they're trying to put their foot in the door. All these old folks and
workers and what-nots. You'll notice under paragraph 2—minorities, we understand that—women, blacks, hispanics and Indians period. Now they were trying
to run these other boobs in in paragraph four. Ethnics, youth, workers over 65,
workers, workers with high school education or less, physically handicapped and
other boobs, trying to run all those in. But the compromise is that the minorities—women, blacks, hispanics, Native Americans, they not only have pro-

grams for affirmative action and for education and recruitment but for remedial action to overcome the effects of past discrimination. That's the key, that's what we're talking about . . . they're one step away but they're not there yet.

It was clear that the caucus did not think highly of the Winograd Commission and its affirmative action proposals.

When Morris Cooper finished his presentation, and there were no more comments from the floor, Marc Stepp addressed the caucus and left no doubt that he also opposed the proposals of the commission: "I always thought minorities were black. And then there was the political definition of minorities. It was who got the votes. And in this state black minorities with votes were represented 20% of the Democrats, 20% or better. . . ." This, it should be noted, did not agree with the position of the McGovern Commission that minorities should be represented in proportion to their percentage of the population. That standard, applied in Michigan, would have reduced black representation below the black proportion of the Democratic vote. It was characteristic and understandable that Stepp, along with nearly every other black Democratic leader, insisted on affirmative action while ignoring the standard of representation affirmative action had originally been designed to achieve. At the moment, however, Stepp was far less concerned with the precise meaning of affirmative action than he was with "a new definition of minorities that's been applied to blacks. . . ." Under this new definition not only blacks but, as Stepp inelegantly and rather intolerantly phrased it, "homos, blue-collar, Chicanos, women and all the others" were called minorities. That, conceivably, could lead to a reduction in black participation while the Democratic party continued to proclaim its commitment to minority representation.

Marc Stepp was a vice-president of the UAW, and Morley Winograd had three times been elected chairman of the Michigan Democratic party with union support, but Stepp obviously felt no obligation to refrain from attacking the commission Winograd had chaired. Stepp, the highest-ranking black official in the UAW, did, however, believe he had an obligation and a debt of loyalty to the mayor of Detroit. "Because of Coleman," Stepp explained to the black caucus, "I am now on the National Committee of the Democratic Party." This would have astonished the white leadership of the Democratic party, all of whom believed that Marc Stepp was on the committee because he was a black vice-president of the UAW. Stepp, however, chose to regard Coleman Young, rather than the union, as his principal benefactor. "Coleman," Stepp continued, "I appreciate that. I hope I never embarrass you." The relation between the mayor of Detroit and the vice-president of the UAW hardly seemed one of equality.

There really was no limit to the lengths Stepp was prepared to go to extol the virtues or exaggerate the importance of Coleman Young. When it was the mayor's turn to speak, Stepp introduced him by suggesting that Coleman Young had not only helped elect, but now controlled, the president of the United States:

> No other region in this country has moved as southeastern Michigan, especially Detroit, for the last few years. And if it were not for the person who serves as vice-chairman of the party who said very early when all the other aspects of ethnic purity and all that and stood steady would we have this today. That's why it seems to me that we are blessed to have among us a man named Coleman Young, along with Jimmy Carter, to bring to this region the kind of blessings we have.

There seemed, then, to be no reason to provide Coleman Young with an introduction any different from the one traditionally given the president.

> You know they say that whenever the President of the United States or the Vice-President speaks anywhere at a podium, there's always the shield of the United States of America. Check it, next time you listen to Carter at a press conference, they never say President Carter peanut farmer and all the background on that person, they just simply say the President of the United States. Cause all intelligent people know who that person is. Intelligent people, the Mayor of the City of Detroit.

Coleman Young had a remarkable ability to express clearly the central issue as he understood it. While most liberal Democratic politicians, both black and white, drew fine distinctions between affirmative action, which they invariably supported, and a system of quotas, which they inevitably opposed, the mayor was not afraid of calling a thing by its real name. In a real sense, as Young put it, "affirmative action began here in Michigan. You remember in 1968 we went to the midnight caucus, I think it was down in the old Book-Cadillac, and we were demanding 20%, I admit it was a quota, far as I'm concerned, I ain't got a damn thing against quotas. That's the only way you can keep matters straight. . . ." The mayor had no sympathy for those who opposed racial quotas. They "will take us back to the old slavery days when we couldn't count. So those who are against quotas have already achieved over their quota and can't stand the count." The 20 percent quota blacks had demanded had been won in 1968, and "since that time I believe we're the only state in the union who's done that consistently every election and we've applied it across the board to politics in Michigan."

Affirmative action, whether in the Michigan or the national Democratic party, was the same as it was in the city of Detroit: "Every time that we advance a mile somebody attacks us and tries to push us back. At every convention we've had there's been an attack on this question. There was first the McGovern Commission, then the Mikulski Commission and, now, the Winograd Commission. The same damn story.'' Young placed the responsibility for the latest attempt to curtail black representation directly on the chairman of the state Democratic party. Winograd ''was the person who came to the Executive Board of the National Committee of the Democratic Party proposing and he called it the Michigan plan proposing language worse than this that would have diluted minorities and all those people you heard about— old folks and working folks and handicapped folks and friends and Lithuanians. That's exactly what it might involve.'' The reason Young was reporting this now was ''to indicate that there has been a hell of a lot of fighting going on,'' and to let everyone know ''that the Chairman of the Michigan State Democratic Party is trying to push the damn thing back and you ought to know about that. . . .''

For Coleman Young and the black caucus the issue of affirmative action was by no means restricted to the internal organization of the Democratic party. If blacks were to be independent, their participation could not depend on the favor of a white majority; they had to obtain recognition of their right to representation at every level and in every branch of government, including even the judiciary. The mayor reminded his audience that ''we've got some judgeships coming up—federal judgeships—you all know about them because there's no need in pussy-footing around.'' Damon Keith, who had served on the federal bench at the district court level, had been appointed to fill the vacancy on the Sixth Circuit Court of Appeals that was created when Wade McCree became the first black ever to serve as solicitor general of the United States.

> Now as far as I'm concerned when Wade McCree went on that court down there, that was our quota and we want a black guy in his place and we got one. Now there were those who said we want to look at all these candidates and pick one on merit. Well I still say that was a black position and we got it replaced with a black so everybody's happy. I'm happy cause I got my quota and they believe the best man got it and I believe that too.

The selection of Keith to replace McCree created a vacancy on the district court. Moreover, Congress was in the process of creating three more positions on the district court for the Eastern District of Michigan. A total of four new judges, in other words, would have to be appointed. Coleman Young's position was clear: ''We ought to have two out of those four. To put it another way, a black should replace Damon so we don't lose ground but right now there's no black at all on the federal bench in Detroit, in Michigan . . . so we get a black in Damon's place we still want one out of three of those others.''

The mayor moved from the federal judiciary to the state's major universities. There were at the time vacancies in the presidencies of both Wayne State University and Michigan State University. Clifton Wharton, who had become the first black to head a major American university when he became president of Michigan State in 1969, had left to become chancellor of New York's state university system. Though Wharton had never become involved in Michigan politics and had had no apparent interest in either the Democratic party or the black caucus, the mayor claimed him and his position: "When we lost Wharton at Michigan State that meant the only black who's president of a big university is gone. Between Wayne and Michigan State, I'm saying we ought to demand one of them too. Anyway you want to cut it." To those who might object that the question of the governance of a university should not become part of a political struggle, Young had a quick reply: "For those who say that we don't want to get in the political process, every damn thing is in the political process." Or would be if the mayor had his way.

For years the Democratic party had apportioned membership on the national committee equally between the sexes and thought nothing of it. From the very beginning of Morley Winograd's tenure as state chairman, the Michigan Democratic party had carefully divided every district delegation to the state convention and every committee appointed by the state party equally between men and women. Coleman Young was one of the very few who seemed able to understand that the party was perfectly prepared to give to women what it seemed determined to withhold from blacks. The mayor pointed to the inconsistency, and observed the irony of it, with rare subtlety.

> Now just one final matter, a word on the matter of quotas. We were successful, I believe, in the Executive Committee in getting them to back off in this opposition to quotas because if you read the language that provides for delegate representation, it says very clearly that every other half of each state's delegation shall be of the opposite sex. If that ain't a damn quota of 50%, I don't know what is. Then they say period. And then they say but this shall not be considered a quota. All I want then is that 20% of the damn delegation gonna be black . . . and this shall not be considered a quota.

Before it adjourned, the black caucus adopted a position paper accusing the Winograd Commission of attempting "with malice and forethought . . . to dilute black representation within the Democratic Party." The caucus warned that "adoption of the Winograd Commission report in its present form by the DNC could result in a demand at the state convention in August by our organization for the removal of Morley Winograd as chairman."[27] State Representative Raymond Hood, a trustee of the caucus, added his own complaint that Winograd was "supposed to be representing us in Michigan and here he's going out trying to dilute our power."[28]

When the press asked Winograd to respond to the accusations of the black caucus, he refused: "I'm not going to respond to a statement like that." Winograd claimed that he did not really know what the black caucus was upset about. "I have no idea," he asserted, "what they're talking about. I don't know what their charges are based on. For one thing, the report of the commission hasn't been released yet."[29] Winograd knew more than he suggested, and he was a good deal more angry than he appeared.

Five days after he was attacked by the black caucus, Winograd took the offensive. In a letter to State Senator David Holmes, chairman of the caucus, Winograd called the caucus resolution

> one of the most shameful and unwarranted attacks upon my personal character and integrity that I have ever had to endure in my political career. It is shameful because it was done "behind my back" without affording me an opportunity to confront my accusers. It is unwarranted because all of the facts alleged in the paper are untrue.

According to Winograd, the affirmative action proposal, which the black caucus believed jeopardized black representation, actually "gave women, blacks and other 'discriminated against' minorities new rights in the selection of delegates to national conventions." The proposal also required "outreach programs for a number of groups which have been underrepresented in our national conventions as compared to their electoral contributions to the Democratic Party." These programs were not "designed to 'take away' anything from the most loyal segment of our Democratic electorate—the black voter." Winograd enclosed materials documenting precisely what his original affirmative action proposal had been and how it had been clarified and then unanimously adopted. "I trust after receiving the material," he suggested, "you will re-examine the position of your organization both as it relates to me personally and as it relates to the Commission's proposal." Winograd wanted something more: "I would hope that in order to repair the damage you have done to my reputation, you will also at that time issue a public apology."[30]

On the same day that he wrote to David Holmes, Winograd wrote to Hubert Holley and Freddie Burton, the chairmen of the First and Thirteenth district organizations, and asked them "to disassociate yourselves from the position paper released by the officers of the Black Caucus, particularly as it regards the threatened demand for my resignation."[31] He also wrote to Coleman Young. After expressing his appreciation for the remarks the mayor had made at the black caucus that "were helpful in attempting to clarify the complex subject which had been confused even further by previous speakers," Winograd indicated his distress at learning "that you indicated to the members that I and other party officers had not consulted you about our original proposals.'' Winograd reminded Young that the entire Michigan delegation to the national committee had been invited to participate in drafting the proposals. ''One of the reasons'' for this invitation ''was out of respect and appreciation for your role as Vice Chairman of the DNC.'' Though the mayor had not attended the meeting at which the original proposal had been put forward, his assistant Malcolm Dade had been there, and Dade had ''indicated afterwards that Libby Maynard should contact you directly on the proposal.'' For three weeks Maynard ''made numerous phone calls,'' but ''she was unable to contact either you or Malcolm until the day of the DNC Executive Committee meeting. It was then that you publicly condemned her, me, and the proposal in a manner for which you later apologized to Libby.'' The chairman of the Michigan Democratic party closed his letter to the vice-chairman of the Democratic National Committee by suggesting that the full Michigan delegation to the DNC meet for dinner to resolve any misunderstandings that might exist. ''Michigan Democrats,'' Winograd wrote with some urgency, ''cannot afford confrontation over racial issues in this critical election year. Complete communication is the only way to prevent such confrontation.''[32]

Winograd had been outraged by what had transpired at the black caucus, but he had managed to exhibit restraint in the letter he wrote to the black leadership. Even in the letter to the chairman of the caucus, in which his anger had shown through, he had observed at least the forms of civility. When he wrote to Marc Stepp, however, he did not even attempt to disguise how he felt. Unlike Coleman Young and David Holmes, who were elected officials, or Freddie Burton and Hubert Holley, who were elected party officers, Marc Stepp was an officer of an organization upon whose loyalty and support Winograd believed he was entitled to rely. In Winograd's judgment at least, Stepp had failed utterly to represent the position of the UAW at the meeting of the black caucus. Coleman Young and David Holmes had opposed Winograd; Marc Stepp had betrayed him.

Winograd wrote to Stepp ''out of a deep felt sense of anger and resentment.'' He accused the UAW vice-president of having ''deliberately distorted and misrepresented the position'' of the Winograd Commission. As a consequence of Stepp's ''unfounded and malicious allegations that I was attempting to dilute black representation in the affairs of our party, the rank-and-file black Democrats of this state have been given a totally false impression not only of my work at the Democratic National Committee but also of me as a person.'' This was not the first time Stepp had helped to create a false impression. Obviously referring to the Willa Mae King episode, Winograd gave notice that he would not ''sit idly by and allow this kind of character assassination to occur once again.'' If Stepp did not fully understand what the commission had done, he had no one to blame but himself.

> As a member of the Democratic National Committee and of the Michigan Democratic Party's Executive Board, you have failed to attend a number of meetings at which this subject has been discussed. I met with you personally several months ago and you did not at that time indicate any disagreement with my actions. Instead you chose to raise it in a forum from which I had been excluded.

Winograd proceeded to explain, as he had done in the letter to Holmes, what the commission had actually proposed. He then asked Stepp to disassociate himself from the position paper of the black caucus, and in addition, to provide the *Michigan Chronicle* with a written clarification of the position taken by Morley Winograd and the Winograd Commission on the question of black representation.[33]

Whatever Marc Stepp thought when he read Winograd's letter, he had no reason to feel any obligation to comply with any of the requests or demands made in it. Stepp was a vice-president of the UAW, and while that had not stopped him from expressing in front of the black caucus his indebtedness to Coleman Young, it was a position from which he could disdain the complaints of a state party chairman. Stepp understood that, but so did his antagonist. After Winograd had written to Stepp, he made a telephone call to Irving Bluestone. Winograd told Bluestone that he was being "cut up by people in the union," and he asked "whether black UAW leaders were considered part of the UAW." He explained that he was tired of arranging things in advance with the union only to be "stabbed in the back." Bluestone agreed that this should not be going on, and to put an end to it, he called an executive meeting of Michigan CAP. It was understood that in addition to the UAW vice-presidents and regional directors who made up the executive board of Michigan CAP, Morley Winograd would attend and present his case.[34] The meeting was scheduled for April 10.

Before the meeting took place, Winograd received replies from two of the black leaders to whom he had written. On March 10, Freddie Burton avoided a direct response to Winograd's request that he disassociate himself from the position paper of the black caucus. He instead reported that it had been "the opinion of the members who attended the Black Caucus meeting that the thrust of the report of the Winograd Commission was to dilute and reduce the representation throughout the country to a percentage that was less than the representation that had been accorded to minorities and women at the last two National Conventions."[35] Burton invited the state chairman to attend the next membership meeting of the Thirteenth District committee to correct any misunderstanding that might exist. He was rather more civil than David Holmes. The chairman of the black caucus waited over a month to respond to Winograd's request for an apology and then sent only a curt reply. Holmes wrote that after meeting with the officers of the black caucus on March 5, "I was instructed to inform you that we have no intention of apologizing for the position which was adopted by the full membership of the Caucus retreat held February 11 and 12, 1978."[36] Holmes also invited Winograd to discuss the recommendations of the commission with a meeting of the membership. Winograd waited only a day to answer. "Dear Dave," he wrote, "At such time as the Black Caucus withdraws its public statement accusing me of maliciously attempting to dilute black representation, I will be more than happy to meet with its membership to discuss the positions taken by the Winograd Commission."[37] It did not seem likely that such a meeting would be held soon. No meeting with the black caucus had been held[38]—nor, for that matter, had any communication from either Coleman Young or Marc Stepp been received—before the executive board of Michigan UAW-CAP met on April 10.

When Morley Winogard walked into the upstairs room at Little Harry's restaurant on East Jefferson in Detroit where the CAP executive board was meeting, he was thoroughly prepared. In addition to a detailed outline of what he was going to say, he had with him documentation with which to support his charge that Marc Stepp had engaged in a systematic attempt to discredit a party chairman who had never done anything without the prior approval of the UAW. This was crucial. Winograd could defend himself against Stepp's attempt to discredit him in the eyes of the black community only if he could discredit Stepp in the eyes of the UAW. To do that he had to show that an attack on him was somehow tantamount to an attack on the union. Winograd wasted no time. He told the executive board that he "would not be here if the dispute between Marc and me was based upon personality differences or was without impact on the UAW and the Democratic Party."[39] It was a dispute, moreover, that had to be resolved, because "it goes to the heart of the relationship between the UAW and the Democratic Party."

Those who believed that the UAW was simply one of the participants in a coalition of interests that made up the Democratic party would have been astounded to hear the chairman of the Michigan Democratic party explain to the executive board of the UAW's political arm his understanding of the relationship between the union and the party. "I don't make any substantive political decision," he asserted, "without checking with the UAW and reaching agreement." Winograd, in other words, went to the UAW before he ever proposed anything to the executive board of the Michigan Democratic party. The chairman had "campaigned for this job and won it with UAW support because I believe you're the essential component of any Democratic victory in

Michigan and because I believe in your goals and principles.'' He did not want ''the job without UAW support because it isn't worth having under those conditions.'' The chairman left no doubt that he believed the union was entitled to have the state party led by someone with whom it felt entirely comfortable: ''All you have to do is let me know when you want me to go and I'll be gone.''

Winograd proceeded to describe the regular procedure he employed to make certain that he never did anything that might conflict with UAW policy. ''When I clear things with the UAW,'' he explained, ''it is done through the appropriate organizational channels.'' He would ''first check'' with Sam Fishman, and then, ''if he or I think it's important enough, we arrange a meeting with the head of UAW-CAP-Michigan (before Doug, now Irv) to review the matter in detail. Sometimes all that's required is a phone call; sometimes, such as this, the matter is referred for a full board discussion.'' Having declared his own dedication to the union, and described the carefully calibrated procedure by which he ensured the compatibility of party policy with union policy, Winograd sprang the trap he had carefully set.

> All of this makes it very hard for me to understand how I can be criticized publicly by a board member like Marc. If he has a complaint about something I've done, he really has a complaint with UAW policy because I've never gone against it and if he has a difference of opinion, it should be ironed out within the UAW (with or without my involvement as you deem necessary) if the organizational structure means anything.

If, in other words, there was a dispute between Winograd and Stepp, then there was also, necessarily, a dispute between Stepp and the UAW.

According to the logic of Winograd's argument, an attack on him was an attack on the UAW. By threatening to call for the resignation of the state chairman, the black caucus, whether it knew it or not, had placed itself at odds with union policy. Worse yet, Marc Stepp and the rest of the caucus had acted in the best interest of the Republican party. Governor Milliken, in Winograd's judgment, was losing some of his rural support and would attempt to make up for it in the black community. That, the chairman suggested, was the reason Milliken had ''been so friendly to Coleman and to Detroit,'' and that was the reason ''why we need united black and white leadership opposition to him.'' The UAW and the Democratic party were ''clearly united on the need to beat Milliken.'' It was therefore ''incredible to me that during the last year, Marc Stepp, officer and leader in the black community, would spend his time trying to undermine my leadership and more importantly publicly criticizing the Democratic instead of the Republican Party.'' An attack on Morley Winograd, it now appeared, was indistinguishable from an assault on *both* the UAW and the Democratic party, and that, in turn, was equivalent to support for William Milliken and the Republican party. Winograd knew what he was doing.

Marc Stepp had attacked Morley Winograd for his remarks about Willa Mae King, but "those remarks," according to Winograd, "were made after I checked her credentials with many black leaders including Buddy Battle and Marc Stepp." The UAW vice-president had then "compounded and worsened the problem by launching a false and unwarranted attack upon me at the last meeting of the Black Caucus with the press in attendance." Stepp had not been deterred when Winograd wrote him privately during the Willa Mae King controversy, so after the attack in the black caucus, Winograd sent all of the members of the Michigan UAW-CAP executive board "copies of my letter this time in the hope that you could collectively convince Marc that there is a clear need for him to publicly correct the very damaging impression created by this latest incident." Winograd was perfectly prepared to let the UAW decide what ought to be done. "I haven't changed since I took the job," he asserted. He was still determined to follow the lead of the UAW: "My policies have been your policies. If you don't like them, then please change your decisions and I'll change mine." He would follow the UAW even if it decided to ask for what he had angrily refused even to hear suggested by the black caucus: "If one of those decisions is that Marc's right and I stand in the way of electing a Governor, then let me know now so I can quit tomorrow." If, on the other hand, the union wanted him to continue and to lead the party during the effort to defeat Milliken, then it was time to remind "the black community that the Democratic Party and its leader is your ally and their friend." Winograd had someone in mind to initiate the campaign to restore the credibility of the chairman with black voters. Looking directly at Stepp, Morley Winograd concluded his remarks with the request, "Marc, I'd like to have you begin that PR barrage; I've been waiting for it to be directed against someone else for a long time."

On the surface the dispute between Morley Winograd and the black caucus had arisen over the question of black representation at the 1980 Democratic national convention. Winograd had denied he had ever intended to dilute black representation, and as Coleman Young had pointed out in his speech to the caucus, that had not actually been proposed by the Winograd Commission. The anger the chairman and the black leadership of the Michigan Democratic party directed at each other derived more from mutual suspicion than from any uncontested fact. Coleman Young, Marc Stepp, and much of the rest of the black leadership believed that Morley Winograd, in concert with, among others, Sam Fishman, had set about to abolish the guarantees of black participation in the Democratic party. Coleman Young did not hesitate to call a quota a quota, and Morley Winograd had run for the chairmanship proclaiming his opposition to them. That neither he nor Sam Fishman nor any other white leader of the state Democratic party had ever uttered so much as a word against party rules that allocated delegates and party office equally between the sexes did nothing to diminish black distrust.

Winograd, for his part, had been subjected to the kind of vicious personal attack that no black had ever experienced at the hands of a white leader of the modern Michigan Democratic party. There was, in addition, a peculiar double standard involved when the chairman of the party was expected to conform to the wishes of the UAW while a union vice-president attacked him with apparent impunity. Winograd, moreover, had to suffer the indignity of watching helplessly while Coleman Young, vice-chairman of the national Democratic party, held the allegiance of the White House while fraternizing with a Republican governor and attacking the Democratic state chairman. All of this was only intensified by the 1978 election, in which a Republican governor carried more than a quarter of Detroit's black vote, an accomplishment that Winograd believed would have been politically impossible without the covert assistance of Mayor Coleman Young. Less than a year later, however, the chairman of the Michigan Democratic party would have what would seem at the time a splendid opportunity for revenge, and the conflict between Morley Winograd and Coleman Young would become part of a national struggle between Jimmy Carter and Edward Kennedy for possession of the Democratic party.

Three months after the 1978 election, Morley Winograd was elected without opposition to a fourth successive term as state party chairman. He had no intention of seeking a fifth and did not really expect to finish the fourth. After six years, he had begun to grow tired of a position that limited both his income and his political opportunities. While Winograd was looking for something else to do, the White House began to recruit him to serve as deputy to Sarah Weddington, assistant to the president. Weddington had replaced Mark Segal after Segal had resigned in protest over what he considered the administration's inadequate commitment to Israel. Segal had been the administration's main contact with the Jewish community and the state Democratic organizations, and Winograd, it was hoped, would take over these two responsibilities. By the summer of 1979 Winograd was not at all certain that a job in the Carter White House had much of a future, but he was at least willing to hear what the president had to say. On Labor Day, Winograd and his wife and daughter had lunch at the White House.

Jimmy Carter was in serious political trouble in the summer of 1979. For more than a year he had run behind Senator Edward Kennedy in every poll taken. In July, 1978, Kennedy had led Carter by twenty-four points.[40] Following his performance at Camp David, Carter had managed to close to within five points of Kennedy, but he had not come that close again. Though Kennedy had "reaffirmed his support" for Carter in March, the president believed "later that spring" that Kennedy's "constant public criticism of my policies was a strong indication that he was planning to run himself."[41] On June 12, the president confided in his diary:

> I met with Ham, Jody, Jerry, Tim, Fritz, Rosalyn, Stu, Frank and Dick Moe to talk about the political situation. To summarize, I told them that they should screen their entire staffs, to tell everybody that we were faced with difficulty now, and that it was very likely to get worse in the future. If they couldn't take the pressure, to get out. I felt personally confident that we were doing a good job for the country, that we would prevail again in this Congress as we have in the previous Congresses, that I would win in 1980 no matter who ran against me, and that I was going to fight to the last vote.[42]

A week later, on June 19, Carter demonstrated his confidence in the future by remarking to a small group of congressmen who "asked me privately if I dared face Kennedy in a primary election," that should it come to that he would whip "Kennedy's ass."[43] The president's comment seemed like nothing so much as the empty boast of a desperate man when, in the middle of July, a New York Times/CBS News poll showed him trailing Kennedy by the incredible margin of fifty-three to sixteen.[44]

Carter was in trouble with the country, with the Democratic party, and, because of Andrew Young, with the Jewish community. As he had proven with both Leonard Woodcock and Coleman Young, he was intensely loyal to those who had helped him when very few were willing to take him seriously as a candidate for the Democratic nomination in 1976. When he appointed Andrew Young, who had been the first black elected to Congress from Georgia in the twentieth century, as ambassador to the United Nations, Carter called him the best person he had ever known in public service and announced that his "status will be equal to that of the Secretary of State or the Secretary of the Treasury or anyone else."[45] It did not take Young long to confuse ambassador to the United Nations with ambassador to the world. From his declaration that Cuban troops in Angola provided some degree of stability to his assertion that there were thousands of political prisoners in American jails, the former congressman exhibited an uncanny ability to generate controversy and to jeopardize the political well-being of Jimmy Carter. Through it all the president seemed either unaware of the damage or unable to control his own ambassador. In the summer of 1979, however, Young "finally outran presidential and public tolerance in Washington when . . . he entered into clandestine negotiations with the Palestinian Liberation Organization in New York, and he was forced to resign."[46]

The Labor Day luncheon at the White House was designed to begin a process of reconciliation between two essential parts of the Democratic coalition, blacks and Jews. A dozen people, half of them black and half of them Jewish, had been invited. Jimmy Carter told them he was certain that any division that might exist between blacks and Jews was probably based on misunderstandings that could, with goodwill, be corrected. Apparently to demonstrate that even serious differences of policy should not disrupt the Democratic alliance, Carter proceeded to inform his small audience that even though he had dismissed Andrew Young from office, Young was still a good friend and, indeed, had spent the previous night as a guest at the White House. If this disclosure provided any assurances to his black guests, it did nothing to reduce the suspicion among his Jewish guests that Young's contacts with the PLO had perhaps not been entirely unknown to or unauthorized by the president.

After the president had expressed his belief that blacks and Jews could be brought back into harmonious relationship within the Democratic coalition, he turned to Winograd and asked, "Morley, don't you agree?" Carter did not expect the answer he received. Winograd did not agree and, when Carter asked him why, explained that he thought there were fundamental differences on a number of issues like affirmative action and the question of Israel and the PLO that made real reconciliation impossible. The president did not appear to appreciate Winograd's opinion or his candor, while another guest, Ted Mann, president of the Jewish Organization Presidents, looked stunned. As if to show that the reconciliation he was urging was really possible, even on the question of the PLO, Carter remarked that the disagreement over this matter was more apparent than real. Israel, he told his guests, had known that a member of the Egyptian delegation at Camp David was a member of the PLO. According to Carter, Israel also knew that the Egyptians were constantly checking with the PLO as they negotiated the Camp David agreement. Morley Winograd listened as the president suggested that Israel had known that in negotiating with the Egyptians they were also negotiating with the PLO and said to himself, "The hell they did."[47]

As the lunch ended and Winograd and his wife were about to fetch their daughter, who had been having lunch with Amy Carter, the president approached him and said he wanted to see him later that afternoon. Winograd nodded. A few minutes later, Winograd told Hamilton Jordan to tell Carter that he did not want the White House job, and because he did not want to embarrass the president, that if the afternoon meeting was for that purpose, not to call. No one did. Winograd left the White House convinced that Jimmy Carter was not a real friend of Israel and certain that both the party and the country would be better served by another candidate for the presidency. By a strange coincidence, at about the same time Winograd was having lunch with

Jimmy Carter, Edward Kennedy "at a cookout at his summer home in Hyannis Port," took his closest political aide, Paul Kirk, "aside and told him he was going to run."[48] The Kennedy campaign, however, had actually begun months earlier, and Morley Winograd was already a part of it.

Winograd had been displeased with Jimmy Carter and his administration almost from the beginning. Appointments to positions in the administration were made without any consultation with the Michigan Democratic party, and on some occasions, without any consideration for the expressed preference of the party chairman. One of the few appointments Winograd actively lobbied for was to have Roger Marz of Oakland County named director of the Great Lakes Basin Commission. Though this was hardly a major policy-making position, Winograd's request was ignored, and Carter appointed a former member of Congress from Ohio. If Winograd's wishes were not considered on matters of patronage, neither he nor Sam Fishman was ever consulted by the White House on matters within the province of the Democratic National Committee. The president named Ken Curtis national chairman without so much as a courtesy call to the Michigan state chairman, and in Winograd's judgment, the White House proceeded to exhibit the intention effectively to dismantle the national committee in order to increase its own control of the party. Winograd, however, had not complained and had suffered in silence as he watched the White House operate as if the mayor of Detroit had somehow been put in charge of the state of Michigan and the Michigan Democratic party. He was, to say the least, in a receptive mood when he began to get telephone calls from his old friend Mark Segal suggesting the imminent possibility of a Kennedy challenge.

Bernard Ryan had worked as an assistant to the chairman of the Michigan Democratic party from 1973, when Morley Winograd was first elected, until the end of 1978. Ryan, a graduate of Notre Dame, where he had won a prize his senior year for the best paper in philosophy, was endowed with a quick mind and a pungent wit. He understood that the future of those who attempt to make a career of party politics is almost always bleak and therefore while he worked for the state party he also attended law school at the University of Detroit. For three years he managed to balance the requirements of his job with the demands imposed by the study of law. He graduated very close to the top of his class and left his position with the Democratic party to join the legal staff of the General Motors Corporation. In 1979, in the middle of July, Morley Winograd called and asked if he would be willing to become involved in a Kennedy campaign. Ryan did not think there was really going to be a Kennedy campaign, because he did not believe Kennedy would actually become a candidate. Winograd, however, insisted that he would: "I can't explain this to you. I can't tell you why, but believe me Kennedy is going to run." Not only was Kennedy going to run, he was clearly going to win.

Winograd had seen polling information that, he assured Ryan, was even more decisive than what the public polls were reporting. Kennedy was going to run, he was going to win, and Ryan was being offered the opportunity to become involved earlier than anyone else in Michigan. Winograd then gave Ryan the telephone number of Mark Segal and told him, "Don't tell anyone about Segal's involvement. Call him. He'll tell you what the plan is."

Segal, as Ryan knew, had become a friend of Winograd's when he served as executive director of the Democratic National Committee before the election of Jimmy Carter. Segal had supported the presidential ambitions of Henry Jackson early in 1972 and had been hired by Carter as his emissary to the Jewish community, especially that part of it most actively involved in promoting the interests of Israel. After leaving the White House because of what he regarded as deliberate deception on whether weapons sold to the Arab nations were useful only for defensive purposes, Segal publicly set up his own lobbying firm and privately began to advance the candidacy of Edward Kennedy. When Ryan called, Segal instructed him, as Winograd already had, not to mention to anyone that he was involved. The movement to draft Kennedy, he informed Ryan, was being orchestrated by Paul Kirk, who, though he had left the Kennedy staff to return to private law practice in Boston, was still Kennedy's closest political advisor. Segal was serving as an intermediary between Kirk and people like Ryan who would become the publicly identified leaders of the draft movement in the states. Kennedy, Segal explained, did not want it to look as if he was taking on an incumbent Democratic president; he wanted it to appear instead as if he were simply responding to an enormous popular demand within the party that he lead the ticket in 1980. This effect would obviously be impossible to produce if it became known that someone as close to Kennedy as Paul Kirk was directly involved. Though they were just beginning, things had to be done quickly. Segal was to create a series of "spontaneous," "grass roots" organizations in a number of states. These organizations were to include credible public figures and important party leaders. Segal wanted Michigan to be the first, and he wanted the organization ready before Labor Day. Ryan agreed to help.

Bernard Ryan was now the leader of the first draft-Kennedy movement in the country, but he faced a formidable obstacle in finding any followers. Mark Segal, Morley Winograd, and Sam Fishman all knew what was going on, but none of them could be publicly identified as having any connection with a Kennedy draft. Ryan needed to have some way to "be able to say I've talked to the right people and this is a scam. He's going to run. Get on board." He discussed the problem with Winograd, and they decided to begin with only those people they needed and could trust. Among those they believed could be trusted were Donald Tucker, an Oakland County attorney who loved Kennedy and, more importantly, was an experienced fund raiser, and Kathy Brown,

who had succeeded Betty Howe as Oakland County chairman and who followed wherever Morley Winograd and Sam Fishman led. Win Rowe, who
had been devoted to all the Kennedys, and Richard Vandermoelen had both
worked for Winograd at the state party and were now both legislative assistants to Joe Forbes, majority leader in the state house of representatives.
Ryan talked to Tucker and told him "I know he's going to run." He talked to
Rowe, Vandermoelen and Brown and told each of them that "Winograd is
somehow involved and Kennedy is going to run." Winograd talked directly to
Joe Forbes.

Ryan now had a small group of trusted allies with which to work, but it
was very far from the formidable committee of public officials and party
officers Segal wanted. Throughout the month of August, Segal continued both
to urge the immediate formation of a draft committee and to insist that his own
involvement remain undisclosed. For Segal, everything was subordinate to
the requirements of the draft movement; for Ryan and Winograd, there were
other considerations. Both of them knew that draft committees seldom survive
a formal declaration of candidacy. If they were to have any chance of direct-
ing the Michigan campaign after Kennedy announced his intention to run,
they had to maintain complete control over the draft committee. Segal clearly
wanted the committee to be made up of the most prominent Democrats willing
to join; Ryan and Winograd wanted a committee made up of the most prominent Democrats willing not only to join but to follow their lead. The most
prominent Democrat they were eager to exclude was Coleman Young, who
they feared might want to have a leg in both the Kennedy and the Carter
camps. Winograd was eager to have the mayor firmly attached to Carter,
because Carter was clearly going to lose to Kennedy. Coleman Young was
never asked to join the draft committee.

Though Segal had wanted a draft committee established by Labor Day, it
was not until the beginning of September that the small group Ryan and
Winograd had assembled began to recruit Democrats to serve. By this time
the national press was beginning to report that supporters of both Carter and
Kennedy were organizing for a straw vote scheduled to take place in October
at the Florida state Democratic convention. Public attention seemed concentrated on the increasing prospects of a Kennedy candidacy. Frank Kelley, the
attorney general, who a few months earlier had dismissed a Kennedy challenge as a futile gesture, now eagerly agreed when he was asked to join the
draft committee. Kelley, however, was not interested in simply serving; he
had talked to Kennedy at a recent meeting of state attorneys general and had
come away convinced that Kennedy was going to run and that he, Frank
Kelley, should lead the campaign in Michigan.

Kelley agreed to serve and then insisted that he lead. He was, after all,
the attorney general of the state of Michigan, and from his point of view, it

was nothing short of ludicrous to suggest that he serve under Bernard Ryan and Donald Tucker, both of whom were twenty years his junior, and neither of whom had ever held or even sought public office. In addition to this, Kelley's last involvement in a presidential campaign had been in 1976, when his appointment as chairman of the Michigan campaign for Henry Jackson had been announced by Jackson himself. Frank Kelley was too important a public figure to be placed under the direction of a couple of former staff assistants. But if Kelley was unwilling to serve unless he could also lead, precisely the same demand could be made by other public officials who, like Dick Austin, held an equal status, or, as in the case of the two Democratic U.S. Senators, Carl Levin and Donald Riegle, occupied higher positions. More important than the potential conflict that might arise over Kelley's insistence that he be treated with greater deference than those who had at least an equal claim to priority was the threat he posed to the control that both Morley Winograd and Sam Fishman wanted to have over an organization with which neither could be publicly associated. Frank Kelley was a problem.

Ryan, Winograd, Fishman, and Kathy Brown had worked together to devise a Kennedy strategy in Michigan. Under their plan, money would be raised to help with the effort in the Florida straw vote as well as to fund a Michigan organization. A draft committee would be formed that was made up of those Democrats sufficiently well known to have an impact on the public. A larger list of supporters would also be assembled to provide the framework for a statewide campaign organization. The Kennedy organization, finally, was to be under Bernard Ryan, who would serve as chairman, and Donald Tucker, who would serve as treasurer. Kathy Brown was to operate as the campaign manager. This plan had been sent to Mark Segal, and it had been approved in broad outline by Paul Kirk. It could now be used to present Frank Kelley with a fait accompli.

On the second Saturday in September, at the Holiday Inn on Telegraph Road in Southfield, Frank Kelley and his assistant, deputy attorney general Stanley Steinborn, met with two state legislators, Morris Hood and Joe Forbes; the chairman of the Wayne County Democratic committee and Sam Fishman's close friend, Bruce Miller; the Twelfth District chairman and another close friend of Fishman's, John Bruff; and the Oakland County chairman, Kathy Brown. Ryan, Tucker, Richard Vandermoelen, and Win Rowe were there as well. After the plan that had been approved by Segal and Kirk had been described, Kelley announced that he did not think Segal was important, and that, moreover, he had spoken directly with Paul Kirk. Apparently Kelley was not going to be denied, even if it meant removing the veil of secrecy behind which Segal and Kirk had been compelled to operate. This was only the beginning. Kelley had not only called Kirk, he had also begun discussions with Carl Wagner. This was, as Ryan put it, "the atom bomb." Wagner had come into Michigan in 1972 to run the McGovern campaign and had managed to antagonize Sam Fishman and most of the other UAW political operatives to the point where he had been asked to leave the state. Nevertheless, he had gained a reputation as a political organizer, and when he joined the staff of Senator Edward Kennedy in December, 1978, it was taken as a sign that a Kennedy candidacy was a serious possibility. Wagner had been unacceptable to Sam Fishman in 1972, and he was considered a danger by Morley Winograd in 1979. Wagner threatened the ability of Winograd and the others to maintain control over the Michigan Kennedy campaign. But he also threatened the legitimacy of the Kennedy draft. Paul Kirk was in private practice in Boston, and Mark Segal was a private consultant in Washington; neither was on the Kennedy payroll, and both had been careful to conceal their participation from all but a few other people. Wagner was known as the political staff assistant to Kennedy, and he was now talking directly to Frank Kelley. Worse, Kelley announced that he had invited Wagner to attend a meeting in Michigan the following Friday to discuss the Kennedy draft committee organization. Incredibly, Wagner had accepted. Kelley wanted to lead the Kennedy campaign, and Wagner apparently wanted to take some measure of revenge for what had been done to him in 1972. Kelley was using Wagner and Wagner was using him. It was a fair bargain.

Carl Wagner did not change his mind. On the following Friday, as scheduled, he attended a meeting at Kelley's Detroit office. Bernard Ryan, however, had decided to pack the meeting with those who agreed with him that Wagner should be kept out and that Kelley should not be allowed to take control. Kathy Brown, Vandermoelen, Rowe, Bruce Miller, and John Bruff were all there. Sam Fishman, whose involvement had to remain secret and who therefore attended only small meetings with people considered reliable, was not. If Wagner noticed that he was facing a largely hostile audience, he did not seem to care. He criticized the plan that Paul Kirk had already approved and indicated his intention to lay down rules that a Michigan Kennedy organization would have to follow. Ryan and the others had decided beforehand that their immediate objective was simply to get through the meeting. Let Wagner say whatever he felt like saying, and let him be as insufferable as he knew how to be. They would nod agreement at what he said and ignore it after he left. For their part, they would use the meeting to try to give Wagner at least some understanding of the political dynamics of the state, and in the process, let him see for himself that Ryan was perfectly capable of chairing the draft committee and that Kathy Brown was adequately equipped to manage the state campaign. When the meeting ended it was not clear that anything had really been accomplished. Wagner said he would return to Washington and report and that he would get back in touch with Kelley.

Frank Kelley was now convinced that he was running the Kennedy campaign. Carl Wagner had let everyone know that he was working with Kelley, and as far as Kelley was concerned, Wagner spoke for Kennedy. Kelley now began to give orders to Ryan—instructing him, for example, to obtain a headquarters, "something visible downtown." Ryan was furious, and he was not alone. Kelley was creating enormous problems for the future ability of Morley Winograd and his allies to control the Kennedy campaign after Kennedy became an announced candidate. Finally, both Winograd and Sam Fishman began talking directly with the attorney general. Kelley was ultimately persuaded that it would be difficult to ask Bobby Crim, Speaker of the House, Richard Austin, the secretary of state, and Donald Riegle, the senior U.S. senator, all of whom had expressed a willingness to join the draft committee, to occupy lesser positions. The solution, it was explained, was to let Ryan and Tucker, who were really technical staff people, head up the committee on paper. This was not the only argument used on Kelley, however. At a meeting at the Dearborn Inn, Ryan and Tucker told Kelley that the draft committee had to file with the Federal Elections Commission and that a decision had to be made as to whose name would be listed as committee chairman. Kelley insisted that his name be on the FEC filing. Ryan, who was barely a year out of law school, informed the attorney general of the state of Michigan that if he became chairman of the draft committee there could be a legal question whether he could then become chairman of the regular, authorized campaign committee that would be established once Kennedy declared his candidacy for the nomination. What he did not say was that in fact there was not even a requirement that the name of the chairman be listed on the FEC filing; only the treasurer of a campaign committee had to be identified when the committee filed. Kelley knew none of this and believed instead what he had just heard. If the chairman of the draft committee was prohibited by federal law from chairing a regular campaign committee for the same office, Kelley preferred that Ryan chair the draft committee. Kelley continued to treat Ryan as if he were staff and continued to give him orders. Bernard Ryan, however, and not Frank Kelley, was the chairman of the Michigan Kennedy for President Committee when the draft committee was announced to the public on September 20. Frank Kelley and three state representatives, Bobby Crim, Joseph Forbes, and Morris Hood, were listed as the four "spokespersons" of the committee. Donald Riegle and Richard Austin had both changed their minds and decided not to become publicly identified with a movement to deprive Jimmy Carter of the Democratic nomination. Carl Levin had never been asked.

While the organizers of the draft movement were struggling with the difficulties of assembling a committee that was both formidable and controllable, Sam Fishman had become convinced that Edward Kennedy had already made up his mind to run. When he informed Douglas Fraser that he had information that Kennedy had decided to become a candidate, however, the president of the UAW said it could not possibly be true. Kennedy, Fraser told Fishman, would not have made any decision that important without first consulting him. As Kennedy had said nothing to Fraser, Kennedy had obviously made no decision. Fraser was not the first person to believe that he was a close friend of a Kennedy, but he had more reason than most to believe that he would be consulted in advance by the senator on anything as politically important as a decision to run against an incumbent president for the Democratic nomination. It was not simply that Fraser was the head of the UAW, nor was it even that he never attempted to conceal that he was a liberal who was much more comfortable with the politics of an Edward Kennedy than those of a Jimmy Carter. It was instead that both of them had worked in concert for several years on the major issue that had come to divide both the UAW and Edward Kennedy from Jimmy Carter.

Douglas Fraser had been the last member of the UAW executive board to give his consent to support for Jimmy Carter during the 1976 campaign for the Democratic nomination, and he had extracted a price. Carter, for the first time, committed himself to a national health insurance program. This commitment, moreover, had not taken the form of private, vague assurances that he would, if elected, do what he could. In April, 1976, "Carter took the liberal Democratic oath on national health insurance in an address to the Student National Medical Association. . . ." Stuart Eizenstat, Carter's advisor on domestic issues, "had negotiated the speech word by word with Lane Kirkland for the AFL-CIO and Leonard Woodcock for the UAW." Carter's speech "stopped barely short of Kennedy's federal cradle-to-grave blanket, the Kennedy-Corman Health Security Act."[49] Once Carter became president, Kennedy began almost immediately to press for action on the program. On May 2, 1977, Carter's secretary of health, education and welfare, Joseph Califano, met with Kennedy and Leonard Woodcock at Kennedy's home in McLean, Virginia. "To Kennedy and Woodcock," according to Califano, "Carter's campaign speech to the medical students was an endorsement of the Kennedy-Corman bill."[50] Two weeks later, at the UAW's annual convention in Los Angeles, "Kennedy charged that 'health reform is in danger of becoming the missing promise' of the Carter administration."[51]

While Kennedy was urging the president to act, Carter was telling Califano, "We can't afford to do everything." While Woodcock and Fraser were supporting Kennedy's view that Carter had made a commitment to national health insurance, another prominent Michigan citizen, the former head of the Bendix Corporation who was the new secretary of the treasury, W. Michael Blumenthal, was among those "moving to influence Carter to postpone, or perhaps even to drop, any national health program because of budgetary problems.''[52] Blumenthal continued to fight against what both Kennedy and the UAW wanted the following March, when he and Califano met with the president to decide whether to send a bill to the Congress in 1978 or 1979. Blumenthal argued against doing anything in 1978: "Sending NHI forward this year will affect the tax bill most adversely.'' Carter replied, "The only bill Mike Blumenthal wants to have before the Congress is *his* bill.'' Blumenthal, though he had done nothing as secretary but resist attempts to secure the passage or even the introduction of national health insurance legislation, corrected Carter: "That is not so, Mr. President. I have believed in national health insurance for twenty years.''[53] While Blumenthal, Califano, and Eizenstat agreed that the best course of action was to renew the public commitment to national health insurance but refrain from recommending specific legislation until 1979, Hamilton Jordan had other ideas:

> The President has a political commitment to the UAW, and the UAW is the best political organization in the country and the most powerful. At a time when our public opinion polls are down, we've got to stay close to powerful organizations like this. The President's commitment was renewed just a few weeks ago in a meeting between the President and UAW President Doug Fraser. The UAW wants to go to every congressman in the country and offer to help them in their campaigns if they will support NHI. That's the way to get the bill passed.[54]

Carter immediately added: "My word is at stake. I have made a commitment. It would be a lie not to send the legislation forward this year.''[55]

Carter, who had promised never to lie, combined a rigid insistence on keeping his word with a marvelous flexibility in the interpretation of the word he was to keep. He would not give in when Califano and Blumenthal tried to convince him that a promise could be broken when circumstances had changed. But when Califano then suggested that "we announce principles in late April, 1978, to be followed by a tentative program, then by legislation,'' Carter said, "That's consistent with my commitments.'' Califano knew it was not, and with honorable devotion to duty, informed Carter that "you should know this is not consistent with what Kennedy thinks your commitments are. He expects a piece of legislation, not principles.'' But Carter never lied. " 'Kennedy is wrong,' Carter said, his eyes icy blue.' '' When the meeting was over, Eizenstat told Califano, "Kennedy may be right about what Carter committed to.''[56]

A month later, Carter met with Kennedy, George Meany, Lane Kirkland, and Doug Fraser. It was "clear" to Califano "that Kennedy was trying to take labor away from him.''[57] Kennedy and the labor leaders with whom he had worked were willing to compromise and support a proposal that would include, as the senator put it, "a role for private insurance, which you want.''

But they would not compromise on "the principles of universality, comprehensive benefits and tough controls."[58] Califano thought Kennedy was "making a speech . . . and of course he was, for the benefit of the labor groups." Fraser indicated his desire to have a bill placed before the Congress before that year's election: "We want these guys campaigning to have to declare on this issue." George Meany agreed. Kennedy, "in a tone so insistent that it was almost disdainful of the President," argued that work should begin immediately to arrive at a bill all of them would support, though the procedure he recommended would give the White House minority participation in the deliberations: "A working group—the administration, organized labor, and my staff—should be set up to negotiate a bill." Toward the end of the meeting, Carter made a statement that must have given Kennedy and Fraser notice that any negotiations would be difficult. "Your views," the president informed them, "will be fully considered—favorably, if possible. I did not support the Kennedy-Corman bill during the campaign; I endorsed a set of principles instead."[59]

Jimmy Carter had been Leonard Woodcock's candidate, not Douglas Fraser's. Fraser had no vested interest in the Carter presidency, and by the fall of 1978, when the White House had still put forward no national health insurance bill, he no longer felt constrained to withhold public comment on the deficiencies of the Democratic administration. On October 26, when Kennedy came to Detroit to campaign for the Democratic gubernatorial candidate, William Fitzgerald, and spent the night as a guest at Fraser's home, the head of the UAW remarked to Remer Tyson of the *Detroit Free Press* that after the defeat of labor law reform and after Carter put aside national health insurance, "We kept looking at those election returns. We thought we had won the election."[60] Two months later, when Kennedy, appearing before the Democratic party's mini-convention in Memphis, made "an arm-waving podium-pounding harangue on the need for national health insurance and an end to social welfare budget cuts,"[61] Jody Powell dismissed it as "demogoguery,"[62] while most of the UAW members in attendance began to believe that the next election returns they consulted would somehow involve Teddy Kennedy.

Douglas Fraser and the UAW clearly preferred Kennedy to Carter, but when Kennedy formally declared his candidacy on November 7 and the Michigan draft committee dissolved itself on November 8,[63] the union did not immediately become involved. It could not. The Carter administration had not yet decided what it would do about the Chrysler Corporation. For the remainder of 1979, Fraser and the UAW could do nothing that might antagonize the White House. The administration understood the leverage it now had with the UAW. National health insurance, whether it was the grand and benevolent social program the union claimed or whether, as Senator Russell Long insisted, the "UAW is engaged in a confidence game" to get "coverage from Uncle Sam so they can take the four percent now spent by the auto companies on health care and turn it into higher wages,"[64] was something the union had managed to live without. It could not so easily live without Chrysler. Jimmy Carter had it in his power to withhold approval of legislation that would provide loan guarantees on which the future existence of the third largest automobile producer in America depended. As one UAW official described it, "Strauss and Mondale were very cagey. They took the leadership up to the mountaintop and showed them how good the goodies are."[65] Once the loan guarantee legislation had been passed by the Congress and signed by the president, however, national health insurance and the promises the president had not been willing to keep became once again the central consideration in the UAW's political calculations.

The UAW endorsed Kennedy in the contest for the Michigan delegation to the Democratic convention, but by then Carter, for all practical purposes, had already recaptured the nomination. Kennedy, it is true, won in Michigan, but he won with a margin of a single delegate, and he won even that paper-thin victory only because the Michigan Democratic party had employed a procedure that years earlier it had led the nation in denouncing when southern states had used it to deny political participation to blacks. It replaced the presidential primary with a system of party caucuses in which only dues-paying members could participate. Theodore H. White had no difficulty recognizing this arrangement for what it really was.

And in all Michigan, only 41,717 Democrats could enter the caucuses—after having paid a new kind of poll tax called a membership fee, costing two dollars for retirees, three dollars for students . . . and up to ten dollars for ordinary citizens. Of these 41,717 enrollees, only 16,048 appeared at the caucuses, less than 1 percent of the 1,661,532 Democrats who voted in November. They gave Kennedy 71 delegates, Carter 70, and Michigan's role at the Democratic national convention was reduced to zero.[66]

The UAW had supported Edward Kennedy because in its judgment Jimmy Carter had broken his word on national health insurance.[67] Kennedy lost, and with the victory of Ronald Reagan in November, the UAW would never know whether Carter had intended to keep during a second term the promise he had made for the first. Under the Reagan administration, national health insurance would become at most a distant memory preserved for the distant future. In the present, the immediate and all-consuming task was simply to somehow survive what appeared to be the impending destruction of the American automobile industry and the utter devastation of the Michigan economy.

Notes

1. Morley Winograd, interview with author, August 22, 1982.

2. Morley Winograd, memo to Democratic Senate Business Committee Members, RE: Public Service Commission appointment, July 18, 1977.

3. Morley Winograd, letter to Douglas Fraser, July 18, 1977.

4. Morley Winograd, letter to William G. Milliken, May 18, 1977.

5. Morley Winograd, letter to William G. Milliken, May 23, 1977.

6. Morley Winograd, letter to Douglas Fraser, July 18, 1977.

7. William G. Milliken, letter to Morley Winograd, June 21, 1977.

8. Morley Winograd, letter to Douglas Fraser, July 18, 1977.

9. Ibid.

10. Ibid.

11. Morley Winograd, letter to Marc Stepp, July 18, 1977.

12. Ibid.

13. Ibid.

14. *Detroit Free Press,* July 7, 1977.

15. *Detroit News,* July 7, 1977.

16. Morley Winograd, memo to Democratic Senate Business Committee Members, July 18, 1977.

17. Morley Winograd, interview with author, August 22, 1982.

18. *Michigan Chronicle,* July 17, 1977.

19. Morley Winograd, letter to Marc Stepp, July 18, 1977.

20. Ibid. A blind copy of this letter was sent to Regional Director Ken Morris.

21. Theodore H. White, *America in Search of Itself: The Making of the President 1956–1980* (New York: Harper and Row, 1982), p. 285.

22. Ibid., p. 286.

23. The Commission on Presidential Nomination and Party Structure, *Openness, Participation and Party Building: Reforms for a Stronger Democratic Party* (Washington, D.C.: Democratic National Committee, 1978).

24. Ibid.

25. Quoted in *Michigan Chronicle,* February 18, 1978.

26. Unknown to the participants in this session of the black caucus, a tape recording was made. This and the other quotations from this session are taken from a transcript of that recording.

27. Michigan Democratic Black Caucus, press release, Lansing, Michigan, February 12, 1978.

28. Quoted in *Lansing State Journal,* February 14, 1978.

29. Ibid.

30. Morley Winograd, letter to David S. Holmes, February 17, 1978.

31. Morley Winograd, letter to Freddie Burton and Hubert Holley, February 17, 1978.

32. Morley Winograd, letter to Coleman Young, February 17, 1978.

33. Morley Winograd, letter to Marc Stepp, February 17, 1978.

34. Morley Winograd, interview with author, August 22, 1982.

35. Freddie Burton, letter to Morley Winograd, March 10, 1978.
36. David S. Holmes, letter to Morley Winograd, March 21, 1978.
37. Morley Winograd, letter to David S. Holmes, March 22, 1978.
38. However, in response to Freddie Burton's invitation, Winograd did debate David Holmes on the commission's proposals before a Thirteenth District meeting.
39. This and the quotations that follow are taken from the text Winograd had prepared in advance of the meeting and which he followed exactly during the course of his remarks. Morley Winograd, interview with author, August 22, 1982.
40. *Detroit Free Press,* October 20, 1978.
41. Jimmy Carter, *Keeping Faith: Memoirs of a President* (New York: Bantam Books, 1982) p. 463.
42. Quoted in ibid., pp. 463–64.
43. Ibid.
44. White, *America in Search of Itself,* p. 270.
45. Quoted in ibid., p. 223.
46. Ibid.
47. Morley Winograd, interview with author, August 22, 1982.
48. Jack Germond and Jules Witcover, *Blue Smoke and Mirrors: How Reagan Won and Why Carter Lost the Election of 1980* (New York: Viking Press, 1981), p. 54.
49. Joseph A. Califano, Jr., *Governing America: An Insider's Report from the White House and the Cabinet* (New York: Simon and Schuster, 1981), p. 89.
50. Ibid., p. 97.
51. Ibid., p. 98.
52. Ibid., p. 99.
53. Ibid., p. 103.
54. Ibid.
55. Ibid.
56. Ibid.
57. Ibid., p. 104.
58. Ibid.
59. Ibid., pp. 105, 106.
60. *Detroit Free Press,* October 26, 1978.
61. Germond and Witcover, *Blue Smoke and Mirrors,* p. 49.
62. Quoted in ibid.
63. Bernard M. Ryan and Donald F. Tucker, letter to Kennedy supporters, November 8, 1979. The chairman and the treasurer of the draft committee informed those who had volunteered that "the present Draft Committee will be dissolved pursuant to Senator Kennedy's request. A new, authorized Michigan Kennedy Committee will be established in the near future. . . ."
64. Quoted in Califano, *Governing America,* p. 108.
65. Quoted in Elizabeth Drew, *Portrait of an Election: The 1980 Presidential Campaign* (New York: Simon and Schuster, 1981), p. 15.
66. White, *America in Search of Itself,* p. 288.
67. Morley Winograd, interview with author, August 22, 1982.

CHAPTER 10

The Common Danger and the
Politics of Necessity

The Michigan Democratic party had waged the 1980 campaign under a new chairman, and after the election it confronted an old problem in a new form. Morley Winograd had resigned on October 13, 1979, to accept a position with the Michigan Bell Telephone Company. Acting under the direction of the UAW, the Democratic state central committee appointed the vice-chairman, Libby Maynard, to fill the unexpired portion of Winograd's two-year term. Under the rules of the national Democratic party, the chairman and one vice-chairman of each state party were automatically members of the Democratic National Committee. At the time Winograd resigned, the Michigan Democratic party, in addition to the two officers, was entitled to elect seven members to the national committee. Out of this nine-member delegation, three, Alex Ott, Shirley Hall, and Coleman Young were black. Once Winograd resigned, Libby Maynard assumed the position he had held on the national committee, while the one she had held as vice-chairman now went to the other vice-chairman, Clyde Cleveland,[1] who was black. Four of the nine members of the Michigan delegation were now black. The black proportion was returned to one-third, however, when, by prearrangement, Coleman Young, who as vice-chairman of the national party was automatically a member of the national committee, resigned as an elected member of the Michigan delegation so that Morley Winograd could fill the vacancy and remain on the national committee. Whether the black percentage on the Michigan delegation to the national committee was a third or, because Coleman Young continued to be a member by virtue of his office, and Marc Stepp was one of the at-large members selected by the national committee itself, closer to half, black representation was more than what it would have been under the quota system Young and Stepp had both urged as a matter of simple justice.

After the 1980 election, the national committee was reapportioned and the Michigan delegation was increased from nine to ten. What some had already suspected now became obvious; Coleman Young's insistence on quotas had never really been more than a political expedient. The principle that black representation within the Democratic party should be apportioned on the basis of the black percentage of the Democratic vote carried the unspoken and unwritten amendment "unless we can get something more." Young had argued eloquently that black representation in the Michigan delegation to the Democratic national convention should correspond to the roughly 20 percent that constituted the black proportion of the Democratic electorate. He did not raise his voice to protest or even to note what according to the principle he professed was an enormous racial imbalance on the Michigan delegation to the Democratic National Committee. To the contrary, under his direction blacks from the First and Thirteenth districts strenuously objected to any reduction in black representation within the Michigan delegation and accused those who now argued for the kind of quota Young had advocated of the worst sort of racism; and no one, in their judgment, was more guilty of racism than their former state chairman, Morley Winograd.

With the defeat of Jimmy Carter in November, Coleman Young lost the source of both his influence with the federal government and his power within the national Democratic party. This would have devastating economic consequences for Detroit. Unemployment was already nearly 20 percent, and the city had somehow to deal with a record $120 million deficit.[2] The state of Michigan, which was now beginning to have enormous financial difficulties of its own, could not help, and the federal government, which during the Carter administration had supplied the city with hundreds of millions of dollars, was now under the direction of a Republican president publicly pledged to do less for the nation's cities than what had been done before. Jimmy Carter was no longer there to help Detroit, and he was no longer in a position to help Coleman Young. If the mayor of Detroit wanted to remain vice-chairman of the national Democratic party, he would have to defeat on his own the challenge of another black mayor, Richard Hatcher of Gary, Indiana. Hatcher, however, had broad support and did not have what was now the distinct liability, even within the Democratic National Committee, of close association with the former Democratic president. Hatcher was expected to win, and Coleman Young wanted once again to be elected to the national committee by the central committee of the Michigan Democratic party.

On December 13, 1980, the Democratic state central committee met to choose the members of the Michigan delegation on the national committee. Two of the ten positions were automatically filled by the state party chairman and the vice-chairman of the opposite sex. The main business before the central committee was the election of the other eight. Coleman Young and the black leadership of the First and Thirteenth districts had decided to insist that blacks were entitled to three of the eight elective positions. By concentrating exclusively on the members to be elected, that is to say, by leaving out of account the two positions filled by the party chairman and vice-chairman, it could be made to appear that blacks were actually giving something up. When the committee delegation was nine instead of ten, and seven instead of eight positions were elected, three of the seven had originally been blacks. Coleman Young had voluntarily reduced that number to two when he let Morley Winograd take his elected position while he had a position on the national committee as vice-chairman of the national party. Young now wanted his original position back. The proposition that blacks were entitled to three of eight because they had held three of seven seemed at least somewhat ambiguous when it was remembered that if the full delegation was considered, blacks, who before had held three of nine, would now (because Clyde Cleveland was vice-chairman of the state party) hold four of ten. Nevertheless, the mayor and the black leadership had done their work. Malcolm Dade, the mayor's principal assistant for political affairs, counted eighty state central committee votes, more than enough for a majority, committed to the black position.[3]

The first two members of the state central committee to speak after Libby Maynard opened the floor to discussion of the process by which national committee members were to be elected were the chairmen of the First and Thirteenth districts. Hubert Holley, chairman of the First, reminded the central committee that black voters had "stuck with the Democratic Party better than 93 percent" in November and suggested that the committee formally declare in advance what "the number of black National Committee persons should be."[4] Holley was followed immediately by George Atkins, chairman of the Thirteenth, who expressed his desire "to echo the sentiments of the chairman of the 1st District."[5] The third state central committee member who rose to speak sounded as if he agreed with the position taken by the black leadership of the two black congressional district committees: "I agree 100 percent with the proposition that we ought to take care to represent the elements of the Party on our National Committee delegation in regard to the degree to which they demonstrate support for the Democratic Party and its candidates."[6] Morley Winograd, however, had not risen to commend or to endorse the position of Coleman Young and the black caucus.

Hubert Holley had pointed to the support given by the black electorate to Jimmy Carter in 1980 as evidence of the loyalty of black Democrats. Winograd now reminded everyone of the 1978 election in order to bring into question the loyalty of Coleman Young and the black leadership.

When I was Chairman of the Democratic Party in 1978, we were in a very close and tough election for Governor of this State. . . . Meetings were held without the knowledge of the State AFL-CIO, called by Tom Turner, President of the Metropolitan AFL-CIO, in order to work out the distribution of a slate . . . that would have Bill Milliken's name at the top. And those people met with the Teamsters, the Building Trades and with certain dissident elements within the AFL-CIO. And eventually their work produced a tabloid which was distributed, but only partially, because Bill Marshall found out about what was going on and he, courageously, at the risk of his own leadership, put an end to it. I filed, on behalf of the Michigan Democratic Party, a complaint against the distribution of that tabloid because it did not contain the name of who was putting it out. I wonder why.[7]

Winograd pointed out that after a hearing, the secretary of state requested the attorney general to "fine and find in violation of the State election law, the Teamsters Union," which, because of the intervention of Bill Marshall, was the only labor union that actually distributed the tabloid.

Morley Winograd did not charge Coleman Young or any other elected party official with participating in the tabloid scheme, but he did suggest that the mayor had acted in concert with the Republican governor: "Over 40 percent of the black votes" in Detroit "voted for Governor Milliken." The state party had "spent a lot of time" trying to "reverse the inroads that Governor Milliken was attempting to make." These efforts confronted obstacles in the black community, however, the largest of which "was the complicity of the Mayor's office in the support of Governor Milliken in 1978." Winograd now made a statement that on the surface mitigated, but in reality only increased the severity of his criticism of the mayor: "Now Mayor Young signed a tabloid on behalf of our gubernatorial candidate and Mayor Young never spoke publicly against our candidate." The mayor, in other words, had been guilty of political hypocrisy and personal deceit. What the mayor had done, or at least what Winograd accused him of having done, could of course be justified. Winograd professed to "understand the problems of a Mayor in tough economic times and the need to have the support of the Governor's office to rescue that city—and he has the interest of the city in mind, and had to have it in mind in his political dealings." This justification, however, might explain and even in some measure excuse Coleman Young's support for a Republican governor, it did "not mean that we have to accept that activity and reward it with further representation on the Democratic National Committee."

By the time Winograd finished his remarks, the issue of black representation within the Democratic party had been drawn with greater clarity and more indifference to the reaction of the black leadership than at any time in recent memory. Blacks demanded three of the eight elective positions; Winograd denied they should have four of the ten positions to which Michigan was entitled. He had reminded the state central committee that the black percentage of the Carter vote in Michigan did not exceed 20 percent of the total. Blacks wanted three out of eight, which meant four of ten, national committee positions, though they had supplied only two out of every ten votes cast. Coleman Young's quotas and Morley Winograd's arithmetic both stood in opposition to the demands of the First and Thirteenth districts. The numbers, however, were less important than the accusations that had been made. Winograd had attacked Young by name, and that could scarcely be ignored. After two or three speakers had made brief comments against racial quotas of any sort—comments which, as Winograd later put it, "did not help any-thing,"[8]—Conrad Mallet was recognized by the chair.

Conrad Mallet, urbane and eloquent, was a close friend of Coleman Young and a leading force in the First District. With an air of studied amuse-ment that would have been the envy of an eighteenth century English aristo-crat, Mallet deftly turned Winograd's point back upon him.

> Fellow Democrats, we seem to be engaged in an activity that while it's not limited to Democrats, seems to be one of our activities that certainly keeps us from winning elections. We are forming a firing squad first by building a circle. We're attacking ourselves. We're good at that. We always name names. We always recount history, especially when it serves our particular purpose.

Mallet demonstrated his disdain for Winograd's attack by refusing to respond directly to it: "I do not rise here to defend Mayor Young. I am absolutely certain that when he hears what Morley Winograd said about him he will defend himself in ways that completely outshadow mine." Mallet devoted the remainder of his remarks to a detached dissertation on the propriety of the black demand for three of the eight elective positions on the national commit-tee. With an unassuming manner that masked numerous and complicated assumptions, Mallet insisted that because of its loyalty to the Democratic president in the last election, the black community should be permitted "to retain what it already had." Blacks had held three elective positions before, and blacks should have three elective positions now. "That's at least as much as simple justice would require. That's all that we're asking for." It was more than they were going to get.

When Mallet finished, Bruce Miller took the opportunity to instruct black Democrats on the nature of their real interests. Miller had few rivals in the art of condescension, and he had rarely displayed it with greater vir-tuosity. He informed his listeners that his initial involvement in Michigan politics, "many, many years ago," had been as "General Counsel of the NAACP," a position he had held for ten years. He had also served "on the General Counsel of the A. Philip Randolph Institute, an organization of black trade unions." As a white adviser to black organizations, Miller had, in his own estimation, "learned an awful lot about strategy and politics and advanc-ing minority causes. . . ." Among the things he had learned was "that when

you're a minority, you need all the help you can get in the Democratic Party."
The thing most necessary was a party that could win elections, he told them,
because "if it didn't win any elections, it ain't worth a damn for blacks and it
ain't worth a damn for whites. . . ." Miller knew that the Democratic party
was good for blacks, and he could therefore assert that "for anybody to say,
and to say it seriously and meaningfully, that this Party does not represent this
minority's cause, it either doesn't understand arithmetic, or it has no notion or
conception of intelligent politics." Miller's lecture, in the judgment of the
black leadership, could only be described as "demeaning."

By now there was an almost automatic alternation between black speakers who supported the demand for three of the eight elective positions on the
national committee and white speakers who, under one guise or another,
supported the opposition begun by Morley Winograd. Shirley Hall exclaimed
that blacks were "being shafted here today," receiving "the same treatment—the white treatment—that they may get in the Republican Party." The
Democratic party was breaking faith: "When you had seven members, the
representation was fine to have three minorities. Today we're electing eight
members and it's not o.k. That's not simple mathematics to me. It doesn't add
up, it doesn't subtract, I cannot understand it. . . ." Sam Fishman was willing to explain it. The problem, as Fishman claimed to see it, was that "we are
not counting accurately," and his solution was to "just count simply on our
fingers . . . and then since we can't disagree, we only have to deal with the
fingers on two hands, let's put the problem to rest." The Michigan delegation
to the Democratic National Committee did not "consist of eight members. It
consists of ten members." This was the major mathematical mistake that had
been made. Once this error was corrected, the basis of disagreement, according to the director of UAW-CAP, would disappear. He agreed "absolutely"
with the proposition that there should be three blacks on the Michigan delegation. Alex Ott had resigned from the national committee when he left the
state. "Coleman Young is running in his place in a way," Fishman explained, and that meant that if the mayor and Shirley Hall were both elected,
and they were both on the slate the UAW supported, there would be three
blacks on the delegation: "Now, I don't have any hat in front of me, I have
nothing to hide anything, but please look to my left where is seated Clyde
Cleveland, the Vice-Chairman of the Democratic Party, who is a member of
the Democratic Party's Democratic National Committee. Now that's three."

Shirley Hall was right, the numbers did not add up. Sam Fishman and the
black leadership agreed there should be three blacks selected, but Fishman
spoke of three of ten total members of the delegation, while the black leadership insisted on three of the eight elective positions. Malcolm Dade understood the difference: "They were counting Clyde Cleveland and we were not
counting Clyde Cleveland."[9] If Cleveland, who as vice-chairman of the state

party had automatic membership on the national committee, was counted, there would then be three blacks and seven whites on the ten-member delegation. If Cleveland was not counted as filling one of the three black positions demanded, there would be four blacks. Everyone understood this. Few understood, however, that in the interest of immediate political advantage the black leadership was abandoning the demand that its power within the party be tied directly to its share of the Democratic electorate. Fewer still seemed to notice that precisely those who had most vigorously rejected demands for racial quotas now invoked them to deny an increase in black representation. It was as if Coleman Young and Sam Fishman had passed each other in the night and failed to notice that each had stolen the other's principles. Fishman was now in a position to state the issue that was before the central committee with clarity and effect:

> If we're going from nine to ten, should we have four blacks out of ten or three blacks out of ten? Now I buy the proposition of several speakers that said let's look at qualifications of people because I think nobody can argue that 30 percent representation of the black in this state is inadequate. Let's take some specific statistics. The black community in this state roughly is between 11 and 13 percent. In my judgment, that figure has very little meaning or significance to me. What is significant is what I and others said here today—that overwhelmingly they support . . . the Democratic Party. . . . To what extent is that vote? I happen to look at the figures and am knowledgeable about those figures and I would say a low figure would be something like 20 percent . . . a high figure would be 25 percent.

In other words, according to a principle that Sam Fishman opposed but now employed, and which Coleman Young embraced but his followers now ignored, if three of the ten national committee positions were filled by blacks they were in no position to complain. But they did more than complain; they left.

While the state central committee was debating the question of black representation, Conrad Mallet had left the room and made a phone call. After Sam Fishman had finished speaking, Mallet announced that he had been instructed to withdraw the name of Coleman Young as a candidate for a position on the national committee. Shirley Hall, who was sitting in the front of the audience, understood the signal that had just been given and took the microphone to announce that she too was withdrawing her candidacy. With that, nearly all of the black members of the delegations from the First and Thirteenth districts walked out. After a brief recess, the central committee reassembled and in the absence of the First and Thirteenth districts decided on a motion by state AFL-CIO president Bill Marshall to elect six members to the

Democratic National Committee. The remaining two members, it was hoped, would be filled when the two black districts again participated in the deliberations of the Democratic state central committee. That, it would turn out, would not be for some time.

One week later, on December 20, the First and Thirteenth congressional district committees held a joint meeting and, without a single dissenting vote, adopted a resolution that accused Morley Winograd of an attack upon "black Democrats . . . that was vicious, unwarranted, and racist." Winograd's "frontal attack," moreover, was "only one of a series of attacks designed to reduce the input and effectiveness of blacks in the Democratic Party." The resolution recounted several of the earlier assaults, beginning with the Willa Mae King episode, in which "this distinguished black female attorney" was attacked "in such ways that it caused embarrassment to many black Democrats because of its racist overtones." The resolution did not bother to explain why at the time one of the two districts had refused to endorse the candidacy of this "distinguished" attorney, nor how the phrase "closet Republican," which Winograd denied ever saying, had "racist overtones." According to the resolution, Winograd had also acted in opposition to black interests in 1978 with the affirmative action proposals recommended by the Winograd Commission. The most interesting charge, however, was that "on more than one occasion he has intruded in the political affairs of the UAW to attack its black membership." Marc Stepp had obviously not yet recovered from the meeting at Little Harry's. Stepp had attacked Winograd in the black caucus of the Democratic party. Winograd had retaliated by attacking Stepp before the executive board of UAW-CAP. Now Stepp or his allies sought revenge in the First and Thirteenth congressional districts of the Democratic party. It was apparently permissible for an officer of the UAW to intrude into the political affairs of the Democratic party to protest the intrusion of the chairman of the party in the affairs of the UAW. Consistency and even simple logic were of little importance. Coleman Young and his allies in both the UAW and the Democratic party were now in a state of open warfare against Morley Winograd. The resolution concluded "that these insults to blacks and the disgrace he has caused to all Democrats can only be corrected by his apology and resignation as a National Committee person from Michigan."[10] Winograd was not inclined to do either.

Three days after the First and Thirteenth districts accused Winograd of racism, Coleman Young wrote the former state chairman and also asked Libby Maynard to arrange a meeting with him.[11] After five weeks passed and Maynard had still not been able to find a time that was convenient for both of them, Winograd responded directly to the mayor's letter. He did not apologize for anything he had said at the central committee meeting, but he did "express regret" that a "type-setting error by the Detroit Free Press" might have made his remarks appear "other than what they were." David Lawrence, executive editor of the *Free Press,* had agreed "that the original story did not accurately convey my statements." Lawrence's letter was enclosed to support Winograd's contention, and Winograd quoted from the transcript of the meeting what he had actually said. This was of course nothing more than an attempt to resolve the dispute by blaming it on a misunderstanding so that neither side would have to back down from positions to which they were now publicly committed. Coleman Young had not attended the December 20 central committee meeting, and he might very well have read the *Detroit Free Press* and the inaccuracy it contained, but his decision to withdraw as a candidate for the national committee and the walk-out of the First and Thirteenth districts had taken place during that meeting and in response to what Winograd had said, not what someone else had later written. The First and Thirteenth had demanded that Winograd apologize and resign from the national committee. He apologized to the mayor for remarks which, because of the inaccuracy of the *Detroit Free Press,* "appeared to be, but were certainly not, 'racist' in tone or content." He did not offer to resign.[12]

The letter did no good. "The type of apology that's been called for has not been extended," Young declared.[13] The mayor claimed that the dispute "was not a personal one between Morley Winograd and me," but was instead a dispute between Winograd and members of the First and Thirteenth districts, "who acted quite angrily and resentfully to what they considered to be slanderous and racist remarks by Mr. Winograd."[14] Winograd had offered the mayor a way to end what had become a racial division within the party, and the mayor had refused. More than that, by insisting that Winograd give the apology insisted upon and give it directly to the First and Thirteenth districts, Young eliminated any possibility that the dispute would soon or easily be resolved. Misunderstanding was no longer available as a formula both sides could use to reunite the party without first having to relinquish their self-respect. The mayor's refusal to grasp the hand Winograd had extended transformed what had at first appeared to be a temporary rupture into the beginning of what threatened to become a permanent break. Black delegates from the First and Thirteenth districts had walked out of the Democratic state central committee in December; in February, they did not even bother to show up for the Democratic state convention.

On Saturday, February 14, while the other seventeen congressional district delegations to the state Democratic convention held their scheduled caucuses, the two rooms in the Detroit Plaza Hotel reserved for the First and Thirteenth districts were virtually empty. Only a dozen of the First District's 235 delegates and only two of the Thirteenth District's 158 appeared; all the others participated in an organized boycott of the convention proceedings.

The AFL-CIO and the UAW opposed the boycott, but the women's caucus adopted a resolution supporting it. One of the members of the women's caucus explained, "We are offended by Morley's remarks and support our black brothers and sisters."[15] Neil Staebler, though he had not been closely involved with party affairs in more than a decade, played the part of party elder to make a statement that sounded serious but had no discernible meaning: "We've had hotheads and flareups before and people got over it in time. But we could easily lose perspective this time. The Michigan party is not racist. We're the best integrated party in the country and we'll continue that way."[16]

Staebler was not the only Democrat of note who seemed to believe that the problem would go away if it was ignored. Douglas Fraser preferred to believe that Coleman Young was yielding to pressure than that he meant what he said. Fraser, according to the *New York Times*, "insisted . . . that Mr. Young was 'conciliatory' and only seemed adamant because hardliners were pushing him."[17] The mayor, however, did not appear very conciliatory when, on March 10, he attributed much of the difficulty to "differences of philosophy between some Jews and some blacks," and then, as if to prove his own hypothesis, attacked Sam Fishman and Morley Winograd for opposing affirmative action because, according to the mayor, it would increase black representation within the Democratic party.[18] When the *Times* contacted Fishman and Winograd for their reaction, both of them said "that they had always supported affirmative action but that they were opposed to specific numerical quotas to enhance the role of blacks." All this had been said before, but now it was beginning to be said in anger and with uncharacteristic candor. For one of the very few times in his political career, Sam Fishman abandoned the manner that rivaled that of Metternich for guile concealed in civility and told a reporter exactly what he thought: "Mr. Fishman denounced Mr. Young's approach as a 'hustle.' He said that Michigan blacks accused anyone who opposed their demands of 'racism' and 'then try to play on the guilt we're supposed to have.' "[19] Fishman was not the only one who had begun to speak openly. Two weeks later, Hubert Holley and the Reverend James Wadsworth told the *Michigan Chronicle* that "The first and the 13th Districts and the Black Community will not stand idly by and be insulted by those persons who represent communities that continually vote Republican and then accuse us of being responsible for losing the election." Blacks in the First and Thirteenth weren't "going to ride in the back of the Michigan Democratic bus any longer."[20] No one, it seemed, had listened to Neil Staebler.

Detroit blacks had boycotted the Democratic state convention in February, and they boycotted the annual Jefferson-Jackson Day Dinner in April. For all practical purposes the First and Thirteenth districts had seceded from the Michigan Democratic party. The mayor continued to call Morley Winograd a racist,[21] and Winograd continued to refuse to apologize for what he had said until the leadership of the First and Thirteenth districts apologized for what they had alleged. Nineteen eighty-one gave way to 1982, but neither side to the party conflict gave way to the other. In April of 1982, the Michigan Democratic party once again put on its annual Jefferson-Jackson Day Dinner, and for the second consecutive year the First and Thirteenth districts continued their boycott by holding an event of their own. The principal speaker at what was called the 1982 Martin Luther King Memorial Dinner was none other than the mayor of Detroit.

Coleman Young made a remarkable speech. He denounced compromise and at the same time called for an end to hostilities. He still insisted that affirmative action meant nothing without quotas and argued that "To say that you should have affirmative action without quotas, is to say you can go to the butcher shop and get a good deal without watching the scale: You know the man is going to weigh his hands and everything else."[22] He still denied that anyone who lived in Oakland County, where only 40 percent of the vote had been cast for the Democratic gubernatorial candidate in 1978, had any business suggesting that black representation be reduced because the Democratic percentage of the vote in the First and Thirteenth districts had fallen from 85 percent to 70 percent. Young was unrepentant, but he was also unprepared to ignore a threat that "is not aimed primarily at the 1st and the 13th Districts." It was "not a threat against Black folks, and it's not a threat against white folks—it's a threat against folks! It challenges America; it challenges the direction of America." The threat Young feared most, the threat that prompted him "to extend a hand of unity to all within the Democratic Party who will adhere to the principles of the Democratic party," was the threat posed by the conservative policies of Ronald Reagan and the Republican party. Reagan and his allies were turning the clock back on civil rights and were proposing to "balance the budget . . . on the backs of the poor." For Coleman Young the threat was immediate: "Time is running out. There is no question that this coming election will be one of the most important in your lives." It was impossible to wait until 1984. "We have to start preparing in '82 for '84." Unknown to the mayor, Sam Fishman and Morley Winograd had begun preparing for 1982 in the last months of 1980.

Within two weeks of the 1980 election, the same group that since 1972 had been meeting privately to plan the strategy for a labor-led Democratic party gathered to discuss the 1982 campaign. Over the years membership in the group had sometimes been larger and sometimes smaller, but the principal participants had never changed. Morley Winograd, Sam Fishman, Bruce Miller, John Bruff, and Betty Howe had always formed the central element that made the final decisions and provided the direction that others followed.

From the election of Morley Winograd as state party chairman through the election of 1980, the group had exercised unbroken control over the internal affairs of the Democratic party. With Fishman as head of the UAW's political arm, Winograd as state chairman, and Miller, Bruff, and Howe leading party figures in the three metropolitan area counties, no one, including the mayor of Detroit, had been able seriously to challenge their hold on the party organization. Domination of the party had not, however, brought with it the ability to influence the outcome of at least the most important elections. A Democrat, it is true, had been elected to succeed Phil Hart in 1976, but most of the members of the inner circle had preferred Jim O'Hara to Donald Riegle in the primary. Carl Levin had defeated an incumbent Republican to capture the second Senate seat in 1978, but few of them had either thought he could or had wanted him to have the chance. Most members of the group had privately supported William Fitzgerald in the last gubernatorial primary. Fitzgerald had won only to be decimated in the general election. Morley Winograd told the other members of the group that in 1982 they had to elect a governor, and that meant they had to find a candidate who could win.

During his tenure as chairman, Winograd had accomplished two of the three things he considered necessary to the election of a Democratic governor. The party organization had been made into an effective instrument with which to wage statewide campaigns, and through the adoption of legislation providing public funding, adequate and equal campaign financing had been guaranteed. There was money and there was an organization. There had not, in either 1974 or 1978, been a candidate sufficiently attractive to compete with William Milliken. The third thing necessary to the election of a Democratic governor was obviously the recruitment of a candidate who could appeal to the Michigan electorate. Though it was probably the most important thing to be done, Winograd, while he was chairman, had not been able to do it. The party had a long tradition of at least formal impartiality toward candidates in party primaries, and the chairman was required to act as a neutral presiding officer while Democratic voters decided which candidates would enter the general election. Winograd was no longer chairman, and he was no longer neutral. He had, indeed, already put together a list of five potential candidates for the Democratic nomination, any one of whom, he told the others at this first meeting after the 1980 election, would give the Democratic party an excellent chance to capture the governor's office in 1982.

Of the five potential candidates on Winograd's list, three were members of Congress from largely suburban districts. William Ford, William Brodhead, and James Blanchard were all immensely popular in their own districts, and each of them had, in different ways, established reputations in the House. Ford chaired the higher education subcommittee in the House, was recognized as one of the most effective members of the House Committee on Education and Labor, and was expected to gain a steadily widening circle of power and influence as his seniority increased. Brodhead and Blanchard, both about to begin their fourth terms, gave away more than a decade in experience to Ford, but had made their marks nevertheless. Brodhead had won a seat on the powerful Ways and Means Committee and had been selected to head the liberal Democratic Study Group. Blanchard sat on the House Banking Committee and had been in a position to play a significant part in the legislative battle to provide loan guarantees to the Chrysler Corporation. "After Chrysler," Blanchard later remarked, "I decided I had more potential than I gave myself credit for."[23] The other two potential candidates were not members of Congress, but one of them also had a connection with Chrysler. Though he had never held any public office and was without political experience, Lee Iacocca was clearly better known than any of the others. The remaining candidate was not nearly so well known as Iacocca but was quite possibly better equipped than any of the others by training and temperament to be not only a formidable candidate but, more importantly, an effective governor. Blair Moody, Jr., was the son of a senator, and had become a member of the state supreme court. He had a brilliant mind disciplined in the law and a presence that commanded respect and invited affection. He had, it is not too much to say, the elements of greatness. In two years he would die suddenly like his father before him in the prime of his life and at the peak of his powers.

During the next two months, four of the five potential candidates were contacted and asked if they might have an interest in running for the Democratic gubernatorial nomination in 1982. Bill Ford quickly and completely removed himself from consideration. The Fifteenth District congressman had too much influence in the Congress and too many prospects for even larger influence in the future to risk it all on the uncertain event of a gubernatorial campaign. Blair Moody, Jr., was flattered to be asked, but he was not interested. Under the Michigan Constitution, he would have had to resign from the bench a year in advance of the election. Moody was content and productive where he was. If Ford and Moody were both unwilling to give up the positions they held, William Brodhead had no such reluctance. He would, he explained to Sam Fishman, very much like to be governor. He did have a problem, however. He had only recently been selected to lead the Democratic Study Group in the House, and because of the obligations that position imposed, he did not believe he could begin to campaign before 1982. The congressman had a problem, but he also had a condition: before he became a candidate he would have to be guaranteed the endorsement of the UAW. Fishman told Brodhead that it was impossible to say what the union was going to do, but that there were going to be a number of state senators who would be running and that he was not going to wait until 1982 to tell them whether the UAW was going to make an endorsement. Brodhead did not want to run until

1982, and he wanted everything arranged, including a guarantee of adequate financing, before he ran at all. Even had he wanted to, Sam Fishman was in no position to agree to the demands of William Brodhead.

Of all the people on Winograd's list of prospective candidates, James Blanchard was considered, at least by Winograd and Fishman, the most attractive. Blanchard had gained public attention and respect as the congressman who had helped save Chrysler. Perhaps more importantly he was, like William Milliken, personable, likeable, and, again like the Republican governor, extremely adept at avoiding close identification with politically divisive issues. As the congressman from a white, blue-collar suburban district, he had proven his ability to acquire and retain the loyalties of conservative Democrats. He had also, though it was not widely noted at the time, worked with Coleman Young to obtain federal funding and approval for a transportation plan under which the mayor would get a subway for Detroit and the congressman would get a ten-mile connection between the two interstate highways that ran through his district. Blanchard, in short, was politically shrewd and had an impressive ability to create political coalitions with which to advance not only his own ambitions but the interests of his constituency. There was only one serious drawback: hardly anyone thought he would be willing to give up what he had made into one of the safest seats in Congress. Sam Fishman simply did not believe Blanchard was likely to take the chance to run for governor. Morley Winograd, on the other hand, thought his old friend just might be interested in a chance at higher office.

In December, Winograd had dinner with Blanchard and Blanchard's wife, Paula. Instead of asking Blanchard whether he had any interest in running for governor, Winograd asked instead about Lee Iacocca. When Blanchard wanted to know why Winograd was interested in learning more about the head of the Chrysler Corporation, Winograd explained that Iacocca was on a list of potential gubernatorial candidates. Unable to contain his curiosity, Blanchard wanted to know what other names were on the list. Winograd told him that his name was among the others, but quickly added, "But you're not interested." It is reasonable to assume that if Winograd had really believed that Blanchard had no interest in the possibility, he would not have included his name in the first place. It is also reasonable to assume that having known Blanchard for as many years as he had, Winograd knew something about how he could be influenced. In any event, before Blanchard could reply to Winograd's assertion that he had no interest in a position for which Winograd had nevertheless listed him as a potential candidate, Paula Blanchard interjected, "Why wouldn't he be?" By the end of dinner, James Blanchard was very interested indeed in the prospect of becoming a candidate for governor of Michigan.

The dinner meeting with Blanchard was followed by a second meeting, during which the congressman began to raise questions about the timing and

the financing of a gubernatorial campaign. In subsequent meetings, Blanchard's closest staff assistants, including, for example, his principal fund raiser,
Ron Thayer, entered into discussions covering the various contingencies for
which a campaign would have to prepare.[24] These were not the only discussions taking place, however. Sam Fishman had been meeting with three
Democratic state senators who, undaunted by the odds, had begun actively to
campaign for the nomination. Gary Corbin, Kerry Kammer, and David
Plawecki were all young and ambitious, and each had been a dependable ally
of labor in the legislature. Fishman had come to believe that there was a very
good chance the UAW would take an active part in the gubernatorial primary.
Irving Bluestone had retired, and his replacement, Donald Ephlin, was from
New England, where, perhaps because the union had little real political
power, the UAW regularly endorsed candidates in party primaries. In addition, Lane Kirkland, who had succeeded George Meany as president of the
AFL-CIO, was suddenly insisting that organized labor had to participate at
every level of the Democratic party and at every stage in the selection of
Democratic candidates. Everyone was talking as if union endorsement in
Democratic primaries was the normal and expected thing to do. Fishman,
who could sense a tendency and detect a trend as well as anyone, told the
three state senators that a union endorsement was a possibility and that each of
them should begin to line up support within the UAW. Having given them this
advice, he extracted an agreement. Corbin, Plawecki, and Kammer agreed
that if the UAW made an endorsement, those who did not receive it would
withdraw from the race.

Fishman was dealing honestly with them. He knew that of the people on
Winograd's list only Blanchard was still a possibility, and Fishman had serious doubts that anything would come of it. When he advised Corbin, Kammer, and Plawecki to gather what support they could within the union it was
because, so far as he could know at the time, the only two other candidates
almost certain to run were Zolton Ferency and William Fitzgerald, and neither
of them was likely to have much chance for the UAW's endorsement. Once
he knew that Blanchard was serious about entering the race, however, Fishman was in a difficult position. It was his responsibility to represent the
political interests of the union, and that required doing what he could to
encourage the strongest potential candidate to enter the Democratic primary.
He had done precisely that. He had encouraged Blanchard to run, and there
was now every reason to believe that he had succeeded. But Blanchard was still
a long way from becoming a publicly announced candidate. Indeed, part of
the strategy of those who organized the Blanchard campaign was to have him
give every appearance of a reluctant candidate responding to a genuine draft.
Fishman did not want the three state senators to stay in the race, but he could
not tell them what he knew. Meeting with the three of them, he explained as

much as he could. Blanchard, he informed them, might become a candidate, and if that were to happen they could have a great deal of trouble getting either the union endorsement or the nomination. They heard the words and ignored their meaning. When no one could any longer doubt that Blanchard would in fact become a candidate, at least Kammer and Plawecki believed they had been betrayed, because they could not believe that Sam Fishman had not known Blanchard's intentions from the very beginning. They were wrong.

By the summer of 1981, the campaign to elect Blanchard governor was precisely where it was designed to be. In July, Hugh McDiarmid, political writer for the *Detroit Free Press*, reported that a draft committee was "quietly being organized within the Michigan Democratic Party, aimed at recruiting U.S. Rep. James J. Blanchard, D-Pleasant Ridge, to run for governor in 1982.''[25] Among the twenty-three members of the draft committee was Betty Howe. In August, Blanchard added to the drama, and thereby ensured continuing coverage by the press, by denying that any decision had been made. "I have not made any decision on the governor's race," he insisted, nor would his decision be dictated by others: "I will not be talked into this race by anybody, a committee, a group, a draft, a union. . . .''[26] While the prospective candidate persisted in his claims of uncertainty, the organization of his gubernatorial campaign continued to increase in size and power. In September, the Draft Blanchard for Michigan committee purchased the entire back page of the monthly party newspaper, the *Michigan Democrat,* to send an open letter to members of the state party. Three weeks after twenty-three people had formed the draft committee, "more than five hundred Democrats whose names appear on this page are joining together to tell Congressman Blanchard: 'You oughta run, Jim. You'd make a great Governor.' ''[27] Whether anyone seriously believed that all this was somehow a spontaneous demonstration of support coordinated without the careful planning and the political influence of some of the most powerful Democrats in the state, it did create, even among those who understood exactly what was going on, the impression of a movement rapidly increasing in strength and likely to sweep everything before it. Two weeks later, Blanchard wrote a letter of his own and sent it to 9,000 potential supporters. He told them: "I will seek the Democratic nomination for governor in 1982.''[28] Though he was careful to add that a formal announcement would not be made until the beginning of 1982, there was no longer any room for doubt. James J. Blanchard was a candidate for the Democratic nomination for governor. William Fitzgerald did not think he had a chance.

Shortly after his defeat in 1978, Fitzgerald was told by Peter Hart, who had done polling for the gubernatorial campaign, that if he did nothing at all for the next several years he would still be able to enter a campaign in 1982 with his name recognized by 70 percent of the electorate. This was a considerable advantage. Blanchard, like most members of Congress, was relatively well known in his own district and hardly known at all in the other districts of the state. That was precisely the situation Donald Riegle had been in at the beginning of the 1976 contest with Richard Austin for the Democratic nomination for the Senate, but if that even occurred to Fitzgerald, it did not for a minute cause him to doubt the ultimate outcome of the 1982 gubernatorial primary. Two weeks after Blanchard indicated his intention to run, Fitzgerald announced his own candidacy and came very close to declaring war on the UAW. Fitzgerald knew that Sam Fishman had been involved in the effort to persuade Blanchard to run, and he understood that Blanchard would almost certainly have the support of both the union and the Democratic party leadership. Without mentioning anyone by name, he accused labor leaders of having "already lined up behind Jamie Blanchard" and added defiance to allegation by claiming that "I am clearly the overwhelming choice of the Democratic voters today."[29] Fitzgerald had polling data to prove it. He sent it to Blanchard before either of them announced their candidacy, while Blanchard, who had polling data of his own that yielded other conclusions, sent his to Fitzgerald.[30] Neither was dissuaded by the helpful information of the other.

As late as the end of March, Fitzgerald and his campaign manager, Wally Long, were certain of victory. Their latest polling information had Fitzgerald running first, with Zolton Ferency, who had apparently decided to lose as many gubernatorial elections as G. Mennen Williams had won, second.[31] Blanchard was running a distant third, and in Fitzgerald's judgment, could not possibly make up the nearly 20 points that separated them. That Fitzgerald himself had barely a 30 percent share of the vote in his own poll did nothing to discourage his enthusiasm. With a half dozen candidates in the race, he explained, 35 or 36 percent would be enough to win, and it was certainly going to be easier for him than for Blanchard to acquire the additional support needed to reach that level. Knowing that he could not obtain any assistance from the leadership of organized labor, Fitzgerald sought support from those who, whether members of the business community or of labor's rank and file, resented the power of that leadership. He accused the president of the state AFL-CIO and other labor leaders as well of conspiring with Sam Fishman to organize the "annointment" of Blanchard.[32] He characterized anyone who agreed with Fishman as having been "Fishmanized,"[33] and he consistently called labor leaders "bosses." He even went so far as to invite reporters to attend the private interviews held by the UAW and the AFL-CIO as part of their endorsement procedure.[34] Twenty years earlier, John Swainson had defeated the heavily favored James Hare in the Democratic gubernatorial primary by appealing directly to local union officials in the UAW and the AFL-CIO. Now William Fitzgerald was trying to win union members by attacking union leaders. "We can't win without the rank-and-file," Wally Long remarked, "but we can win without the support of 100 labor leaders."[35]

The labor leaders did not agree. In April, the UAW, for the first time in twelve years, endorsed a candidate for the Democratic nomination for governor. For Frank Garrison, the union's legislative director, the issue was very simple. This time "we don't have Milliken" to contend with, and, he added, "we know we can win." If a Democrat was likely to win, then the UAW did not "want others deciding who the Democratic candidate is going to be."[36] No one was surprised when it decided that the Democrat it wanted to win was James Blanchard. The AFL-CIO quickly followed the UAW's lead. With only a single dissenting vote, its executive board endorsed Blanchard in the Democratic primary.[37] Within days the MEA, for the first time in its history, endorsed a candidate in a statewide party primary. By a simple majority, Blanchard, instead of Zolton Ferency, who was also "highly considered," received his third major union endorsement in ten days.[38] With the endorsements of the UAW, the AFL-CIO, and the MEA, which together represented 1.4 million members, James Blanchard had the organized support of more people than any other candidate had had for any primary for any office in Michigan history. From dinner with Morley Winograd at the end of 1980 to a draft committee of 23 in August, 1981 to a committee of 500 in September to the endorsement of institutions representing 1.4 million people was a progress that constituted perhaps the most effective and intelligent use of political power and influence in at least the modern history of the Michigan Democratic party. Morley Winograd and Sam Fishman had a candidate who could win, and, thanks to them, Blanchard had the best opportunity to become governor any Michigan Democrat who did not already hold the office had had in more than a third of a century.

The primary was held in August, but it had really been decided in April, if not much earlier. With the UAW, the AFL-CIO, the MEA, and much of the leadership of the county and district organizations of the Democratic party behind him, Blanchard was unstoppable. But none of the others gave up. Fitzgerald insisted that "Jamie Blanchard's endorsements will work against him,"[39] and that he, not Blanchard, was the candidate who was really "for the rank-and-file worker."[40] Ferency accused labor of ignoring the principles of the Democratic party in its eagerness "to get a middle-of-the-road, personable, inoffensive looking sort of guy—because that's what the Republicans have been doing."[41] The three other candidates, state senators Kerry Kammer, David Plawecki, and Edward Pierce,[42] each had his own version of why Blanchard would not win. Kammer, who had been so angered by the UAW endorsement that he wrote a letter of complaint to Douglas Fraser, had the endorsement of the National Rifle Association[43] and believed his opposition to gun control would appeal to enough voters, including Republican defectors,[44] to win him the nomination. But then, by his own admission, Kammer had "never been in a campaign where I've had such little feel for what's going on."[45] Plawecki complained that the UAW had been afraid to endorse him because he was considered too pro-labor to win a general election.[46] Presumably, the rank and file would be more inclined than the leadership to repay his past allegiance. Edward Pierce, a physician and first-term member of the state senate, who, like most Ann Arbor Democrats, considered himself (despite a 69 percent rating by the Michigan Chamber of Commerce, which placed him one point higher than the reactionary John Welborn) more liberal than the UAW, was the most direct. "The voters will be extremely discerning," Pierce decided. "They won't buy Blanchard because they don't want Sam Fishman . . . running the state."[47] After the primary was over, Pierce remarked, in something of an understatement: "I think I was unable to realistically evaluate my status in the race. . . ." He also admitted to having "underestimated the strength of the UAW."[48]

With only a week to go before the primary election, the Fitzgerald campaign had a poll that seemed to offer the possibility of victory. Blanchard held a 7-point lead over Fitzgerald, but 34 percent of those likely to vote were still undecided.[49] The *Royal Oak Tribune*, the *Macomb Daily*, the *Ann Arbor News*, the *Kalamazoo Gazette*, and the *Grand Rapids Press* had endorsed Blanchard, but they were the only major newspapers to do so. Of the two Detroit papers, which were the only ones that could claim to have statewide influence, one, the *Detroit News*, endorsed Fitzgerald, and the other, the *Detroit Free Press*, endorsed what it conceded was the long-shot candidacy of Edward Pierce. Moreover, both Detroit papers devoted considerable portions of their endorsement editorials to what they regarded as the deficiencies of Blanchard or the dangers of his association with the UAW. The *Free Press* lamented the absence of any discernible political principle in the leading contender for the Democratic nomination. "We have sat down with him many times over the last several years," the *Free Press* editorial writers sorrowfully reported, "and we cannot tell you what his core beliefs are."[50] The *News* warned that the "unions, especially the UAW, are pouring everything into this race, not just to elect Mr. Blanchard, but to preserve their iron-clad control of the Democratic Party apparatus."[51]

Neither the warnings of the *News* nor the reservations of the *Free Press* had any apparent effect. With the active assistance of the UAW, the AFL-CIO, and the MEA; with the endorsements of both Lee Iacocca and W. Michael Blumenthal; with the help of the overwhelming majority of county and district party officers and members; with the support of Coleman Young; with all of the 1.2 million dollars available under the public funding arrangement; with the unions telephoning their own members in an effort the Fitzgerald campaign estimated to be worth half a million dollars; with the most massive and well-organized campaign any candidate for the Democratic nomination for governor had ever had—with all of this James Blanchard took 50 percent of the vote, carried eighty-one of the state's eighty-three counties, and defeated his nearest rival, William Fitzgerald, by a margin of nearly three-to-one.[52]

More surprising than the margin of Blanchard's victory, however, was the selection of his Republican opponent. Instead of lieutenant governor James Brickley, a moderate, the Republican party turned to the very conservative Richard Headlee, who opposed the Equal Rights Amendment with almost as much energy as he attacked Coleman Young for the mayor's alleged mismanagement of the city of Detroit.[53] Blanchard had had the support of the unions for months; Richard Headlee now guaranteed him the allegiance of women and blacks.

In April, Coleman Young had called for a reunited Democratic party to wage the battle against the conservative social and economic policies of the Reagan administration and the Republican party. Two weeks after the Democratic primary, the mayor declared the twenty-month-long boycott conducted by the First and Thirteenth districts against the Michigan Democratic party to be at an end. "The basic strength of the Democratic Party," he declared in the time-honored manner of Democratic politicians who wish to end a quarrel without dealing with any of the issues that created it, "is . . . that we have very frequent fights about principled positions. But we're able to come together and be strengthened by our diversity and our ability to disagree with each other."[54] It wasn't even clear what the fight had been all about or what the principled positions had been. What had seemed to be an unyielding determination to insist on proportional representation on every public body and at every level within the organization of the Democratic party was now replaced with the desire to have a Democratic slate that could defeat the Republicans in November. Young did not demand or even suggest that Blanchard choose a black as the Democratic candidate for lieutenant governor. "The issue here," he said, "is advocating a program that will be a positive one for the people of Detroit and for minority groups. I don't think the inclusion of a black candidate necessarily guarantees that. . . . Whether or not the person is from the City of Detroit, I don't think is that basic."[55] Coleman Young, nevertheless, no doubt noticed the irony of it all when Blanchard chose former U.S. Representative Martha Griffiths for his running mate and the Democratic slate therewith continued the party's policy of a 50 percent quota for women.

When the Democratic state convention opened in Flint, the First and Thirteenth joined the other seventeen districts in a demonstration of unity that refused to yield even to the normal workings of democratic procedure. For the first time in twenty years the Michigan Democratic party was entering a gubernatorial election without facing a popular Republican incumbent. Moreover, the decision of Governor Milliken to retire, which had seemed certain to provide his designated successor, James Brickley, with the Republican nomination, had instead made it possible for the Republican right wing to stage a remarkable resurgence. Even with three conservative candidates, L. Brooks Patterson, John Welborn, and Richard Headlee, to divide the conservative vote, Brickley had not been able to win. The party had repudiated Brickley, and in doing so had turned its back on the moderation and the political success of the Milliken administration. This was unexpected good fortune for Blanchard and the Democratic party. With a Republican nominee who parroted the economic and social theories of Ronald Reagan while the state of Michigan suffered from the highest unemployment in the nation and the worst it had experienced since the darkest days of the Great Depression, Michigan Democrats seemed to understand intuitively that this was an election they could lose only through their own mistakes. The usual mindless enthusiasms of party conventions were this time replaced with a sober determination not to do or say anything that might jeopardize what everyone understood was for all practical purposes a victory already won.

Nothing was permitted to give even the slightest impression of disagreement, much less disunity. Libby Maynard had selected Flint as the site of the convention not simply because of its staggering unemployment or even because it was the hometown of Senator Donald Riegle, who was seeking reelection to a second term. Flint was chosen because the Democratic party had gathered there in convention following the primary victory of G. Mennen Williams in 1948. Hicks Griffiths, who had managed that Williams campaign, was there on stage with his wife, Martha, who at age seventy had become Blanchard's running mate. The Williams era, the most successful one in the history of the Michigan Democratic party, had been made to merge with the Blanchard campaign. Nineteen eighty-two, it was understood, was not just another election; it was not even just an election the Democratic party had every reason to expect to win. Nineteen eighty-two was to be the beginning of a new era, an era that would close the circle on the Williams era by beginning the cycle all over again. Neil Staebler spoke to the convention about the Democratic party that he had made his life's work, and G. Mennen Williams, still a member of the state supreme court, extolled the virtues of the Democratic ticket and showed by his very presence how many years of power the election of a Democratic governor could bring. Led by the recollections of past triumphs and controlled by the power of the UAW, the state convention proceeded to nominate candidates without risking the danger that contested elections sometimes pose to party unity. Every nomination, from Richard Austin for secretary of state and Frank Kelley for attorney general to the candidates for the governing boards of the state's three major universities, was accomplished without competition. Those who had wished to run but whom the union did not support were persuaded against having their names placed in nomination. Every candidate nominated by the party had the support of labor, and every nomination was by acclamation. Nothing, absolutely nothing, was going to threaten the unity of the Democratic party. Late in the afternoon on the second and last day of the convention, Coleman Young remarked to his old adversary, Morley Winograd, "I haven't seen this much unity since World War II." Winograd replied: "I'm not old enough for that." The mayor had to leave: "I'm getting out of here before it softens me up."[56]

The general election was almost anticlimactic. Blanchard left the Democratic state convention at the end of August with an enormous lead in the public opinion polls and with the knowledge that the margin would be much closer in November. Richard Headlee continued to alienate women and antagonize Coleman Young. Blanchard, on the other hand, did nothing and said nothing that was in any sense controversial. While the defection of several leading Republican women and the unwillingness of William Milliken to mask the disdain in which he held the candidate of his own party attracted widespread attention, the most important Democratic advantage continued to be the existence of the economic conditions that had, half a century earlier, called into being the original New Deal coalition. Even the budget director of the Milliken administration described the Michigan economy as in the midst of a depression, a depression, moreover, that he announced would last at least two more years. It was not a good year for Republicans, and it was certainly not a good year for Richard Headlee. James Blanchard won the election by a comfortable seven-point margin, and twenty years of Republican rule came to a close.

The Democratic party had held its August convention in Flint to symbolize its intention to repeat in 1982 what had been begun in 1948. The parallel between the election of G. Mennen Williams and the election of James J. Blanchard, however, was even closer than anyone who had planned the state convention could have realized. A week after the convention, the UAW, which had already reaffiliated with the AFL-CIO at the national level, merged with the AFL-CIO on the state level. The union, which had nearly 500,000 members in Michigan, acquired majority power on the executive board of the state AFL-CIO, which before reunification had had only 300,000 members. By prearrangement, the merger was formalized at a convention in which Sam Fishman was elected secretary-treasurer of the AFL-CIO. It was understood that Bill Marshall, who continued as president, would retire in June and that Fishman would be his successor. The understanding was followed with fidelity. Marshall retired on schedule, and on June 28 Fishman became the president of the Michigan AFL-CIO. Sam Fishman was now the principal political spokesman for the combined forces of the UAW and the AFL-CIO, while James Blanchard controlled a Democratic administration. There had not been such a close relationship between organized labor and the chief executive of the state of Michigan since the days when the president of the AFL-CIO was Gus Scholle and the governor of Michigan was G. Mennen Williams.

Notes

1. Under the rules of the Democratic party there were two vice-chairmen. The vice-chairman of the opposite sex of the chairman was entitled to automatic membership on the Democratic National Committee.

2. Kirk Cheyfitz, "The Survivor," *Monthly Detroit*, February, 1981, p. 42.

3. Malcolm Dade, interview with author, August 26, 1982.

4. Transcript of Democratic State Central Committee meeting, December 13, 1980, p. 1.

5. Ibid., p. 2.

6. Ibid.

7. Ibid., pp. 3–4.

8. Morley Winograd, interview with author, August 22, 1982.

9. Malcolm Dade, interview with author, August 26, 1982.

10. Resolution, First and Thirteenth Democratic Congressional Districts, December 20, 1980.

11. Coleman Young, letter to Morley Winograd, December 23, 1980.

12. Morley Winograd, letter to Coleman Young, February 1, 1981.

13. *Detroit News*, February 17, 1981.

14. Ibid.

15. *Detroit News*, February 15, 1981.

16. Ibid.

17. *New York Times*, March 30, 1981.

18. Ibid.

19. Ibid.

20. *Michigan Chronicle*, April 11, 1981.

21. See Hillel Levin, "City vs. Suburb: Is It Really Black vs. White?" *Monthly Detroit*, August, 1981, p. 41. In this article Coleman Young is quoted as stating, in reference to the 1978 gubernatorial election: "Now Morley says blacks in the First and Thirteenth Districts were responsible for the defeat of the Democratic candidate because thirty-one percent voted for the Republican. . . . Morley says we should have voted ninety percent. For blacks to prove their loyalty, they have to vote eighty percent or better, but for a white like him from Oakland County, they can vote only forty percent and still be loyal. Now if that isn't racism, I don't know what is" Ibid., p. 45. This is not what Winograd had said, however. Instead, he had argued that because the black proportion of the Democratic vote had gone down it was difficult to see why black representation on the national committee should go up. Winograd, as has already

been pointed out, used the principle of proportional representation against the political interests of the mayor.

22. Remarks of Mayor Coleman A. Young at the Martin Luther King Memorial Dinner, Barth Hall, Detroit, April 3, 1982.

23. Hillel Levin, "The Next Deal: Jim Blanchard," *Monthly Detroit*, September, 1982, p. 120. For the story of Blanchard's involvement in the Chrysler legislation see Michael Moritz and Barrett Seaman, *Going for Broke: The Chrysler Story* (Garden City, N.Y.: Doubleday and Co., 1981). Blanchard's own account is contained in: James Blanchard, "How Chrysler Went to Washington and Blanchard Went to Bat," *Detroit Magazine,* May 25, 1980. For a contemporary report, see *Congressional Quarterly Weekly Report,* November 17, 1979.

24. In July, Hugh McDiarmid reported: "It is known that well-placed Michigan Democrats approached Blanchard early this year about running and he told them he wasn't interested." McDiarmid was misinformed. *Detroit Free Press,* July 15, 1981.

25. Ibid.

26. *Flint Journal,* August 13, 1981.

27. *Michigan Democrat,* September, 1981.

28. *Detroit Free Press,* September 21, 1981.

29. *Detroit Free Press,* October 6, 1981.

30. Wally Long, interview with author, August 24, 1982.

31. *Detroit Free Press,* July 20, 1982.

32. *Detroit Free Press,* May 24, 1982.

33. Ibid.

34. *Lansing State Journal,* April 18, 1982.

35. Ibid.

36. Frank Garrison, interview with author, August 29, 1982.

37. Daryl Tennis, interview with author, August 29, 1982.

38. *Detroit News,* April 25, 1982.

39. *Detroit News,* July 21, 1982.

40. *Macomb Daily,* June 4, 1982.

41. *Ann Arbor News,* July 4, 1982.

42. Gary Corbin dropped out of the race when it became apparent that Blanchard was going to run and was going to have labor support.

43. *Detroit Free Press,* July 20, 1982.

44. *Detroit Free Press,* July 22, 1982.

45. *Detroit News,* July 10, 1982.

46. *Detroit Free Press,* July 23, 1982.

47. *Detroit News,* July 10, 1982.

48. *Ann Arbor Observer,* September, 1982.

49. Wally Long, interview with author, August 24, 1982.

50. *Detroit Free Press,* July 23, 1982.

51. *Detroit News,* July 25, 1982.

52. *Detroit News,* August 12, 1982.

53. Two days before the election, Brickley remarked, "It's going so well that it's scary." *Detroit Free Press,* August 8, 1982.

54. *Detroit News,* August 26, 1982.
55. *Detroit Free Press,* August 26, 1982.
56. Morley Winograd, interview with author, August 29, 1982. The exchange was also reported by Hugh McDiarmid, who Winograd knew was listening to his conversation with the mayor. *Detroit Free Press,* August 31, 1982.

Selected Bibliography

Abramson, Paul R.; Aldrich, John H.; and Rohde, David W. *Change and Continuity in the 1980 Elections*. Washington, D.C.: Congressional Quarterly Press, 1982.

Baker, Howard H., Jr. *No Margin for Error: America in the Eighties*. New York: Times Books, 1980.

Bishop, George F.; Meadow, Robert G.; and Jackson-Beeck, Marilyn. *The Presidential Debates: Media, Electoral, and Policy Perspectives*. New York: Praeger Publishers, 1978.

Broder, David, et al. *The Pursuit of the Presidency, 1980*. New York: Berkley Books, 1980.

Califano, Joseph A., Jr. *Governing America: An Insider's Report from the White House and the Cabinet*. New York: Simon and Schuster, 1981.

Carter, Jimmy. *Keeping Faith: Memoirs of a President*. New York: Bantam Books, 1982.

Cleage, Albert B., Jr. *The Black Messiah*. New York: Sheed and Ward, 1968.

Drew, Elizabeth. *American Journal: The Events of 1976*. New York: Random House, 1976.

————. *Portrait of an Election: The 1980 Presidential Campaign*. New York: Simon and Schuster, 1981.

Ferguson, Thomas, and Rogers, Joel, eds. *The Hidden Election: Politics and Economics in the 1980 Presidential Election*. New York: Pantheon Books, 1981.

Foley, Michael. *The New Senate: Liberal Influence on a Conservative Institution 1959–1972*. New Haven: Yale University Press, 1980.

Frisch, Morton J., and Stevens, Richard G., eds. *The Political Thought of American Statesmen: Selected Writings and Speeches*. Itasca, Ill.: F. E. Peacock, 1973.

Germond, Jack, and Witcover, Jules. *Blue Smoke and Mirrors: How Reagan Won and Why Carter Lost the Election of 1980*. New York: Viking Press, 1981.

Gold, Vic. *PR as in President*. Garden City, N.Y.: Doubleday and Co., 1977.

Hadley, Arthur T. *The Invisible Primary*. Englewood Cliffs, N.J.: Prentice-Hall, 1976.

Hart, B. H. Liddell. *T. E. Lawrence: In Arabia and After*. London: Jonathan Cape, 1965.

Kraus, Sidney, ed. *The Great Debates: Carter vs. Ford, 1976*. Bloomington: Indiana University Press, 1979.

Lawrence, T. E. *Seven Pillars of Wisdom, a Triumph.* Garden City, N.Y.: Doubleday, Doran and Co., 1935.

MacDougall, Malcolm D. *We Almost Made It.* New York: Crown Publishers, 1977.

Malbin, Michael J., ed. *Parties, Interest Groups, and Campaign Finance Laws.* Washington, D.C.: American Enterprise Institute for Public Policy Research, 1980.

————. *Unelected Representatives: Congressional Staff and the Future of Representative Government.* New York: Basic Books, 1982.

Moore, Jonathan, and Fraser, Janet, eds. *Campaign for President: 1976 in Retrospect.* Cambridge, Mass.: Ballinger Publishing Co., 1977.

Moritz, Michael, and Seaman, Barrett. *Going for Broke: The Chrysler Story.* Garden City, N.Y.: Doubleday and Co., 1981.

Nash, George H. *The Conservative Intellectual Movement in America Since 1945.* New York: Basic Books, 1976.

Nie, Norman; Verba, Sidney; and Petrocik, John R. *The Changing American Voter.* Cambridge, Mass.: Harvard University Press, 1976.

Patterson, Thomas E. *The Mass Media Election: How Americans Choose Their President.* New York: Praeger Publishers, 1980.

Pomper, Gerald M. *The Election of 1980: Reports and Interpretations.* Chatham, N.J.: Chatham House Publishers, 1981.

Pomper, Marlene M., ed. *The Election of 1976: Reports and Interpretations.* New York: David McKay Co., 1977.

Procopius, *Secret History.* Translated by Richard Atwater. Ann Arbor: University of Michigan Press, 1963.

Ranney, Austin, ed. *The American Elections of 1980.* Washington, D.C.: American Enterprise Institute for Public Policy Research, 1981.

Rawls, John. *A Theory of Justice.* Cambridge, Mass.: Harvard University Press. 1971.

Sandoz, Ellis, and Crabb, Cecil V., Jr., eds. *A Tide of Discontent: The 1980 Elections and Their Meaning.* Washington, D.C.: Congressional Quarterly Press, 1981.

Schram, Martin. *Running for President: A Journal of the Carter Campaign.* New York: Simon and Schuster, 1977.

Shoup, Laurence H. *The Carter Presidency and Beyond: Power and Politics in the 1980's.* Palo Alto, Calif.: Ramparts Press, 1980.

Stacks, John F. *Watershed: The Campaign for the Presidency, 1980.* New York: Time Books, 1982.

Storing, Herbert J., ed. *What Country Have I?: Political Writings by Black Americans.* New York: St. Martin's Press, 1970.

Stroud, Kandy. *How Jimmy Won: The Victory Campaign from Plains to the White House.* New York: William Morrow and Co., 1977.

Sullivan, Denis G.; Pressman, Jeffrey L.; and Arterton, F. Christopher. *Explorations in Convention Decision Making: The Democratic Party in the 1970's.* San Francisco: W. H. Freeman and Co., 1976.

Sullivan, Denis G.; Pressman, Jeffrey L.; Page, Benjamin I.; and Lyons, John L. *The Politics of Representation: The Democratic Convention of 1972.* New York: St. Martin's Press, 1974.

Tacitus. *Annals*. Translated by John Jackson. Cambridge, Mass.: Harvard University Press, 1962.

_____. *The Histories*. Translated by Kenneth Wellesley. Baltimore: Penguin Books, 1964.

Thucydides. *The Peloponnesian War*. Translated by Thomas Hobbes. Edited by David Greene. Ann Arbor: University of Michigan Press, 1959.

Tocqueville, Alexis de. *Democracy in America*. Translated by George Lawrence. Garden City, N.Y.: Doubleday and Co., Anchor Books, 1969.

U.S. Government Printing Office. *The Presidential Campaign 1976*. Vol. 1. Washington, D.C., 1978.

Verba, Sidney; Nie, Norman H.; and Jae-on Kim. *Participation and Political Equality: A Seven-Nation Comparison*. London: Cambridge University Press, 1978.

White, Theodore H. *America in Search of Itself: The Making of the President 1956–1980*. New York: Harper and Row, 1982.

_____. *The Making of the President 1972*. New York: Atheneum, 1973.

Wills, Garry. *The Kennedy Imprisonment: A Meditation on Power*. Boston: Little, Brown and Co., 1982.

Wilson, James Q. *Political Organizations*. New York: Basic Books, 1973.

Wooten, James. *Dasher: The Root and Rising of Jimmy Carter*. New York: Summit Books, 1978.

Index

AFL-CIO, 35, 97, 246, 273
Agnew, Spiro, 89
Albert, Carl, 93
Amalgamated Clothing Workers, 97
Amalgamated Meat Cutters, 97
American Civil Liberties Union
    (ACLU), 79
American Independent party, 93
Americans for Democratic Action
    (ADA), 79
Angelo, Frank, 211
Ann Arbor News, 270
Annulis, John, 90–92, 109, 113
A. Philip Randolph Institute, 256
Arnold, Stan, 211
Atkins, George, 254
Atlanta Constitution, 154
Austin, Richard, 47, 55, 56n.18, 132,
    142, 176, 195, 243, 245, 268, 272;
    as mayoral candidate, 73–74, 77–78,
    81, 127; and 1976 Senate primary,
    162, 165–68, 170

Bagehot, Walter, 10
Bailey, Richard, 176
Baker, Howard, 194
Baldini, Tom, 48, 52
Ballenger, William, 119
Bannon, Ken, 150, 152
Barkan, Al, 29, 163
Barnes, James, 131
Battle, Buddy, 52, 78, 149, 164, 221,
    223, 236

Battle Creek "manifesto," 22, 24–25,
    27, 29, 37
Bay City, 94
Bay County Democratic party, 94
Bendix Corporation, 246
Berry, Michael, 49–50, 220
Bieber, Owen, 90–91
Bielawski, Anthony, 66, 94–95, 97
Blanchard, James, 19, 26, 32n.64, 54,
    274; and 1974 congressional cam-
    paign, 121–25; and 1982 election,
    271–73; and 1982 primary, 263–71,
    275n.24
Bliss, Ray, 59
Bluestone, Irving, 187, 202–3, 220,
    233, 235, 266
Blumenthal, W. Michael, 246–47, 270
Bourne, Peter, 153
Braithwaite, Joyce, 212
Brickley, James, 137, 197, 271–72,
    275n.53
Brodhead, William, 118, 263–65
Brooke, Edward, 162
Broomfield, William, 17–18
Broomfield Amendment, 13, 17
Brouillette, Francis, 175
Brown, Basil, 181
Brown, Garry, 100
Brown, Haywood, 80
Brown, Jerry, 154
Brown, Kathy, 241–44
Bruff, John, 41, 54–55, 66, 82, 134,
    160, 186, 243–44, 262–63; and 1973

Bruff, John (*continued*)
  election of party chairman, 48–50;
  and unity caucus, 67, 71
Building trades, 211, 255
Burch, Betty, 66, 72, 176
Burton, Freddie, 223, 231–33, 251n.38
Burton, John, 72–73
Bush, George, 93
Busing, 7–17, 19, 21–30, 39, 50, 61,
  82, 117, 121–23, 151, 160

Cadell, Pat, 158
Calhoun County, 34
Calhoun County Democratic party, 34
Califano, Joseph, 246–48
Campaign Spending Reform Act, 182
Carr, M. Robert, 118–20, 125, 200
Carter, Amy, 239
Carter, Jimmy, 163, 169–71, 175,
  191–92, 194, 209, 212, 220, 228,
  239–41, 253–55; and National
  Health Insurance, 246–49; and 1976
  primary, 146–60; and 1980 cam-
  paign, 237–38, 242, 245, 249
Cartwright, Arthur, 183, 186
Catholic Conference, 181, 184–85
Catholic voters, 46, 178–79, 192,
  206–7, 209
Cavanagh, Jerome, 47, 126–29
Chamberlain, Charles, 118–20
Chapple, Si, 211
Chicago Tribune, 158
Chrysler Corporation, 248–49, 264–65
Churchill, Winston, 190
Citizen's Lobby, 133
Civil Liberties Clearinghouse, 4
Cleage, Albert, 79
Cleveland, Clyde, 252, 254, 257–58
Coffey, Bert, 172n.40
Cohan, Leon, 23, 27, 124
Collins, John J. "Joe," 53
Commission on Presidential Nomination
  and Party Structure (Winograd Com-
  mission), 225–27, 229–34, 236, 259
Communication Workers of America,
  97, 147, 211

Congressional Record, 40, 161
Conyers, John, 11, 16–17, 52, 55, 153
Coomes, Jerry, 181, 184–85
Cooper, Daniel, 18, 185–86
Cooper, Morris, 226–27
Copeland, William, 135
Corbin, Gary, 180, 266, 275n.42
Council of Black Baptist Ministers, 79
Crim, Bobby, 47, 187, 245
Curtis, Ken, 220, 240

Dade, Malcolm, 146, 212–13, 223,
  232, 254, 257
Daley, Richard J., 44
Damman, James, 137–38, 197
Deardorff, John, 131
DeFrancis, James, 20, 22
Democratic centralism, 59–60, 64
Democratic liberals, 40, 44, 47, 50, 53,
  58, 61–62, 71–72, 148, 155–56,
  175
Democratic National Committee, 7, 27,
  37–39, 65, 72, 89, 103, 147, 220,
  225, 230, 232, 240–41, 252–55,
  257–59
Democratic party, 44, 51, 87–88, 225,
  227–28, 230–31, 237, 252–54, 257–
  59, 262, 266. *See also* Michigan
  Democratic party
Democratic Study Group, 264
Derezinski, Anthony, 180, 196, 199,
  204–5
Detroit, 42, 64, 151, 153, 211–13,
  228, 235, 253, 255, 271; black Baptist ministers, 156, 158; black proportion of population in, 74–75, 77,
  81–82; and busing, 7, 21–24; 1973
  mayoral election, 73–82
Detroit Board of Education, 117–18
Detroit Common Council, 197, 204
Detroit Economic Club, 29, 135–36,
  208
Detroit Free Press, 60, 73, 137–38,
  146, 154, 167, 204, 206, 210–11,
  224, 248, 259–60, 267, 270
Detroit News, 13, 28–30, 60, 81, 129,

133, 136, 138, 166–67, 169–70, 204, 206–7, 209, 212, 224, 270

Devries, Walter, 20–21

Dewan, John, 123

Diggs, Charles, 11

Dingell, John, 11–14, 17, 117, 132–33

Dodd, William, 97, 147

Donahue, Paul, 40–42, 48, 50–52, 55n.1, 132

Drew, Elizabeth, 149

Eagleton, Thomas, 29

Eastern Michigan University, 197

Eastland, James, 10

Edwards, Nelson "Jack," 77–78, 221

Eighteenth Congressional District, 17–19, 48, 118, 121–22, 124

Eighth Congressional District, 94, 96–98, 116–17

Eizenstat, Stuart, 246–47

Eleventh Congressional District, 48, 52–53, 175

Elliott, Walter, 56, 166

Ellis, Don, 164–65

Elsman, James, 162, 166, 168

Ephlin, Donald, 266

Equal Educational Opportunities Act, 13–14

Equal Rights Amendment, 271

Esch, Marvin, 14, 169–70

Farnum, Billy Sunday, 17

Faust, William, 184–85

Ferency, Zolton, 35–37, 53–54, 63, 126, 129–30, 176; and 1978 gubernatorial primary, 187–90, 192; and 1982 gubernatorial primary, 266, 268–69

Fifteenth Congressional District, 16, 49, 66, 117, 264

Fifth Congressional District, 91–94, 103–4, 107, 117

Finkbeiner, Joe, 71

First Congressional District, 49, 52, 72, 79, 159, 221, 223, 231, 253–54, 256, 258–62, 271, 274n.21

Fishman, Sam, 36–39, 63, 65, 67, 79, 97, 103, 126, 130, 132–33, 145, 157, 160, 237, 240, 242–43, 273–74; and black representation in Democratic party, 257–58, 261; and Coleman Young, 220, 236, 258, 261; and James Blanchard, 265–67, 274; and Morley Winograd, 54, 59, 63–64, 70, 220, 235; and 1973 election of party chairman, 40, 49, 51; and 1978 gubernatorial primary, 187, 189–90, 209; and 1978 Senate primary, 200, 202; and 1980 Kennedy campaign, 241, 243–46, and 1982 gubernatorial primary, 262–70

Fitzgerald, George, 128, 180

Fitzgerald, William, 180–81, 263; as majority leader, 183–86; and 1978 gubernatorial primary, 182–83, 185–86, 188–90, 192; and 1978 gubernatorial campaign, 205, 207–13, 248; and 1982 gubernatorial primary, 266–71

Fitzgerald, William, Sr., 180

Fitzpatrick, Robert, 117–18

Flint, 272

Forbes, Joe, 242–43, 245

Ford, Gerald, 89–94, 96, 98–99, 102, 104, 109–11, 113, 116, 170, 175, 194; and 1974 Fifth District election, 107–8; and 1976 Michigan presidential primary, 142–46; and Nixon pardon, 101, 104–5

Ford, Henry II, 153, 159, 202

Ford, William, 117, 196, 263–64; and busing, 11–12, 16–17, 26

Fortas, Abe, 20

Fourteenth Congressional District, 13, 40, 49, 55, 117

Fourth Congressional District, 64

Frank, David, 111

Fraser, Donald, 225

Fraser, Douglas, 38, 150, 152, 186, 203, 220–21, 235, 269; and Coleman Young, 76, 261; and Edward Kennedy, 246–48; and Morley

Fraser, Douglas (*continued*)
  Winograd, 60, 63; and National
  Health Insurance, 246–48
Frost, Douglas, 94

Garrison, Frank, 186, 269
Garth, David, 131
Geiger, Keith, 203
General Motors, 240
Goebel, Paul, 104–8, 111
Goldwater, Barry, 33n.69, 59, 138,
  179
Gordon, Lou, 80, 138, 156, 167–68
Grand Rapids, 90–91, 105, 110
Grand Rapids Press, 91, 106–8, 111,
  139, 270
Gravel, Mike, 39–40
Gray, Tom, 54, 55n.3, 59, 61–63, 82
Great Lakes Basin Commission, 240
Greene, Tom, 60
Gribbs, Roman, 47, 74, 76, 127, 212
Griffin, Robert, 19, 89, 121, 127,
  140n.54, 145; and busing, 22–25,
  27–30; and 1972 Senate campaign,
  19–25, 27–30; and 1978 Senate cam-
  paign, 194–99, 205–6, 213
Griffiths, Hicks, 53–54, 272
Griffiths, Martha, 31n.18, 117–18,
  271–72; and busing, 11–13
Guastello, Thomas, 186

Hall, Shirley, 252, 257–58
Harbolt, Larry, 34–35
Hare, James, 36, 268
Harris, Fred, 17
Harris, Laird, 132
Hart, Jerome, 181
Hart, Peter, 155, 194, 198–99, 205,
  207, 267
Hart, Philip A., 10, 13, 18–19, 40, 47,
  91, 99–101, 109, 120, 124–25, 132,
  150–52, 160, 163, 165, 168–69,
  173n.66, 175, 179, 194, 196, 209,
  263; and busing, 7–11, 14, 17; decision of, not to seek fourth term,
  161–62; endorsement of Udall, 152–

53; and Nixon, 89, 93, 98–99, 101–
  2; and race relations, 4–6
Harvey, James, 94, 97
Hatcher, Richard, 253
Headlee, Richard, 271–73
Headlee Amendment, 190
Heidegger, Martin, 87
Hertzberg, Stuart, 53–54, 220
Hoffa, Jimmy, 180
Holley, Hubert, 223, 231–32, 254, 261
Holmes, David S., 175, 226, 231–34,
  251n.38
Holmes, Robert, 211
Hood, Morris, 243, 245
Hood, Raymond, 230
House Armed Services Committee, 15
House Banking Committee, 100, 264
House Committee on Education and La-
  bor, 15, 263–64
House Judiciary Committee, 13
House Ways and Means Committee, 264
Howe, Betty, 66–67, 123, 137, 242,
  262–63, 267
Hubbard, Orville, 26
Huber, Robert, 18–19, 121–24
Huffman, Bill, 181, 184–85
Human Rights party, 187
Humphrey, Hubert, 34, 37, 40, 55n.1,
  150, 152, 163

Iacocca, Lee, 264–65, 270
Ingham County Democratic party, 71
International Association of Machinists,
  97
International Brotherhood of Electrical
  Workers, 97
Irving, Helen, 55
Ivory, Marcellius, 36, 50, 52, 78

Jackson, Henry, 150, 152, 160, 163,
  172n.40, 241, 243
Jackson, Robert, 76
Johnson, Lyndon B., 7, 33n.69, 39,
  95, 121, 147, 179, 190, 224
Jordon, Hamilton, 147, 158, 209, 239,
  247

Kalamazoo Gazette, 270
Kammer, Kerry, 180, 266–67, 269–70
Karoub, James, 184–86, 193
Keith, Damon, 229
Kelley, Frank, 47, 82, 84n.25, 121, 132, 142, 160, 176, 195, 205, 272; and busing, 22–30, 122; and 1972 Senate campaign, 20–30, 33n.69; and 1980 Kennedy campaign, 242–45
Kennedy, Edward, 29; and National Health Insurance, 246–48; and 1980 campaign, 237–38, 240–46, 249, 251n.63
Kennedy, John F., 7, 11, 121, 126, 147, 190
Kennedy, Robert F., 26, 35
Kennedy-Corman Health Security Act, 246, 248
Kent County, 90–91
Kent County Democratic party, 48, 90
Kent County UAW-CAP, 90
Killeen, George, 18
King, Willa Mae, 223–24, 232, 236, 259
Kirk, Paul, 240–41, 243–44
Kirkland, Lane, 246–47, 266
Kleiner, Robert, 66
Klimist, Sheldon, 54
Knox, Patti, 200
Kowalski, Joseph, 95
Kuthy, Gene, 200

Landrum-Griffin Act, 19
Lansing State Journal, 120
Lawrence, David, 260
Leach, Russell, 34–35, 165
Lesinski, T. John, 91, 204
Levin, Carl, 243, 245, 263; and 1978 Senate campaign, 205–6, 213; and 1978 Senate primary, 197–205
Levin, Charles, 197
Levin, Joseph, 117
Levin, Sander, 34, 37, 40, 53, 121, 164, 187; and 1970 gubernatorial election, 19, 62, 91; and 1974 guber-

natorial campaign, 109, 126–36, 138–39, 140n.54, 178–79, 206–8, 212
Levine, Ken, 102–3, 105–6, 108–13
Liberal Conference, 118
Liberal-labor coalition, 53
Lindsay, John, 62
Long, Russell, 248–49
Long, Wally, 268–69
Longstaff, Robert, 134
Lyons, Dee, 52

McCabe, Irene, 12, 22
McCarthy, Eugene, 35, 51, 53–54, 71, 177
McCloskey, Pete, 125
McCollough, Lucille, 183
McCollough, Patrick, 183–84, 186, 188–92, 193n.18, 210
McCree, Wade, 229
McDiarmid, Hugh, 267, 275n.24, 276n.56
MacDonald, Jack, 17–18
McDonald, Patrick, 117–18
McEwan, John, 222, 224
McGovern, George, 27–30, 40, 46, 50–51, 53–54, 57n.23, 71, 89, 103, 119, 142–43, 177, 225, 244
McGovern Commission, 38, 43–44, 225, 227, 229
Mack, Joe, 183, 186
Mackie, John, 125
McLaughlin, William, 93, 96, 144–46, 221
McNamara, Patrick, 127
McNamara, Robert, 187
McNeely, James, 7, 37, 39–41, 53, 65
Macomb County, 7–8, 10, 15, 17, 25, 30, 117, 204, 213
Macomb County Democratic party, 7–8, 10, 41, 48
Macomb Daily, 270
McPhail, Scotty, 92, 110
Maddox, Lester, 154
Major, Jim, 210
Mallet, Conrad, 256, 258

Manatt, Charles, 39–40
Mann, Ted, 239
Market Opinion Research, 105
Marquette County Democratic Women's
  Caucus, 43
Marshall, William, 55, 59, 100, 132,
  145, 150, 163, 211, 255, 258, 273;
  and 1973 election of party chairman,
  40, 51–53
Martilla, John (Martilla and Associates), 92, 94, 102–3, 112, 117
Marz, Roger, 240
Maynard, Libby, 133, 199, 232, 252,
  254, 259, 272
Meany, George, 13, 28–29, 51, 97,
  247–48
Metropolitan Detroit AFL-CIO, 150,
  164, 211, 254
Michigan AFL-CIO, 13, 17, 28–29,
  35, 37, 55n.1, 58, 100, 118, 143,
  150, 163, 254–55, 258, 261, 273–
  74; and Democratic party, 58, 66,
  69–70; and 1973 election of party
  chairman, 40, 42, 51–52; and 1978
  election, 203–4, 211; and 1982
  gubernatorial primary, 268–70
Michigan Chamber of Commerce, 270
Michigan Chronicle, 224, 233, 261
Michigan Democrat, 267
Michigan Democratic party, 6, 19, 23,
  34, 38, 40–42, 45, 53–54, 58, 61,
  73, 101, 166–67, 169, 185, 187–88,
  205, 220, 224, 227, 229, 237, 240,
  249, 252–53, 255, 259; black boycott, 260–62, 271; black caucus,
  226, 230–34, 236, 254, 259; and
  busing, 7, 21, 23, 25, 28; and Democratic centralism, 59–60, 64; and
  Michigan AFL-CIO, 66, 69–70; and
  1973 Detroit mayoral campaign, 80;
  and 1973 state convention, 50–53;
  and 1974 gubernatorial campaign,
  129–30, 132; and 1974 state convention, 130; and 1978 campaign, 194,
  197, 208–9; and 1982 election, 263,
  267–69, 271–73; and 1982 state con-

vention, 271–73; and public service
  commission, 221–22; and question of
  black representation, 252–58, 261;
  racial divisions of, 82–83, 219–20,
  232; and results of 1974 congressional races, 125–26; State Central Committee, 7, 23, 25, 41, 54, 65–66,
  125, 143, 221, 252–53, 258–59; and
  UAW, 35, 39, 64–66, 68–70, 72–
  73, 177, 186, 234–36, 252, 272;
  Unity Caucus, 67–72, 221; under
  Winograd, 59–61, 63, 65–73, 175–
  76, 230; Women's Caucus, 46
Michigan Education Association, 185,
  203, 269–70
Michigan House of Representatives, 95,
  179–80; Judiciary Committee, 196,
  204; Ways and Means Committee, 135
Michigan Public Service Commission,
  188, 191, 221–24
Michigan Republican party, 93, 104,
  142, 144–45, 194, 205, 271–72
Michigan State Senate, 179–86, 222–
  23; Appropriations Committee, 181
Michigan State University, 20, 71,
  119–20, 134, 230
Michigan Supreme Court, 76, 175,
  182, 264
Michigan UAW-CAP, 36, 39, 163,
  165, 233, 235–36
Mikulski, Barbara, 225, 229
Millender, Robert, 75, 79, 81–82
Miller, Arnie, 103
Miller, Bruce, 41, 54, 67, 243–44,
  256–57, 262–63
Miller, Mike, 147
Milliken, William, 18–19, 21, 62, 73,
  126–27, 193n.18, 206–7, 235–36,
  255, 263, 265, 269, 272–73; and
  1974 campaign, 129–31, 133–39,
  140n.54, 178–79; and 1974 Fifth
  District election, 106, 109; and 1976
  presidential primary, 142–46; and
  1978 campaign, 182, 194–95, 197–
  98, 205, 207–13; and Willa Mae
  King appointment, 222–23

Milliken v. Bradley, 122–23
Miriani, Louis, 126–27
Mississippi Freedom Democratic party, 224
Mitchell, Clarence, 10
Mitchell, Robert, 39, 41, 48, 50–53, 56n.23, 58, 69, 175
Mondale, Walter, 249
Moody, Blair Jr., 264
Morris, Ken, 49–50, 52, 79, 250n.20
Mott, Stewart, 109
Murphy, George, 33n.69
Murphy, Gerald, 129
Murphy, Reg, 154
Murray, Tom, 71
Muskie, Edmund, 57n.23

National Action Group (NAG), 12, 22–23, 25
National Association for the Advancement of Colored People (NAACP), 10, 79, 256
National Education Association, 97
National Health Insurance, 150, 246–49
National Rifle Association, 269
Nedzi, Lucien, 40, 117, 132, 150; and busing, 11–17, 27
Nelson, Earl, 180, 185
New Deal, 54, 64, 87, 273
New Democratic Coalition, 46, 58
New York Times, 159, 261
Nichols, John, 76–77, 80–81
Nineteenth Congressional District, 17–18, 124
Ninth Congressional District, 64, 93
Nixon, Richard, 13, 27, 29–30, 37, 51, 89–90, 92–95, 98–101, 103–5, 108, 116, 127, 138, 142–43, 153, 156, 182, 194, 212, 225; and race relations, 3, 4, 5, 6; and special election in Eighth Congressional District, 96, 97
Northwest Mothers Alert, 14
Notre Dame, 240
Nowakowski, Adam, 122–23

Oakland County, 12, 18, 40–41, 48, 50–51, 137, 204, 213, 262
Oakland County Democratic party, 37, 41, 122–24, 137
O'Brien, Lawrence, 31n.18, 89
O'Hara, James, 41, 117, 186, 196, 263; and busing, 7–8, 11–12, 15–17, 27, 32n.37, 39; and 1976 Senate primary, 162–66, 168–69
Olmstead, David, 159
O'Reilly, Jack, 26
Ott, Alex, 72–73, 252, 257
Otterbacher, John, 180, 195, 199, 205

Palevsky, Max, 149
Patterson, L. Brooks, 272; and busing, 12, 22–23; and 1978 Senate primary, 197–98, 205–6
Patterson, Pat, 125
PBB, 207, 210, 213
Petitpren, Vincent, 66
Pew, Robert, 109
Pierce, Edward, 269–70
Pisor, Robert, 60, 81
Plawecki, David, 266–67, 269–70
Pope John Paul I, 209
Powell, Jody, 148, 153–54, 248
Power, Philip, 195, 197, 200–204
Prather, Charles, 133
Proposition C, 133–36, 138–39

Ralls, William, 188–92, 221–22, 224
Ravitz, Mel, 73, 77–81, 164
Reagan, Ronald, 249, 272; and 1976 Michigan presidential primary, 143–46
Republican party, 3, 59, 100, 104, 116, 136, 138, 235, 257
Retail Clerks, 97
Reuther, Walter, 12, 34–36, 75, 78, 150, 186
Rhodes, John, 18
Riccardo, John, 159
Riegle, Donald, 120, 125, 161, 175–76, 195, 199, 201, 243, 245, 263, 268, 272; and busing, 11–12; and

Riegle, Donald (*continued*)
  1976 Senate election, 169–71; and
  1976 Senate primary, 162, 164–66,
  168–69
Rizzo, Frank, 103
Robertson, Cliff, 155
Rome, Louis J., 128–29
Romney, George, 18–20, 33n.69, 36,
  125–27, 170, 187, 189
Romney, Lenore, 18, 91, 125
Roosevelt, Franklin D., 113, 179
Rosenbaum, Paul, 196, 199, 203–5
Ross, Douglas, 26–27, 133
Roth, Stephen J., 7, 13, 21, 23–26,
  31n.8, 82, 84n.25, 122
Rowe, Win, 242–44
Royal Oak Tribune, 59, 270
Runyon, Damon, 133
Ruppe, Philip, 14, 197–98
Rush, Barney, 111
Ryan, Bernard, 147, 240–45
Ryan, William, 47, 95, 181, 184

Saginaw, 94
Sain, Danny, 147
Salinger, Pierre, 33n.69
Sanders, Carl, 154
Scholle, Gus, 17, 35–36, 40, 274
Schroeder, H. Bernard, 120
Seale, Bobby, 80–81
Second (Wayne) Congressional District,
  48
Segal, Mark, 237, 240–44
Senate Judiciary Committee, 10
Serpe, Mike, 11–12
Seventeenth Congressional District, 49,
  117–18
Sheffield, Horace, 77
Shelton, Herman, 211
Shrine of the Black Madonna, 80
Shrum, Robert, 156
Sigler, Kim, 127
Sixteenth Congressional District, 25–
  26, 48–50, 66, 72, 117, 176
Sixth Congressional District, 118–20
Skubick, Tim, 63

Sparling, James, 94, 96–97
Staebler, Neil, 35, 38, 53–54, 128–29,
  261, 272
Steelworkers, 52–53
Steinborn, Stanley, 243
Stepp, Marc, 78, 164, 221–24, 226–
  28, 232–36, 252, 259
Stevenson, Adlai, 121
Stokes, Louis, 14
Strauss, Kathleen, 118
Strauss, Robert, 39–40, 98, 147, 249
Student Transportation Moratorium Act,
  13
Swainson, John, 35–36, 91, 268
*Swann v. Charlotte-Mecklenburg Board
  of Education,* 30n.6

Taylor, Clifford, 119–20
Teamsters, 128, 203–4, 211–12, 255
Tenth Congressional District, 64
terHorst, Jerry, 104
Thayer, Ron, 266
Third Congressional District, 100
Thirteenth Congressional District, 49,
  52, 72, 79, 159, 221, 223, 231,
  251n.38, 253–54, 256, 258–62
Ticket-splitters, 178–79, 198
Todd, Paul, 100–101
Traxler, J. Robert, 94–98, 116–18, 200
Treska, Paul, 150
Tucker, Donald, 241, 243, 245
Turner, Tom, 150, 164, 211–12, 254
Twelfth Congressional District, 15, 48,
  117
Tydings, Joseph, 26
Tyson, Remer, 73–74, 154, 167,
  172n.40, 248

UAW, 12, 14, 34, 36–37, 52, 60, 64,
  72, 75, 92, 97, 100, 103, 118, 120,
  123, 125–26, 129, 143, 145, 147,
  150, 160–61, 180, 220, 227, 232,
  246, 257, 259, 261, 273–74; CAP,
  60, 150, 187, 202, 220, 257, 259;
  and AFL-CIO, 35–36; internal racial
  divisions of, 77–79; and Michigan

Democratic party, 35, 38–39, 58, 64–70, 72–73, 177, 186, 234–36, 252, 272; and Michigan State Senate, 181–86; and Morley Winograd, 60, 63, 73, 132, 227, 233–37; and National Health Insurance, 246–49; and 1972 Senate campaign, 28–29; and 1973 Detroit mayoral election, 73–74, 76–82; and 1973 election of party chairman, 40, 42, 49–52, 56n.23; and 1974 gubernatorial campaign, 129, 132, 136; and 1975 Fifth District election, 109–13; and 1976 presidential primary, 148, 150, 152, 156–59; and 1976 Senate primary, 163–65; and 1978 gubernatorial election, 211; and 1978 gubernatorial primary, 185–87, 189–90; and 1978 Senate primary, 196, 202–4; and 1980 Kennedy campaign, 248–49; and 1982 gubernatorial primary, 264, 266–70; Region 1, 189, 203; Region 1-A, 50, 149, 221; Region 1-B, 49, 79; Region 1-C, 125, 147, 164–65; Region 1-D, 90, 112–13; Region 1-E, 50, 157, 203; and William Fitzgerald, 182

Udall, Morris: and 1976 primary, 146, 148–49, 151–53, 155, 160

United Transportation Union, 97, 150

University of Detroit, 240

University of Michigan, 71

U.S. Chamber of Commerce, 106

Vallely, Tom, 92

Van Dam, Philip, 20–22, 140n.54

VanderLaan, Robert, 90, 93, 104, 116

Vandermoelen, Richard, 242–44

VanderVeen, Richard, 116–17, 161; and Fifth District special election, 90–93, 97; and 1974 congressional campaign, 102–13; and 1978 Senate primary, 195, 199–200, 203–4

Voting Rights Act of 1965, 7, 9, 151

Wadsworth, James, 261

Wagner, Carl, 243–45

Wallace, George, 17, 28, 37, 143–45, 154, 178, 196; and 1976 presidential primary, 148–50, 152–53, 159

Washington Post, 10

Washtenaw County Democratic party, 71

Watergate, 89, 93, 96–97, 100–101, 105, 116–18, 121, 123, 131, 138

Wayne County, 133, 168, 204–5, 213

Wayne County Board of Commissioners, 117

Wayne County CIO, 76

Wayne County Democratic party, 41, 48, 55n.1, 147, 243

Wayne County Road Commission, 49

Wayne State University, 230

Webb, Wilfred, 122–23

Weddington, Sarah, 237

Welborn, John, 270, 272

Western Michigan University, 180

Westwood, Jean, 40

Wexler, Anne, 102–3

Wharton, Clifton, 230

White, Theodore, 3, 224, 249

Williams, G. Mennen, 19, 35, 40, 127–29, 195, 205, 268, 272, 274

Williams, Salome, 165

Winograd, Bernard, 48, 54, 124

Winograd, Morley, 69, 82, 123, 171, 181, 185, 229, 233, 252, 276n.56; and Affirmative Action, 231, 237; and black leadership, 214, 219–20, 223, 230–33, 236–37, 251n.38, 253–54, 259, 262; on black representation in party, 254–57, 261; and Coleman Young, 176, 220, 231–32, 234, 237, 242, 252, 254–56, 259–60, 273, 274n.21; and Jimmy Carter, 239–40; and Marc Stepp, 222–24, 232–36; 1973 campaign for party chairman, 40–53, 56n.18; and 1974 gubernatorial campaign, 130, 132–34, 136; and 1976 Senate primary, 160; and 1978 campaign, 177, 179,

Winograd, Morley (*continued*)
182, 194–96, 205, 207–8, 213; and
1980 Kennedy campaign, 240–41,
243–45; and 1982 gubernatorial primary, 262–63, 265–66, 269; as party
chairman, 54–55, 59–61, 65–68,
70–73, 175–77, 230, 263; and Public Service Commission appointment,
221–24; and quotas, 43–44, 219; and
Sam Fishman, 54, 63–64, 70, 220,
235; and UAW, 60, 63, 73, 234–37
Woodcock, Leonard, 29, 39–40, 186,
246; and Jimmy Carter, 147–50,
152–54, 156–60, 163, 238, 248
Workmen's Compensation Appeal
Board, 222

Yokich, Steve, 189, 203

Young, Andrew, 238–39
Young, Bard, 50, 157, 203
Young, Coleman, 38, 52, 164, 200,
221, 226–27, 232–34, 242, 262,
273; and black representation within
Democratic party, 252–54, 256, 258,
261; and James Blanchard, 265,
270–71; and Jimmy Carter, 146,
149, 151, 153–54, 156, 158–60,
163, 238, 242, 253; and Morley
Winograd, 176, 220, 229, 236–37,
252, 254–55, 273, 274n.21; and
1973 mayoral campaign, 75–83; and
1978 gubernatorial campaign, 212–
13; and racial quotas, 228–30, 236;
and Sam Fishman, 220, 236, 258,
261
Younglove, Charles, 52–53